Cities as part

**The challenge to strengthen urban governance through
North-South city partnerships**

Cities as partners

**The challenge to strengthen urban governance through
North-South city partnerships**

Steden als partners
De uitdaging lokaal bestuur te versterken door stedenbanden tussen Noord en Zuid

(met een samenvatting in het Nederlands)

Ciudades como socios
El desafío del fortalecimiento de la gobernanza local por medio de hermanamientos Norte-Sur

(con una síntesis en español)

Städte als Partner: die Herausforderung städtische Regierungsführung mithilfe von Nord-Süd-
Städtepartnerschaften zu stärken

(mit einer Zusammenfassung in deutscher Sprache)

PROEFSCHRIFT

ter verkrijging van de graad van doctor aan de Universiteit Utrecht
op gezag van de rector magnificus, prof.dr. J.C. Stoof,
ingevolge het besluit van het college voor promoties in het openbaar te verdedigen
op dinsdag 31 maart 2009 des middags te 4.15 uur.

door

Marike Christine Bontenbal

geboren op 22 januari 1978
te Voorburg

Promotor: Prof.dr. O. Verkoren

Co-promotor: Dr. P.H.C.M. van Lindert

ISBN 978-90-5972-313-9

Uitgeverij Eburon
Postbus 2867
2601 CW Delft
tel.: 015-2131484 / fax: 015-2146888
info@eburon.nl / www.eburon.nl

Dit proefschrift werd mogelijk gemaakt met financiële steun van NWO binnen het onderzoeksprogramma 'Bestuur in beweging', Urban and Regional Research Centre Utrecht (URU) en de Treub-Maatschappij voor Wetenschappelijk Onderzoek in de Tropen.

Grafische vormgeving, cartografie en omslag ontwerp:
GeoMedia [7351], Faculteit Geowetenschappen, Universiteit Utrecht

Table of contents

THE CHALLENGE TO STRENGTHEN URBAN GOVERNANCE THROUGH NORTH-SOUTH CITY PARTNERSHIPS

List of Boxes

List of Figures

List of Tables

Abbreviations

ACOPOE	Asociación Comunitaria Los Poetas [Community Association Los Poetas]
AMUNIC	Asociación de Municipios de Nicaragua [Association of Nicaraguan Municipalities]
C2C	City-to-City Cooperation
CBO	Community Based Organisation
CCL	Consejo de Coordinación Local (Peru) [Local Coordinating Council]
CCR	Consejo de Coordinación Regional (Peru) [Regional Coordinating Council]
CCSE	Coordinating Civil Society Entity
CDM	Comité de Desarrollo Municipal (Nicaragua) [Municipal Development Committee]
CE	Cooperación Externa [External Cooperation]
CEMR	Council of European Municipalities and Regions
COS	Centrum for Internationale Samenwerking (Netherlands) [Centre for International Cooperation]
CPC	Consejo del Poder Ciudadano (Nicaragua) [Council of Citizen Power]
EU	European Union
FISE	Fondo de Inversión Social de Emergencia (Nicaragua) [Emergency Social Investment Fund]
FODEL	Federación de Organizaciones para el Desarrollo Local (Nicaragua) [Federation of Organisations for Local Development]
FSLN	Frente Sandinista de Liberación Nacional (Nicaragua) [Sandinista National Liberation Front]
GRUFIDES	Grupo de Formación e Intervención para el Desarrollo Sostenible [Training and Intervention Group for Sustainable Development]
GSO	Gemeentelijke Samenwerking met Ontwikkelingslanden (Netherlands) [Municipal Cooperation with Developing Countries]
GST	Gemeentelijke Samenwerking met Toetredingslanden (Netherlands) [Municipal Cooperation with Accession Countries]
HDI	Human Development Index
HR	Human Resources
IC	International Cooperation
IDP	Integrated Development Plan/Planning (South Africa)
INIFOM	Instituto Nicaragüense de Fomento Municipal [Nicaraguan Institute of Municipal Development]
INWENT	Internationale Weiterbildung und Entwicklung (Germany) [Capacity Building International]
IT	Information Technology
IULA	International Union of Local Authorities
KATE	Kontaktstelle für Umwelt und Entwicklung (Germany) [Centre for Ecology and Development]
LA21	Local Agenda 21

THE CHALLENGE TO STRENGTHEN URBAN GOVERNANCE THROUGH NORTH-SOUTH CITY PARTNERSHIPS

LBSNN	Landelijk Beraad Stedenbanden Nederland-Nicaragua *[National Organisation of Twinnings Netherlands – Nicaragua]*
LED	Local Economic Development
LGA	Local Government Association
LOGO South	Local Government International Capacity Building Programme (Netherlands)
LOTA	Lokale Overheden Tegen Apartheid (Netherlands) *[Local Governments Against Apartheid]*
LSE	León Sur Este *[León South-East]*
MCLCP	Mesa de Concertación para la Lucha Contra la Pobreza (Peru) *[Concertation Board for the Fight Against Poverty]*
MDGs	Millennium Development Goals
MMTP	Municipal Management Training Programme (Netherlands)
MoU	Memorandum of Understanding
NCDO	Nationale Commissie voor Internationale Samenwerking en Duurzame Ontwikkeling (Netherlands) *[National Committee for International Cooperation and Sustainable Development]*
NGO	Non-governmental organisation
NPM	New Public Management
OECD	Organisation for Economic Cooperation and Development
OECD-DAC	OECD Development Assistance Committee
PDI	Plan de Desarrollo Institucional (Peru) *[Institutional Development Plan]*
PDM	Plan de Desarrollo Municipal (Nicaragua) *[Municipal Development Plan]*
PEDM	Plan Estructural de Dessarollo Municipal *[Structural Municipal Development Plan]*
PIA	Plan de Inversión Anual (Nicaragua) *[Annual Investment Plan]*
PIDC	Plan Integral de Desarrollo Concertado (Peru) *[Concertated Integrated Development Plan]*
PMS	Performance Management System (South Africa)
PROPOLI	Programa de Lucha Contra la Pobreza en Lima Metropolitana *[Programme to Fight Against Poverty in Metropolitan Lima]*
SALGA	South African Local Government Association
SAP	Structural Adjustment Programme
SCI	Sister Cities International
ToR	Terms of Reference
UCLG	United Cities and Local Governments
UN	United Nations
UNACLA	United Nations Advisory Committee of Local Authorities
UNAN	Universidad Nacional Autónoma de Nicaragua *[National Autonomous University of Nicaragua]*
UNDP	United Nations Development Programme
UN-Habitat	United Nations Human Settlements Programme
URB-AL	Decentralised cooperation programme of the European Commission for European and Latin American local communities
VES	Villa El Salvador

VNG	Vereniging van Nederlandse Gemeenten *[Association of Netherlands Municipalities]*
WACAP	World Alliance of Cities Against Poverty
WACLAC	World Association of Cities and Local Authorities Coordination

THE CHALLENGE TO STRENGTHEN URBAN GOVERNANCE THROUGH NORTH-SOUTH CITY PARTNERSHIPS

Preface

"Ein Kleingeist hält Ordnung, ein Genie überblickt das Chaos" luidde de spreuk op een tegeltje dat ik in april 2008 kocht in een porseleinwinkel in Heidelberg. Hoewel het waarschijnlijk bedoeld is om sloddervossen en chaoten een hart onder de riem te steken, schuilt in deze spreuk ook een krachtige les, die mij het schrijven van een proefschrift in een ander daglicht hielp plaatsen. Ik pretendeer geenszins een genie te zijn, maar het 'overzien van chaos' is precies hetgeen je dient te doen als je promotieonderzoek uitvoert. Ik heb ervaren dat hoe meer chaos je toestaat, hoe beter het resultaat uiteindelijk wordt. De geest de vrije loop laten, levert nieuwe inzichten en invalshoeken; teveel orde en structuur houden het denkproces beperkt. Dit was voor mij een grote uitdaging (ik hecht aan orde): loslaten, met opzet op zoek gaan naar ongemak door de grip op het onderwerp en de onderzoeksdata te verliezen, verstrikt raken in observaties, gedachten en ideeën. Het is de enige manier om uiteindelijk verbanden te leggen, vergelijkingen te maken, verschillen en overeenkomsten te ontdekken, patronen te herkennen. Dit proces is essentieel om uiteindelijk uit te komen op – inderdaad – een ordelijk verhaal. De lezer ziet dikwijls niet de worstelingen die zijn ondergaan om het resultaat in deze 'aangename' vorm te presenteren.

Twee mensen zijn onlosmakelijk verbonden aan dit proefschrift, en aan hen heb ik de kans te danken om chaos te scheppen en daarna weer te ordenen in een promotieonderzoek. Mijn promotor Otto Verkoren: je bracht veel nieuwe ideeën en wijsheid in, maar wist me ook te remmen wanneer ik te enthousiaste, ambitieuze plannen had. Je zorgde ervoor dat de chaos realistisch bleef en resulteerde in een concreet product. Je gaf me vertrouwen om mijn eigen weg te kiezen in deze vier jaar. Paul van Lindert: de termen 'co-promotor' of 'dagelijks begeleider' zijn niet toereikend om de rol te beschrijven die jij hebt vervuld. Het was veel meer. Je schreef een ambitieus onderzoeksvoorstel, kreeg dat gefinancierd en vertrouwde mij de invulling toe. Samen hebben we gepubliceerd, congressen bezocht, een special issue geredigeerd en seminars georganiseerd. Het onderwerp van gemeentelijke internationale samenwerking meer op de kaart gezet. Onze gezamenlijke verre reizen waren ontzettend leuk. Er was altijd ruimte en tijd voor overleg (en koffie!) en je interesse in het onderwerp werkte aanstekelijk.

In addition, there are several people who have contributed to my chaos and to whom I want to express my gratitude. First of all, Mayors, councillors, local officials, representatives of businesses and organisations and citizens from Utrecht, Amstelveen, Alphen aan den Rijn, Treptow-Köpenick, León, Villa El Salvador, Oudtshoorn and Cajamarca: I am thankful for our conversations and your willingness to share information, participate in meetings and help me in any possible way to collect meaningful data.
Some special people have given me a home away from home during fieldwork journeys. I would in particular like to mention Alie and Lehana Killian in Oudtshoorn and Frau Beier in Köpenick, who selflessly and without knowing me invited me as a guest to their homes. Your hospitality and our discussions and meals together meant a lot to me and have left a lasting impression.

Special thanks to 'partners in crime' Edith van Ewijk from the University of Amsterdam and Ulrike Devers-Kanoglu from the University of Cologne: we shared a passion for the research subject and have held endless discussions (in airplanes, municipal libraries, conference rooms and at home) on partnerships, mutuality, knowledge, learning and so on.

Also thanks to my colleagues at the Department of Human Geography and Planning, the International Development Studies group, Geomedia, fellow PhD candidates Bram, Edo, Rizki, Efsane, Dinu, Maarten, Daniël, Martin, Leendert, Rebecca and Sonja, and other researchers who I have met at conferences, training courses and workshops. You have added to the chaos by raising critical questions, but have also helped me to find comfort in ordering information and confirming my conclusions.

Ik wil ook velen buiten de wetenschap danken die hebben bijgedragen aan het voltooien van dit werk. Lieve ouders, jullie hebben mij een omgeving geboden waarin ik kon groeien en kon worden wie ik wil zijn. Dit is het mooiste geschenk voor een kind. Alle lieve vrienden en familie bedankt voor jullie interesse, afleiding en steun. Liesbeth, onze hardloopuurtjes en het trainen voor de halve marathon waren ideaal om uit de intellectuele chaos te stappen. Katinka, je dagelijks ontvangen zet-'m-op kaartjes in de laatste paar weken betekenden veel voor me. Beatrijs en Martine, de dineetjes bij jullie thuis brachten ontspanning na een dagje Uithof. Joyce Wigboldus, dank voor je inzet om het Engels in dit boek op te poetsen. Familie Lopes Cardozo, mijn weken 'retraite' op de Meulenhof in Renesse waren doorslaggevend om mijn verhaal op papier te zetten. Als laatste genoemd maar met stip bovenaan: Gideon. Mijn Genie. Je stimuleert me steeds het besef van mijn kunnen op te rekken. Tijdens mijn onderzoek was je mijn rots, mijn meest kritische meedenker, mijn gezelligste reisgenoot, de beste kopjes-thee-brenger, effectieve *stick* én *carrot*. Jij maakte het verschil, en ik draag dit boek aan jou op.

Marike Bontenbal Lopes Cardozo
Den Haag, Februari 2009

Introduction[1]

1. Backgrounds

This study on city-to-city cooperation and urban governance appears at a special time. During the French presidency of the European Union in the second half of 2008, France put forward an initiative to value the importance of the local dimension of development and to recognise the role of local governments in international cooperation.[2] The fact that local level governance and development are placed high on the EU agenda reflects an accumulation of attention and consolidates the recognition built up over the last years from donors, governments and practitioners alike to decentralised cooperation, in which cities take up a key role. Already in 2002, UN-Habitat chose city-to-city cooperation (C2C) – a term introduced by UNDP in 2000 – as the theme of World Habitat Day. It drew attention to the rapid growth of the number of city partnerships and networks world-wide. It has been estimated that today 70% of the world's cities are engaged in some form of international cooperation, sister city agreements, international city networks, partnerships and programmes (UCLG, 2006). Many of these links connect the developed and the developing world, or in different terms, the global North and global South. It puts cities at the core of international cooperation, both as development agents and beneficiaries.

In the light of world-wide ongoing decentralisation of government, globalisation and urbanisation trends, a growing sense of *global citizenship*, the changing role of local government and increased attention to good governance as a precondition for development, municipal partnerships are more and more employed as instruments for cities and communities to assist one another by means of knowledge sharing, transfer of resources and technology, and joint cooperation. Cities – both local administrations and civil societies – partner up and their partnerships seek to contribute to a variety of objectives, including poverty alleviation, institutional strengthening, democracy and peace building, knowledge exchange, and the attainment of the Millennium Development Goals. Moreover, city-to-city cooperation has been increasingly incorporated in supranational, national and local policy making. Various support programmes from donors, national governments and international local government associations, including the World Bank, UNDP, UN-Habitat, the European Union and United Cities and Local Governments (UCLG) facilitate local governments to be prominent players in the international development cooperation arena.

Not only has the number of international city arrangements increased, the regional and thematic scopes of these partnerships have also become more diverse. Since the emergence of C2C various stages in time have passed, leading to what has been described as different generations of C2C and 'twinning arrangements'. Not every C2C structure is related to development-oriented objectives (although this study deals with this type in particular) and motives to participate have varied from cultural exchanges and the exchange of people, to a

---

1   Part of this Introduction has been published elsewhere (Bontenbal & Van Lindert, 2009).

2   See http://www.localgovernance-coop-charter.eu/

   THE CHALLENGE TO STRENGTHEN URBAN GOVERNANCE THROUGH NORTH-SOUTH CITY PARTNERSHIPS

solidarity-driven perspective, often fed by political-ideological ideas, and to seeking mutual benefits to tackle urban challenges or to get inspiration from good practice of partner cities.

Although the number of C2C arrangements, city networks and local authorities involved in international cooperation is substantial, C2C is a newcomer in the academic debate on development cooperation. The number of academic studies on municipal international cooperation is limited, and relatively little is known about their objectives and results, organisational structures, success factors and weaknesses. The body of knowledge remains modest and anecdotal, and highly isolated in disciplines. This was one of the reasons to develop a research project on city-to-city cooperation, from which this dissertation and a range of publications are the offspring. The research aims to further conceptualise the phenomenon of C2C and moreover, to increase its empirical knowledge base. The intention of this research and its findings is to help put mainstream opinions, beliefs, and observations on city-to-city cooperation into perspective and to synthesise, measure, evaluate and critically assess existing policies and practices.

2. Raising the issues: towards a research objective and questions

Before turning to the introduction of the objective and main questions of the research, it should be stressed here that there is no agreement in the literature on the definition of city-to-city cooperation. This makes the use of the term somewhat ambiguous. Moreover, a plethora of synonyms is used,[3] which may add to the confusion. At the same time this diversity is a reflection of the richness and variety of the international activities of cities. A second key notion central to this research is *urban governance*. As with C2C, governance is a complex concept; its definition and meaning continues to be hotly debated. In section 3 the various concepts of the study and the underlying motives for their applications are defined in greater detail.

Chapter 1 and 2 provide a literature review of the main concepts of this research. In Chapter 1 the academic body of knowledge with regard to city-to-city cooperation in relation to development is discussed and compared. Chapter 2 examines the concept of urban governance. Starting from the debates on urban governance and C2C partnerships that are explored in these Chapters, the research aims to gain insight into the relevance and potential of North-South city-to-city cooperation with regard to strengthening urban governance in the South. Moreover, it seeks to gain a better understanding of the factors affecting this potential of C2C.

Below a brief account is given of the assumptions and issues emerging from the literature review. These form the foundation of the five research questions of this study. Ongoing urbanisation, especially in the developing world (the 'South'), and changing donor policies have made the 'urban' more prominent in development thinking. There is an increased recognition that the solutions to tomorrow's development and poverty challenges are to be found in cities. At the same time, as a result of government decentralisation and public reform, the nature of local administration and local policy making has been changing rapidly

---

3   E.g. town or city twinning, municipal partnerships, municipal international cooperation, decentralised cooperation, and city partnerships. In Chapter 1 these synonyms will be discussed in greater detail and the choice for using city-to-city cooperation as the main concept used in this study will be justified.

in many developing countries. In its turn this has increased both rights and responsibilities of local governments in the South, making their position in government systems more prominent (Devas & Grant, 2003; Campbell, 2003). The new responsibilities include the taking up of a more significant role in fostering local development and the improving of the quality of urban life. Changes in the legal and administrative framework in which local governments operate have raised a wide range of issues regarding the lack of organisational capacity and the needs to improve basic service delivery (Grindle, 2006). At the same time it offers opportunities for new forms of urban governance, in which municipalities, at the level closest to citizens, may become more responsive to local needs.

During the last decades local governments have increasingly become recognised as active actors in international development cooperation. Through various city-to-city (C2C) cooperation structures and organised city networks linking municipalities in North and South, cities are committed to improve municipal performance and enhance local development in partner cities in the South. The body of knowledge on municipal international relations has however been largely restricted to general international activity of local authorities (e.g. Hobbs, 1994; Shuman, 1994) or international municipal relations involving mainly the developed world (Zelinsky, 1991; Cremers et al., 2001; O'Toole, 2001). Only few academic publications have discussed the concept of C2C in detail (e.g. Hafteck, 2003; Bossuyt, 1994; ECDPM, 2004) thereby truly focusing on C2C as development modality, or in other ways, as form of decentralised cooperation. Practitioners have published several studies on C2C, either by municipalities involved in C2C or by supporting agencies e.g. IULA (Schep et al., 1995), UNDP (2000), IULA & ICLEI (Rademaker & Van der Veer, 2001) and UN-Habitat (2003).[4] Only a thin body of empirical case studies has been published (e.g. Hewitt, 1999, 2000, 2004; Tjandradewi et al., 2006; special issue on city-to-city cooperation, edited by Bontenbal & Van Lindert, 2009).

In order to understand the effects and the potential of city-to-city cooperation there is a need to examine the institutional and policy context in which these initiatives and activities occur. In the first place it is relevant to understand how cities and their local authorities are encouraged and supported in establishing and sustaining North-South relations. Multilateral organisations and national governments offer a range of incentives to municipalities, which often do not have sufficient resources to engage in international network and partnership activities. Secondly, it is imperative to understand the national institutional context in which urban governance in the South is placed, in order to gain insight into the question how the quality of urban governance in the South can be improved. This includes the role of local governments in the governance of society, their mandate and competencies, and their role in local (participatory) development processes. From these knowledge needs the following question is formulated:

Research Question 1: Which national and supranational institutional and policy conditions shape the role of local governments in international cooperation and local development processes?

---

4   Practitioner studies on the developmental role of city-to-city cooperation have existed for a longer time than academic studies, and have unravelled key issues at an early stage. A good example of an early practitioner study is Kussendrager (1985).

Descending from the (supra)national level reflected in research question 1, we arrive here at the level of the cities. The analysis and review in the academic discourse on development cooperation has been largely geared towards bilateral and multinational donor assistance on the one hand and the role of NGOs and CBOs on the other hand. The former category is largely concerned with development cooperation at the macro level by national governments and international donor institutions, often focusing on public sector reform and good governance. The latter type of cooperation is usually directed at local level development and poverty reduction dealing with civil society, with NGOs in the North working in direct partnership with locally based organisations in the South. In the dichotomy of bilateral macro donor assistance versus local, NGO-based cooperation with civil society, there has been limited space for academic attention to development cooperation initiated by and aimed at government at the local level. Indeed, so far there has been insufficient focus on development cooperation geared towards municipalities and performed by partner municipalities, and a need for further research has been indicated in order to understand the content, objectives and implications of such interventions (e.g. Tjandradewi et al., 2006; Hewitt, 1999). As Hafteck (2003) observes, in C2C local governments are at the core of North-South partnerships, making it a unique form of development cooperation. At the same time however, local institutions are primarily concerned with their area of jurisdiction and their own constituency for which they are politically accountable. They usually do not have a clear mandate for international cooperation, which has been traditionally confined to national governments. Although Hafteck (2003) considers it an advantage that municipalities engage in C2C on a voluntary basis and are not dependent on it for their existence, it also brings about a number of challenges with regard to the availability of resources and capacities. In this light, participation of local governments in the international cooperation arena raises a number of questions with regard to their suitability. Are local governments sufficiently tailored to provide development assistance, in terms of skills (to transfer knowledge and facilitate learning), knowledge (of urban development issues in the South) or cultural awareness (the way of 'doing business' in the partner country)? Moreover, as a clear mandate for international cooperation is often lacking, a high level of institutional consolidation within the municipal administration and political will have been found to be critical factors to sustain international activities (UNDP, 2000; UN-Habitat, 2003; Van Lindert, 2001; Spence & Ninnes, 2007). In local governments in the South it is assumed that similar capacities and conditions apply, although their implications are expected to differ, especially when the partner organisations vary in input of resources and knowledge. It is important to consider the various political-institutional factors and conditions in both North and South that shape the role of local governments in international cooperation, and to understand the implications for the practice of C2C, especially with regard to its potential for strengthening urban governance in the South. What are the (political) motives for local governments to be engaged in C2C? How are resources mobilised? What capacities are needed to perform their role? From this discussion, the following research question is distilled:

Research Question 2 Under which local political and institutional conditions do local governments operate in international cooperation and what are the implications for the practice of city-to-city cooperation?

A second distinguishing feature of C2C as form of development cooperation is that it is not confined to the participation of local authorities alone. In Hafteck's view (2003), while the concept of a relationship between local authorities is at the core of the partnership, the participation of civil society is a feature of equal importance. The interest of civil society and other non-public stakeholders in local city-to-city cooperation initiatives, and the extent and scope of their involvement has been considered a critical factor for success (UNDP, 2000; Rademaker & Van der Veer, 2001; UN-Habitat, 2003; Van Lindert, 2001, Tjandradewi et al., 2006). C2C thus usually involves a range of urban actors – with both an authoritative and a civil society background – as partners in C2C interventions and as the perceived beneficiaries of these interventions. Civil, private and public sector representatives collaborate in initiatives and together constitute a network of C2C actors. Although the existence of such municipal C2C networks has been identified in the literature (Schep et al. (1995, p. 4) refer to a 'web of links' consisting of different sectors and institutions), very little research has been done on how they function. Actors have their own objectives, capacities and resources that define their engagement. Together these actors constitute the 'partner city' of C2C cooperation structures. In order to understand how cities operate in international cooperation, it is essential to unravel this concept of 'partner city' and study its components and their interrelations in more detail. Hence, the distinguishing element of multi-stakeholder participation in C2C raises a number of issues. How do the individual actors collaborate in C2C efforts? Which roles can be distinguished and which factors affect them? Do discrepancies in preferences cause conflict and disagreement? How do cooperation or conflict within the networks affect the C2C initiatives performed? These issues are summarised in the following research question:

Research Question 3: Which actors constitute municipal C2C networks in partner cities, what are their roles and responsibilities and which interrelations can be found among them?

In order to understand the potential of C2C, one should not only observe the processes that take place in the two partner cities *per se*, but also consider the interrelations and cooperation between the two cities. From this angle, C2C partnerships are viewed as mechanisms for urban capacity development, conceptualised in this study as urban governance strengthening. In the literature ample attention has been paid to partnerships. Various strands of literature provide insight into such relationships in a North-South context, taking into account the often asymmetrical power relations as a result of differences in knowledge and resources (e.g. Jones & Blunt, 1999; Lister, 2000). Issues in this respect include the notion of ownership for beneficiaries in setting out their development strategies in capacity building initiatives, partnerships as sites for learning, and mutuality with regard to opportunities for learning and benefits that derive from the partnerships to participants in North and South (e.g. Milèn, 2001; Fowler, 1998; Ubels et al., 2005). McFarlane (2006) states that the linkages between learning, knowledge and development are of growing importance in the study of development, but attempts to explore how learning between North and South might be envisaged have been rare. Moreover, the literature, with some exceptions (e.g. Johnson and Wilson, 2006, Van Lindert, 2001), remains silent on how these concepts can be applied to the context of cities and local authorities in particular. This raises various questions in the discussion on city partnerships as to how the *process* of exchanging knowledge and expertise and capacity development can be made effective. Who sets the agenda of the partnership? What modalities of capacity development are most successful and what defines their success? To what extent does C2C offer opportunities for learning, and to whom? In short, the partnerships between cities themselves, as mechanisms of exchange, learning and capacity building, deserve to be studied in more detail. The guiding question to meet this demand is formulated as follows:

Research Question 4: Under which conditions and to what extent do C2C partnerships function as mechanism for capacity development and knowledge exchange?

Finally, it is apt to introduce the key question to this research. It brings together the two core concepts of the study. 'Good' governance, also at the urban level, is increasingly considered the *sine qua non* for sustainable development (UN-Habitat, 2002). Governance can be approached as a theory, as an empirical object of study and as a normative model (Pierre, 2005). The latter approach often interprets how governance 'ought to be'. Although a common definition of the concept remains debated (see Grindle, 2007), there is a growing agreement on the criteria for such a desired model. The review of literature in Chapter 2, in particular the work of Gaventa (2001) reveals that in order to improve the quality of governance in cities, the building of a strong local state as well as a strong citizenry are imperative. Development interventions with objectives corresponding to either need are believed to make urban governance developmental and make local development processes inclusive, offering opportunities to public and non-public stakeholders alike. The increased focus of the international donor community on governance (Bergh, 2004) underlines the recognition of the value of 'good governance' with regard to poverty alleviation and development. Within C2C cooperation strengthening urban governance has been a common objective (Hewitt, 2004; Rademaker & Van der Veer, 2001). However, in order to understand the implications of this objective, there is a need to appreciate on the one hand the urban governance processes taking place in the South, and on the other C2C cooperation seeking to contribute to these processes. Here, we touch upon the core of the research, where urban governance and C2C meet. How does city-to-city cooperation perform with regard to strengthening local governments and civil society in cities in the South? How can the external forces of C2C function as a mechanism to strengthen the quality of governance in partner cities? In other words:

Research Question 5: To what extent and in what way do C2C partnerships contribute to strengthening urban governance in the South?

In Chapter 2 a model is introduced which provides a methodological starting point for assessing the impact of city-to-city cooperation on urban governance. In order to answer this fifth research question, the study builds on the conceptualisation of the two-sided condition for 'good' urban governance. It first investigates how C2C can strengthen municipal administrations and their services. Secondly, it identifies the contributions that C2C can make to fostering citizen participation in local decision-making processes. The rationale of linking city-to-city cooperation to this two-sided approach is the following. As stated above, as a decentralised form of development cooperation, C2C has the unique feature that it involves a range of urban actors with both a public and non-public background. This diversity is reflected in the wide scope of objectives pursued. First, C2C is perceived as being instrumental in enhancing the capacities of local institutions. North-South city partnerships facilitate the transfer of know-how and expertise among municipalities to tackle needs in urban management and service delivery. This often takes the form of technical *practitioner-to-practitioner* exchanges between local politicians and administrators (Johnson & Wilson, 2006; Schep et al., 1995; Buis 2009). Secondly, C2C aims to contribute to community strengthening and provision of services, especially for the poor. Interventions of this category are often pursued by civil society groups e.g. through strengthening the capacity of NGOs or neighbourhood committees in the South (UNDP, 2000; UN-Habitat, 2003). It is therefore assumed that C2C partnerships may affect urban governance from different angles, drawing on the participation of a wide variety of stakeholders in North and South.

3. Conceptual model and guiding concepts defined

The guiding concepts of this study are defined as follows:

1. **The 'global North'; the 'global South'.** 'North' and 'South' are used here as metaphors to stress the socio-economic division between the industrialised, (economically) developed countries, known collectively as 'the global North' and the poor, developing countries or 'the global South'. Although the majority of countries which make up 'the North' are in fact located in the Northern Hemisphere, the divide is not primarily geographically defined. Rather, the terms 'North' and 'South' are used to express a development gap, also known as the 'North-South divide'. The North is understood as having obtained a high level of 'development', which is usually correlated to high income per capita and a high Human Development Index.[5]

2. In this study, **city-to-city cooperation** (C2C in short) refers to formalised, long-term, bi-lateral partnerships between two local authorities, one comprising of the 'North' and one comprising of the 'South', in which a range of development initiatives are performed by local public, private and civil actors. In order to avoid reader fatigue, various synonyms are used including *city partnerships, municipal partnerships* and *city links*. Unless otherwise specified, they are used as equivalents for city-to-city cooperation.

3. **Local governments** are defined as the governing authorities of municipalities by locally elected public bodies. The geographical territory and area of jurisdiction of local governments is defined by the politico-administrative organisation of the state to which it pertains. The area of jurisdiction of local or sub-national authorities may hence refer to regions, counties, districts, or municipalities. In this research local government concerns the governing authorities of municipalities and district municipalities. Synonyms used in this study include local authorities and municipalities.

4. **Municipal C2C actors** are defined as individuals and organisations from local public, private and civil sectors that are involved in C2C structures. Their involvement may be expressed in direct participation in C2C activities, or the funding thereof. As Hafteck (2003) notes, while local governments are lead actors in C2C, other 'locally-based actors' from civil society, the non-profit and private sectors collaborate with local authorities

---

5   The Human Development Index (HDI) measures the achievements of an economy in three basic dimensions of human development, namely life expectancy, literacy and income.

THE CHALLENGE TO STRENGTHEN URBAN GOVERNANCE THROUGH NORTH-SOUTH CITY PARTNERSHIPS

and the international activities carried out by them. Together, these actors constitute a **municipal C2C network**, which refers to a multi-actor model of international cooperation in which C2C actors are connected to participate jointly in C2C efforts.

5. Based on the perspective that both a strong local state and a strong local civil society are needed to improve the quality of urban governance, the concept of **urban governance strengthening** therefore builds on this two-sided condition in this study. Local government strengthening with regard to its effectiveness and responsiveness, and civil society strengthening with regard to enhancing opportunities for citizen and other non-state participation in urban decision-making are considered. Chapter 2 defines these concepts in greater detail.

Figure 0.1 shows the conceptual model, discerning the central elements of the research and their assumed relations and interdependencies. At its centre the key subject of city-to-city cooperation is placed. It is assumed that the practice of C2C is influenced by processes and conditions in both North and South. The 'global North' and the 'global South' are constructed in an identical way, i.e. they consist of a municipal C2C network, in which various actors in C2C are represented. Local government is one of them, and as its participation is a key feature of city-to-city cooperation, its objectives, activities and motives are highlighted in this study, in particular the political and organisational conditions affecting them. The model shows that with regard to the municipal C2C networks the various actors as well as their interrelations are expressed in the research. 'North' and 'South' differ to the extent that they operate in dissimilar institutional and policy contexts. The dotted lines in the model represent these contexts and demonstrate that they both affect the processes taking place in the cities in North and South and the practice and partnership of C2C itself (i.e. the interaction as a result of linking the partners). Finally, the model demonstrates the assumed relationship between city-to-city cooperation and urban governance strengthening. Urban governance is further specified, based on the two-sided conceptualisation of urban governance in this study explained above.

It should be noted from the model that the emphasis of this study is on the local level. City-to-city cooperation takes place in a complex structure of actors, power, and policies at local, national and international level. It is beyond this study to examine this complete structure. Instead the focus of analysis is on local processes and practice. It is useful to refer to Hafteck's (2003) conceptual mapping exercise which demonstrates that decentralised cooperation (or C2C in this study) is embedded in complex frameworks of development cooperation as well as local government (and governance), while at the same time it is confined to where these frameworks overlap.

4. Methodology

This section briefly considers some general methodological issues with regard to the case studies selected and used in this research and the methods applied to collect empirical data. Annex I contains a detailed overview of the methodology and research methods employed in this study.

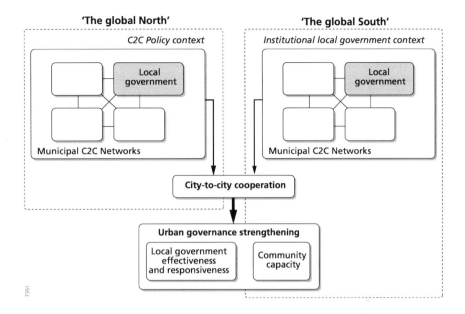

Figure 0.1 Conceptual model of the study

A multiple case study strategy

The research uses qualitative research methods and takes a multiple-case study approach. The choice of research strategy has been largely based on Ragin's retroduction model (1994) and is further clarified in Annex I. The Annex provides also more detail on the process of the selection of case studies, based on a combination of factors, such as existing knowledge base, theory-driven considerations, the prospect of analytic generalisation, and more practical factors i.e. access to the field. As C2C is a variable phenomenon it is not easy to make a meaningful selection. At the same time, given the exploratory nature of this study, this very diversity was an important criterion on which to base the choice of cases. The following four North-South C2C partnerships have been included in the study:

1. Amstelveen (The Netherlands) – Villa el Salvador (Peru)
2. Treptow-Köpenick (Germany) – Cajamarca (Peru)
3. Utrecht (The Netherlands) – León (Nicaragua)
4. Alphen aan den Rijn (The Netherlands) – Oudtshoorn (South Africa).

Box 0.1 briefly introduces the four partnerships. In Chapter 5 a more detailed account is provided of these cities and their respective partnerships. It is important to emphasise here that the case studies in this research refer to city-to-city partnerships, and not to individual cities. Therefore each case study consists of two geographical and administrative components, i.e. the Northern and the Southern city of the partnerships.

THE CHALLENGE TO STRENGTHEN URBAN GOVERNANCE THROUGH NORTH-SOUTH CITY PARTNERSHIPS

Box 0.1 The four C2C partnerships cases

- The municipalities of **Amstelveen** and **Villa El Salvador** (VES) became official partners in 1997. Recent cooperation projects (2004-2007) aimed at strengthening the local administration of VES with a focus on municipal finance and environmental management.
- Since its inception in 1983, the partnership between **Utrecht** and **León** has known both municipal and civil society participation. From 1998, Utrecht Municipality has supported León in its urban expansion ambitions in the León South East project to build 15,000 dwellings by 2020.
- The partnership (1998) between the Berlin District **Treptow-Köpenick** and the Municipality of **Cajamarca** is an example of C2C as North-South component in the framework of Local Agenda 21. Mainly driven by civil society, the municipal role is more limited. The partnership aims at fostering exchanges (e.g. schools), awareness raising and fundraising.
- **Alphen aan den Rijn** ('Alphen') signed a twinning agreement with **Oudtshoorn** in 2002, focusing on strengthening institutional performance and community development in Oudtshoorn. The municipality has been assisted with policymaking on HIV/Aids, gender and social housing, and the implementation of a Performance Management System.

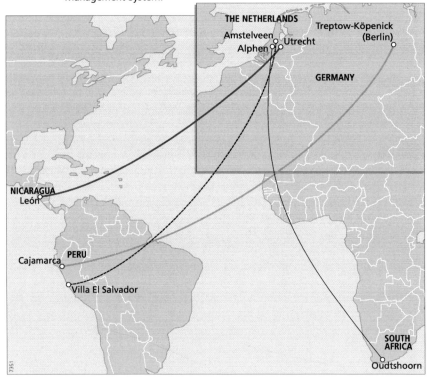

Figure 0.2 The four C2C partnership cases

Methods

Research was performed between 2005 and 2008 in the eight cities under study. Various qualitative research techniques were applied. The number of interviews, observation opportunities and documents varied per case. These methods have been employed to gather data from individuals and organisations that are either involved in C2C partnerships, affect it or experience impact from it: local politicians, local government officials, representatives of public-private partnerships, (twinning) development projects, local government associations, civil society groups, NGOs, embassies, etc.

Semi structured (in-depth) interviews have been used to explore various topics and to allow respondents to share their knowledge and express their opinions and views. A list of respondents is attached as Annex II. In addition, a survey was held to assess the individual characteristics, motivations, learning experiences and visions with regard to respondents' participation in municipal exchanges and C2C delegation missions. Representatives from municipal councils and local administrations in both Northern and Southern cities were interviewed; in Oudtshoorn, entrepreneurs were included as well.

The opportunity to use observation as a research tool largely depended on whether situations occurred during the fieldwork period that were relevant to the research. Examples include shadowing members of delegations visiting their partner cities, being present at workshops and meetings organised in the framework of partnership activities, and attending public forums and other local participatory decision-making structures such as public consultation for approval of annual municipal budgets.

Documents that have been analysed include (municipal) policy documents, C2C partnership evaluations, urban strategic plans, urban development plans, reports from civil organisations, speeches, local newspaper articles, mission reports, personal diaries, etc. As with observing, document collection has varied from case to case. Some partnerships are better documented than others and some local authorities have extensive policy documentation where others have not.

Finally, in some cities there was an opportunity to organise dissemination workshops in the final stages of the research project. Sharing the research findings and results with the respondents is not only of ethical and societal importance, it proved also to be a unique method to fine-tune and reflect on the research outcomes, as the meetings allowed to directly incorporate feedback from respondents.

5. Detailed outline of the study

Having introduced the concepts behind the theme of this dissertation and having raised the key questions that emerge from the discussions on city-to-city cooperation and urban governance strengthening, the outline of the study is presented here (Figure 0.3).

In *Chapter 1 and 2* respectively, the two key concepts are explored in more detail, based on a literature review. Although together they provide the theoretical foundation of the research, it was decided to discuss the discourses on city-to-city cooperation and urban governance separately in different Chapters, for a number of reasons. The conceptual model clearly shows their distinction, one being an instrument (means) to attain the other (end).

Moreover, the notion of 'partnership' is widely used in the governance debate,[6] mainly to indicate local relations between public and non-public sectors (such as public-private partnerships, see e.g. Krishna, 2003; Pierre, 1998). This could confuse our understanding of C2C partnerships, which (as section 3 pointed out) refer explicitly to partnerships between two different local authority entities in North and South.

Chapter 3 and 4 provide an institutional framework and respond to research question 1. *Chapter 3* discusses current policies with regard to urban development and municipal partnerships and explains the increased attention among donors, national governments and practitioners for C2C. It reviews several shifts in development thinking that have resulted in a growing role of municipalities as development partners. Moreover, it considers the response of donors and national governments to this growing recognition, presents various C2C policy instruments and examines how they affect C2C practice. While Chapter 3 focuses on policies and support programmes that encourage municipalities in the 'North' to engage in C2C, in *Chapter 4* attention is turned towards the 'South'. The institutional frameworks in which the Southern partner cities operate are equally important. National legislation, municipal mandates and existing urban governance structures in Peru, South Africa and Nicaragua are discussed, as they affect the question to what extent the objective of strengthening urban governance through C2C can be achieved.

Chapter 5 is an intermezzo. It serves to bridge the theoretical and institutional frameworks of the preceding Chapters with the empirical analysis carried out in the subsequent Chapters. This Chapter introduces the empirical cases – i.e. partner cities in North and South and their respective C2C partnerships. It examines the local socio-economic and institutional dynamics of the cities and reviews the history of the partnerships and how it has affected the current C2C practice today.

Chapters 6, 7, 8 and 9 are empirically grounded and present the main findings of the study. In *Chapter 6* research question 2 is considered. It discusses the political and organisational conditions under which local governments operate as partners in international development, in both North and South. The Chapter analyses the critical conditions that have an impact on the role of local governments in development cooperation in the North, and also defines the extent to which partner cities in the South apply C2C partnerships as a strategy to meet municipal development objectives.

Chapter 7 is linked to research question 3. This means that the level of analysis will move away from the institution or organisation to the wider municipality or city. In this Chapter various actors from public, private and civil sectors are reviewed. Together they form C2C networks in partner cities, and their interrelations are considered. As will be demonstrated, these latter range from cooperation to conflict.

While Chapter 6 and 7 analyse the conditions and factors that define the role and position of the respective partner cities and their (municipal) organisations in city-to-city cooperation, *Chapter 8* turns towards the mechanism of partnership itself. Connected to research question 4, it analyses the conditions that shape capacity development for urban governance strengthening through municipal partnerships, and provides insight into how partnerships could possibly be sustained and which challenges they are confronted with.

---

6   The concept of partnership is not only applied in governance literature but it is also extensively used in (sustainable) development literature (e.g. Ros-Tonen, Hombergh & Zoomers, 2007; Glasbergen et al., 2007). The use and meaning of the concept however varies drastically, which is considered in more detail in Chapter 2.

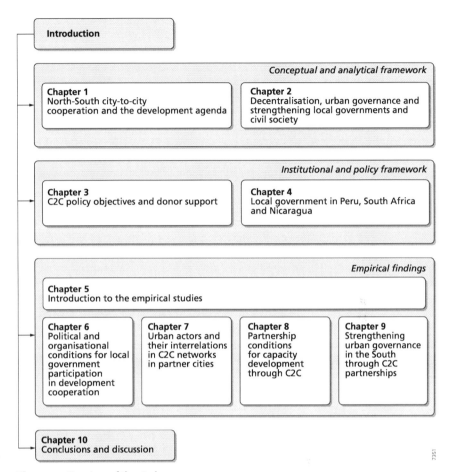

Figure 0.3 Structure of the study

The final empirical *Chapter (9)* reviews the effects and contributions C2C has made with regard to urban governance strengthening in the partner cities in the South. As such, it aims to answer research question 5. Empirical results of C2C initiatives are discussed and compared against the background of the analytical framework of urban governance strengthening introduced in Chapter 2.

Chapter 10 summarises the study, reviews its findings and discusses the implications in the light of the theoretical context, guided by the research questions.

THE CHALLENGE TO STRENGTHEN URBAN GOVERNANCE THROUGH NORTH-SOUTH CITY PARTNERSHIPS

1 North-South city-to-city cooperation and the development agenda: lessons from practice[7]

During the last decades, local governments have increasingly become recognised as relevant actors in international development cooperation through city-to-city cooperation structures. This Chapter seeks to review various strands of literature to explore the nature and implications of city-to-city cooperation and to examine to what extent C2C provides an instrument for meeting some of the challenges local governments and communities in the South are faced with. This Chapter aims to contribute to the discussion in three ways. First, a further conceptualising of city-to-city cooperation is given to understanding the significance of the practice of C2C in the international arena of development cooperation. The Chapter therefore starts with a brief review of the role of local government in development in the South and the needs for capacity development, which will be considered in more detail in Chapter 2. Second, as too little is known as yet about the present and potential developmental role of partnering cities, a first synthesis of the perceived benefits of C2C partnerships and critical factors affecting them is provided. The next session thus discusses what is understood by city-to-city cooperation and how it has evolved over the years. Subsequently, based on a comparative analysis of documented studies of C2C partnerships and support programmes, the Chapter seeks to gain more insight into the benefits of C2C partnerships to the participating cities and their local administrations and the critical factors that improve or undermine C2C practice. Third, lessons from practice emerge from the meta-analysis, drawing attention to a number of key issues that are connected to the practice of North-South city-to-city cooperation. The subsequent section of the Chapter discusses these issues in more detail, further exploring various strands of literature.

1.1 Shifting mandates for local government in the South: the capacity imperative

Since the mid-1980s, decentralisation reforms have been introduced in developing nations. Governments have reshaped and strengthened their systems of local government and have devolved responsibilities and resources to sub-national levels (Devas & Grant, 2003). The diminishing role of the State runs parallel with the trend towards new opportunities for citizen participation and democratisation. The belief that decentralisation will result in better use of resources is based on the assumption that local citizens have an influence on the decisions made by local governments. This would result in more efficient service delivery and urban development planning that is inclusive and provides equal opportunities for those

---

7 Parts of this Chapter have been published elsewhere in adapted version (Bontenbal & Van Lindert, 2006; Bontenbal & Van Lindert, 2008a; Bontenbal, 2009a).

concerned. Changes in the institutional frameworks of developing countries have resulted in new mandates, responsibilities and financial resource bases for local government. Campbell (2003) refers to this process as the 'quiet revolution'. Local governments have gained many new responsibilities, dealing with basic service delivery and urban infrastructure. In addition, a primary competency has emerged since municipalities are increasingly expected to become 'developmental' through taking a lead role in local development processes. A municipal approach that is development-oriented and encourages the community to participate is considered an important precondition for local governments to take an active role in the local development processes. In that sense, developmental local government structures provide a foundation on which the interrelations between local government, civil society and local development are brought together. Indeed, it has been argued that conditions of *urban governance* (dealt with in more detail in Chapter 2) – which addresses these interrelations contribute to the creation of partnerships and decision-making that is inclusive and reflects broad consensus in society, and hence may lead to a reduction of poverty (Chapter 2).

The quality of local government performance in this respect however has been severely undermined by the many problems municipalities are faced with. Under highly centralised political systems, local governments had long been without any significant authority or resources. The changing nature of local administration steered by decentralisation processes in combination with a continuous weak financial resource base challenges organisational capacity and basic service delivery: service provision has to be created or restructured, officials need to be trained and new legislation and procedures need to be put into effect (Grindle, 2006). Local governments keep lacking financial and human resources to perform their tasks adequately. With so many difficulties today, the institutional strengthening of local governments in the South continues to be a major task for the future.

With the process of decentralisation and the need to strengthen local governments, the potential role for local authorities in the North to provide development assistance to cities in the South through city-to-city cooperation structures is intensified. As Chapter 2 and 3 will demonstrate, the evolution in development assistance has partly led to a growing emphasis on the decentralised and urban level. The understanding that nation states no longer represent the sole milieu for solving current problems (Gaspari, 2002) has strengthened the role of non-state actors and micro-order players in development aid. Moreover, the increased attention to *good governance* on the development agenda of donor agencies has not been confined to the macro level. Only recently the majority of the human population is urban. This reality, along with the fact that urbanisation is most rapid in developing countries means that poverty is becoming increasingly urbanised. This calls for an intensified focus on good urban government, governance and development intervention that is geared towards meeting this goal. It is in this context that local authorities world wide have stepped up to become actively involved in development aid and C2C is considered an innovative way of development cooperation. The overall objective of C2C is indeed contributing to development at the local level (Hafteck, 2003). The exchange of information and technology among municipalities allows for capacity building to strengthen urban governance in developing countries and assist local authorities in taking up their newly ascribed competencies.

1.2 Understanding city-to-city cooperation

The evolution of international municipal relations in the 20th century

In order to better understand the contemporary phenomenon of C2C, it is useful to look into the history of international municipal relations. Although the municipal movement has now reached global dimensions, its European practice was undoubtedly the most highly developed until the second part of the 20th century (Gaspari, 2002).

The emergence of international municipal relations in Europe and the 'networked European municipality' (Ewen & Hebbert, 2007) can be traced back to the beginning of the 20th century, partly as a working class initiative to lobby for socio-economic improvements, partly as a utopian vision of those striving for unity of all people in a universal brotherhood (Dogliani, 2002; Gaspari, 2002). The ideas and ideals of the International Union of Local Authorities (IULA) founded in 1913, which developed into the "most immediate progenitor of today's organised transnational companionship among communities" (Zelinsky, 1991, p. 5), underline the objectives of international municipal relations at that time: the exchange of technical knowledge and, more from an ideological viewpoint, bringing together institutions from all over Europe (Gaspari, 2002). World War II caused an intensification of international municipal relations. According to Zelinsky (1991), a major impulse was the work of war relief organisations that channelled assistance from North America to the allies in Europe, occasionally from one specific place to another. After the war, a growing reconciliation movement evolved in Europe, creating active twinning relationships between municipalities, initially in France and Germany but later involving other countries as well. The 1950s can be marked as the effective period of origin of international twinning relationships between cities (Mamadouh, 2002).

The political crisis that nation states encountered after the Second World War allowed room for municipalities to appear on the international scene. A new municipal association was initiated in 1951, the Council of European Municipalities (CEM). It was founded by fifty European municipalities whose primary objective was to achieve European integration in accordance with the principles of subsidiarity and local democracy through the encouragement of municipal exchanges and projects. In 1984 the Council of European Municipalities and Regions (CEMR) evolved from the CEM and merged with IULA in 1990, whereby the former became the European section of the latter (Hafteck, 2003). Various other national and international organisations were founded to foster town twinning, such as *Monde Bilingue* in France.

Whereas in Europe town twinning originated from bottom-up initiatives, the American twinning program was established top-down. The US movement materialised with President Eisenhower's 'People-to-People' program in 1956 that was intended to involve individuals and organised groups in citizen diplomacy, encouraging exchanges fostered through sister cities (the American equivalent of the European town twinnings) to reduce the chance of future world conflicts (Mamadouh, 2002; Vion, 2002). The initiative was reorganised in 1967 as a separate non-profit organisation known as Sister Cities International (SCI). Nowadays, SCI presents itself as a 'non-profit citizen diplomacy network' and functions as clearinghouse, catalyst, matchmaker, and advisor. SCI claims to have the world's largest number of twinnings today on a national scale (Hafteck, 2003).

The pattern that evolved in Europe and the USA from the 1950s onwards have turned into a world-wide trend of long-term international municipal relations. Attempts have been made to estimate the total number of town twinning relationships. Zelinsky (1991) calculated that by the end of the 1980s more than 11,000 pairs of cities in some 159 countries had entered into twinning agreements. Mamadouh (2002) suggested that the total number of CEMR twinning arrangements in 1995 was around 14,000. Today, there are close to 30,000 European twinnings registered with CEMR, giving Europe the highest density of town twinning (Ewen & Hebbert, 2007). In the United States, SCI claims to represent more than 2,400 communities in 124 countries around the world compared to 1,205 communities in 87 countries in 1988.

Today, 70% of the world's cities participate in C2C programmes (UCLG, 2006). The figures thus indicate that the number of twinnings has increased substantially over the last twenty years and that twinnings are a ubiquitous phenomenon and practice of local administration worldwide.

The links that originated directly after world war II were predominantly cultural and involved primarily the countries of the North (Zelinsky, 1991). From the 1980s onward, the scope of twinning became more varied in terms of regional distribution and objectives. As Giezen (2008) notes, shifting ideologies resulted in a different use of twinning structures. Twinning now also involved communities in the socialist countries of Eastern Europe, a means for Western cities to express solidarity and protest against the Cold War. After the collapse of the Iron Curtain, West European twinning initiatives assisted in the institutional reforms of their now transitional partners in Eastern Europe (Buček & Bakker, 1998). Also, some twinnings obtained a more economic character, fostering entrepreneurship, city marketing and trade (Giezen, 2008; Cremer et al, 2001; O'Toole, 2001). One of the most obvious shifts in scope and goals, however, has been the emergence of town twinning as an expression of decentralised development cooperation. The idea of 'cooperation twinnings' was launched in the 1960s after the independence of several African states, and was practiced essentially by municipalities from France and West Africa, in particular Senegal. Such decentralised cooperation developed further in the 1970s and 1980s, becoming more project-based and technically oriented (Hafteck, 2003). While twinning arrangements of cooperation between municipalities or institutions were first developed primarily as aid delivery mechanisms, they now increasingly aim to build capacity and facilitate the exchange of local governance knowledge and practices between cities.

Numerous municipalities involved in North-South twinning are now functioning on an equal footing with other international cooperation agencies. Hafteck (2003, p. 338) points out the comparative advantages of local governments over NGOs and other stakeholders: their possession of in-house technical expertise, their experience with medium to long-term project cycle planning and budgeting, and their approach of involving relevant stakeholders from civil society in decision making processes. Further, Hafteck maintains that local governments, as established institutions, "can engage in development cooperation by choice rather than necessity" – i.e. their existence is not dependent on it.

Defining city-to-city cooperation in a developmental context
The trends in the international municipal relations described above are important in order to understand city-to-city cooperation and its development potentials. With its objective to improve local governance and urban development, C2C is more than an instrument linking populations of different cities through cultural exchange. Cities set up and support projects,

and provide knowledge and expertise through capacity building in their partner cities, often organised in a peer-to-peer setting for local government officials and politicians.

A serious attempt to define and conceptualise C2C is made by Hafteck (2003). In his article he gives an overview of the existing definitions and terminology used by various support programmes and local government associations. Terms used to describe C2C practice include 'Municipal International Cooperation' (Schep *et al.*, 1995), 'International Municipal Cooperation' (Hewitt, 1999, 2000), 'linking' (UNDP, 2000) and 'city-to-city cooperation' (used by UN-Habitat and the world's largest local government association United Cities and Local Governments – UCLG). In this study the term 'city-to-city cooperation' is used to refer to the practice of North-South city partnerships. A number of arguments can be put forward to motivate this choice. For example the term 'twinning' should be avoided to prevent confusion with the use of the term in a more general sense in development practice, when it refers to cooperation efforts between institutions, universities, hospitals and other public services (see Jones & Blunt, 1999; Avskik, 1999). 'Twinning' does therefore not sufficiently stress the central position given in this study to local governments and their communities in North-South partnerships. Another reason to avoid 'twinning' is to distinguish municipal relations with substantive development objectives, from twinnings focusing on cultural or people exchanges. Furthermore, 'municipal international cooperation' may imply that North-South city partnerships are confined to the participation of local governments and city councils alone. Instead, as will be demonstrated in this Chapter and in Chapter 7, these partnerships often move beyond local government and include the participation of a wide range of stakeholders from civil and private spheres as well. City-to-city cooperation has become an umbrella covering all possible forms of relationships between local authorities at any level in two or more countries which are collaborating over matters of mutual interest leading to sustainable urban development. Being used by UN-Habitat and UCLG in policymaking and widely acknowledged by their partner organisations, the term fits best the current thinking on municipal development cooperation and its practice. Moreover, C2C has increasingly gained ground as an accepted concept in the academic debate on North-South city partnerships, especially in recent years (see e.g. Tjandradewi et al., 2006; Tjandradewi & Marcotullio, 2009; Buis, 2009; De Villiers, 2009; Van Lindert, 2009).[8]

Much discussion as there is about the terminology to describe the C2C movement, there is discussion about an overarching, inclusive definition that reflects all C2C activities and characteristics. As Hafteck (2003) notes, a single definition for C2C does not exist. He provides an overview of the definitions used by various organisations involved in development cooperation. Although there is variety in approach, lead actors, purpose and means involved, he finds some points of convergence: the overall goal of sustainable development, the concept of some form of partnership between local authorities at the core of the partnership, the notion of territory (i.e. the area of jurisdiction of a local authority), and the participation of civil society. Hafteck's (2003) view of decentralised development

---

8   Hafteck (2003) prefers to use the term Decentralised Cooperation (DC) and notes that using the term C2C may lead to misunderstandings: the term 'city' may not be ideal as it does not reflect the entire range of sub-national governments that are involved in such partnerships. DC itself is however also a controversial term, assuming that all project-implementing entities other than central administrative bodies can engage. As such, DC is often understood for example to include NGOs as well, whereas in this study, local public institutions, representing 'the city', are at the core of the concept.

cooperation based on these insights includes the elements of "consist[ing] in substantial collaborative relationships between sub-national governments from different countries, aiming at sustainable local development, implying some form of exchange or support carried out by these institutions or other locally based actors" (p. 336).

From the literature no blueprint can be distinguished for the activities, involved actors, geographical scope, or contact frequency of decentralised development cooperation. Various authors have reviewed these elements in their work (Cremer et al., 2001; Hafteck, 2003; Mamadouh, 2002; Vagale, 2003; Zelinsky, 1991). Although C2C cooperation is highly diverse in content, some general characteristics can be discerned, which distinguish C2C as a unique form of international development cooperation.

A first general characteristic of decentralised development cooperation is that it is usually founded on two pillars; the local state apparatus and its constituency, i.e. the citizens themselves. As far as the local administration is concerned, its involvement is most visible in the formal political and technical encounters between mayors, municipal councillors, and technical personnel. Such C2C programmes, providing monetary and in-kind contributions (including training sessions and advisory services), are designed to encourage regular, direct, and on-going contact between municipal officers and technicians, allowing the transfer of technical information and exchange of expertise and best practice (Hewitt, 1999). Thus, the exchange of know-how and experience is a central aim, servicing the overall objective of attaining sustainable urban development through improved municipal performance. The second pillar consists of the participation and contributions of civil society, the non-profit and the private sector. Civil society may cooperate with the local authority in C2C activities, or it may execute its own programme. In fact, there are many hybrid forms of North-South partnerships incorporating municipal and civil society efforts. Civil society activities include fundraising for projects and facilitating the exchange of people (e.g. students) and information by means of organising exhibitions and festivals. Raising awareness on global issues and development cooperation is an important goal, as well as generating public support for the international cooperation efforts of the local government. Mamadouh (2002) and Buček & Bakker (1998) point out that these activities in the civil society sphere have a substantial symbolic meaning, reinforcing the link between the cities and further stimulating public support.

A second characteristic of C2C is its North-South dimension, bringing together local governments from the 'North' (the industrialised, developed world) and South (the developing world). This North-South component is fundamentally connected with the fact that C2C cooperation specifically aims at strengthening the developmental capacity of local governments and thus contributing to local development, liveability and productivity, and reducing poverty in the South.

Third, C2C cooperation is characterised by a formal agreement of a long-term, bilateral partnership between the participating local authorities and their respective civil society groups. In general, the relationship does not limit itself to carrying out a single project but opens a way for a variety of shared activities, usually for an indefinite period (Zelinsky, 1991, Cremer et al, 2001).

Fourth, funding is usually provided from the Northern donor municipalities' budgets and through non-public fund raising campaigns in these cities. Additional funds derive from national governments, local government associations, or through various international donor-funded programmes.

Finally, the potential mutuality of effort and benefit between the partners distinguishes C2C cooperation from other types of development cooperation. It has been perceived that in practice, Southern partners are supported by means of financial aid and capacity building activities, whilst Northern partners benefit from C2C through an increased awareness and knowledge of global issues and the opportunity for the public at large to participate in development efforts. Thus, the exchange of knowledge and expertise through peer-to-peer programmes for local government officials and citizens implies two-way capacity building. However, with a few exceptions (cf. Van Lindert, 2001), empirical evidence on this subject has so far been limited (see also 1.4).

1.3 A comparative analysis of selected C2C programmes and partnerships: benefits, strengths and weaknesses

The academic body of knowledge on the benefits and underlying mechanisms affecting C2C, has remained limited and mainly anecdotal and based on localised experiences (see Table 1.1). There is no common agreement on what constitutes good city-to-city cooperation in the sense that it utilises its full potential to contribute to urban development and poverty alleviation in the South. Too little is known as yet about the present and potential role of cities in exchanging knowledge and expertise that helps improve urban governance practice. What are strengths that constitute 'good' C2C? And which weaknesses can be observed that may undermine the functioning of city partnerships? Below, a first comparative meta-level analysis of documented studies of C2C partnerships and support programmes is presented. It focuses on, respectively, the perceived benefits of C2C cooperation, its strengths and, finally, its weaknesses. Table 1.1 summarises the main findings.

Benefits for cities engaging in C2C partnerships

The wide variety of results and benefits that was found from the literature and document analysis reveals that the effects and impact of C2C partnerships are highly diverse, and that a range of objectives and outcomes has been obtained. Three main categories of C2C benefits can be pointed out, which are related to, respectively, the fostering of global citizenship; the strengthening of municipal institutions; and the improvement of liveability and access to services.

The positive effect that C2C partnerships may have on global citizenship is especially felt among the Northern partners. Many city councils that formally approve of municipal development cooperation as being one of the municipality's responsibilities hold the legitimate argument that such cooperation will foster a better understanding of globalisation and development cooperation issues among citizens. Related are the advantages of increasing international accountability among local authorities to address global challenges (Van Lindert, 2001) and that of 'creating a global culture of peace' through the linking of populations from different countries (UNDP, 2000). Indeed, many Northern municipalities consider citizen education an important objective to engage in C2C partnerships. In practice, however, it is not easy to measure the impact of such efforts. Analogous to awareness-raising among citizens (e.g. Hewitt, 2004), perceived learning benefits for Northern participants in North-South technical exchanges have been mentioned. In the framework of the South African/Canadian programme on Governance, six sub-national government twinning relationships were examined (Proctor, 2000). The study found that

Table 1.1 Benefits, strengths and weaknesses of documented C2C cooperation

Study	Benefits	Strengths	Weaknesses
UNDP (2000)	Contributions to combating poverty Greater international understanding, creating a global culture of peace 'Concrete improvements to the lives of the poor' e.g. in sanitation, health, education Improved municipal performance e.g. management, finance, administration Awareness-raising and development education in the North	Commitments in terms of time and resources Community-wide participation Mutual understanding partners Mutuality of effort and benefit	Partners want quick results with high expectations Threat of paternalism and donor domination Lack of expertise and knowledge of development cooperation Concentrated political and administrative support risks discontinuity
UN-Habitat (2003)	'Tangible benefits' for cities and their citizens e.g. in municipal finance, infrastructure, health and social services C2C initiatives less formal and bureaucratic and more flexible than external programmes	Political commitment Clear, realistic and long-term objectives and work plans Mutual understanding of partners' expectations Joint action local authority and civic society initiatives	Misunderstanding of partners' behaviour patterns, working styles and ethics Multiplied international commitments go beyond manageable level Lack of monitoring and evaluation
IULA/ICLEI Local Agenda 21 Charters Programme (Rademaker & Van der Veer 2001; Van Lindert 2001; Knowles & Materu, 1999)	Putting sustainable development planning on municipal agendas in South and North Increased international accountability to address global challenges Sharing of 'good practices' between North-South partner cities and all (20) members of the programme Promotion of public education and debate through joint action	Programme based on real needs and a shared vision Political commitment Organised community groups Knowledge exchange: 'teach and learn' Permanent and fluid communication between partner cities	Matching of partners sometimes based on wrong assumptions Lack of regulatory frameworks Lack of resources and capacities Expectations unrealistically high Stakeholder groups underrepresented
Swedish International Development Cooperation Agency – SIDA (Jones & Blunt, 1999)	Provision of physical resources Educational opportunities Work with professionals Stronger organisational confidence Enhanced international profile	Long-term relations Sharing of professional skills Involvement in organisation, management, values and attitudes	Risk of being unsuitable partners Unequal power relations Staff loss after capacity building
Norwegian Agency for Development Cooperation – NORAD (Askvik, 1999)	Direct contact to professional milieus in Norway Access to resources and expertise	Long track record of cooperation between institutions	Objectives unclear – technical or institutional change?

Partnership	Outcomes/Activities	Success factors	Challenges/Constraints
Canada/South Africa Programme on Governance (Proctor, 2000)	Constant and diverse supply of Canadian expertise Learn to employ skills in different ways Spin off: trade missions	Selection partners on mutual suitability Mix of project techniques used Sharing the English language Area of focus and activity determined by South Africans	Visits became ends rather than means due to lack of focus on clear objectives Periodic disruptions: political change, elections, staff turnover
Penang – Yokohama partnership (Tjandradewi et al., 2006)	Urban design and road administration Solid waste management Staff training and planning & research unit established Enhanced language and international cooperation skills Job satisfaction	MoU stating objectives and timeframe yet flexible for modification Political support from higher government levels Consistent leadership Public awareness Free information flows	Lack of community participation Lack of demand-driven focus and donor understanding of local government needs
Toronto – São Paulo partnership (Hewitt, 1999)	Equipment and operations upgrading Staff training and spin off to all staff levels Improvements of new systems and procedures	Priority areas defined based on joint consultation Hands on approach Focus on specific initiatives Quality of working relationships and personal contacts Diffuse cooperation prevents disruptive personnel changes	Lack of resources to implement changes Project based support threat to continuation of partnership agreement Political and administrative change
Australian – Timorese partnerships (Spence & Ninnes, 2007)	Revitalising community action and community building through closer local government-civil society relations Cross-municipal relationship building	Relationship and trust building Remunerated project officer Workable, joint evaluation procedures Bi-partisan political support and effective leadership	Threat of paternalism and dependency relations Limited access to communication means High staff turnover obstructs relationship building Lack of finances
Charlesbourg – Ovalle partnership (Hewitt, 2004)	Employee seminars and exchanges Awareness-raising and development education in the North Personal reward, enhanced job satisfaction and productivity Increased public consultation in municipal planning Improved strategies and means for citizen communication		Long-term effects on local democracy building not clear

through exchange with South African counterparts, Canadian participants "observed and worked in a very different governance environment and within it were sometimes able to employ their skills in new and different ways" (p. 323). In their empirical analysis of twinning arrangements of Swedish public institutions with counterpart organisations in Namibia and Laos, Jones and Blunt (1999) found that benefits for Swedish partners included opportunities for expanding professional competence and providing professional challenge to staff members, and the possibility to achieve an enhanced international profile. The studies by Tjandradewi et al. (2006) and Hewitt (2004) further mention increased job satisfaction and enhanced language, working and international cooperation skills for Northern participants. Spence & Ninnes (2007) found that the friendship ties with Timorese communities revitalised community building in Australian municipalities by bringing together local authorities and citizens through joint action. Such intangible benefits for partners in the North are also referred to as the 'soft' skills[9] or benefits of city-to-city cooperation against the more tangible results regarding services upgrading and project investments found in the South (see also 1.4).

In current North-South C2C cooperation programmes, municipal institutional strengthening in the South is one of the most common objectives and it may be achieved through a variety of activities. Many programmes indeed focus on the development of administrative and organisational systems, upgrading of municipal operations, and improvement of municipal services and equipment. Instruments for institutional strengthening include the exchange of knowledge and experience, technical training and general exchanges between local officials and technicians from both cities. Jones and Blunt (1999) draw conclusions on the effects of twinning as mechanism for such institutional capacity building. For the partners in the South, the benefits of these twinnings include the attainment of technical equipment such as vehicles and computers, and enhanced opportunities for individuals to travel, receive further education and work together with fellow professionals. Furthermore, the "backing of an empathetic partner organisation" (p. 389) provided organisational confidence for the recipient partner. Askvik (1999) analysed the inter-organisational cooperation projects in Norwegian development assistance where benefits for partners in the South included the direct contacts the partnerships provided with a professional environment in Norway and consequent access to resources and expertise for the recipient organisation. The example of Proctor (2000) showed that exchanges between Canadian and South African public servants repeatedly resulted in new insights on public management issues on both sides, which promoted greater understanding of the problems that needed to be tackled. In the Toronto (Canada) – São Paulo (Brazil) partnership which aimed at the improvement of emergency service delivery in the latter, managers and technicians of both municipalities met regularly. Information and technical exchanges resulted in improvements in equipment, operations, the implementation of new emergency systems and staff training (Hewitt, 1999). Improvement of municipal performance in terms of finance, administration and management was also found to be a benefit in a survey among several C2C partnerships done by UNDP (2000). The partnership between Yokohama (Japan) and Penang (Malaysia) resulted in the creation of an urban design plan for the latter

---

9   Johnson & Thomas (2007) define 'hard' skills as techniques and tools of particular content areas and general tools for analysis and action. 'Soft' skills refers to learning how to be reflective, how to negotiate or how to think differently in a given context.

which acknowledged cultural heritage, green areas and space for pedestrians. Practice and knowledge of solid waste management from Yokohama was applied in Penang through staff training and establishing a planning and research unit in the local authority. Results contained the introduction of a waste management information system and a recycling programme, including environmental public education (Tjandradewi et al., 2006).

The scope of many C2C programmes is not limited to strengthening the municipal organisation, but reaches beyond, with a focus on strengthening local governance. The Local Agenda 21 Charters Programme, executed to support local governments and their respective partnerships through linkages of ten cities in Europe (8) and Canada (2) with ten cities in Africa (6) and Latin America (4), is a good example in this respect (Rademaker & Van der Veer, 2001).[10] The main objective of the programme was the implementation of the Agenda 21 principles (see Box 5.1) in each of the twenty partnered cities. Establishing linkages between each pair of cities was not the programme's aim, the linkages were rather considered an instrument to exchange experience and provide mutual support in the field of Local Agenda 21 (LA21). Examples of local governance strengthening through the programme included fostering public-civil sector cooperation, local level participatory planning, and decision-making mechanisms (Van Lindert, 2001). In the case of Ovalle (Chile), Hewitt (2004) found that the partnership with Charlesbourg (Canada) resulted in increased public consultation in municipal planning and improved strategies and means for local government communication with its citizens, opening opportunities for citizens to participate in local decision-making.

In addition to the aim of municipal institutional strengthening, almost all of the C2C partnerships included in the literature review focused on urban service upgrading, such as health care, education, and infrastructure improvement. A third category of benefits therefore entails C2C projects that deliver tangible results for the partner community in the South with respect to the improvement of living conditions and the alleviation of poverty, especially through improved access and quality of social services. Such efforts can be made by both the partners' municipal organisations and civil society initiatives. As UNDP (2000) puts it: C2C makes "contributions to combating poverty", mainly through improving the lives of the poor with projects on health, sanitation, and education. Today, many of the Northern municipalities that engage in North-South partnerships have incorporated one or more of the Millennium Development Goals as guiding principles in their international cooperation programme (Chapter 3).

With respect to the benefits of C2C cooperation for the Southern partner municipalities, it should be noted that questions can be raised regarding the tangible community results achieved by C2C cooperation. There are ample examples of C2C projects contributing to housing, sanitation, education and other important elements of service provision. However, one should be hesitant to suggest that such projects automatically contribute to poverty alleviation. C2C activities, especially those of a donor-driven nature, may run the

10   The Local Agenda 21 Charters Programme ran from 1997 to 2000 and was funded by the Dutch government. The executing agencies were IULA (International Union of Local Authorities), ICLEI (International Council for Local Environmental Initiatives – now Local Governments for Sustainability) and T&D (Towns and Development). Participants in the Programme included the city linkages of: Johannesburg-Birmingham; Kumasi-Almere; Mutare-Haarlem; Mwanza-Tampere; Nakuru-Leuven; Windhoek-Bremen; Cajamarca-Köpenick; León-Utrecht; Porto Alegre-Hamilton Wentworth; Santiago de Chile-Ottawa.

risk of becoming isolated events that have only little impact beyond the project level. It is therefore of crucial importance that C2C cooperation be institutionalised through municipal partnership structures and strong civil society organisations with long-term development objectives to achieve sustainable change.

Critical factors aiding C2C partnerships – Strengths

Various conditions can be detected as determinants of success for city-to-city partnerships. These vary from political commitment and constant adjustment and reshaping of the cooperation programmes to making use of local expertise and setting realistic goals and objectives. Below two major categories of critical strengths are discussed, relating to – respectively – the levels of institutionalisation of the partnership and the quality of the partnership as an effective vehicle for decentralised development cooperation.

With regard to the first category, ample evidence was found that C2C cooperation can only be successful if it is institutionally consolidated at both ends of the partnership (UNDP, 2000; UN-Habitat, 2003; Van Lindert, 2001; Spence & Ninnes, 2007; Tjandradewi et al., 2006). Such consolidation includes a wide variety of aspects, most important of which is the institutional embedding within the municipal political-administrative apparatus and local civil society. Critical factors include the process of political decision making and strategy development, the political view of municipal councils on international cooperation, the level of political commitment to C2C and the presence of partnership champions in key positions within the administration. Political will in the local government apparatus, and support and consistent, effective leadership from the mayor and formal city council resolutions for C2C support help build commitment and prevent possible disruption caused by changes in political leadership.

The employment of professional coordinators on both sides of the partnership helps to maintain an organisational structure which allows constant coordination and monitoring of projects and facilitates adequate communication between the partners. Ideally, such coordinators should be remunerated (Spence & Ninnes, 2007). Moreover, they should be on the payroll of the municipality instead of being persons outside the formal municipal apparatus who are being 'contracted' for their services (Van Lindert, 2001). In addition, institutional embedding will be more solid if international cooperation is supported by a wide range of municipal departments, which may be involved by providing technical services and devoting part of their departments' budgets to specific C2C project support (Van Lindert, 2005a).

Commitments in terms of time and resources to support C2C partnerships are of crucial importance (UNDP 2000). From the human capacity perspective several factors are believed to affect the functioning of the partnership and its involved participants, e.g. professional skills, expertise and experience in development cooperation, language proficiency, and personal commitment to the partnership. From the financial capacity perspective, sufficient resources not only help achieve the objectives set, it also ensures follow up and sustainability of projects and capacity building efforts. In general terms it may be held that the larger Northern cities are, the more support they can mobilise for international development cooperation. In the Netherlands an unwritten rule of thumb is that municipalities should allocate one Euro per inhabitant for international cooperation. However, they can decide to have larger funds for C2C, by contracting money from decentralised municipal departments or third parties. A high level of professionalism and institutionalisation regarding C2C allows the Northern partner to expand its C2C budget through fundraising through national and supranational funding schemes (Chapter 3). Important in this respect is also the political support needed from higher government levels which may result in financial support, as was the case in Malaysia (Tjandradewi et al., 2006). Such support is also imperative in countries which are strongly state-led and where bilateral and multilateral cooperation have traditionally been a task of national governments, which may require that all official international relations of municipalities be reported to obtain approval.

A final element which determines the level of institutionalisation of the partnership is the effective coordination and alignment of civil society actors and municipal efforts. Important in this respect is public awareness, community-wide participation and a strong commitment from civil society. It is believed that the wider the participation (e.g. of community organisations, chambers of commerce, housing associations, universities), the more a link is likely to bear fruit. The Local Agenda 21 Charters Programme specifically aimed at deepening civil society commitment to local sustainable development. The formally signed Charters between the partner cities were to be based on identified local stakeholder needs and a vision for future local development developed through joint consultation. In addition, the Charters functioned as accountability mechanisms between the local authorities, citizens and executing agencies of the support programme (Rademaker & Van der Veer, 2001; Van Lindert, 2001).

A second type of strength entails the quality of the partnership as an effective vehicle for development cooperation. Quality of the partnership refers here to the mechanisms for exchange of knowledge and learning among the partners, decision – making and agenda setting, focus and scope of the partnership and level of mutuality in the relationship.

It was found that mutual understanding between the partners, and having clear plans and objectives (e.g. based on a Memorandum of Understanding) on which both partners agree, are contributive. Long-term objectives and realistic progress stages should be defined. The long-term character of twinning partnerships provides sustainability (Jones & Blunt, 1999; Askvik, 1999). Mutual understanding, aided by free information flows, building trust and respect among partner cities and their individual participants, and working on the basis of mutuality are of vital importance (UNDP, 2000; UN-Habitat, 2003; Spence & Ninnes, 2007). C2C as a development mechanism is promising since it is less formal and bureaucratic and more flexible than external aid programmes (UN-Habitat, 2003). Evaluation procedures should be followed carefully in a workable, jointly-executed way (Spence & Ninnes, 2007).

A demand-driven determination of the scope and focus of the programmed activities by the recipient partner is identified as a crucial success factor (Hewitt, 1999; Proctor, 2000). In addition, the mix of project techniques used in the South African/Canadian programme proved relevant, enabling a variety of administrators to participate, even those with tight agendas who had no time for long classroom training sessions (Proctor, 2000). In the Toronto – São Paulo case, the focus on specific initiatives and project areas, the hands-on approach, and the personal contacts between the parties contributed to positive outcomes (Hewitt, 1999).

Findings from the Local Agenda 21 Charters Programme show similarities with the above-mentioned conditions. According to the programme, good practice in C2C is based on three principles: shared goals, shared planning and 'something to teach and something to learn'. The latter means that the transfer of knowledge and skills is not a one-way flow from North to South (Knowles & Materu, 1999). Learning and teaching should thus replace the paternalistic approaches that are still practised in many multi- and bilateral development cooperation programmes. Northern partners need to acquire a solid understanding of the needs in the South and aid should be demand-driven rather than donor-driven (Rademaker & Van der Veer, 2001). In this respect, it is interesting to note that Southern participants greatly valued the regional knowledge exchange conferences that were organised. Representatives of African and Latin American cities remarked that South-South partnerships and networks would flourish more on the basis of equity and mutuality than in the case of North-South cooperation (Van Lindert, 2001).

Critical factors undermining C2C partnerships – Weaknesses
Similar to conditions positively affecting C2C partnerships, there are several factors identified that may harm cooperation efforts. The documented studies reveal various weaknesses, mostly represented as a certain lack of critical strengths, i.e. an incomplete process of institutionalisation and a lack of quality in building and maintaining a development partnership with partner cities in the South.

A first weakness relates to a lack of institutional embedding, which will make C2C vulnerable and hardly sustainable. Political volatility due to elections or the substitution of personnel on both ends of the linkage may interrupt relationships, a factor that was found to be a threat to the Toronto-São Paulo case (Hewitt, 1999), the Australian – Timorese partnerships (Spence & Ninnes, 2007) and to various city twinnings in the Local Agenda 21 Charters Programme, e.g. the partnerships of Mutare-Haarlem, Cajamarca-Köpenick and Nakuru-Leuven (Van Lindert, 2001). Individuals who have acquired skills and knowledge through a partnership programme may leave the organisation, especially because salary levels in developing countries tend to be relatively low in the public sector (Jones & Blunt, 1999). The continuity of the partnership can also be threatened if the management of the partnership is in the hands of a single official or political leader who may leave office. Hence, concentrated political and administrative support may lead to discontinuity (UNDP, 2000), although this is certainly not always the case. An interesting counter example in this respect is the Dutch municipality of Eindhoven, which has a high profile in Dutch decentralised development cooperation and maintains five C2C partnerships at the same time. Although on the one hand Eindhoven administratively has organised all of its municipal international contacts through one central office for international cooperation – thereby somewhat marginalising the potential role of the various municipal departments – on the other hand a successful system of shared political responsibility has been put in place that cuts across all political parties. In Eindhoven's multi-party city council, each of the political parties' leaders is the 'ambassador' of a particular municipal partnership. This mechanism creates high levels of political commitment for municipal international cooperation and institutionalises it, which makes it less vulnerable to local regime changes (Van Lindert & Van Dooren, 2001).

With respect to the provision of financial and human resources, Hewitt (1999) stresses that partnership initiatives and efforts will not be sustainable if there are no sufficient resources available to implement changes. This is according to UN-Habitat (2003) also a motive for cities not to "multiply their international commitments beyond a manageable level" (p. 29) since partnerships require consistent and reliable inputs from all partners. Limited access to communication means may further obstruct efforts (Spence & Ninnes, 2007). Moreover, in the North, lack of expertise and knowledge of development cooperation may undermine good intentions. Partnerships fail when Northern partners wrongly assume to have all the necessary professional expertise and knowledge needed to engage in development cooperation: "Many [Northern municipal partners] see themselves walking into the aid business with none of the knowledge which has built up in NGO circles over the years, so there is a danger if guidance is not sought, of their taking part in very amateurish aid efforts" (Knight, quoted in UNDP, 2000, p. 28). Tjandradewi et al. (2006) also found that a lack of donor understanding of local government needs undermines a demand-driven focus. Indeed, the practice of C2C compared to NGO assistance has both advantages and disadvantages. A positive aspect is that the so-called 'peer-to-peer' or 'colleague-to-colleague' approach is considered a vehicle for knowledge and skills transfer that is unique to C2C partnerships and scarcely found among other modalities of development cooperation. It stresses the values of equity and mutuality in municipal cooperation and the fact that professional colleagues from both cities speak the same technical 'language'. A disadvantage is the above mentioned lack of development expertise among municipal staff in the North, e.g. regarding knowledge of local contextual conditions, taking into account adequate evaluation and monitoring criteria, or possessing the required advisory skills (Schep et al., 1995). The dilemma of well-intended aid ambitions versus the lack of professional expertise has been well expressed in the title of a Dutch Government evaluation of national C2C support programmes: "On Solidarity and Professionalisation" (IOB, 2004).

This leads to the second category regarding the quality of the partnership as a vehicle for development cooperation. In addition to a lack of development professionalism, weaknesses may include paternalism and donor domination in project design and decision-making; partners looking for quick results; unrealistic expectations; misunderstanding of partners' behaviour and intentions; and unequal power relations. If partners fail to set clear objectives, it may result in visits becoming ends in themselves rather than a basis on which to systematically build the partnership (Proctor, 2000). While one of the strengths of C2C derives from the time horizon which is often considerably longer than the average development programme's time span, a key pitfall appears to be the fact that partners expect results too quickly. In this respect, UN-Habitat (2003) and UNDP (2000) point out that it takes time to engage in a C2C partnership and develop an effective relationship with the partner. Focusing too hurriedly on achieving results while not taking the time to understand behavioural patterns, working style and ethics of the partner local authority may seriously undermine the success of the partnership. In addition, partners are exposed to the risk of being unsuitable partners with dissimilar political, social, historical and geographical contexts, resources, experiences and organisational cultures which may obstruct twinning (Jones & Blunt, 1999; Van Lindert, 2001). Paternalism and donor domination in C2C partnerships harm the spirit of partnership and mutuality (UNDP, 2000; Spence & Ninnes, 2007). Indeed, there is a danger of an unequal relationship in which the 'developed' partner takes a superior attitude and expects a passive, dependent partner (Jones & Blunt, 1999).

Discussion
The review of documented studies of North-South city twinning programmes may be considered a first synthesis of the perceived benefits, strengths and inherent weaknesses of C2C cooperation. The analysis has provided insight into the question how to optimally organise and manage C2C partnerships as instruments to achieve the developmental objectives of municipal cooperation. This refers to the level of institutionalisation of the partnership in the municipal partner organisations and the quality of the partnership as

an effective vehicle for decentralised development cooperation. The review suggests that institutional consolidation is of crucial importance to guarantee sustainability and continuity of C2C practice. It is expressed in the municipality's political commitment or mandate to international cooperation, the administrative embedding of C2C activities, financial and human resources available including knowledge of development cooperation in the North and working on C2C in joint action with civil society and other stakeholders. It was found that partnership conditions that foster good practice of city-to-city cooperation are based on mutuality of understanding and learning, where peer-to-peer cooperation is claimed to be beneficial for knowledge and skills transfer and to overcome some of the persistent unequal power relations in international development cooperation. In addition, C2C cooperation should be demand-driven, based on a solid understanding of the partner's needs.

The analysis has further shown the rich scope that decentralised international cooperation may have for championing global citizenship in the North, and for municipal institutional strengthening and improvement of service provision in the South. The literature suggests that C2C has the potential to improve local governance structures in the South: strengthening municipalities to be more effective and responsive, while at the same time supporting civil society through the improvement of living conditions and access to services. The comparative study has revealed, however, that based on the evidence available it proves difficult to demonstrate a systematisation of the beneficial effects of this potential to improve local governance. While there are many examples of C2C activities in building municipal capacity, little is known on the effects on implementing sustainable institutional change. Hewitt (2004) for example points out that although cooperation between Charlesbourg and Ovalle has improved communication between public authorities and citizens in the Chilean city, the wider long-term effect on local democracy building is not clear. Analogous, while the review has found a wide range of tangible community benefits resulting from C2C projects, there is insufficient evidence of the effects these tangible results have on poverty alleviation in general. Moreover, there is a need to understand more clearly the role that C2C could play in empowering civil society and other non-state actors in order to strengthen their capacities to participate in urban decision making processes. Hence, there is a need to further investigate the greater institutional and societal impact of C2C on municipalities and communities in the South.

1.4 Key issues of North-South municipal partnerships

The review of twinning programmes in the previous section has raised a number of key issues inherent to the practice of North-South municipal partnerships, that deserve further attention. The next step is therefore to conceptualise a number of these issues and discuss them in more detail. They include: a) the notion of 'partnership' in North-South cooperation b) capacity building in the public sector c) learning and knowledge exchange in North-South partnerships d) mutuality in partnerships and e) meanings and values attributed to North-South learning and knowledge.

A. The notion of 'partnership' in North-South cooperation
The notion of *partnership* has become omnipresent in the field of international development cooperation referring to any form of North-South cooperative relationship between NGOs, universities, or bi-lateral or multilateral donor coordination of national governments. It

dominates current development jargon and even forms the basis of one of the Millennium Development Goals (Goal 8: 'To develop a global partnership for development'). The notion of partnership entails a redefinition of the power relationship between Northern and Southern actors in development cooperation in favour of the latter. Aid relations between donors and recipient countries or organisations that have prevailed in international cooperation during the 20th century, are increasingly renamed into *partnerships*, emphasising equality and promoting recipient partners to take up a leading role and exercise more ownership in their own development strategies. New donor strategies urge Northern actors to step away from a dominating donor interventionist role, while Southern actors should take leadership in setting out development priorities. This has not only occurred at macro level.[11] On the decentralised level, a similar trend can be observed. Various authors mention the (desirable) redefinition of the relations of Northern NGOs and private voluntary organisations with local NGOs in the South (Lister, 2000; Fowler, 1998; Ahmad, 2006), that would grant more decision-making power to the South. At the same time, critical questions are raised about the real changes in roles of partners and power balance, which is often found to continue to be tipped towards the Northern side of partnerships.

There has thus far been little consensus on the meaning of 'partnership', and its practice varies. Theoretical backing or conceptual frameworks to inform the design and management of partnerships have been meagre (Brinkerhoff, 2002).[12] An underlying cause is that the notion of partnership is not always critically assessed, as much of the literature tends to be of a normative nature, especially from the side of NGO advocacy. According to Brinkerhoff (2002), partnerships are in that case considered the most ethically appropriate approach to e.g. sustainable development or service delivery, and its rhetoric and language are employed to promote better public relations for business, government and donors alike.[13] Therefore, she argues, the meaning of partnership, and our understanding thereof, is unavoidably value-laden.

From a development intervention perspective, partnerships and capacity building are often part of the same vocabulary. Partnerships are considered instruments to develop and build capacity in partner organisations in the South. The notion of *capacity development* gained ground during the 1990s as a result of the limited success of technical and externally induced development efforts, focusing on creating the conditions to set out sustainable development strategies based on the needs expressed by local actors (Ubels et al., 2005). Today, capacity development, alike good governance, is seen as panacea for sustainable development and poverty alleviation. It is defined as "…the process by which individuals,

---

11 Macro-level examples include the development of Poverty Reduction Strategy Papers (PRSPs) and the OECD's Paris Declaration on Aid Effectiveness (2005), both meant to allow poor countries to govern their own development strategies. Also, according to Abrahamsen (2004), the Heavily Indebted Poor Countries (HIPC) initiative is an example which holds poor partners responsible for designing poverty reduction strategies as a precondition for debt relief.

12 A workable definition of 'partnerships' is given by Baud et al. (2001): "Highly structured forms of co-operation, with long-term commitments, concrete activities, a form of contract, and autonomous participating partners".

13 Brinkerhoff (2002) distinguishes additional strands of literature on partnerships, including pragmatic-analytic (e.g. the effectiveness of partnerships), 'how-to' literature discussing types and purposes of partnerships, the business alliance literature (see e.g. De Villiers, 2009 in relation to C2C), network theory, political economy and New Public Management and new governance models literature.

THE CHALLENGE TO STRENGTHEN URBAN GOVERNANCE THROUGH NORTH-SOUTH CITY PARTNERSHIPS

organisations, institutions and societies develop abilities (individually and collectively) to perform functions, solve problems and set and achieve objectives" (UNDP, 1997a). However, as with 'partnership', the term is used and abused to refer to a wide variety of interventions which makes its meaning highly ambiguous.[14]

The rhetoric on North-South partnerships is based on a number of values and conditions for good partnerships. Milèn (2001) states that ownership and genuine partnership are preconditions to successful capacity development. *Ownership* is important in the sense that organisations invest in capacity development when they feel the need and desire to improve. Moreover, ownership entails that organisations build on their own capacity to formulate their development plans. It thus guarantees that cooperation is tailored towards the organisation's existing capacity, a 'locally owned' strategy and expressed needs. Working in *genuine partnership* means partners have a mutual understanding of issues, a greater sharing of goals and a shift of decision-making authority and control of program resources to the beneficial partner (Milèn, 2001). Fowler (1998) defines such 'authentic partnerships' as "mutually enabling, inter-dependent interaction with shared intentions" (p. 144).

Land (2000) notes that seeing *capacity development as a process* is crucial in understanding its sustainability implications and requires rethinking the roles performed by partners. Building on existing knowledge, capacity and practice is considered important to induce real change. The question is how external agencies can support endogenous capacity development processes (Ubels et al., 2005). Land (2000) further observes that… "increasingly, it is accepted that capacity programmes are more successful, and are more likely to be sustainable when they respond to an internal initiative, and when they are supported through a process approach, and not through single one time events". Issues of ownership, commitment and leadership are important in partnerships in respect to seeing capacity as a process.

It is widely debated whether the partnership concept has truly altered North-South relationships and whether they can truly be considered 'partnerships'. As Ashman (2000) notes, while partnership is understood "to indicate relationships based on equity and mutual benefit", the authenticity of such criteria is contested in two ways. First, it is suggested that partnerships are 'old wine in new bottles', by presenting a more political correct account of what eventually is a disguise of the same practice of donor dominance (Ahmad, 2006; Lister, 2000; Fowler, 1998). Secondly, many barriers are noted to achieving 'true' or 'genuine' partnership based on equality, shared objectives and mutual benefits (e.g. Ubels et al., 2005; Milèn, 2001). Structural inequalities are persistent in North-South partnerships that continue to represent the much criticised 'classic linear model of North-South transfer of knowledge' (Baud, 2002): the North retains financial, technological and institutional

---

14 The literature classifies capacity building into various dimensions and levels, for example outlining a hierarchy of capacity on the individual, organisational, institutional and systems level or rather distinguishing the areas of capacity e.g. technical versus 'soft' capacities, such as leadership skills (Leibler and Ferri, 2004; Milèn, 2001; Grindle et al., 1997; Rhebergen, 2006; Grindle & Hilderbrand, 1995; Land, 2000; UNDP, 1997a). There is agreement that developing the capacity of a certain level or area requires also the need to enhance other capacities in order to achieve sustainable change. In other words, the mutual influence of capacity in various areas and hierarchical levels is evident. However, there is little known about how the various levels of capacity interact and how their complex and interrelated structure leads to performance and development.

advantage over the South, making working in partnership between donors and recipients difficult to achieve in reality (Milèn, 2001).

Johnson & Wilson (2006) observe that the literature about North-South partnerships, in particular donor-recipient relations, focuses on dimensions of power, participation, trust, and mutuality. Issues raised in this debate include: working in partnership with ample attention for local culture and knowledge and where differences in values and work ethic are respected, finding a 'balance' in aid relationships, even though they are 'inherently unequal, with financial, decision-making and professional power unevenly distributed' (Ubels et al., 2005), and shaping partnerships to be more demand-driven, making donors responsive to the greatest needs.

B. Capacity building in the public sector: political dynamics shaping processes and outcomes

In the public sector capacity building is mainly directed towards the institutional strengthening of public institutions and administrations, aiming at 'getting good government' (Grindle et al., 1997) through increased institutional performance. Promoting good government and especially good governance has become a central development objective. Democratic and decentralised governance is increasingly considered a requisite component of development initiatives: development aid both aims to contribute to the decentralisation process itself (reforming legal, political and fiscal systems) and to strengthen the capacity of local authorities in response to the changing legal framework (resource management, social services delivery and civil participation) (Work, 2002).

As Grindle (2006) notes, capacity building initiatives are considered a solution to the often poor performance of (local) public institutions in the South. How can the capacity of local institutions for improved local governance be developed? Public sector reform as a response and in relation to (donor driven) decentralisation programmes has been reviewed extensively in discourses on e.g. New Public Management and private sector organisational change and change management, which support the idea that the performance of local governments can be increased. Efforts may be aimed at institution creation, organisational engineering, information technology and technical input for electronic government (Grindle, 2006), but also at more institutional issues of participatory decision making, transparency and responsiveness, and contributing to the developmental role of local governments particularly. Grindle et al. (1997) distinguish three areas of capacity building for institutional strengthening which form a hierarchy. First, capacity building may be aimed at *human resource development*, e.g. by training of staff and improving recruitment procedures and work conditions. Secondly, *organisational strengthening* focuses on improving management systems on the micro level, through changing management structures or the organisational culture of the institution. Thirdly, *institutional reform* targets institutions and systems at the macro level. This includes policy and legal change and constitutional reform (Chapter 2). In a study on capacity building in Mexican local governments, four strategies for improving the performance of municipalities were detected (Grindle, 2006): 1) Reorganising the local administration, especially to increase transparency and reduce corruption; 2) Professionalisation, partly to increase the quality of staff and recruitment practices, partly through introducing long-term planning systems and strategic plans; 3) Training and technology, e.g. computer literacy, customer care and personal effectiveness including time management and communication skills; 4) Introducing new systems for measuring performance and quality management systems.

Technical capacity development interventions are especially well-received and popular as they are believed to be free from political controversy. Grindle (2006) however demonstrates that capacity building in the public sector is not free from "partisan politics, decision making processes, political conflict or policy debates" (p. 56). Therefore, there is a need to focus more on the contextual factors affecting public sector capacity building initiatives in order to understand its implications. Such factors relating to contextual, political dynamics include:

1. The orientation and preferences of political leaders define to a large extent the direction and effectiveness of capacity building initiatives. Leadership preferences are thus a determinant factor, especially since local political leaders in developing countries have much influence on policies and municipal organisations and consequently on the openness to and priorities in capacity building initiatives;

2. Electoral cycles and political calendars are a temporal framework to capacity building initiatives that affect priorities and actions undertaken. Especially in newly democratic but weakly institutionalised systems, elections and new political leaders often cause drastic changes in political priorities and administrative compositions;

3. The scope of local administrations to introduce change and take an adoptive attitude depends largely on existing political institutions, including the 'rules of the game' – how authority and power are distributed in formal and informal ways, despite of electoral systems.

Grindle (2006) thus argues that capacity building in local governments in the South are affected by political preferences, calendars and institutions. This may impose risks and dangers while it provides opportunities at the same time: it encourages change on the one hand by allowing room to manoeuvre and thus facilitate change. On the other hand, especially due to the cyclic nature of local administrations and policies, it sets constraints to institutionalise performance and address capacity and performance needs in the long term.

The political factor is therefore key in public sector capacity building policies and practice. Koonings (2007) stresses that political dimensions are generally insufficiently valued in development thinking. He argues that both formal and informal mechanisms shape the political context in which capacity building and development aid takes place.[15] Hence not only capacity building initiatives, but development cooperation at large is affected by political conditions. Donor agencies are political actors and partnerships are politically value-laden. Moreover, beneficiaries of aid programmes may not be reached due to *local elite capture* and local partisanship and patronage structures which are reflected and sustained in local bureaucracies and public administrations. As Gillespie et al. (1996) note, local development projects face many potential opponents including village elites whose economic interests and political authority may be challenged by successful development. As projects take place in a context in which coalitions of interest among the 'haves' oppose the interests of the 'have-nots', they may fail due to political reasons (Gillespie et al., 1996).

---

15 Formal mechanisms include electoral mandates, rational policy formats, accountability structures and legal framework. Informal mechanisms refer to issues such as clientelism, patrimonialism, charisma, ethnicity and religion. Such formal and informal aspects affect for example the position of the poor, and issues of exclusion from voice and power, which are currently understood as key factors explaining poverty (Koonings, 2007) – see also Chapter 2.

C. Learning and knowledge exchange in North-South partnerships

A crucial issue that emerges from the literature review on city-to-city cooperation in 1.3 refers to the element of learning and knowledge exchange and more specifically, the mutuality of learning benefits to individuals and organisations collaborating in partnership structures in both North and South. While C2C rhetoric implies mutuality of efforts and benefits, the review showed that in practice persistent inequalities often result in one-way flows from North to South of money, expertise, and information. Other studies seem to corroborate such a *mutuality gap* (Johnson & Wilson, 2006) in North-South partnerships and question the opportunities for learning and benefiting in the North that allow municipal partnerships to truly become sites for learning to all stakeholders involved.[16] While the general aim of North-South C2C is to provide development assistance to the South, it is also said that C2C brings benefits and opportunities to the North. Indeed, a shared sense of learning has been considered one of the key guiding principles of municipal partnerships (Devers-Kanoglu, 2009). Various references are made to the benefits (also other than learning) that may accrue to both Southern and Northern cities and their participants of partnership activities. At the same time challenges are mentioned. The potential mutuality of effort and benefit between the partners makes municipal partnerships distinct from conventional North-South aid flows. However, a difference in benefits was also observed, with 'solid' or 'tangible' benefits in the South (technical knowledge, financial resources) versus 'soft' benefits in the North: awareness-raising and education in the sphere of development and global citizenship. Such benefits in the North are in need of more scrutiny in order to understand their practical implications (Johnson & Wilson, 2009; Van Ewijk & Baud, 2009).

The practice of *development education* emerged from the idea that learning in the North had been neglected at the expense of learning in the South, which has always been considered the prime objective of development cooperation (Devers-Kanoglu, 2009). Learning or awareness-raising in the North was considered a welcome side-effect of development cooperation, but it was never the main intention of engaging with the South. When development education gained ground, it was criticised at the same time for approaching the developing world merely as a 'learning object' rather than an equal partner for dialogue and exchange (Devers-Kanoglu, 2009). Local level partnerships have traditionally been considered sites for development education in the North. As C2C is not confined to the work of local governments alone, it offers opportunities for citizens to be exposed to development cooperation and issues related to global poverty and inequality, and the possibility to establish intercultural contacts, obtain greater cultural awareness, 'friendship' and mutual understanding. As a form of development cooperation which directly involves communities, C2C has the potential to translate the abstract matter of far away places and large-scale donor development assistance to the world of the citizen. At city level, development cooperation becomes more tangible and visible and is supported by a range of learning and exchange mechanisms, such as 'learning through action' in partnership projects, school exchanges and technical exchanges of similar institutions (local authorities, hospitals, fire brigades etc.).

Many municipalities see a role for themselves as development educators vis-à-vis their citizens. Awareness-raising may range from understanding the need for emergency aid

---

16   See e.g. Johnson & Wilson; Devers-Kanoglu; and Van Ewijk & Baud in a forthcoming special issue on city-to-city cooperation edited by Bontenbal & Van Lindert in Habitat International, 2009.

for natural disasters and wars world-wide to the relevance of development cooperation with the South or with pre-accession countries of the European Union (VNG, 2000). In 2000 more than 50% of the medium-sized cities in the Netherlands engaged in C2C undertook awareness-raising activities. Among the large cities (over 100,000 inhabitants) this percentage was 92% (VNG, 2000). Indeed, in the Netherlands public awareness-raising has traditionally been a key objective of municipal partnerships, although national subsidy schemes for Dutch cities have insufficiently acknowledged this in the past. Also they do not provide funding to municipalities for such activities today (IOB, 2004).[17] Schep et al. (1995) found that C2C partnerships led by civil society initiatives have been more successful in raising public awareness than local authority-led partnerships.

Recent studies suggest that there is more to gain in the North than merely awareness-raising and a growing understanding of world poverty among citizens. Descending to the individual level, a relevant subject of study in C2C has been the *learning benefits of participants* in partnership arrangements, such as local officials and politicians in municipal exchanges, and volunteers and citizens engaged in civil society partnership initiatives and exchanges. In the literature review in 1.3, a number of individual and organisational benefits in the North were discussed, which include job satisfaction, acquiring new skills and learning 'to do things differently', language proficiency and professional challenges to participants. In a study by Johnson & Wilson (2006), UK local government staff engaged in partnerships with Ugandan municipalities stated that these brought them a range of advantages, including new skills with regard to carrying out informal training, team working, communication, negotiation and public speaking, which had a positive effect on their performance in the workplace in the UK. The officials responded that they "gained confidence, they were better able to negotiate projects, and they built working relationships across conventional professional and departmental divides" (p. 78).

On North-South partnerships in general (and not solely in the North) McFarlane (2006) observes that the linkages between knowledge, learning and development are of growing importance in development,[18] but there have been few attempts to explore how learning between North and South might be envisaged. Part of the literature tends to focus on various forms of knowledge and learning that are exchanged in partnerships and how the transfer of knowledge and learning occurs (e.g. Van Ewijk & Baud, 2009;[19] Johnson & Thomas, 2007; Wilson & Johnson, 2007; Gaventa, 1999; King, 2002; Drew, 2002). Van Ewijk & Baud (2009) distinguish between knowledge exchange as a process and learning as the outcome of the process. They stress – following Argyris (1999) – that learning only occurs when knowledge is practically applied, for example to find solutions to problems.

Among the benefits of C2C discussed in the literature review in 1.3, the second type, i.e. improving municipal performance, mainly shows evidence of advantages for individual

---

17   Although public awareness-raising was one of the main objectives under the former national funding programme for C2C partnerships with the South ('GSO', jointly executed by the Ministry of Foreign Affairs and the Association of Dutch Municipalities), supporting modalities and funding were never formulated (IOB, 2004). Under the current funding scheme (LOGO South) the objective has disappeared altogether (see also Chapter 3).

18   See e.g. special issues of *Development in Practice* (2002; 2006).

19   Forms of knowledge identified by Van Ewijk & Baud (2009) include tacit knowledge, embedded knowledge based on experience and more 'universally codified knowledge'.

participants or departments that are directly involved in C2C projects and programmes. The scaling up of individual learning experiences to (sustainable) organisational change is a common subject in the literature on capacity development and organisational learning. Johnson & Wilson (2006) argue that such scaling up is challenging. A learning culture is needed in the organisation, also referred to as the 'learning organisation' the origin of which lies mainly in the work of Kolb et al. (1971) on experiential learning and of Argyris & Schon (1996) on organisational learning. In the context of municipal partnerships and C2C however, most of the existing documentation tends to neglect the question as to how such *individual learning can be transformed into organisational change*. Few authors elaborate on how institutional strengthening at large can really be achieved. Both Jones and Blunt (1999) and Askvik (1999) draw the conclusion that, while the twinning arrangements under study have brought tangible improvements at the operational level of recipient organisations (i.e. technical-administrative upgrading and general competence building), there is less evidence of this at the organisational level or at the level of institutional capacity building. Changes at the institutional-strategic level are also less notable and the projects tend to have less impact on the main goals of the recipient organisations. Askvik argues that changes at the organisational and institutional levels of public agencies have more political implications and meet more resistance than measures to improve technical skills and procedures at the operational level. It may be controversial to give advice on how to (re)organise an administration. Furthermore, the Northern partner may not possess the skills to engage in organisational development. On the other hand, Askvik correctly observes that the institutional value of transferring *technical* competence should not be underestimated: "In a country like Mozambique, developmental needs are many and varied, and an overzealous interpretation of institution building as primarily directed towards managerial and strategic changes can be counterproductive" (Askvik, 1999, p. 406). In this respect it is relevant that partners clarify to what extent institution building is a significant objective of the cooperation. Johnson & Thomas (2007) conclude that individual learning can only be transformed into organisational capacity building when the individual has sufficient influence in the organisation to act as a 'change agent'. Not only the 'learning style' of the individual and the quality of the education, but also organisational factors are of crucial importance in this process. These include opportunities (e.g. resources available to implement what has been learnt) and support both for the individual learner and the "uncomfortable process of organisational change" (p. 46). They observe however that in practice it is difficult to reach the ideal situation where opportunities and support are widely available, and that a direct translation from individual to organisational learning is never the case. This may be especially true for local administrations in developing countries.

A final strand of literature that is worth mentioning in the discussion on North-South learning in a C2C context moves from the level of individual learning back to the level of 'learning cities' (Campbell, 2009). While at city level fostering global citizenship and awareness-raising are important objectives of partnerships, the question arises whether city-to-city cooperation should also generate more tangible benefits to the partner cities in the North. The notion of mutual benefit links up with the recent trend of the adoption in the North of innovations in democratic governance that have emerged in cities in the South. The exporting of ideas and knowledge on urban governance from South to North is specifically related to experiences in participatory budgeting,[20] first practised in Porto Alegre, Brazil. This countermovement to traditional North-South flows is referred to as 'the return of the caravels' (Allegretti & Herzberg, 2004) and is promoted by various international donor programmes including UNDP, UN-Habitat, the World Bank and particularly European Union's URB-AL Thematic Network on participatory budgeting. Especially in cases where the Southern partner has a long tradition of community participation and has innovative forms of urban governance in place, including participatory budgeting methodologies, the question arises to what extent it has inspired partner cities in the North. Significant research would therefore be to assess to what extent C2C brings innovative forms of governance and participatory democracy also to cities in the North – going beyond conventional one-way flows from North to South – and which factors promote or undermine such mutual processes.

D. Mutuality in partnerships

To what extent are North-South city partnerships mutual, and more in particular, what type of mutuality is referred to here? Mutuality refers to mutual dependence and entails respective rights and responsibilities and complementary roles to all actors involved (Brinkerhoff, 2002; Johnson & Wilson, 2006). It seeks to maximise benefits for each party and is based on a strong mutual commitment to the partnership. Mutuality is important, since it has been claimed that when partners benefit equally, partnerships tend to be more enduring (Austin, 2000 quoted in Brinkerhoff, 2002) and it allows partners to contribute to the partnership with fewer constraints and greater legitimacy and sense of ownership.

   Much work on mutuality in (municipal) partnerships has been done by Johnson & Wilson (2006, 2007). A clarifying exercise is the idea of the 'mutuality gap' (2006), which might provide a different approach to partnerships by addressing more explicitly levels of inequality and power relations. They observe two approaches in the literature on partnerships. One can be seen as the *ideal* view, based on the rhetoric of shared benefits and mutuality for all parties involved. The other view is *sceptical,* i.e. it claims that there is a huge gap between rhetoric and reality and that shared benefits are hindered by unequal power relations and other inequalities among the partners. The mutuality gap describes to what extent a partnership approaches the ideal or sceptical view. Seeing partnerships as 'learning models' may help to close this gap, especially when it offers explicit opportunities for Northern participants to learn. In the ideal view, Johnson & Wilson argue, such opportunities for learning are driven by *difference.* Hence, difference is a virtue in partnerships and promotes mutuality because it offers benefits to both. In the sceptical view, difference is a vice, which hinders mutuality because of the power and resource inequalities that underlie. If partnerships are regarded as learning spaces, "inherent differences between the partners are seen as opportunities rather than constraints". As a consequence, mutuality does not refer to resemblance or equality that should be pursued, but flourishes thanks to difference and distinction.

   One of the issues that was raised in 1.3 was the practice of peer-to-peer exchanges as instruments for learning and knowledge exchange in municipal partnerships. They have

---

20   Participatory budgeting is a process and an instrument that enables the inhabitants of municipalities to formally participate in decision-making on planning, public policies and their implementation (Van Lindert, 2005b). From the 1990s it has spread over many municipalities in Latin America and beyond (see Cabannes, 2004).

also been dubbed colleague-to-colleague exchanges (Schep et al., 1995) and practitioner-to-practitioner partnerships (Johnson & Wilson, 2007). Since peer-to-peer exchange implies horizontal cooperation, such partnerships offer opportunities for mutual learning, as "like-minded people of similar professional backgrounds" work together on municipal issues and problems (Johnson & Wilson, 2007). Notions of professional equivalence, a relative parity of status, trust and knowledge sharing on a collegiate basis provide opportunities to overcome inequality (Johnson & Wilson, 2006):

- Peer-to-peer cooperation claims 'knowledge parity' ("speaking the same language") based on similar theoretical knowledge, frameworks and applications
- It creates a shared professional challenge to succeed in resource-poor environments and therefore a strong commitment to joint learning
- Exchanges are based on similar professional characteristics, which facilitate mutual understanding and 'dialogic learning'. In peer-to-peer exchanges, counterparts are generally treated as genuinely equal and consensus is sought.
- Trust, which can be viewed as an informal form of contract, is characteristic based[21] and is intensified by positive personal relations and friendship in peer-to-peer relationships. In the discourse on municipal partnerships, trust is often mentioned as a key success factor (or failure when absent).

Peer-to-peer exchanges allow for interaction with the 'other' – who operates in different social, political, economical and cultural contexts, speaks a different language and has different attitudes and values. The 'other' may provide a mirror that allows for critical reflection of one-self and one's own working conditions, work ethic, and outlook on life (Wulf, 2001, quoted in Devers-Kanoglu, 2009). The process of alienation that emerges from North-South encounters can be beneficial in this respect e.g. for personal development, however only when differences encountered are accepted and valued. City-to-city cooperation offers opportunities for comparison, in which difference is a trigger to reflect and learn. This offers opportunities for North-South mutuality.

E. Meanings and values attributed to learning and knowledge in North and South
A final issue worth discussing is the question of meaning and value placed on learning and knowledge in both North and South and how they differ. Two streams of thoughts emerge from the literature. The first states that learning in the North from the South is undervalued and insufficiently acknowledged. The second argues that benefits in the North from working in partnership with the South are overvalued, and claimed mutuality is often used as a token of appreciation.

In their study on community based volunteer work in Ontario, Mündel & Schugurensky (2005) found that informal learning is often not brought up as a motive or objective to participate in the activities that bring about learning experiences, rather it remains incidental, and therefore, often unconscious.[22] Such unintended learning is vulnerable (Devers-Kanoglu, 2009): Especially when it is not expressed in political objectives of partnership

---

21   Characteristic based trust refers to trust based on shared characteristics, such as kinship, ethnicity, religion, and profession (Zucker, 1986 quoted in Johnson & Wilson, 2006).

22   They define informal learning as not structured in terms of learning objectives, time or support. It is more often non-intentional (incidental/random) than deliberate. Moreover, they argue that informal learning has a level of intentionality and consciousness: Intentionality refers to the degree of deliberate versus implicit learning.

agreements, learning may not be recognised and remains implicit. In practice, there is a risk that learning from C2C in the North goes unnoticed and remains undervalued. Van Ewijk & Baud (2009) argue that Northern partners often feel they have more advanced knowledge than Southern partners (political or cultural inequalities) while implicit knowledge is often perceived as inferior to codified knowledge (knowledge inequalities). Johnson & Wilson (2006) also found that in peer-to-peer exchanges different values were placed on different forms of knowledge. It may obstruct organisational change in the North when participating municipalities do not conceptualise C2C as a potential source for learning.

On the other hand, the benefits with regard to learning in the North are often overemphasised. As Devers-Kanoglu (2009) notes: "The discourse on mutuality and shared learning in municipal partnership has raised high expectations, but tend to be normative placings i.e. desirable outcomes", which may be exploited at the expense of individual learning opportunities. She correctly warns that the discourse risks the danger to be overly optimistic and normative, while the real benefits remain insufficiently questioned. The claim that learning in the North is taking place may be used as a token of appreciation towards the Southern partner. A myth of equality and mutuality emerges, based on the belief that the North is compensated with learning for the financial and technical assistance delivered to the South and fed by the use of a common discourse understood by both partners.

1.5 Conclusions

The repertoire of competencies and responsibilities assigned to local governments in the South has been growing rapidly due to ongoing decentralisation processes. Municipalities have become more autonomous and proactive development agents, and their role with regard to service delivery, poverty alleviation and improving the quality of urban life has expanded. After the concise discussion of the current capacity imperative in local government in the South resulting from these processes (which is discussed in more detail in Chapter 2), this Chapter pointed out that, from an evolutionary perspective of international municipal relations, C2C partnerships specifically targeting development are a relatively new but growing phenomenon. The international activities of municipalities and in particular 'twinning' partnerships have undergone dynamic changes over the last sixty years, accumulating to 70% of the world's cities involved in international cooperation today. Many of these C2C partnerships are between the North and the South.

As Chapter 2 and 3 will demonstrate, recent trends in development practice towards decentralisation and good local governance provide a policy context that together with the increasing recognition that aid can be delivered by a wide variety of partners and agents, allow local authorities to play an active role in fostering sustainable local development through city-to-city cooperation. As such, local governments have given international development cooperation a more decentralised dimension. City-to-city cooperation is aimed at supporting municipalities in institutional capacity building and improvement of local governance issues such as service delivery, thereby creating and enabling legal and institutional environment and fostering partnerships with key local public, private and community actors. Cities set up and support projects, and provide knowledge and expertise

---

Consciousness relates to evident, planned learning versus unconscious learning, which learners may be unaware of or which may be elicited upon reflection.

through the delivery of technical assistance to their partner cities, which is often organised in a peer-to-peer setting for local government officials and technicians. C2C features include the overall goal of sustainable development, the concept of a relationship between local authorities being at the core of the partnership, and the participation of civil society.

Although the number of North-South city partnerships worldwide is immense, there is still a dearth of knowledge of the underlying mechanisms that affect the outcomes of such structures and processes. The meta-study on documented C2C in section 1.3 has provided a first synthesis of mainly anecdotal, isolated evidence. A number of interesting conclusions was drawn, but an equal number of questions remain unanswered.

First, as was underscored in section 1.4, the political context in which local government capacity building takes place, shapes C2C initiatives and hence has implications for its practice. While the literature assumes that a high level of institutionalisation of partnerships is a key strength, there is a need to explore the politico-administrative dimensions that affect the opportunities for institutionalisation in greater detail, and to understand the consequences for C2C.

Secondly, this Chapter pointed out that C2C is usually not confined to the involvement of local government alone. As the meta-study revealed, the participation of a wide range of actors, especially from civil society was found as one of the success factors to C2C. This aspect of C2C has however been little reflected upon. Such 'webs of links' (Schep et al., 1995) of local government, citizens, organisations, churches etc. that collectively constitute C2C networks in partner cities, need to be studied more closely, including their interrelations, roles and responsibilities. One relevant question in this respect is whether such a wide diversity of actors engaged is inducive to the practice of C2C or obstructive, e.g. when conflicting interests among actors arise.

Thirdly, the notion of 'partnership' has received wide attention in this Chapter. Various strands of literature were discussed to gain a better understanding of how 'good' partnerships can be defined in the context of North-South city-to-city cooperation. Many of the issues that emerged are concerned with the question whether North-South C2C are mechanisms of equal, horizontal exchange or whether they are just another form of the traditional model of aid flowing from North to South. While the former implies learning and knowledge exchange that benefits both partners, which is popular rhetoric in the C2C discourse, the latter questions such reciprocity since unilateral flows of resources, technical knowledge and expertise from North to South appear to be practice, at least at first sight. More research is therefore needed to assess the real impact of municipal partnerships with regard to shared learning and benefits, without neglecting donors' intentions to employ C2C partnerships as instruments for local public sector capacity building in the South.

Indeed, finally, there is a need to further investigate the impact of C2C on strengthening the quality of urban governance in the South. In order to understand these processes, it is essential to gain more insight into the notion of governance in an urban context first, and to explore how such strengthening can be assessed analytically. This will be done in the next Chapter.

THE CHALLENGE TO STRENGTHEN URBAN GOVERNANCE THROUGH NORTH-SOUTH CITY PARTNERSHIPS

2 Urban governance reconsidered[23]

Urban governance is, in addition to city-to-city cooperation, a key concept of this study. The aim of this Chapter is to review and analyse current processes in governance with a specific focus on the urban context, based on a literature study. The local level poses both challenges and opportunities to participatory and collective decision-making, as it implies that institutions and the people to which they are accountable are closely connected. It will be argued that in order to obtain 'good' governance in cities in the South, local governments need to be effective and responsive, while civil society and citizens need a strong position in collective decision-making processes. The Chapter starts with an overview of urban development thinking from the 1970s to the present, which emphasises the current focus on good governance as precondition for urban development and poverty alleviation. Then, the process of decentralisation of government in developing countries is reviewed, as it has shaped the current role of local institutions, also in development. As such, decentralisation is intimately related to local governance. Subsequently, the concept of urban governance is considered in greater detail. An analytical framework is presented that describes the various conditions necessary to strengthen urban governance. It hence provides a methodological starting point to assess the potential of city-to-city cooperation to affect these conditions positively.

2.1 The evolution of urban development thinking

For the first time in 2007, the majority of the human population was living in urban areas. While this milestone is the result of rapid urbanisation in the last decades (see Figure 2.1), growth is expected to continue in the next decades at an unprecedented rate. Urbanisation is most rapid in developing countries. It is expected that in Africa and Asia the urban population will double between 2000 and 2030, and that by 2030 cities in the developing world will make up 80% of the world's population (United Nations, 2008). It implies that poverty is becoming increasingly urbanised. It also means, as donors argue, that the challenges in the future are strongly correlated with global urbanisation, and that both the cause of these challenges and their solutions are to be found in cities. The management of urban areas and their populations will become more multifaceted, and cities will be under increased pressure in finding solutions and improving their planning strategies to accommodate the poor, enhance urban living conditions, infrastructure, services and employment opportunities, and strengthen governance in increasingly complex urban systems.

---

23   Parts of this Chapter have been published elsewhere in adapted version (Bontenbal & Van Lindert, 2008b; Bontenbal, 2009b).

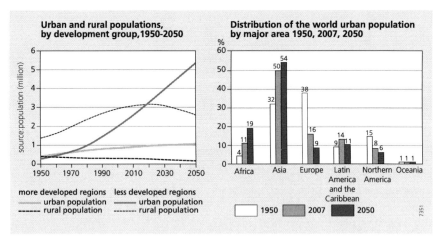

Figure 2.1 Urban and rural population by development group, 1950-2050 - Source: United Nations, 2008

In the early days of development planning, the growth of cities and their population was generally considered an undesirable and negative development, as overpopulated and congested urban areas were seen as unhealthy, prone to crime and without sufficient opportunities to accommodate newcomers from the rural areas. Planners held the opinion that urban growth had to be controlled, rural-urban migration mitigated and urban slums eliminated. From the 1970s however, the traditional rural-oriented development model was challenged by a new paradigm which revolved around urban development (Van Lindert, 2006). It was based on a 'new realism', which recognised that urban growth could not be prevented but should rather be accommodated by paying attention to flexible planning, an enabling and supportive government and a realistic standard of service delivery (Devas & Rakodi, 1993). The establishment of the United Nations Centre for Human Settlements (UNCHS-Habitat) in 1977 and the first UN-Habitat conference held in Vancouver in the previous year can be marked as the effective origin of donor commitment to urban poverty issues.

Figure 2.2 shows the evolution of urban development thinking from the early days in the 1970s until today (*cf.* Van Lindert, 2006). In the 1970s urban development was rather narrowly defined and focused essentially on meeting housing needs, in particular through settlement upgrading and self-help housing, the provision of 'sites and services' and security of land tenure. The urban development approach became more multidimensional in the following decade. With the start of the Urban Management Programme (UMP) in 1986 – a joint effort of UN-Habitat, UNDP and the World Bank – a more integrated perspective towards urban development began to include a range of urban sectors such as markets and the financial sector, infrastructure management, land and environmental management, and poverty alleviation. Capacity building and institutional strengthening of local authorities became major strategies to increase urban productivity, raise local revenues and improve urban socio-economic conditions.

In the 1990s, the concept of 'good governance' gained ground, also in urban development thinking. The 1990s can also be marked as the heydays of decentralisation policies. Democratic, decentralised governance was considered more and more an essential

Agenda Setting	Concepts	Strategic Focus	Policies & Practices
1970s	• Self-help housing	• Housing needs • Housing priorities	
1976 *Vancouver Habitat -1*	• Affordability • Cost Recovery • Replicability	• Enable self-help initiatives • Security of land tenure	• Sites and services • Settlement upgrading • Tolerance of squatter settlements
1986	***Urban Management Programme***	• Strengthening of markets and financial sector • Private sector construction	• Urban management • Capacity building • Institutional strengthening
1992 *Rio Earth Summit*	***Local Agenda 21***		
1996 *Istanbul- Habitat-2 (City Summit)*	***Habitat Agenda*** • Decentralisation • Good local governance • Sustainable urban development	• Holistic planning frameworks • Institutionalised multi-stakeholder, multi-sector consultation mechanisms • Local government-national state relations	• Good urban governance • Integrated development planning • Strategic planning • Capacity strengthening • Participatory planning • Partnerships and networks
2000 *Millennium Summit*	• Millennium Development Goals (MDGs)		
2001 *City Summit+5*	***Urban Development And Local Government Strategy*** • Liveability • Good governance and management • Competitiveness • Bankability	• Environment, Safety, Security, Health • Municipal finance	• Performance based urban management • Transparent municipal budgeting • Participatory budgeting

Figure 2.2 The evolution in urban development thinking, planning and policies - Source: Adapted from Van Lindert, 2006, p. 54.

component of urban development initiatives. Strategies aimed to contribute to the decentralisation process itself as well as to strengthen local institutions and the capacities of local governments. Such capacity building of local authorities was indispensable in order to respond adequately to the new responsibilities that decentralisation has brought to these institutions. Thus, some programmes have provided support to central governments in designing and implementing decentralisation plans (reforming legal, political, and fiscal systems), while others have addressed local government capacity building and strengthening, e.g. resource management, social service delivery, and civil participation (Romeo, 2003; Work, 2002).

In the new Millennium, urban development strategies are generally based on three main principles (Van Lindert, 2006): a multi-disciplinary, integrated and pro-poor approach with a long-term perspective, supported by institutional capacity building initiatives; public

THE CHALLENGE TO STRENGTHEN URBAN GOVERNANCE THROUGH NORTH-SOUTH CITY PARTNERSHIPS

participation as essential component of both local decision-making procedures and donor-supported development programmes; and the establishment of multi-sectoral partnerships to facilitate cooperation between public, private and civil actors. Also, external partnerships between cities and donors are important strategic alliances to tap from additional resources and know-how. Hence, in addition to targeting the narrowly defined role of local government as service provider (institutional strengthening, bankability, competitiveness) that manages cities, the wider role of local government as community developer (transparency, participatory budgeting, accountable management) which governs cities, became more integrated in urban development strategies. Before turning to the debate of governance, in which these concepts will be further clarified, this Chapter will first explore the process of decentralisation more closely.

2.2 Decentralisation: new opportunities for participation and poverty reduction?

During the last decades, many countries of the South have gone through an unprecedented fast and fundamental process of decentralisation and devolution of government authority, administration and resources to subnational levels (Devas & Grant, 2003). This reshaping of public administration has given local governments a more prominent role. The different reasons why decentralisation is pursued, many of which lie in the political sphere[24] have been widely discussed (e.g. Smoke, 2003; Nijenhuis, 2002; Litvack et al., 1998; Heller, 2001; Crook, 2003). The state is no longer seen as the sole framework for organising space, people and economic activities (De Jong & Broekhuis, 2004). Decentralisation is generally considered a response to failure of the state and need for reform to counter economic inefficiencies, macroeconomic instability, and ineffective governance (Work, 2002). It can be defined as the transfer of responsibility for public functions and services from the central government to lower levels of government. Decentralisation is closely connected to the subsidiarity principle, meaning that functions should be devolved to the lowest level of social order that is capable of completing them (Work, 2002). An underlying rationale for decentralisation is that bringing government closer to the people will make it more responsive to the needs of ordinary citizens – the majority of whom are 'the poor'. The relationship between decentralisation, participation, local development and poverty alleviation has been an issue that has received wide academic attention (e.g. Schneider, 1999; Steiner, 2007; Blair, 2000; Crook, 2003).

Three functional dimensions of decentralisation can be distinguished (Smoke, 2003; Work, 2002). *Fiscal decentralisation* refers to the resource reallocation to sub-national levels of government, such as the assignment of responsibilities of own-source revenues. *Institutional or administrative decentralisation* aims at transferring decision-making authority, resources and responsibilities for the delivery of public services from the central government to sublevels of government. It concerns administrative bodies, systems and mechanisms which help to manage and support decentralisation. It also comprises mechanisms that link formal government bodies to other key local actors such as NGOs and

---

24 In Latin America, democratisation was an important objective of decentralisation policies in the 1980s, when most military regimes were replaced by democratically elected governments (Van Lindert & Nijenhuis, 2004). In Eastern Europe, it has been a response to the shift to market economies and democracy. In Africa, it is part of a process of national reform and viewed as a path to national unity (Devas & Grant, 2003; Work, 2002).

the private sector. Finally, through *political decentralisation*, political power and authority is transferred to sub-national levels of government. It allows for the creation of an inclusive local political process necessary for local authorities to understand and act on the needs and preferences of local people. Political decentralisation requires the restructuring of institutions and the legal framework, and stronger linkages with civil society and the private sector.

In addition to functional dimensions, decentralisation has been classified by degree or intensity. Rondinelli (1999) distinguishes between deconcentration, delegation and devolution, in which the former is considered the weakest form of decentralisation, with a geographical dispersion of state responsibilities rather than the actual transfer of authority to sub-national governments. 'Delegation' implies a transfer of decision-making authority and the administration of public functions to subnational level. Subnational authorities are not controlled by the state but are accountable to it. 'Devolution' finally concerns the strongest form of decentralisation, with transfer of competencies, especially in service delivery, to local authorities that elect their own mayors and councils, gain revenue autonomy, and have independent decision-making authority in the allocation of investments. Devolution is therefore an inherent political process and has also been termed 'democratic decentralisation' (see Litvack et al., 1998).[25]

The literature assumes that decentralisation of government has some generic benefits, mainly concerning the potential it offers for increased political participation of ordinary citizens whose voices are better heard. Smoke (2003) notes that the majority of these advantages can be broadly captured as improved efficiency, governance and/or equity. These results are also associated with poverty alleviation. Advocates of decentralisation say it will lead to greater responsiveness to the needs of the 'poor' through new initiatives and greater citizen participation (Crook & Sverrisson, 2001; Grindle, 2006). Local governments thus are expected to contribute to local development through a more efficient allocation of resources, by providing tailor-made services and an enabling legal and institutional environment, by offering innovative solutions to persistent problems, and by creating partnerships with key local public, private and community actors. At the same time local populations may be given more space to participate in local decision-making (Crook & Manor, 1998 quoted in Bergh, 2004).

Some pitfalls of decentralisation however have also been discerned (Devas & Grant, 2003; Gaventa, 2001; Smoke, 2003; Bergh, 2004; McCarney, 1996). Two of the elements that have been identified as crucial in order to link decentralisation to local development and poverty reduction include the availability of financial resources and an adequate administration at the local level (Nijenhuis, 2002). The transfer of administrative responsibilities to local governments may however not be accompanied with the provision of adequate financial resources which impedes appropriate service delivery. Besides the mismatch between financial authority and functional responsibility, a deficit in technical and administrative local government capacity may even cause service delivery to deteriorate. Mechanisms of participation and accountability are in practice often 'captured' and dominated by local

---

25 Bergh (2004) argues that the political dimension of decentralisation should not be ignored, given the disproportionate attention paid in literature and policy debates on the administrative and fiscal aspects of decentralisation. Important in this respect is the extent to which decentralisation is an instrument to deepen democracy.

elites to the exclusion of the marginalised (Baud, 2004). Decentralisation efforts are in some cases a guise for national political elites to expand their control by means of developing new local institutions or restructuring existing ones. Obstacles of power, social exclusion and minimal organisational capacity mean that little will be gained by the poor. Furthermore, decentralisation may undermine macro-economic control, worsen interregional income disparities and increase local government budget deficits. Perhaps the greatest pitfall is that the assumed causality of decentralisation leading to poverty reduction has thus far lacked solid empirical confirmation. According to Devas & Grant (2003) there is no evidence of such a connection between decentralisation and the development of more pro-poor policies or poverty-alleviating outcomes. A study by Blair (2000) found a similar weak link with poverty reduction. More recently, Steiner (2007) has observed that the academic backing for the relationship between decentralisation and poverty is still restricted and ambiguous.

2.3 Exploring 'urban governance': local state responsiveness, public participation and partnerships

Whether the pitfalls outweigh the gains or vice versa, it is evident that decentralisation brings government and civil society closer together, and challenges all urban stakeholders involved to take up new responsibilities. In particular the 'devolution' form of decentralisation offers strong linkages with democracy, popular participation and empowerment. The symbiotic relationship between decentralisation and government proximity to the people introduces participation and responsiveness into the debate, as decentralisation provides opportunities for participation, while participation challenges local institutions to be responsive to community needs (Bergh, 2004). Indeed, historically, the 'local' has been considered a key site for democracy building and citizen participation. Citizenship was thought to derive largely from community identification and locally concentrated political participation (Lowndes, 1995 quoted in Gaventa, 2001). In their comparison of four countries, Crook & Manor (1998) found a positive link between decentralisation and local citizen participation. Decentralisation thus offers enhanced possibilities to include a wide range of stakeholders in urban decision-making.

In response to ongoing decentralisation processes, and what Cornwall & Gaventa (2001) have called a 'growing crisis of legitimacy' in the relationships between citizens and the institutions that affect their lives, notions of urban governance and collective urban decision-making have become more relevant. At the same time the current emphasis in development thinking on promoting 'good governance' has re-intensified the attention for decentralisation, efficient local government and popular participation. As McCarney (1996) notes, the 1990s were characterised by a shift from the rather technical aspects of *managing* cities towards more political aspects of *governing* cities. As such, the importance of local government was not only expressed in management capacity but also in terms of serving the community including the role of participation in service delivery and representative local government structures. Local governance has been increasingly considered imperative for the sustainable management of urban areas. The governance debate has been dynamic since the introduction of the initial concept of governance as "good government" in 1989 by the World Bank (Helmsing, 2000). While its definition remains a hotly debated issue (see Grindle, 2007; Doornbos, 2001), there is a growing consensus that governance is important in the light of development and poverty reduction, also at city level (Barten et al., 2002; UN-Habitat, 2002).

Governance is broadly understood as the system of formal and informal values, policies and institutions by which a society organises collective decision-making and action related to political, economic, socio-cultural and environmental affairs through the interaction of the state, civil society and private sector (based on UNDP, 1997b; Hyden et al., 2004, and World Bank, 1992, quoted in Santiso, 2002). Governance comprises the complex mechanisms, processes and institutions through which citizens and groups articulate their interests, mediate their differences and exercise their legal rights and obligations (Work, 2002). It recognises that it is not local government alone, but various other actors as well that shape the political urban agenda and its implementation. Harpham & Boateng (1997) observe that the crucial distinction between government and governance is the notion of civil society, which they define as "the public life of individuals and institutions outside the control of the state", whereas government is understood as institutions that "make and implement laws" (p. 66). Governance refers to governing with permeable boundaries between organisations in the public and private sectors. This recognises the interdependence of these sectors but also involves a blurring and sharing of responsibilities (Stoker, 1998).

Entering the normative debate on *good* governance,[26] the creation of effective partnerships between these spheres are needed to base political, social en economic priorities on broad consensus which includes taking into account the needs of the poor (Work, 2002). This has implications for the role of institutions and citizens alike. Gaventa (2001) argues that in order to achieve good, participatory local governance,[27] people and institutions need to be brought together. He stresses that rebuilding the relationship calls for 'working both sides of the equation' i.e. strengthening local institutions while at the same time enhancing the empowerment of civil society to participate in local decision-making: "…[T]here is growing consensus that the way forward is found in a focus on both a more active and engaged civil society which can express demands of the citizenry, and a more responsive and effective state which can deliver needed public services" (Gaventa, 2001, p. 2). Moreover, good governance is driven by advancing the intersection of the two, in which issues of citizen participation and state responsiveness and accountability are taken into account. Cornwall & Gaventa (2001) argue that focusing on just one of these perspectives holds the risks of leading to either 'voice without influence', when participation is not linked to power and politics, or to reinforcing the status quo when reform of political institutions

---

26 Although a normative debate, there is increasing agreement on what constitutes good governance, also in the urban context. According to the UN-Habitat Global Campaign on Urban Governance, the fundamental principles of good governance (based on experiences of cities participating in the Campaign) include sustainability, subsidiarity, equity, efficiency, transparency and accountability, civil engagement and citizenship, and security (UN-Habitat, 2002).

27 In comparison to 'governance', 'local governance' emphasises the opportunities that are offered at the local level for individual citizens and their representative organisations to directly engage in governance affairs. Shah & Shah (2006, p. 1-2) define local governance as "the formulation and execution of collective action at the local level [encompassing] the direct and indirect roles of formal institutions of local government and government hierarchies, as well as the roles of informal norms, networks, community organisations, and neighbourhood associations in pursuing collective action by defining the framework for citizen-citizen and citizen-state interactions, collective decision-making, and delivery of local public services".

THE CHALLENGE TO STRENGTHEN URBAN GOVERNANCE THROUGH NORTH-SOUTH CITY PARTNERSHIPS

does not include consultation and participation. Also Krishna (2003) concludes that the discussions on decentralisation and community-based development have proceeded separately from each other for too long. He observes that by working together local government and civil society can achieve what neither can achieve on its own. They both have a part to play in forging mutual beneficial influences: local government stability and institutional performance will be more effective when community organisations are engaged in government programmes at the local level, providing access and information to citizens. At the same time, the value and utility of community organisations are enhanced when they can provide mobilisation capacity to citizens in order to connect with government institutions and markets. Local governance thus calls for collective action. A strong state and a strong civil society are therefore needed for better conditions for service delivery and high responsiveness to poverty needs. How can this be achieved?

With respect to the first issue, capacity building for local governments has become a common element of donor driven decentralisation programmes, decentralised cooperation and interventions aimed at public sector reform. The role of local administrations in urban governance can be narrowly defined – the municipality as a service provider – or more widely: the municipality as a community developer. With regard to the former role, effective municipal administration is an important precondition. The changing nature of local government steered by decentralisation processes in combination with a continuous weak financial resource base poses difficulties to organisational capacity and basic service delivery. As has been noted, decentralisation policies have not automatically led to financial autonomy of local governments and many local governments suffer from a serious lack of financial and human resources. As Van Lindert (2005c) states, municipalities usually spend the major part of their annual budgets (up to 70-80 per cent in some cases) on personnel costs due to the labour intensive provision of services, facilities, and infrastructure in their area of jurisdiction. Owing to a huge lack of revenue-raising capacities, local governments in the South continue to heavily depend on transfers from the state. Moreover, local governments need to devise policies and adopt particular regulations and by-laws, through which they may complement and expand what has been predefined by the central or intermediate government tiers. The design and implementation of local policies require specific knowledge and skills within the local government apparatus, which is often lacking (Baud, 2004; Grindle, 2006; Olowu & Wunsch, 2004).

In development thinking and practice, 'public sector reform' and 'New Public Management'[28] have become mainstream notions to reflect the increased attention for improving the technical and organisational performance of local governments. They respond to the questions of 'what local governments should do' and 'how they should do it better' (World Bank, 2008; Shah & Shah, 2006). Many of the capacity building programmes for the public sector are directed towards the institutional strengthening of public institutions and administrations: aiming at what Grindle (1997) has phrased 'getting good government'. She distinguishes three areas of capacity building for institutional strengthening which are hierarchically related. First, capacity building may be aimed at *human resource development*,

---

28 New Public Management (NPM) is a broad term used to describe the worldwide trend of public sector reform that has started in the 1980s. The NPM perspective is primarily concerned with market failures and how to deliver public goods efficiently and effectively through better management of public budget. It focuses in particular on new approaches to management from the bottom-up rather than top-down (Shah & Shah, 2006).

e.g. through the training of staff, and the improvement of recruitment procedures and work conditions. Secondly, *organisational strengthening* focuses on improving management systems on the micro level, through changing management structures or the organisational culture of the institution. Thirdly, *institutional reform* targets institutions and systems at the macro level. This includes policy and legal change and constitutional reform. Andrews & Shah (2003) put 'conformance' and 'fiscal health' central in the assessment of institutional performance of local governments. The former considers whether local authorities conduct their operation within the parameters of legislation, the latter addresses resource use in local government, and whether an adequate level of fiscal health and discipline is maintained.

The broader governance perspective of municipalities as *community developers* implies that a shift in their mandate as well as in their position vis-à-vis civil society and other non-public actors is necessary. As Andrews and Shah (2003) argue, these issues also need to be taken into account in the evaluation of local government performance, especially in developing countries where local institutions are often created in response to low efficiency, responsiveness and accountability in central governments. Local governments should then not only operate according to legislation and manage their finances properly, but also "provide the 'right' services (in response to citizen need) in the 'right' (or most efficient) way and with the highest degree of accountability to constituents" (p. 3). As a result of government reforms, municipalities have increasingly become legally mandated to take a lead role in the development of the area of their jurisdiction, or to become 'developmental'.[29]. This role may be explicit, e.g. taking an active approach towards local development that is based on identified community needs, or implicit, for example through the position of municipalities as local agents in the redistribution of national fiscal and donor transfers based on pro-poor indicators. Moreover, it has been noted (e.g. Krishna, 2003; Andrews & Shah, 2003) that while the decentralisation agenda has been mainly concerned with making local governments effective and enhancing their technical and financial capacity, a similar concern should be how local governments interact with their constituents in order to foster local development. Linked to the concept of local government as community developer is the notion of institutions' *responsiveness* to the needs of the poor (e.g. Gaventa, 2001; Crook & Manor, 1998). Responsiveness is defined as the achievement of congruence between community preferences and government policies such that activities of the institution are valued by the public (Crook, 2003). Also closely related is the concept of *accountability*, which implies that people will be able to hold local government responsible for how it is affecting them (Blair, 2000). Accountability has a bureaucratic dimension – local government officials must be accountable to elected representatives, and a representative dimension, i.e. elected officials must be accountable to the public (Blair 2000; Crook, 2003). Crook & Manor (1998) found that a *culture of accountability* to a high degree explains local government performance.

To increase government responsiveness, accountability and transparency in relation to its citizenry, innovations have taken place in the design of local governance instruments and tools. Legal frameworks now demand local governments to draw up municipal development

---

29 The term 'developmental local government' is particularly employed in South Africa, where it was formally introduced in the Local Government White Paper (1998) as "local government committed to working with citizens (…) to find sustainable ways to meet their social, economic and material needs and improve the quality of their lives" (RSA, 1998, p. 17).

THE CHALLENGE TO STRENGTHEN URBAN GOVERNANCE THROUGH NORTH-SOUTH CITY PARTNERSHIPS

plans in such a way that public participation is embedded in the entire cycle of urban decision-making. This may include participatory budgeting processes that are interlinked with development plans.[30] The participation of citizens in local decision-making processes and the extent of poverty focus in local government investment allocations have been identified as key evaluative criteria for assessing local government responsiveness (Andrews & Shah, 2003). The intensification of the mutual relationship between local state and civil society requires local governments to open up spaces (Harpham & Boateng (1997) refer to the term 'action space') that allow non-public actors to participate in decision-making and policy implementation.

In order to improve the quality of urban governance, strengthening the capacity of local governments *to respond* should be accompanied by strengthening community capacity *to demand* (Romeo, 2003). Regarding the second precondition for good governance – to build a strong local civil society,[31] much of the literature focuses on issues of citizenship, participation and voice. Hordijk (2005) distinguishes between citizenship as a political right – associated with representative democracy as well as passive, indirect decision-making e.g. through the right to vote – and citizenship as an act of agency and practice. The latter is a more active and direct approach to decision-making (participatory democracy),[32] in which citizenship can be 'practiced' by influencing municipal planning and demanding government accountability and transparency. The distinction is illustrated by the notions introduced by Cornwall & Gaventa (2000) of citizens as 'users and choosers' versus 'makers and shapers' of governing structures and service delivery. Participation, explained by Gaventa (2001) as the way in which poor people exercise voice through new forms of inclusion, consultation and mobilisation, is important with regard to informing and influencing local institutions and policies and to tap from existing potential and knowledge from non-public actors for policy making and implementation. As Krishna (2003, p. 369) notes, there is a greater need to not only study how community organisations can improve their own functioning, but also how they can improve the "environment for development initiatives" through networking and partnerships. Intimately linked with the poverty debate is the concept of 'empowerment', which Schneider (1999, p. 524) defines as "the gaining of strength in the various ways necessary to be able to move out of poverty". Building a strong civil society thus implies being able to overcome the lack of means which are the basis of power in the

---

30 Participatory budgeting is one of many innovative approaches local governments employ to be better able to respond to the needs and priorities of their communities and constituencies (Cabannes, 2004; Hordijk, 2005; Souza, 2001).

31 In an urban development context, civil society can be defined as those non-public organisations which have roles in reducing poverty (directly by providing services to the poor or indirectly through ensuring a better use of resources or lobbying external agencies) and strengthening local democracy, by representing the interests and needs of the poor to decision-making processes and structures (Mitlin, 1999). Organisations include community-based organisations (CBOs) which are membership organisations of low-income groups, and non-governmental organisations (NGOs) which promote the interests of groups other than its members (Edwards, 2004 quoted in Baud, 2004).

32 Participatory democracy emphasises the broad participation and decision-making of constituents in the direction and operation of political systems. Representative democracy refers to indirect participation in decision-making through the right to vote, leaving actual governing to political institutions.

urban society. These means include knowledge, education, resources, organisation, rights and voice (Schneider, 1999).

In Mitlin's view (2004) a success factor of empowerment and local, participatory governance is in the capacity to create opportunities for groups with distinct but related agendas. This is especially important as the poor are often not a homogenous group (Schneider, 1999). Conditions need to be created that allow interest groups to define objectives and strategies. Building institutional capacity that enhances negotiation and participation power is hence an important ingredient for actors to become involved in the processes of local development, and to 'practice citizenship' to influence decision-making. With high-level engagement in governance at the local level, civil skills will become more effective which again leads to better local governance structures (Etzioni, 2001 quoted in Krishna, 2003). Cornwall & Gaventa (2001) also mention that 'new spaces and places' for citizenship participation need to be created, and existing mechanisms need to be better utilised, such as public meetings and committees, and participatory municipal planning and budgeting. NGOs and CBOs can fill the gap between government and citizenry through providing intermediary participation mechanisms. Promoting citizenship learning and awareness-raising, building civil society organisations, fostering social movements engaged in governance issues, and supporting other empowerment strategies have been mentioned as preconditions of participatory governance (Gaventa, 2001). Obstacles to citizen participation in local governance have been identified by Gaventa & Valderrama (1999) and include poor levels of citizen organisation (e.g. a tradition of social movements), low participatory skills to effectively exercise influence, lack of political will, low levels of participation (e.g. consultation instead of decision-making), and insufficient financial resources, inhibiting local governments to facilitate effective participation.

2.4 Towards an analytical framework of assessing urban governance strengthening

In addition to concerns about definitions of governance and good governance, and the question how the latter can be achieved, there is an ongoing and at times controversial debate about the measurement of governance. According to Grindle (2007), such debates are important as they offer insight in questions on how characteristics or indicators of governance can be operationalised and compared across or within countries. Moreover, they deal with relevant cause-and-effect relationships that are assumed to exist between governance and development, which helps to clarify development thinking. The measurement of good governance is 'problematic and inexact' (Grindle, 2007). In many instances, indicators are used among scholars and donor agencies to allow for cross-national and longitudinal comparisons (Kaufmann et al., 2008; Hyden et al., 2004; Dfid, 2001; UN-Habitat, 2002).[33] Especially studies that examine the relationship between governance and development rely on large-scale quantitative cross-national analysis. It has been argued however, that the use of indicators that allow for broad generalisations have some drawbacks: it would for example ignore the role of institutional and leadership history (Hewko, 2002 quoted in Grindle, 2007) and pay little attention to the unique experiences

---

33 The UNDP user's guide to governance indicators, available from http://www.undp.org/oslocentre/docs04/ UserGuide.pdf, lists over 33 indices of what may be broadly considered good governance indicators projects.

THE CHALLENGE TO STRENGTHEN URBAN GOVERNANCE THROUGH NORTH-SOUTH CITY PARTNERSHIPS

of countries or regions, including international contexts, elite-mass relationships, regime characteristics and institutional and organisational structures (Grindle, 2007). Moreover, indicators are inherently normative, usually based on Western-derived standards and often reflect "the way donors are used to perceive and handle the world around them (...) from their own particular and cultural perspective, even though they may be presented as having 'universal' value" (Doornbos, 2001). It can be argued that especially at the urban level, local contextual political and socio-economic conditions shape to a large extent the relationship between development and governance, and therefore the use of quantitative indicators to measure good governance can be empirically ambiguous.[34]

In this study therefore, bearing in mind the multi-dimensional nature of city-to-city cooperation efforts that aim to improve the quality of urban governance in the South, a more qualitative approach to assessing governance is applied that is tailor-made to the urban context and the characteristics of C2C highlighted in Chapter 1. The perspective of building both a strong local state and a strong citizenry provides an interesting methodological starting point for assessing the impact of city-to-city cooperation in urban governance. How does C2C perform with regard to strengthening local governments and civil society? To what extent and in what way can the external forces of C2C function as an intermediary to bridge gaps and enhance responsibility and responsiveness of all urban stakeholders? This study builds on the conceptualisation of this two-sided condition for good governance. It first investigates how C2C can strengthen municipal administrations and their services. Secondly, it identifies the contributions that C2C can make to fostering citizen participation in local decision-making processes.

Based on the literature reviewed in this Chapter, and in order to build an analytical framework that serves the assessment of urban governance strengthening in the South through C2C, the following considerations need to be taken into account. The different elements of urban governance strengthening and the potential effect of C2C on these elements are presented in Figure 2.3.

1. Two concepts are put central in order to make institutional performance operational. First, *effectiveness* refers to the role of local government as service provider, whereby notions of legal and process conformance, fiscal health, adequate service delivery and technical and operational management capacity prevail. Secondly, *responsiveness*,[35] as explained above, deals with the position of local governments that defines the interaction of participation and institutional performance through the mechanisms of

---

34   Since 1996, the World Bank has published good governance ratings for 212 countries, using several hundred indicators addressing six key aspects connected with good governance: voice and accountability; political stability and absence of violence; government effectiveness; regulatory quality; rule of law; and control of corruption (Kaufmann et al., 2008). The World Governance Indicators or Kaufmann indicators of the World Bank have been criticised in various ways (e.g. Arndt & Oman, 2006, Thomas, 2006, Knack, 2006), mainly to stress that governance cannot be compared over time or across countries due to difference in underlying data sources and that indicators are too imprecise to provide meaningful comparison.

35   Crook and Manor (1998) used 'effectiveness' and 'responsiveness' as key measurements for institutional performance to assess popular participation, representation and institutional accountability.

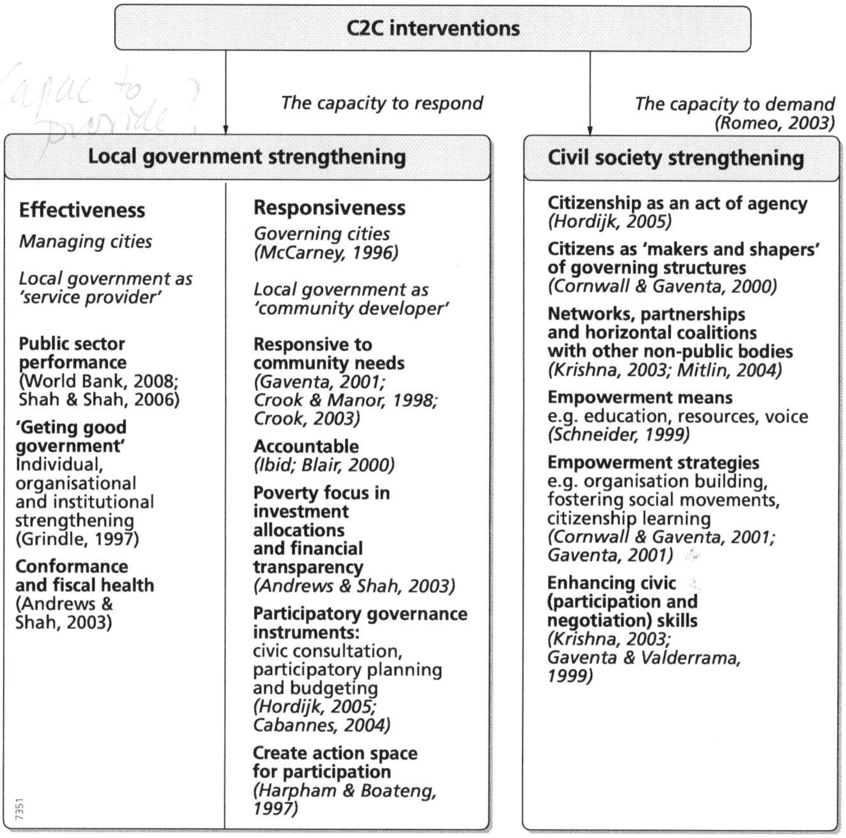

C2C interventions

The capacity to respond

The capacity to demand
(Romeo, 2003)

Local government strengthening

Effectiveness

Managing cities

Local government as 'service provider'

Public sector performance (World Bank, 2008; Shah & Shah, 2006)

'Geting good government' Individual, organisational and institutional strengthening (Grindle, 1997)

Conformance and fiscal health (Andrews & Shah, 2003)

Responsiveness

Governing cities (McCarney, 1996)

Local government as 'community developer'

Responsive to community needs *(Gaventa, 2001; Crook & Manor, 1998; Crook, 2003)*

Accountable *(Ibid; Blair, 2000)*

Poverty focus in investment allocations and financial transparency *(Andrews & Shah, 2003)*

Participatory governance instruments: civic consultation, participatory planning and budgeting *(Hordijk, 2005; Cabannes, 2004)*

Create action space for participation *(Harpham & Boateng, 1997)*

Civil society strengthening

Citizenship as an act of agency *(Hordijk, 2005)*

Citizens as 'makers and shapers' of governing structures *(Cornwall & Gaventa, 2000)*

Networks, partnerships and horizontal coalitions with other non-public bodies *(Krishna, 2003; Mitlin, 2004)*

Empowerment means e.g. education, resources, voice *(Schneider, 1999)*

Empowerment strategies e.g. organisation building, fostering social movements, citizenship learning *(Cornwall & Gaventa, 2001; Gaventa, 2001)*

Enhancing civic (participation and negotiation) skills *(Krishna, 2003; Gaventa & Valderrama, 1999)*

7351

Figure 2.3 A model for assessing urban governance strengthening through city-to-city cooperation

accountability. It refers to the role of local government as community developer.[36] It should be noted that these two capacities of local government are interdependent: An effective administration is necessary to promote participation and partnerships, while responsiveness is essential to improve the performance of the local public sector (*cf.* Romeo, 2003).

2. On the other side of the equation i.e. civil society strengthening, analysis should include the assessment of the potential of civil society in cities, how organised groups would respond to specific incentives or disincentives (Bergh, 2004) and their level of empowerment to participate in collective decision-making.

---

36 The effectiveness vs. responsiveness capacity can be compared with what Romeo (2003) has termed the 'internal' and 'interactive' capacities of local government. The former comprises the ability to carry out core functions of public sector resource mobilisation and expenditure management. The latter refers to the view that local government is recognised as just one element in a network of multiple actors who take decisions collectively.

2.5 Summary

The challenges to urban areas and their authorities that are the result of decentralisation and public sector reform, ongoing urbanisation and persistent poverty, call for new forms of urban governance. Paradigm shifts in urban development policy and planning have resulted in a movements from projects in housing and infrastructure in the 1970s, via city-wide urban management activities in the 1980s, to an increasing emphasis on strengthening local government and creating 'good governance' at the urban level in the 1990s and in the new Millennium. This Chapter considered this historical context which explains the current focus on good governance in urban development thinking today. Subsequently it discussed processes of decentralisation of government which have brought new mandates and responsibilities to local government in the South. Further, the Chapter explored the second key concept of this study, urban governance. In order to improve the quality of governance in cities in the South, institutions and people need to be brought more closely together. To achieve this, a strong local state as well as a strong civil society are needed. It is therefore imperative to increase local government performance in terms of administration, service delivery and level of responsiveness to community needs, while at the same time it is necessary to encourage citizenship and citizen participation in urban decision-making. An analytical framework was presented which indicates potential ways in which the various necessary conditions for good urban governance may be fostered through city-to-city cooperation. The framework will be tested and applied to the empirical cases of this study in Chapter 9. However, before moving from theory to empirical findings, the next Chapters first consider the institutional and policy contexts in which city-to-city cooperation and the institutional reform of local governments in the South can be placed.

3 The policy framework: C2C in the development debate[37]

In Chapter 1 the substance and potential of city-to-city cooperation were reviewed and the practice of C2C was introduced as an ever growing form of development cooperation in which cities take centre stage. Chapter 2 examined the theoretical notions with regard to strengthening urban governance in the South. Moving from practice and theories to policy, this Chapter is directed at discussing past and current policies with regard to urban development and decentralised cooperation. How can the increased attention among donors, national governments and practitioners for C2C be explained? Which shifts in development thinking have taken place that clarify the growing role of municipalities as agents for local development? How have multi-lateral donors and national governments responded to this growing recognition? How are C2C policy instruments shaped and how are they applied to affect C2C practice?

The Chapter is divided into three sections. It starts in the first section with an overview of trends in development thinking and practice that have resulted in the fact that local governments have increasingly become full-fledged players in the international development arena. The section concludes with a review of the plethora of C2C policy and support programmes that have emerged over the last two decades. In 3.2, attention turns towards the Netherlands (and Germany to a lesser extent), both to present a policy framework for the empirical case studies of this study and to provide a more detailed example of existing C2C policy instruments. The final section of this Chapter is of a more evaluative nature and explores the question as to how C2C policy and urban governance strengthening are related, by evaluating Dutch C2C policy with regard to South Africa from 1995 to present.

3.1 The rise of city-to-city cooperation explained

The rise of city-to-city cooperation as a mechanism for development assistance can be explained by a number of trends. A first trend concerns the fact that local governments are increasingly recognised as important players in development. This is reflected in a more general tendency in which the international donor community has become more receptive to incorporating non-conventional donors including NGOs, civil society and local authorities and communities. The recognition of the role of local government in development has not been limited to national states assigning increased authority to municipalities in the context of national decentralisation programmes (Chapter 2). Agendas of various international development institutions point out that local governments play a major role in attaining sustainable development. Chapter 28 of Agenda 21, the outcome of the 1992 Rio Conference (Earth Summit) is a very clear example in this respect. As a result of this international agreement local governments worldwide have taken the lead in devising

---

37 Parts of this Chapter have been published elsewhere in adapted version (Bontenbal, 2006a; Bontenbal, 2006b; Bontenbal, 2007; Bontenbal, 2008).

their own Local Agendas 21 (LA21), and put them into action. In a similar vein the Habitat Agenda (outcome of the Habitat II conference in Istanbul, 1996) emphasises the crucial role of local governments as the 'closest partner' in the Habitat process and encourages national governments to strengthen municipalities. This paradigm shift away from the former central state orientation towards a new emphasis on strengthening the capacities of local governments, including their ability to become efficient and effective agents for local development, can be observed in the latest World Bank policies. In the Cities Alliance programme, for instance, Local Government Associations (LGAs) are fully participating in the Consultative Group and negotiations are taking place directly with the local authorities of the cities involved. More recently, at the UN World Summit on the Millennium Development Goals in 2005, the vital importance of cities and communities in achieving these goals was stressed.

The understanding that nation states no longer have a monopoly on solving current problems (Gaspari, 2002) has strengthened the role of non-state actors and micro-order players in development aid. Decentralised international cooperation, including C2C, implies that the venture of development assistance is no longer limited to multilateral donors and national governments. In the new vision the role of local governments in both North and South in international development cooperation has been increasingly recognised by all leading development institutions. For example, in the framework of the French presidency of the European Union in the second half of 2008, France put forward an initiative to value the importance of the local dimension of development and to recognise the role of local governments, community-based organisations, and other local actors in international cooperation. Indeed, one of the thematic programmes of the European Union for development cooperation for 2008-2013[38] is aimed at 'non-state actors and local authorities in development'. Being at the grassroots, these actors are claimed to have a thorough knowledge of local communities and access to them through their extensive networks. The placing of local level governance and development high on the EU agenda is just one example of the accumulation and consolidation of attention and recognition that has been built up over the last years by donors, governments and practitioners alike to decentralised cooperation. At the end of this section a number of C2C policy and support programmes run by multi-lateral organisations and national governments – which further reflect this recognition – are discussed.

A second trend has occurred in urban development thinking, which more and more embraces the importance of institutions and good governance at the local level: urban development requires strong local governments. This trend, explained in more detail in 2.1, has led to a central position of 'good governance' in current development thinking, both at a national and an urban level, and has been backed by an increased attention for the role of institutions (Nijenhuis, 2002). Accordingly strategies for institutional reform have emerged at the expense of strategies for neoliberal reform that dominated the 1980s and part of the 1990s. The concept of 'good urban governance' is particularly employed by UN-Habitat's Global Campaign on Urban Governance, launched in 1999, which aims to contribute

---

38   As outlined in the Communication from the Commission to the Council, the European Parliament, the European Economic and Social committee and the Committee of the Regions regarding the Thematic Programme "Non-state Actors and Local Authorities in Development" (COM/2006/0019 final).

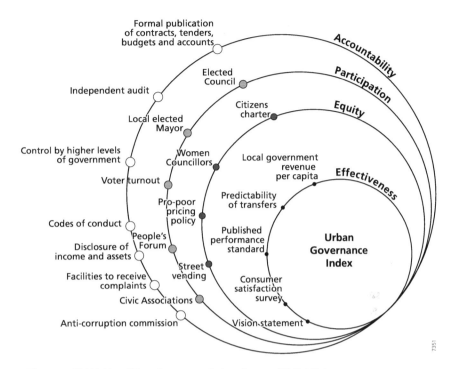

Figure 3.1 UN-Habitat Urban Governance Index - Source: UN-Habitat, 2002

to poverty alleviation through improved urban governance. Capacity building for local governments is a key strategy to realise 'the inclusive city', i.e. "a place where everyone (…) is enabled to participate productively and positively in the opportunities cities have to offer" (UN-Habitat, 2002, p. 3). The key principles to reach inclusive decision-making and good urban governance include sustainability, subsidiarity, equity, efficiency, transparency and accountability, civil engagement and citizenship, and security. An Urban Governance Index has been developed to measure the quality of urban governance and cities are encouraged to benchmark their performance based on these principles and their indicators (Figure 3.1).

A final trend that is discussed here to explain the contemporary position of C2C is the rise of city networks and the growing importance of the notion of 'partnership' in international cooperation. In section 2.4 it was already emphasised that the introduction of the concept of 'partnership' as a central theme in the international cooperation debate has indicated a move away from the traditional hierarchical patron-client relationship between donor and recipient partners towards a more balanced North-South power relationship in which partners cooperate on a peer basis. In an urban context, an opportunity for partners (i.e. cities) to achieve such relationships and learn from peers is through the networking of cities, in order to exchange knowledge and seek best practices elsewhere to find solutions to urban problems. Keiner & Kim (2007) found that between 1982 and 2004, the number of such international city networks grew from eight to 49. The call to cities of Agenda 21 to participate in international sustainability city networking was a key driving force for this trend. With regard to city-to-city cooperation, which Keiner & Kim (2007) view as the "most basic building block of city networking" (p. 1373), a major impetus was given by UN-Habitat

THE CHALLENGE TO STRENGTHEN URBAN GOVERNANCE THROUGH NORTH-SOUTH CITY PARTNERSHIPS

that chose C2C as the theme of World Habitat Day in 2002.[39] It goes beyond the scope of this Chapter to give a full account of the range of city networks that exist today. The study of Keiner & Kim (2007) can be referred to for that purpose. Also, Tjandradewi & Marcotullio (2009) have reflected on one of such networks, CITYNET in Asia, in more detail. Instead, the most significant policy and support programmes of national governments and multilateral organisations are reviewed below. They are specifically geared towards the practice of city-to-city cooperation with regard to contributing to urban development and urban governance in the South.

C2C policy and support programmes

The emergence of donor support programmes to facilitate C2C cooperation has allowed stimulated professionalism and institutionalisation of city partnerships that have often evolved out of informal or solidarity-based grassroots initiatives (see for example section 3.2 and Chapter 5). A range of programmes provide funding of C2C projects and enhance capacity building and the creation of knowledge networks. The existence of these programmes reflects the broad acknowledgement by bilateral and multilateral institutions for development cooperation carried out by local authorities. Which are the organisations that facilitate North-South city-to-city cooperation?

United Cities and Local Governments (UCLG) was launched in January 2004, when three traditional local government associations (International Union of Local Authorities; United Towns Organisations; Metropolis) united their respective global networks of cities and national associations of local governments in a single organisation. Being the largest organisation of cities and local governments in the world, with members in over 127 countries, it is the principal local government partner of the United Nations. It coordinates local government representation to enhance the role and status of local government at the United Nations and to increase the role of local government in the global development agenda (UCLG, 2006). Based on the values of development, local democracy and decentralisation, UCLG focus areas include the UN Millennium Goals (through the Millennium Towns and Cities Campaign), decentralisation, and innovation in local governance.

In recent years the *United Nations* have increasingly become a key player in the facilitation and promotion of local authority networks and international municipal relations. The establishment of the World Associations of Cities and Local Authorities Coordination (WACLAC) in 1996 reflected the call for further development of partnerships between international local government associations and the UN. WACLAC's main objectives have been promoting local autonomy and strengthening the voice of local authorities on the international stage. Another important aim has been to advance the role of these latter in international development cooperation. In these efforts, WACLAC has cooperated with UN-Habitat (UN-Habitat, 2003). In the new millennium, its role has been largely taken over by UCLG.

---

39   World Habitat Day (every first Monday of the month of October) is celebrated by the UN to draw attention to the importance of human shelter and urban settlements in development. Each year, the Habitat Scroll of Honour and the World Habitat Awards are given to promising initiatives in a particular thematic field.

CITIES AS PARTNERS

Today, various UN programmes and institutes liaise with local governments through UCLG including UN-Habitat, UNDP, UNEP, UNITAR and UNESCO.[40] The United Nations Advisory Committee of Local Authorities (UNACLA) was established in January 2000 as the first formal advisory body of local authorities to the United Nations for dialogue on the implementation of the Habitat Agenda. The United Nations Development Programme (UNDP) considers C2C "not only an effective modality for local community and institutional development but also a promising vehicle for building more bridges across the world's ethnic, religious, cultural and material divides" (UNDP, 2000, p. 41).

UNDP established the World Alliance of Cities against Poverty (WACAP), a worldwide network of cities "to help municipalities face up to the challenge of poverty on the spot" (WACAP, undated, p. 1). WACAP was initiated in 1996, the International Year for the Eradication of Poverty. With the signing of the Millennium Declaration in 2000, the Alliance's main objective has been to contribute to achieving the Millennium Development Goals, by "providing a framework for pooling [municipalities'] human, material and financial resources in order to achieve specific objectives that make it possible to reduce poverty and reduce its effects" (WACAP, undated, p. 1).

In 2005, UN-Habitat established a Centre for City-to-City Cooperation in Seville, Spain. The Centre aims to "facilitate methodologies and tools for cities and local governments to undertake projects of international cooperation in support of the MDGs" (UN-Habitat, 2006, p. 3) with the overall objective to improve the effectiveness of the North-South city co-operation in support of the Millennium Development Goals.

Other institutions and programmes that recognise the potential role of C2C to assist cities in the South include the *European Union* (e.g. the previously mentioned thematic programme for non-state actors and local communities, the Tacis City Twinning Programme, URB-al and Asia Urbs), the previously mentioned *Cities Alliance*, a multi-donor coalition of cities and their development partners including the World Bank that provides funding and assistance to local authorities in slum upgrading and city development strategies, and the *CEMR* (Chapter 1), which since 2002 has supported North-South cooperation and the work of European local authorities in international development aimed at capacity building.

Besides international organisations and initiatives, national governments play an active role in facilitating C2C. From the 1980s onwards the establishment of national cooperation programmes and changes in legislation, mainly in Europe and Canada, greatly supported municipal cooperation (Hafteck, 2003). Four such national programmes are presented in Box 3.1, highlighting some of the key innovative players in the international field of decentralised development cooperation.

---

40   United Nations Human Settlements Programme (UN-Habitat), United Nations Development Programme (UNDP), United Nations Environmental Programme (UNEP), United Nations Institute for Training and Research (UNITAR), United Nations Educational, Scientific and Cultural Organization (UNESCO). UN acknowledges that 'UN inter-agency communication and cooperation is often deficient' with a significant lack of knowledge of the respective UN programmes and projects targeting local government. Mandated to fill this gap, the UNDP Hub for Innovative Partnerships has attempted to categorise all UN local development actions working for and with local authorities. It concluded that over 300 UNDP local government projects ran in 2006 while over 20 UN institutes, entities and programmes were involved in local government initiatives (UNDP, 2006).

THE CHALLENGE TO STRENGTHEN URBAN GOVERNANCE THROUGH NORTH-SOUTH CITY PARTNERSHIPS

- One of the first national twinning associations was Sister City International, serving US initiatives. Recently, SCI has administered the US Government funded Sister Cities Network for Sustainable Development, a capacity building programme focusing on local governance and sustainability. It includes the Africa HIV/AIDS Education and Prevention Program (to support innovative education and prevention programs addressing HIV/AIDS in African communities), and the Millennium Development Goals City-to-City Challenge Pilot Program, in collaboration with the World Bank.
- Since 1987, the Federation of Canadian Municipalities (FCM) has represented the international relations of Canadian municipalities. Its mission stresses the strong role of municipal governments in global affairs, striving for the "development and empowerment of municipal governments worldwide to improve the quality of life and the sustainability of local communities". It promotes a range of activities including knowledge and (institutional) capacity development and the development of policy and regulatory frameworks.
- City-to-city cooperation in the UK is coordinated through the Local Government International Bureau (LGIB). Its aim is to foster capacity building in developing countries and the promotion of peace and stability in conflict areas. The Commonwealth Local Government Good Practice Scheme, funded by the UK Department for International development (DfID), is intended to support technical cooperation projects between local authorities around the world.[1]
- VNG International is the International Cooperation Agency of the Association of Dutch Municipalities and is committed to strengthening democratic local government worldwide. It co-finances various programmes for C2C carried out by Dutch municipalities and their partners in developing countries. VNG International is a key player in international networks of local authorities. It plays an active role in the North-South Network of the Council of European Municipalities and Regions and is member of the advisory committee for the Asia Urbs programme of the EU. It further chairs the Capacity and Institution Building Platform of UCLG.

Sources: Websites SCI, FCM, LGIB, VNG-International, CEMR, UCLG

---

1 Evans (2009) gives a detailed account of the lobby and advocacy work in the UK to get C2C on the policy agenda. In a discourse-based analysis, she demonstrates how various institutions in the UK have started to provide support to C2C initiatives and how British local governments have become increasingly recognised as development partners.

3.2 The C2C policy framework in The Netherlands

This section deals with Dutch national policy on decentralised development cooperation. In order to understand the (potential) role of Dutch municipalities in international cooperation, it is important to consider a few general policymaking trends that have shaped Dutch C2C during the last years. The section explains the view of the central government on C2C as a form of development cooperation, discusses the role of the Association of Dutch Municipalities as broker between national development cooperation policy and municipalities as partners in C2C, and reviews the programmes that have been implemented to support the role of Dutch municipalities in international cooperation. Specific attention will be given to South Africa and Nicaragua as the main partner countries for Dutch C2C initiatives. This section also briefly describes the C2C policy framework in Germany to give contrast to and context for to the Dutch situation, and also to serve as a background to the German case study of this research.

3.2.1 Dutch C2C policy: strengthening local government in the South

According to a survey by VNG International (2006), 72% of the Dutch municipalities are involved in international cooperation (VNG, 2006). NCDO (2006) estimates that 10% of these efforts are directed to developing countries, i.e. OECD-DAC countries (Van Ewijk & Baud, 2009). National development policy in the Netherlands has traditionally supported C2C cooperation albeit with different motives. During the 1990s municipal C2C efforts were primarily considered relevant for awareness raising and creating public support for international development cooperation. A second task was the provision of technical assistance and the transfer of knowledge and expertise to Southern partner cities. Strengthening local government in developing countries was seen as a precondition that would allow marginalised communities access to political decision-making (IOB, 2004). Some years later, capacity building to strengthen municipalities and good governance in developing countries became a more central objective, in which the principles of reciprocity and mutual learning were emphasised. Throughout the 1990s policies in favour of C2C received strong parliamentary backing, partly because it was seen to help maintain public and political support for development cooperation in general. Between 1998 and 2002 national support experienced a temporary decline when the effectiveness of C2C towards the reduction of poverty was questioned. There were doubts whether Dutch municipalities, despite their knowledge on governance and urban policies, also possessed the relevant expertise necessary to act in the domain of development cooperation (IOB, 2004). In the last few years, C2C has again become more prominent on the agenda. Current development cooperation policy stresses the importance of partnerships, which certainly applies to C2C. For 2005-2008 the C2C budget, commissioned through the Dutch local government association VNG, has expanded to €12.4 million, an average of €3.1 million per year.[41] In previous years, this average was €2.2 million.[42] The main objective has shifted from awareness raising to local governance capacity building in the South.

Dutch C2C intervention is based on the following logic: The Ministry of Foreign Affairs allocates national budget to the strengthening of local governance in the South through capacity development and modest investments. The implicit assumption is that the transfer of knowledge and skills by means of exchange of personnel, as well as the funding of small-scale tangible activities contribute to capacity development. Subsequently this leads to improved performance of local government, e.g. in the field of management, service delivery and public participation (Cornelissen, 2004).

---

41 Apart from external funding, Dutch municipalities spend an estimated aggregated €8 million per year on international cooperation (VNG, 2001). For the majority of municipalities involved in C2C, C2C is a separate budget item on the municipal budget. This is on average an amount of €55,826 per municipality, or €0.59 per inhabitant (SEOR, 2003)

42 Interview with representative VNG-International, January 19, 2006.

Financial contributions from the Ministry are channelled through the International Co-operation Agency of the Association of Netherlands Municipalities, VNG International (VNG-I). VNG-I in turn is responsible for support programmes to which Dutch municipalities can turn to for financial and technical assistance. Between 1993 and 2003 VNG-I implemented the GSO programme (Municipal International Cooperation with Developing Countries), supporting over 100 Dutch municipalities, local NGOs, municipal water boards and provinces in their international cooperation efforts. Parallel to GSO, a similar programme provided a support framework for C2C with (former) Accession Countries of the European Union in East and Central Europe, the GST programme. Many of these municipalities involved in the GSO programme maintain formal twinning partnerships with Southern counterparts. In the framework of these existing international relations, the method of a peer-to-peer approach would allow for municipal exchange of knowledge and expertise, based on trust and mutual understanding (VNG, 2005).

Between 1997 and 2001, 89 Dutch local governments applied for a GSO subsidy, accounting for 18 percent of the total number of Dutch municipalities. These applications targeted 41 different countries (Cornelissen, 2004). The large majority of contacts existed with local governments in Nicaragua and South Africa, with each over 15 long-term or occasional relations. The GSO programme consisted of four implementation modalities (VNG, 2001; IOB, 2004):

1. Programme for temporary deployment of Dutch local officials and councillors (PUGA). On request of the partner city, dedicated missions for advisory, project formulation or training purposes took place.
2. Internship Local Government (STAGE). Practical on-the-job training provided experience to local officials and councillors from developing countries in a Dutch municipality.
3. Municipal Management Training Programme (MMTP), involving group training for local officials and councillors from developing countries frequently followed by a STAGE. The group composition corresponded to a common thematic background, job position in the local administration or country of origin.
4. Municipal initiatives programme (GI), providing financial support to local governments and NGOs with a structural C2C partnership for concrete projects contributing to exchanges between the partner cities and investments for development projects with a maximum duration of three years.

After the turn of the Millennium, VNG-I replaced the GSO programme by the Good Local Government Programme LOGO South 2005-2008, in short LOGO South. Much of the adjustments made are the result of an evaluation carried out by the Ministry of Foreign Affairs (IOB, 2004) – see Box 3.2. The objective is to 'strengthen good local government as a condition for poverty reduction' by means of capacity building to develop human capital in local government organisations, i.e. councillors and officials. A *Country Programme* has been developed for each of the 12 countries[43] targeted in LOGO South. This is done in consultation with relevant actors, with specific objectives that project applications will

43   They include: Benin (local taxes), Egypt (local water supply and sanitation), Ghana (financial management), Indonesia (local water management), Namibia (HIV/AIDS), Nicaragua (local government), The Palestinian Territories (solid waste and waste water management), Sri Lanka (waste management) , Sudan (water supply and waste management), Surinam (capacity development of decentralised districts), Tanzania (financial management) and South Africa (social housing).

Box 3.2 Policy evaluation "On Solidarity and Professionalisation"

For the first time in history, Dutch city-to-city cooperation policy was evaluated on a national scale. In August 2004, a report titled "On Solidarity and Professionalisation" commissioned by the Ministry's Policy and Operations Evaluation Department (IOB) presented the evaluation results of the GSO and GST programmes from 1997 to 2001. The outcomes of the evaluation has been important guidelines for reshaping current national C2C policy and the objectives and regulations of the LOGO South programme. It was found that two-thirds of the GSO projects had been implemented effectively and efficiently. The PUGA modality was found to be less effective than the STAGE and MMTP modalities. While more than 50% of the projects brought structural institutional or process related change in the partner organisations, it was also concluded that local knowledge had not been tapped sufficiently to aid implementation. Recommendations included making policy formulation more results-oriented and flexible while taking into account the local context. A stronger thematic and geographical focus should prevent scattered, isolated activities. This has resulted in the use of country and thematic programmes under LOGO South. Moreover, it was suggested that C2C as specific form of development cooperation should be more aligned and harmonised with other aid modalities, to facilitate mutual synergies (IOB, 2004).

have to observe. It thus acts as a framework for analysis, policy and strategy for individual project formulation and evaluation. It is meant to be connected to the existing problems, policies, initiatives and actors of the target country (VNG, 2005). The contribution from the Ministry accounts for an estimated 60 to 70% of the finance of LOGO South projects, while the remainder is covered by the participating Dutch municipalities, provinces, municipal water boards, and waterworks (Buis, 2008). As of January 2008, some 40 Dutch local governments participated with 46 projects in LOGO South. In 2006, the programme was extended until 2010 and received an additional grant of €24 million, which reflects the Ministry's continued acknowledgement and commitment to decentralised cooperation in the Netherlands.

Ownership, genuine partnership and local expertise have been given increased attention in project design under LOGO South. The four GSO modalities have been replaced by a multi-annual municipal programme for strengthening the organisational capacity of local governments and supra-municipal projects that are executed in the context of the country programme. The latter allow for the exchange of experience, dissemination (including South-South exchanges) and the influencing of national policies. Partner cities in North and South submit a joint project proposal written in the language of the target country based on a local problem analysis that is jointly conducted. Ideally both partners contribute equally to the project formulation and implementation, while previously this process was mainly conducted by the Northern partner in the Dutch language.[44] Projects need to refer to the

---

44 Attention to ownership is especially relevant as Buis (2008) has observed that content and objectives of Dutch C2C cooperation have traditionally been defined by the Dutch partner cities rather than their counterparts. This is a result of the underlying ideological and political motivations that have led to the mere establishment of these twinnings.

central objective of the *Country Programme* and to four core elements of local governance and municipal organisation. These elements are based on previous experience that has revealed that the exchange of expertise of Dutch municipalities with developing countries is most beneficial in the following aspects:

- Urban policy formulation and implementation
- Institutional development and management strengthening of local governments
- Improved urban service delivery
- Improved municipal financial management and policy making.

In addition to contributing to attaining good governance in the partner cities in the South, which links intimately with the subject of this study, there are other rationales for North-South C2C. They include meeting the Millennium Development Goals at the local level through tackling urban challenges, and cooperation with migrant countries for fostering integration of migrant groups in Dutch cities. These approaches differ in objectives, geographical orientation, and funding opportunities, but also show similarities with regard to contribution to poverty alleviation, democracy building, and improving basic service delivery. Box 3.3 deals with some recent policy trends in Dutch city-to-city cooperation. Finally, Box 3.4 considers the C2C policy framework in Germany. It compares the German to the Dutch situation, and together with the Dutch framework discussed above, it serves as a background to the empirical case studies of this research.

Box 3.3 Recent trends in Dutch C2C policy

A number of recent policy trends in Dutch city-to-city cooperation that have emerged analogous to the policy objective of strengthening urban governance in the South include:

1. The Millennium Development Goals: a new guiding concept to Dutch C2C?
A relatively new trend is the attention for the Millennium Development Goals (MDGs) in C2C, in which the idea is launched to make the MDGs the guiding concept to city-to-city cooperation in the Netherlands. In April 2007 (halfway the start of the global UN Millennium campaign in 2000 and 2015 when the goals are to be met) VNG-I started a campaign to promote Dutch municipal participation in meeting the MDGs. With their focus on poverty alleviation, (access to) education, equal rights for men and women, health care, reduction of child mortality and sustainable development, the MDGs relate well with the scope of most international projects of Dutch municipalities. Furthermore, municipalities in the Netherlands are in a position to contribute to sustainable development e.g. by saving energy, use Fair Trade products and practice sustainable (green) procurement. Hence, through C2C the contribution to achieving the MDGs may occur simultaneously in North and South. The Campaign invites Dutch municipalities to become a so-called 'Millennium Municipality'. As of November 2008, 85 municipalities have signed up, representing 34% of the Dutch population.[1] The Campaign has been praised for its capacity to trigger municipalities that have not been active in C2C before to start initiatives. In that sense, it could also

---

1 The changing number of participating municipalities is tracked on www.millenniumgemeente.nl.

provide a new impulse for political C2C support both at municipal and central levels (Bontenbal & Van Ewijk, 2008).

2. Partnerships with migrant countries

A second new focus is the growing interest of Dutch municipalities with large immigrant groups in establishing contacts with municipalities of the main migrant countries of origin (e.g. Morocco, Turkey, Surinam and the Netherlands Antilles). The majority of these ties have been initiated from 1999 and 2000 onwards as a result of their policies connecting international cooperation to issues related to integration. In addition to strengthening urban governance and improving service delivery in the partner cities, Dutch municipalities aim to contribute to the social, economic and cultural integration of migrant groups in their neighbourhoods and the municipality at large. Municipal strategies include involving migrants in technical and cultural exchanges, gaining knowledge on migrant groups in their cities to inform policy making, and promoting public participation of migrant groups in urban decision making. Fostering trade has been mentioned as additional objective to start C2C activities related to migrant countries (Van Ewijk, 2007; Van Ewijk & Baud, 2009).

3. Partnerships for European unification

The former GST programme, run by VNG to provide resources to Dutch municipalities engaged in city partnerships and projects with the so-called Accession Countries of the European Union and bordering EU countries, has been replaced by the LOGO East programme. The main objective is to strengthen the political and administrative capacity of local government in Romania, Bulgaria, Turkey, Ukraine, Serbia, and the Russian Federation through decentralised cooperation. The establishment of new twinnings is particularly encouraged, especially to extend bilateral partnerships to tri-partite relationships (called *trinnings*). In such structures, third counterparts from the ten countries that joined the EU in 2004 are included to provide EU transition experience.

4. City diplomacy

City diplomacy refers to the international activities of local governments in the spheres of conflict prevention, peace building and post-conflict reconstruction. It has been defined as "the institutions and processes by which cities (…) engage in relations with actors on an international political stage with the aim of representing themselves and their interests to one another" (Van der Pluijm & Melissen, 2007, p.6). While such a broad definition of diplomacy may incorporate a range of objectives including city marketing and branding, cultural exchange and trade opportunities, in practice city diplomacy is strongly related to peace and democracy building, human rights protection and conflict resolution in localities prone to war and conflict. In June 2008, VNG hosted the First World Conference on City Diplomacy in the Hague. It furthermore takes a lead role in UCLG's Committee on City Diplomacy established in 2005. The increased attention for City Diplomacy in Dutch C2C can be seen as a localised reflection of the recent focus in Dutch development cooperation on fragile states and conflict areas.[2]

5. Cross-cutting trends
Besides the above-mentioned policy orientations in Dutch city-to-city cooperation, at least two cross-cutting trends can be identified. First of all, it has been noted that Dutch municipalities have started to seek ways to benefit from international cooperation themselves (Van Ewijk & Baud, 2009; Hoetjes, 2009). The key motive of international solidarity has raised discomfort among a number of municipalities. Reciprocity appears more important today and may substitute altruistic motives. This would reflect a more businesslike attitude towards international cooperation and a reorientation towards mutual profits, such as economic cooperation and trade and the integration of migrants in Dutch society. A second major tendency is the shift from longer lasting sister cities based on friendship and trust built up over the years towards a more project oriented approach. Many municipalities do no longer want to commit themselves to infinite twinning relations. Moreover, municipalities need to demonstrate the impact of their international efforts; especially since municipal international affairs are often followed with considerable scepticism by city councils and the electorate (Van Ewijk, 2007).

---

2   Policy note on development cooperation 2007-2011 "Een zaak van iedereen: Investeren in ontwikkeling in een veranderende wereld", Ministry of Foreign Affairs.

Box 3.4 C2C policy and practice in Germany

German development cooperation policy and practice at community level takes a holistic and multi-faceted approach in comparison to the more narrowly defined Municipal International Cooperation (the Dutch terminology for C2C) in the Netherlands which emphasises the partnership element in particular. *Kommunale Entwicklungszusammenarbeit* (communal development cooperation) incorporates fair trade projects and events, fair procurement policies in German local authorities, and development education and 'global learning' (Nitschke & Wilhelmy, 2009). It has been estimated that the German cities together maintain at least 5,000 but possibly up to 7,000 international partnerships.[1] However, the bulk of relations is within Europe and only 3% of partnerships are with developing countries (Heinz et al., 2004 quoted in Nitschke & Wilhelmy, 2009). Communal development cooperation is characterised as civil society driven (mainly by churches and community organisations), operating with small budgets and mainly financed by donations (Nitschke & Wilhelmy, 2009). Many North-South initiatives are framed in Local Agenda 21 processes. The LA21

---

1   On a total of some 12,000 Germany municipalities, these figures suggests that 40 to 56% of German communities are engaged in international partnerships. The figure however does not take into account the distribution of the number of partnerships among the municipalities.

movement has been successful in Germany, where it has been adopted by 20% of the municipalities (SKEW, 2007). In the Netherlands on the contrary, LA21 is not an issue in urban planning.

Local political support in Germany is ubiquitous. It is however not accompanied with the necessary financial and administrative support. This is in contrast to the Netherlands where local political support is generally expressed by providing financial resources (from the municipal budget or by attracting external funding) to C2C initiatives. As will be demonstrated for the case study of the Berlin district of Treptow-Köpenick, the lack of a clear mandate for development cooperation for German local governments poses makes it difficult to actively engage, especially in communities facing budget debt and struggle with adapting to legislative changes after German reunification.

The main organisation in Germany supporting communal development cooperation is the 'Service Agency Communities in One World' (SKEW), which is a subdivision of the non-profit organisation Capacity Building International (InWent). A commonality with VNG-I in the Netherlands concerns its role in motivating and informing communities (with various publications, newsletters and an interactive homepage). The situation in Germany differs from the Netherlands to the extent that SKEW does not fund community projects. Cities work generally much more independently in development initiatives. In addition, while the Dutch central government provides funding for C2C projects, in Germany such resources are not available to municipalities. Moreover, as Nitschke & Wilhelmy (2009) observe, an unresolved constitutional debate on the limitations of municipal self-government and the monopoly that the federal government maintains on having foreign relations, causes the legal conditions for the use of the municipal budget for North-South city partnerships to remain unclear.

As a result, German municipalities operate in a rather different financial, juridical and political reality than Dutch cities. This has implications for the role of local governments as partners in development, the objectives set in North-South twinnings, and the capacities, resources and political backing available to support these initiatives. In Chapter 6, it will be demonstrated how the differences in the institutional frameworks of the two countries are manifested at community level.

3.2.2 Focus on South Africa and Nicaragua

Many Dutch city twinning relationships originate from the 1980s, an era which is characterised by the rise of several international political solidarity movements. This was expressed at the grassroots level by e.g. support to Eastern European communities under Soviet regime, solidarity with the Sandinista revolution in Nicaragua, and the disapproval of and political lobby against the Apartheid system in South Africa. Community solidarity groups pushed their local authorities to enter into twinning relations (Buis, 2008). It explains why today the large majority of twinnings still consist of partners in the former Soviet block, Nicaragua and South Africa. Over 15 long-term or occasional relationships exist between Dutch cities and cities Nicaragua and South Africa, respectively.

THE CHALLENGE TO STRENGTHEN URBAN GOVERNANCE THROUGH NORTH-SOUTH CITY PARTNERSHIPS

Figure 3.2 Dutch – South African C2C partnerships [1]

---

1   South African municipalities have been going through of process of administrative reform (Chapter 4), in which
     city names dating from the colonisation and Apartheid eras are being replaced by African names. Pretoria for
     example is today called Tshwane, and Durban is now eThekwini. As a consequence, the twinnings between
     Dutch and South African cities need to reconsider their names. The city of Uitenhage for example has been
     incorporated in Nelson Mandela Metropolitan Municipality, however the twinning still refers to Uitenhage. The
     Figure displays the official name of the partner city in brackets when it differs from the original.

South Africa

Nicaragua and South Africa each have their particular history that explains their position as
the two principal Southern partner countries for Dutch municipalities. Regarding the latter,
in the 1980s an increasing number of Dutch municipalities openly declared themselves
'anti-apartheid', Amsterdam being the first in 1985. In 1988 the municipal network *Local
Governments against Apartheid* (LOTA) was established with 69 members (VNG, 2001).
Dutch municipalities took a stand by openly supporting the informal Civics that emerged in
black urban areas in South Africa, and by responding to the boycott call on South African
products.

When apartheid was abolished in the 1990s in South Africa, the anti-apartheid position
of Dutch municipalities and LOTA shifted towards supporting the new democracy and to
institution building. Many new international municipal linkages emerged between the
Netherlands and South Africa and older ones were formalised with the newly established
local governments. Today, around 12 Dutch municipalities have maintained long-term
contacts with South African counterparts (VNG, 2005). In addition, a large number of
Dutch municipalities have been involved in *individual* projects. Between 1997 and 2001, 30
out of 132 (23%) Dutch municipalities involved in C2C[45] received funding through the GSO
programme for their international contacts with South African partners (IOB, 2004), with a
total amount of €2.7 million (Cornelissen, 2004).

Although most Dutch-South African municipal partnerships originate from the anti-
apartheid movement in the 1980s, it was only in the post apartheid years that these
partnerships became official, often with the signing of an agreement (Figure 3.2). The first

---

45   This is an aggregate of municipalities participating in both the GSO and GST funding schemes.

CITIES AS PARTNERS

official partnerships were signed between Culemborg – Villiersdorp (1992) and Alkmaar – Uitenhage (1993). Other partnerships have been made official only recently, such as Alphen aan den Rijn – Oudtshoorn (2002).

The strong historical ties between South Africa and the Netherlands have undeniably contributed to the mutual interest of Dutch and South African cities to establish partnerships. This is underscored by the fact that some links exist of cities carrying the same name, such as the Dutch city of Dordrecht with Dordrecht (Emalahleni) in South Africa. The fact that the Dutch village Oudshoorn has been under jurisdiction of Alphen aan den Rijn since 1918 has inspired the signing of a twinning agreement between Alphen and Oudtshoorn (Chapter 5).

Figure 3.3 Dutch – Nicaraguan C2C partnerships

Nicaragua

From the early 1980s various cities in Europe and North America developed a partnership with municipalities in Nicaragua, including the Netherlands (Box 3.5). It was an international response to the Sandinista revolution, which resulted in the defeat in 1979 of the military dictatorship of President Somoza. The end of the Somoza dynasty, which had ruled the country since 1936 in an aggressively authoritarian way, brought a new political era to Nicaragua. The Sandinista National Liberation Front (FSLN)[46] aimed to implement a new development model for the country in which a just and fair society was put central. In the West, the ideology and objectives of the Sandinistas were perceived with great sympathy and respect which resulted in a global solidarity movement. Solidarity was not only expressed verbally and morally, but also in a practical way of small-scale development aid. The established city partnerships provided the opportunity to maintain personal relations and functioned as a channel to direct such development assistance to Nicaragua.

---

46   Frente Sandinista de Liberación Nacional.

Box 3.5 Nicaragua: 'King of twinning' in Latin America

The recent socialist history of Nicaragua has been an important trigger to the numerous city partnerships that have emerged between the country and particularly North America and Europe. The Sandinista Revolution to overturn the Somoza dynasty and to implement a socialist development system raised much sympathy in the West. Further fuelled by the disagreement of these movements with the Contra actions support by the U.S. government under Reagan, local North-South partnerships emerged to express solidarity. They were later formalised into municipal twinnings. In 1988 – the heydays of the twinning movement – Zelinsky (1991) counted 323 twinning arrangements between Nicaraguan cities and 'the West': 91 with the United States, 49 with Germany, 43 with Spain, 20 with the UK and 16 with Italy, the Netherlands and Sweden each, making it the leading Latin America country in terms of number of twinnings. Shuman (1994) estimated that until 1986, despite hostile relations at country level, some 100,000 US citizens visited Nicaragua through twinning links and that over US$20 million in humanitarian aid was delivered (quoted in Zelinsky 1991, p. 27). Today, *hermanamientos* ('sisterhoods' or twinnings in Spanish) continue to be a common phenomenon in Nicaragua and many cities maintain more than one international city partnership. The capital Managua for example has 19 partnerships, both of a diplomatic nature with other capital cities in Latin America[1] and North-South partnerships. León has 9 city partnerships, exclusively with Europe and North America. The German embassy in Nicaragua counts 28 German-Nicaraguan *hermanamientos*. Sister Cities International reports 23 US city links with Nicaragua. For the Netherlands, Nicaragua is the principal twinning partner, with over 20 active partnerships.

---

1   Mamadouh (2002, p. 24) refers to 'a case of national policy in local disguise'.

Today, around twenty city partnerships between the Netherlands and Nicaragua are maintained (Figure 3.3). In the Netherlands, the umbrella organisation LBSNN[47] (National Organisation of Twinnings Netherlands – Nicaragua) was established in 1986 and has functioned as a platform for exchange of knowledge and experiences with the Dutch cities as members. Moreover, it acts as a clearing house on urban issues in Nicaragua and provides input to municipal policymaking with regard to city partnerships with Nicaragua. An important objective is to share best practices among partner cities. The field office of LBSNN in Managua plays an important role in organising networking events and workshops to facilitate South-South exchange among the Nicaraguan partner cities.

3.3   Illustrating the link between C2C policy and strengthening urban governance: the example of South Africa

This section aims to illustrate Dutch policy on decentralised development cooperation and national support to Dutch C2C partnerships by providing the example of South Africa. It analyses Dutch national C2C policy vis-à-vis South Africa and its implementation through

---

47   Landelijk Beraad Stedenbanden Nederland-Nicaragua

funding programmes for partnerships between Dutch and South African local authorities. It sheds light on the question how C2C and urban governance strengthening are interrelated and it specifically indicates whether Dutch C2C policy instruments – the GSO and LOGO programmes – have contributed to improvements in local government in South Africa. The policy analysis has been performed by means of desk research of reports, evaluations, annual plans, programme formulations and personal conversation with key informants.

3.3.1 Dutch C2C partnerships and projects with South Africa

Under the GSO programme between 1995 and 2004, 42 projects of the various modalities explained above were financed for South Africa (Table 3.1). 39 of these projects applied to municipalities, of which the majority received one project grant (9), while three applicants received five or more project grants (Culemborg, Alkmaar, Rotterdam). An analysis by Cornelissen (2004) shows that 11 of 19 PUGAs consisted of missions with either a representative or political character, such as visits by mayors and councillors (signing of agreements) or missions for project formulation. Frequently, PUGAs therefore had a wider intention than merely capacity building. Fifteen PUGAs had a strong thematic orientation towards housing. Most PUGAs were undertaken by Alkmaar (4) and Culemborg (3) (VNG-I documentation). 9 internships (STAGEs) have been carried out by South African local officials in a Dutch municipality of which the majority were focused on social housing.

Twelve long-term projects have been financed through the GI modality between 1995 and 2004. GIs were all directly related to social housing, except for Oudtshoorn, where the project has a wider approach to municipal Integrated Development Planning (IDP).[48] Examples of long-term housing projects include support to social housing associations (Uitenhage, Durban, Govan Mbeki, Tshwane), assistance in the construction and renovation of houses (Villiersdorp, Buffalo City, Govan Mbeki) and housing policy (Emalahleni). MMTPs have been organised by VNG-I in cooperation with the South African Local Government Association (SALGA) for local government officials and councillors since 1993. After 1998 these annual courses concentrated on the subject of municipal development planning, and were attended by 15 different Dutch and 20 South African municipalities. Between 1993 and 2003, over 220 persons received training through the MMTPs (VNG-I documentation).

Table 3.1 GSO projects South Africa (1995-2004)

Project modality	Number
PUGA	19
GI	12
STAGE	9
MMTP	2
Total	**42**

Source: VNG-I documentation

---

48 In the new South Africa, municipalities are no longer concerned with traditional service delivery alone; rather they take up a more significant role in establishing 'Developmental Local Government'. Key instrument for municipal planning is the Integrated Development Plan (IDP), involving community consultation to assess needs and identify development priorities in an integrated way (Chapter 4).

The above figures indicate that the large majority of projects and partnerships have been oriented towards social housing and spatial planning. Nine out of the approximately 12 structural C2C partnerships focused on these subjects. Cornelissen (2004) found that 70 percent of the activities were directly related to housing and that between 1995 and 2001, 85 percent of all GSO disbursements in South Africa were aimed at the housing sector. Within the theme of social housing, there is a wide variety in scope. Examples include the support to housing associations in strengthening the organisational capacity, support to developing a municipal housing policy and to the construction of (low cost) houses.

Various reasons can be given for the prevalence of housing as a theme in Dutch-South African C2C relations. VNG-I considers housing and planning a priority in South Africa. Historically, the support to the Civics during apartheid by Dutch local government was mainly directed to urban development and social housing. Moreover, on the national level, the Dutch response to South African housing needs has been expressed in long-term cooperation between the Dutch Ministry of Housing and the South African Department of Housing. This cooperation has further motivated Dutch municipalities and Dutch housing associations to become involved in housing projects. Another reason may be the high visibility of results: constructing houses is a concrete and attractive activity for creating public support for C2C among the Dutch population.[49]

An extensive evaluation of the GSO programme for the Ministry of Foreign Affairs (IOB, 2004; Cornelissen, 2004 – see also Box 3.2) provides insight into the effects of the programme in South Africa. First, it was noted that over 70 percent of MMTP/STAGE participants had introduced changes in their daily work situation in local governments in South Africa as a result of the programme. Changes were observed in e.g. the organisation, working procedures, occasionally resulting in new departments or units. Secondly, it was frequently mentioned that Dutch partners hardly made use of local expertise and that some Dutch participants of PUGAs were "too eager to start and to produce immediate results after arrival", undermining existing local knowledge and conditions (Cornelissen, 2004, p. 85). In addition, project proposals were mainly written in the Dutch language with little consultation of the partner municipality. Thirdly, various partnerships and projects had a weak link with the main current challenges encountered in South African local government. Not all activities could be correlated to local government capacity building, rather they contributed to improvements at a more operational level, mainly in the field of social housing. In Kimberley and Emfuleni, the C2C projects were not included in the municipal plan. Furthermore, the activities supported by the GSO-programme were not integrated into other development efforts to establish synergies (Kimberley, Oudtshoorn, Emfuleni). In Kimberley, Tshwane, and Durban it was noted that the housing programmes targeted the middle class while leaving the real poor to the merit of municipal housing schemes (Cornelissen, 2004).

The C2C funding programme for South Africa 2005-2008

The GSO programme has recently been replaced by the Good Local Government Programme LOGO South 2005-2008, in short LOGO South. South Africa is one of the 12 target countries of LOGO South and therefore continues to receive much attention under the new funding scheme, with a continued focus on housing. An evaluation (VNG, 2002) carried out on GSO

---

49   Interview with representative Stichting Habitat Platform, January 24, 2006.

supported housing projects, showed that in order to truly contribute to improved local governance, a stronger correlation between the housing projects and municipal housing policy was necessary. Knowledge exchange on municipal housing policies that are fully integrated into municipal Integrated Development Plans (IDP) is required to receive support for housing associations. The central objective of the South African LOGO South *Country Programme* 'to strengthen the capacity of South African municipalities in the field of housing' seems to reflect this shift towards a more integrated approach that is closely linked to the municipal organisation and its capacity. The approach includes:

- To develop a spatial planning policy for the municipality in which housing is integrated. Municipalities need to develop adequate spatial planning before they start building houses
- To develop and implement a municipal housing policy. Housing is mentioned in many IDPs; however, few municipalities have developed an actual municipal housing policy
- To increase and incorporate the Social Housing Policy in the municipal housing policy. More knowledge is needed on the new Social Housing policy that came into effect in 2004
- To start implementing concrete social housing activities
- To increase the capacity of South African municipalities in relation to Social Housing Institutions for the institutional development of the latter.

3.3.2 Is Dutch C2C beneficial to urban governance in South Africa?

The question remains whether Dutch national C2C policy, expressed in the funding schemes, policy objectives and the C2C partnerships described above, has had substantial effects in institutional strengthening. As a capacity building mechanism through the exchange of knowledge and expertise on local government affairs, does C2C contribute to improved urban governance in South Africa?

Summarizing the previous sections, South African local governments have taken a central position in both the GSO and LOGO South programmes. A relatively large number of structural twinning partnerships exist between Dutch and South African municipalities, whilst a considerable share of the Dutch national C2C budget is allocated to South Africa. The main themes are social housing and planning. In recent years, IDP has become an increasingly important area. Since 2002, support has increasingly been directed towards an integrated, structural municipal housing policy rather than approaching housing as a separate concern in a relatively *ad hoc* fashion.

Under GSO a large variety of projects has been carried out of which the majority were considered to have had positive effects. The training courses and internships for South Africans were especially valued high. Various concrete changes and results have been found in relation to C2C activities. Cornelissen (2004) identified several additional benefits of international contacts, including:

- South African local authorities gain more legitimacy with international experience
- International contacts trigger other international funding sources
- C2C contacts lead to new linkages with Dutch entities, including funding sources and the private sector. Tourism development by Dutch operators in the Western Cape Province and port and trading contacts between Rotterdam and Durban are examples.

Partnership and ownership principles

Human capacity development in local authorities takes centre stage in the VNG-I funding schemes. The underlying thought is that exchange of knowledge and expertise between peers fosters equal partnership. Referring back to the partnership principles outlined in Chapter 1, the introduction of LOGO South seems to have led to some improvements with regard to working in a context shaped by asymmetrical North-South conditions. The fact that project formulation and the corresponding problem analysis are now conducted in a joint fashion allows for improved conditions of genuine partnership in which local expertise can be significantly and properly used and ownership of the process and input is promoted. LOGO South requires project proposals to be written in the language of the target country. Ownership in project design and implementation may lead towards more demand driven C2C policies meaning that South African local governments more evidently indicate the priorities and scope of cooperation. The established twinning partnerships allow for continuity which is a favourable condition to achieve results. The *Country Programme* is meant to act as a framework to better take into account existing policies, initiatives and capacities in South Africa and make better use of local expertise. Improvements in capacity building and partnership principles are expected to have a positive impact on the effectiveness and efficiency of improving urban governance through C2C.

It remains however to be seen whether such a framework of a *Country Programme* does not undermine instead of enhance the principle of ownership and demand-driven partnership. The framework could impose limitations to C2C initiatives of Dutch and South African municipalities and NGOs that do not relate to the objectives and themes set out in the *Country Programme*, although these initiatives may be equally beneficial to local governance in South Africa. Expertise and experience may become underutilised and specific needs may not be responded to adequately, or can only be attended to with municipalities' own resources, outside the framework of the programme. The commitment of Dutch municipalities to social housing moreover is not always evident (See Chapter 8). Although ownership may be enhanced by an increasing number of local authorities in South Africa responding to the Municipal International Relations Policy adopted in 1999, and developing their own international cooperation strategy (e.g. Emfuleni, Tshwane), De Villiers (2005) found little evidence that this policy is actually implemented in South African municipalities, which prevents a demand-driven intensification of mutual cooperation relevant to local reality. It will be interesting for future research to further assess the municipalities' preferences and concerns regarding the *Country Programme*.

Targeting the operational vs. the institutional level

Housing remains the single most important element of Dutch – South African C2C partnerships. There are however doubts whether housing is indeed the most important theme on the agenda of South African local governments. Cornelissen (2004) found that housing has long been only a minor component of municipal IDPs and has not been among the highest priorities of municipalities. The case of Oudtshoorn-Alphen aan den Rijn illustrated this very strongly, and suggests that partnerships focusing on housing in South Africa are certainly not always demand-driven (Chapter 8).

From an institutional capacity building perspective, support should have focused on the municipal political and administrative cadres in order to enable local authorities to manage housing systems through policies, instruments, and management. This is confirmed by the work of Jones & Blunt (1999) and Avskik (1999): while capacity building through C2C may foster beneficial changes at the operational levels of receiving local authorities (housing), the – often – wider goal of institutional and organisational change is more difficult to achieve. VNG-I acknowledges that C2C may be more beneficial to concentrate on "…practical problem solving rather than pretending to deal with complex enabling environment issues since these more often than not require a large scale intervention" (VNG, 2005, p. 9).

The LOGO South programme dictates that more attention will be paid in the future to the IDP and the municipal housing policy which intrinsically entails a stronger focus on institutional strengthening. The *Country Programme's* objective clearly underlines that housing should be considered an integrated aspect of the municipal institutional capacity and policies. Dutch C2C would then be more directed towards one of the major bottlenecks but also a core element of local governance in South Africa, i.e. design and implementation of IDP, of which housing is merely an element.

The analysis of Dutch-South African C2C partnerships, with specific attention to Dutch national C2C policy and implementation programmes, shows that various benefits to local governance in South Africa can be detected. Moreover, the partnerships seem to increasingly become more genuine. The new implementation programme that started in 2005 reflects more awareness of ownership. Projects in the past however appear to have been too much directed towards the operational level of local government which undermined the objective to strengthen institutional capacity. Newly defined objectives are promising in respect to targeting key urban governance aspects. One should bear in mind however that C2C efforts on institution building will have limited effect if they are not in line with intervention resulting from national legislation and policy context and other factors that obviously have much wider implications. Therefore, integration of C2C activities in municipal plans is essential. Also, intervention objectives may not always be in line with the priorities, capacity and willingness of municipalities on both sides of twinning partnerships.

3.4 Conclusions

During the last two decades, local governments have increasingly become recognised by multi-lateral institutions as important actors in development. Due to ongoing urbanisation, donors are more and more convinced that tomorrow's problems call for finding solutions in the city. The current focus in urban development planning on attaining strong local institutions and promoting good urban governance provides a policy context that, together with the increased recognition that aid can be delivered by a wide range of different agents, allows local authorities to play an active role in urban development through city-to-city cooperation. The rise of city networks and partnerships as instruments for capacity building and peer-to-peer knowledge exchange further reflects the potential of C2C. National governments, local authority associations and UN agencies have set up a wide range of support programmes which underline the increased recognition of local governments as stakeholders in global governance and development and the growing importance of C2C as a means to provide development assistance to cities affected by poverty.

Dutch C2C policy responds to these trends in urban development thinking: it considers urban governance strengthening as the main objective of city twinning with the South. Part of Dutch development aid becomes decentralised and is allocated to Dutch cities to support the institutional development of their partner municipalities in terms of service delivery, organisational and financial management and policy making. Improvements made in recent years with regard to the policy instruments employed include more attention to ownership, flexibility to incorporate local context and a stronger awareness of local knowledge and experience. Still, questions remain to be asked whether Dutch C2C policy does focus on the most pressing urban needs and municipal priorities in the target countries, as the case of South Africa demonstrates. Moreover, at times, C2C policy seems to tackle mainly issues at the operational and sectoral levels (housing, HIV/AIDS) while the wider goal of institutional and organisational reform that is required to make change sustainable, appears more difficult to achieve.

It has furthermore become clear that the contribution that C2C can make with regard to urban governance and urban development does not only depend on the policies and support programmes that encourage municipalities in the 'North' to engage in C2C. At the same time, the institutional frameworks in which the partner cities in the 'South' operate, seem to be equally important. National legislation, municipal mandates and existing urban governance structures in the South will affect the question to what extent the objective of strengthening urban governance through C2C can be achieved. Therefore, in the next Chapter, the focus will shift from the policy framework in the North to the institutional framework in the South to address these issues.

4 Developmental local government in Peru, South Africa and Nicaragua[50]

Decentralisation of government responsibilities, as discussed in Chapter 2, and the subsequent changing role of local government have been recent phenomena in the three countries under study. In this Chapter the respective trends in local governance and decentralisation in these countries are discussed. It reviews the historical processes and the changing role of local government which partly explain the current governance structures in the case study cities. Peru has known a long and bumpy decentralisation process, during which the role of municipalities in the country only recently significantly altered. When South Africa changed into democracy, local government was given a completely new role, but the drastic changes greatly challenge the capacity of today's municipalities. Nicaragua is among the last countries in Latin America to decentralise, a process that is severely undermined by a weak and inconsistent institutional framework.

The objective of this Chapter is to provide insight into the legal and political-institutional frameworks which have shaped the role of local governments in local development processes. Specific attention is given to various instruments that have been designed to foster participatory governance. These instruments, framed by municipal legislation, are meant to make municipalities more responsive to the needs of their constituents and to allow a stronger participation of non-public actors in urban decision-making. The analysis provided here serves as a context for both understanding local development and urban governance processes in the cities under study (Chapter 5) and to assess the outcomes of C2C interventions with regard to local government strengthening and civil society capacity building in the empirical cases (Chapter 9). Moreover, it justifies the selection of the case studies in this research, as explained in the Introduction, as this Chapter will demonstrate the need for local government capacity development and urban governance strengthening as a result of rapid institutional changes and public sector reform in the countries and cities under study.

Thus, while the previous Chapter discussed the institutional framework for C2C partnerships in the *North*, the current Chapter focuses primarily on the research areas in the *South*, from a national-institutional perspective. In the next Chapter, the analysis will shift to the urban level, examining the case study cities in the South, including their main socio-economic characteristics and urban governance context.

---

50   Part of this Chapter has been published elsewhere in adapted version (Bontenbal, 2006b).

THE CHALLENGE TO STRENGTHEN URBAN GOVERNANCE THROUGH NORTH-SOUTH CITY PARTNERSHIPS

4.1 Peru

The institutional framework

The Republic of Peru has a turbulent political history, in which periods of military rule and dictatorship have alternated with democratic leadership and institutional hybrids such as the *democradura*[51] under president Fujimori (1990-2000). During the last decades, analogous to the volatility of political orientations and leadership, the road to decentralisation of public administration has been long and uneven. Centralisation, regionalisation and decentralisation have alternated, and their conflicting messages have long prevented local government to take up a significant role in the government of society. Since 1980 three main phases can be distinguished (*cf.* Flores, 2005).

1980-1990 The 1980s mark the beginning of the political decentralisation process in Peru. Decentralisation is first mentioned in the Constitution of 1979, which acknowledges municipalities as independent administrative entities and allows the restoring of municipal elections in 1980. Specific responsibilities and functions were transferred from the central government to municipal governments, granting the latter a greater ownership of public services, such as the organisation of urban transport and planning, and municipal tax revenue (Flores, 2005). In this first phase however, real decentralisation failed due to a lack of resources transferred to the municipal level which inhibited municipalities to adequately perform the tasks assigned to them. An attempt to increase local revenues through the restructuring of the tax system did not have significant results. Hordijk (2000) observes that the share of local government in total government expenditures remained very modest, less than 4% of the national budget, while the financial transfers to municipalities as a component of total transfer to the public sector dropped significantly from an average 4.5% in 1975-1985 to 0.6% in 1987.

1990-2000 Because of scanty progress in decentralisation and the chaotic regionalisation process of the 1980s,[52] the transformation of public administration failed to gain momentum. The government model of the 1990s, under President Alberto Fujimori, was marked as authoritarian and centralist and left no room for political powers towards subnational governments. Despite the 1993 Constitution in which decentralisation is mentioned more explicitly, a reverse process of re-centralisation of political authority and fiscal resources took place. After Fujimori's 1992 *autogolpe* (self-coup) he did away with the regional governments and municipalities became devolved extensions of the State. Financial transfers and the devolution of tasks to the municipalities came to an end and the municipal

---

51   The term *democradura* (an amalgamation of 'democracy' and 'dictatorship') refers to a dictatorship with organised elections, alleged freedom of press and commercial activity, while based on military and state control (Paredes, 2007).

52   At the end of the 1980s, regions were formed by the uniting of two or more departments, and corresponding regional authorities were created. This first step of *regionalización* was of an improvised and inefficient character which led to serious administrative hurdles. Under the Constitution of 1993 the regions became administrative entities by the establishment of an intermediate government level, the *Gobiernos Regionales*. A reform in 1990 allowed for the direct election of departmental governors, but Fujimori later removed them and suspended further elections. In 2002 the regionalisation process was reactivated and finally administrative power was given to the Departments of Peru. Sabatini (2003) stresses however that the functions and authority of this level of government remained highly unclear and unspecified.

tax revenue schemes were abandoned.[53] Moreover, institutions related to subnational governments were closed, such as the National Institute for Urban Development (INADUR) and the Institute for Municipal Promotion (INFOM). National government was strengthened at the expense of the position and power of municipal governments. The rigid and exclusionary regime of Fujimori's government is therefore referred to as 'the lost decade of decentralisation in Peru' (Ugarte Ubilla, 2006).

2001-today With the end of Fujimori's presidency, a fragmented and weak national political elite and civil society were left behind. Especially the rural areas suffered from a lack of autonomous political institutions (Schneider & Zúniga-Hamlin, 2005). The return of democracy in Peru under President Alejandro Toledo (2001-2006) started a new decentralisation movement, aiming at re-establishing the regional governments and consolidating the position of municipalities. Only very recently the devolution of government responsibilities has taken off again.

Today, Peru is divided into 25 regions (formerly: departments), 194 provinces and 1829 districts, with corresponding tiers of government, each with proper functions and mandates. The regions are governed by Regional Governments (*gobiernos regionales*), that were finally given administrative power in 2002 under the Organic Law of Regional Governments.[54] Peru has two levels of Municipal Government (*gobierno municipal*): Provincial Government (*gobierno municipal provincial*) and District Government (*gobierno municipal distrital*), presided by provincial and district mayors, respectively.

In 2002 two key regulations were passed, which significantly structured the framework towards the decentralisation process. The Organic Law of Regions and the Organic Law of Municipalities[55] established a new set of norms to govern decentralised authorities (Schneider & Zúniga-Hamlin, 2005). It outlines functions, assignments and required competencies that correspond to the various government levels. The tiered nature of government – national, regional, provincial and district – is mandated to become more intertwined and more clear on the division of tasks among the various levels.

The developmental role of local government

The current decentralisation process, which effectively started in 2003, redefined the role of local institutions. First, as illustrated in Chapter 2, an underlying argument of decentralisation is to tackle poverty effectively. As local governments are closest to the poor, they are allegedly better equipped to foster development that is tailor-made to the needs and demands of the community. Peru is no exception to the rule. Changes in the legal framework encourage local governments to devise various strategies to take up a stronger role in local development and to actively engage in the 'Fight against Poverty' *(Lucha contra la pobreza)* in the country.

An important mechanism in this respect is the distribution of national transfers and social funds, which is based on pro-poor indicators, giving preferential treatment to poor

---

53 They were replaced by an alternative model of tax distribution, the Municipal Compensation Fund (Fondo de Compensación Municipal-FONCOMUN).

54 Ley Orgánica de Gobiernos Regionales N°27867.

55 Ley Orgánica de Municipalidades N°27972.

Box 4.1 Canon minero: blessing or burden?

In 2007, Peru was the world's second largest producer of silver, the third of zinc, copper and tin, the fourth of lead and the fifth of gold (MEM, 2007). The increased demand for minerals and the correlated price boom on the world market have generated a high national economic growth level for Peru, 8% in 2006. The regions that are richest in natural resources are among the poorest in the country, such as Loreto, Cajamarca and Puno (INEI, 2007a). Various mechanisms for natural resource revenue allocation (*Canons*) have been developed to transfer revenues, profits and taxes from the centre to the producer region. In 1992, the *Canon Minero* was created which stated that 20% of the income tax paid by (foreign) mining companies must go to the territory where the minerals are extracted. In 2001, this percentage was augmented to 50%. Some resource-rich municipalities have hugely benefited financially from the *Canon Minero*. In the Province of Cajamarca for example, the transfers have gone up tenfold from 8.2 million Nuevos soles in 2003 to 87.9 million Nuevos soles in 2007 (MIM, 2007). Although such increase in revenues at first hand seems promising for the poor regions and localities of Peru, it has also been received with much criticism. In the first place the geographical allocation of public resources creates high inequality among the Regions. Further, the fight over revenues makes conflicts between mining companies and mining communities (usually over environmental issues, see e.g. Bebbington, 2007) increasingly complex. Moreover, the performance of local institutions to manage unexpected and substantial amounts of public investment resources is challenged by a lack of technical expertise, complex and strict procedures to allocate resources, and high pressure from the state and mining companies to disburse quickly (Arellano Yanguas, 2008). Often, money is not spent wisely and the transfers hardly contribute to poverty eradication. The burden of the responsibilities that are now laid on the shoulders of subnational governments has also been referred to as a case of 'decentralising the resource curse' (Arellano Yanguas, 2008).

rural and marginal urban areas.[56] To illustrate, in the case of FONCOMUN (which entails revenue sharing of 2% of the national sales tax), distribution criteria include mortality rate, literacy rate, specific indicators to measure the level of unmet basic needs such as the quality of housing and sanitation, and level of rurality. Through various forms of *Canon,* subnational governments get a share of the financial resources generated from the extraction of natural resources in their territories, the most important of which is the Mining Canon *(Canon Minero)*. The Canons play an increasingly important role in the geographic redistribution of resources in the country and are an important source of income for resource-rich municipalities (Box 4.1). Historically, municipalities in Peru have largely depended on transfers

---

56   The Ministry of Woman and Social Development is mainly in charge of the transfer of social funds and executes a wide range of programmes for the fight against Poverty. This includes the National Programme for Food Assistance (*Programa Nacional de Asistencia Alimentaria*-PRONAA), and the National Compensation and Social Development Fund (*Fondo Nacional de Compensación y Desarrollo Social*-FONCODES) which aims at improving the living conditions of the poor through investments in sanitation, health care, education, as well as creating employment and production generating opportunities.

from central government, due to a weak capacity to raise local revenues. By increasing financial transfers to the local level, local governments are granted a stronger position in fostering local development and in the fight against poverty.

A second task for local government is to actively involve the public to participate in local decision making and the urban planning process. It is seen as an important component of the developmental role of municipalities. Mechanisms and opportunities for public participation have become more diverse and ubiquitous, and the options for the poor to deal with poverty have in this sense become more explicit. Peru has had a rich tradition in public participation, mainly at neighbourhood level, that started under the military rule of Juan Velasco (1968-1975). Today, public participation has been institutionalised through a series of legislation and orders local governments to promote citizen participation in the

---

Box 4.2 Participation structures in Peru

At a subnational level, public participation is organised through various mechanisms. These include:

- Consultative Local Coordinating Councils (**CCL**) at municipal level and Regional Coordinating Councils (**CCR**) at departmental level were set up in 2002 to enable coordination between government representatives (e.g. mayor, councillors) and civil society representatives (CBOs, private sector, neighbourhood committees) – guaranteeing 40% of their membership to civil society organisations. The councils function through consensual decision-making and may consult on and supervise the district participatory budget and district integrated development plans (see below).

- The Concertation Boards for the Fight against Poverty *(Mesas de concertación para la lucha contra la pobreza*-**MCLCP***)* created in 2001, bring together actors from government and civil society to coordinate policies and strategies regarding poverty. Legislation demands that *MCLCPs* be established on Departmental, Provincial and District level, however at the end of 2006, only 20% (372) of the District Boards were in place while many other boards have become inactive or have merged with other participation initiatives, such as the CCL (MCLCP, 2007).

A wide range of mechanisms for citizen consultation exist at the local level, which allow citizens to interact with local administration in planning and formulation, but also implementation, control and evaluation. The distinction between the various initiatives is however not always clear. Therefore there is co-existence, even competition and duplication of efforts. In the Province of Cajamarca for example, the government-induced MCLCP and CCL have spread confusion among authorities and civil society since the Province has been used to work with locally designed Concertation Boards for over 10 years. The ambivalent interpretation of the role, mandate and (legal) decision making power of the various mechanisms and their often weak performance led in some cases to the merging of MCLCPs with CCLs. At the same time, additional voluntary thematic or regional *Mesas* (e.g. the Mining Dialogue Board and Transport Board) mushroom in the area, further mystifying participatory decision-making.

THE CHALLENGE TO STRENGTHEN URBAN GOVERNANCE THROUGH NORTH-SOUTH CITY PARTNERSHIPS

formulation, discussion and concertation[57] of their local development plans and budgets (Skinner, 2004). Moreover, it gives citizens the right to access public information and participation mechanisms. A wide (and at times confusing) range of forms and structures for public participation has been elaborated during the last years (Box 4.2).

The implementation of the legislative requirements has obviously not been without difficulties. Much of the planned transfers have not materialised or have been delayed. Flores (2005) maintains that two years after the start of re-decentralisation the results had been very disappointing, as less than 50% of municipalities had received transfers. He blames the delay on the lack of official accreditation municipalities need to have to receive transfers. Flores further points out that the State has failed to adequately facilitate the transfer process with capacity building, technical assistance and close general guidance to local institutions. Moreover, it took time to formulate and approve the Fiscal Decentralisation Law, which regulates the redistribution of financial resources associated with the increased responsibilities of subnational governments. Finally, politicians did not consider decentralisation a priority on their agendas (Flores, 2005).

Instruments for local governance

In the institutional design and organisation of local governance in Peru today, three governance *instruments* are employed to generate local development in a participatory manner. District municipalities are instructed to conduct local planning in an integrated and participatory way, and to design a local integrated development plan *(Plan integral de desarrollo concertado –* **PIDC***)* which outlines the vision, mission and main development priorities and objectives of the district on a medium and long term scale. It is interlinked with the **participatory budget** that enables citizens to participate in decision making of the investment of municipal resources which are allotted to the various thematic strategic lines outlined in the PIDC. The interlinkage of the PIDC and the participatory budget design is believed to guarantee ample attention for the most urgent needs of the poor as well as effective municipal planning that is based on the main development needs of the district. Chambi & Marulanda (2001, quoted in Skinner, 2004) outline a number of additional perceived advantages to the combined PIDC and participatory budget structure:

- It is seen as an opportunity to strengthen local democracy, transparency and legitimacy of local governments
- It promotes awareness among citizens for local tax contributions who observe the reinvestment of their capital into projects they have decided on
- It builds stronger relations between local administration and civil society
- It provides an opportunity for developing participation capacity for civil society organisations and to align their budgets to the participatory budget
- It raises awareness among citizens about the main development problems in their district.

The third legal instrument to control and regulate government planning and expenditures is the National System of Public Investment (**SNIP**). SNIP was introduced in 2004 in Provincial and District municipalities to assure the rational and efficient use of public

---

57 The term *concertación* does not translate easily. As Miranda & Hordijk (1998) note, "it goes beyond consultation and brings the different stakeholders around the table so that solutions can be negotiated and responsibilities assigned".

investments to achieve maximum benefit from economic growth and social development. SNIP intends to raise viability of investments and to guarantee sustainable investment spin-offs by requiring public institutions to comply with all phases of investment (feasibility study, project implementation, control and evaluation) in an organised way.

Challenges to local governance

Although public administration in the country is still highly centralist in comparison to other countries in Latin America, Peru has taken some important steps in granting subnational governments more legal and fiscal authority. This process has been frustrating and complex. An ongoing difficulty to a successful transformation and the emergence of new forms of governance is the huge lack of capacity, education of staff, and experience and resources in municipal governments to adjust properly and respond adequately to their new mandates. Assistance from the State to guide the process to both local governments and civil society organisations is insufficient. Today, municipalities are left with many weaknesses, financial, organisational and where personnel capacity is concerned, to implement their newly assigned tasks and comply with new legislation.

Skinner (2004) observes that in the participatory budgeting process, lack of clarity on regulations allows for wide interpretation which makes budgeting inconsistent. Lack of political will and resistance within the local administration to reach out to the community is another obstacle. Skinner further underlines that Integrated Development Plans in general are not used sufficiently as instruments for public management. They are even not always existent in municipalities or their functioning is weak. Also, the participatory budget is not always linked to the PIDC. This becomes clear when during the participatory budgeting process new priorities are identified instead of the development priorities of the PIDC. In short, local governments still are severely limited to raise local revenues, to design and implement projects, to improve the efficient use of resources and gain access to international development assistance (Flores, 2005). The latter will be discussed in more detail in Chapter 6 for the case of Villa el Salvador. In the light of decentralisation and changing of authoritative power in the country, institutional strengthening continues to be a mayor necessity for Peruvian municipalities.

4.2 South Africa

The institutional framework

South Africa has gone through dramatic changes since the abolition of Apartheid and the subsequent introduction of democracy in the 1990s. The transformation had a significant impact on the organisation and structure of local government. Under Apartheid local government had not played a significant role in the government system of South Africa, being a devolved extension of the central Apartheid regime. The new democratic constitutional settlement brought about changes in legislation and policy that require significant local government reform.

In the first years of post-apartheid, much attention was paid to the new position that municipalities were to take in the government of the country. As it should no longer be a function of national or provincial government, the concept of *co-operative governance* was introduced. The shift from a three-level intergovernmental system to a three-sphere system took place, stressing the non-hierarchical nature of intergovernmental relations and making

THE CHALLENGE TO STRENGTHEN URBAN GOVERNANCE THROUGH NORTH-SOUTH CITY PARTNERSHIPS

local government an integral component of the government system. These *spheres* of government (national, provincial and local), according to the Constitution, are 'distinctive, interdependent and interrelated'. The system is designed to guarantee coordination between the different forms of government. It should prevent duplication and assuming power or functions that is not conferred to the respective spheres. Cameron (2001) observes that the three-sphere system has uplifted local government from a subordinate level of government (in a hierarchical system) to a significant sphere in its own right.

South African local government has undergone a three-phase transformation process, based on the Local Government Transition Act (1993). During the transitional years, a range of legislation was developed that pertains to local government. These are outlined in Box 4.3.

- During the pre-interim phase (1994/95), interim local authorities with appointed councillors came into effect until the local council elections of 1995/6. Their task was to deliberate on appropriate post-apartheid structure of municipalities and to run the municipalities until the post-apartheid system was in place (Wittenberg, 2003).
- The interim phase, guided by the Interim Constitution, took place between 1995/6 and 2000 and brought Transitional Local Councils and Transitional Metropolitan Councils to municipalities. In 1998 the Municipal Demarcation Board was set up to redraw the municipal borders of the country. The number of municipalities was reduced from 843 to 284.[58] Various institutional frameworks for local government came into effect, distinguishing between metropolitan, urban, and rural areas.

Box 4.3 Local government legislation in South Africa

- The key basis for all legislation in the country, the national Constitution (1996) creates three spheres of government, a system of co-operative governance and constitutionally guaranteed functions for local government.
- The Local Government Transition Act (1993) provided the legislative framework for the three-phased transition to a new local government system.
- The Local Government White Paper (1998) considers local government a strong player in development and defines the principle of Developmental Local Government as "local government committed to working with citizens and groups within the community to find sustainable ways to meet their social, economic and material needs and improve the quality of their lives".
- The Local Government Municipal Structures Act (1998, amended in 2003) regulates local governments to consult their communities in performing their functions and exercising their power.
- The Municipal Systems Act (2000) gives direction to the IDP process, public information and transparency, and calls for methods to be established to assess community needs. It further emphasises the importance of capacity building both within local government and amongst civil society to encourage public participation.

---

58   The 284 municipalities were divided into 6 Metropolitan Areas (Category A), 231 local municipalities (Category B) and 47 District Councils (Category C).

- The elections in 2000 ended the transition phase and introduced the third, final stage of democratic, autonomous local government. By that time the new Constitution had been passed, which provided for a system of governance that guaranteed a substantial role for local governments which were allocated the right to govern local affairs subject to national and provincial legislation as well as constitutionally guaranteed functions (Olowu & Wunsch, 2004; Cameron, 2001).

Today however, many legislative, policy, and organisational preconditions for a stable local governance framework remain unresolved. This hinders effective local governance (Olowu & Wunsch, 2004). Intergovernmental relations remain weak with poor coordination among various levels and departments of government (Tapscott quoted in Olowu & Wunsch, 2004). Wittenberg (2003) notes that a lack of transparency in the intergovernmental system questions the division of responsibilities and that – for a proper functioning of the administration – a more profound understanding needs to diffuse downwards.

The developmental role of local government

Service delivery has historically been the prime concern for local governments in South Africa. Also in the new government system, municipalities continue to have a key role in the provision of basic services, in particular water, sanitation, waste collection, electricity, and organised urban planning and urban infrastructure. In South Africa every citizen has the right of adequate housing, healthcare, food and water, social security and a healthy environment. Local governments are required to act upon these rights and provide the necessary resources and investments to realise them in a sustainable manner. Especially meeting the basic needs of historically disadvantaged populations (the political term used to refer to non-whites) is a widely accepted priority of the post-apartheid government (Beall et al., 2000).

In the new South Africa municipalities are however no longer concerned with traditional service delivery alone; they take up a more significant role in establishing 'Developmental Local Government'. Local government is now considered an important development agent to overcome unemployment, segregation, lack of funding and poor services in order to actively tackle poverty. It is legally mandated by the Constitution to 'promote social and economic development'. The Constitution thus states that public administration must be development-oriented (Cameron, 2001). As Nel & Binns (2001) observe, developmental local government represents a shift in political expectations and legal provisions and marks a radical break from the previous service-orientated local government focus.

The principle of Developmental Local Government was formally introduced by the 1998 Government White Paper and defines it as "local government committed to working with citizens and groups within the community to find sustainable ways to meet their social, economic and material needs and improve the quality of their lives". Four developmental approaches for local government are contained in the White Paper: integrated development planning, service delivery, local economic development and democratisation. Cashdan (2000, p. 15) summarises the developmental logic of this White Paper: "Poverty is a condition which resulted from past policies. It can be addressed through the actions of local government, primarily those aimed at increasing responsiveness and efficiency, and especially through partnerships with civil society. The result will be *development*, an improved state of affairs, beneficial to all. A municipality which takes the required actions is, by definition, developmental."

THE CHALLENGE TO STRENGTHEN URBAN GOVERNANCE THROUGH NORTH-SOUTH CITY PARTNERSHIPS

As one of the four approaches mentioned above, fostering Local Economic Development (LED) is a new concept to most municipalities. Prior to 1994 only a very minimal role of economic involvement was permitted (Nel & Binns, 2001). The role in LED includes the creation of employment, the advancement of local competitiveness and the provision of marketing and investment support to businesses. LED is also relevant for raising local revenues, which is an urgent problem in many South African municipalities, since the poor are often not paying for municipal services. While provincial government is financed mainly through transfers from the State, local government has to raise over 90 percent of its own revenue on average (Beall, 2005). The main sources of finance include fees for services provided by the municipality and property tax. Especially rural areas suffer from lack of resources and depend largely on central government transfers which are allocated through the 'Equitable Share' system.[59]

Instruments for local governance
With the changing mandate to become more developmental, municipalities need to become more strategic and visionary. The three main challenges they are faced with are: first, overcome the legacy of the Apartheid past with its segregation and widespread poverty among the previously disadvantaged people. Secondly, the challenge is to make the principle of developmental local government operational (formulate projects, allocate resources efficiently) and thirdly, to foster a culture of co-operative governance, to coordinate development efforts with other stakeholders.

The key instrument for municipalities to incorporate all of the above mentioned objectives is the Integrated Development Plan (**IDP**), legislated by the Municipal Systems Act of 2000. It contains the municipality's development vision, needs assessment, development priorities, short, medium and long term objectives and strategies, and financial plans for investments and implementation. IDPs integrate the municipal functions of planning and service delivery and should contain institutional, spatial and financial components that also take into account national and provincial government planning.

The IDP process is based on an integrated, participatory approach to planning and development. This involves widespread consultation with the community to assess needs and identify development priorities. Municipalities are required to be responsive and base their service delivery on the basic needs identified by the community, and ensure that marginalised groups have a say in decision making. Project implementation and investments also require the involvement of community stakeholders and business partners through multi-sectoral partnerships. The IDP process thus institutionalises participation, to involve citizens and stakeholder groups in the development process and to build social capital and generate a sense of common purpose to find local solutions for sustainability (Nel & Binns, 2001).

Participation mechanisms involve *imbizos* which are public forums organised by the government to facilitate the cycle of consultation, planning, budgeting and public feedback,

---

59 The Equitable Share is a single basket of revenue that is distributed *vertically among* the three spheres of government. A main objective is to enable local governments to carry out their constitutionally mandated functions, despite financial constraints. Through the *horizontal* equity principle, the Share is meant to favour poorer municipalities with infrastructural backlogs and a low level of basic services. It is measured by the number of poor households in the area of jurisdiction (Mase, 2003).

including making amendments to the IDP. The latter is done through the annual *IDP and Budget Review Process* which enables citizens to provide input on changes to be made in the IDP and to approve the annual budget, which is integrated in the IDP. Community participation in these processes is mainly structured through *imbizos*, although citizens, organisations and businesses can also react in writing. Consultation with sectoral clusters or forums is another mechanism for participation, which brings together stakeholders involved in e.g. security or LED.

Challenges to local governance
New roles and responsibilities challenge the institutional performance of local governments in South Africa. The rapidly changing legal environment impedes organisational capacity, and institutional weakness persists in terms of personnel skills, leadership and management. As South African municipalities are faced with many new responsibilities, local officials and councillors need training and support from provincial and central government to ensure that municipalities have the resources, powers and capacity to implement IDPs (Cashdan, 2000). Nel & Binns (2001) note that while limited training is already provided to local officials and councillors, much greater support is needed: "The lack of capacity seriously undermines the new position of municipalities since well-intentioned but poorly funded, supported, structured and managed projects have little chance of success" (p. 361).

Municipalities find it difficult to implement IDPs and target development issues. A study of Johannesburg shows that the IDP "failed to provide a sufficient strategic framework for action towards either growth or poverty alleviation and (...) the process had failed to establish an overt poverty focus" (Beall et al., 2000, p. 120). Also, the study revealed that pursuing integrated objectives instead of the traditional line department budgets proved difficult. The pitfall of IDPs is that they become technocratic processes that do not correspond to reality. In a different study on women's participation in local governance processes, Beall (2005) states that municipalities have difficulties incorporating the multiple and often contradictory views that citizens express. Participation of all population groups is not properly in place. Although local government provides opportunities for locally organised women, it seems to be more responsive to the interests of conservative groups and existing powers which inhibit women's full participation and decision-making power.

Beall et al. (2000) observe that the challenge for local government in South Africa is twofold, i.e. there is both a technical challenge to establish effective local institutional and administrative structures and a governmental challenge to alter into an agent of local development: "First, there is a major technical task underway to establish effective planning, administrative and service delivery systems out of the chaos inherited from the apartheid era. Second, there is a political reconceptualisation of the governance process, focused on reorienting state resources and regulatory powers towards the needs of the poor" (p. 118).

Constitutionally, South Africa today has one of the most advanced local government systems in the world, with entrenched rights, powers and functions (Cameron, 2001). In sum, local government is expected to maximise social development and economic growth, to take a leadership role, involving citizens and stakeholder groups in the development process, to find local solutions for sustainability, to become more strategic, visionary and ultimately influential in the way they operate. Municipalities have a crucial role as policy makers, as thinkers and innovators, and as institutions of local democracy (Nel & Binns, 2001). With so many new challenges faced today, and in order to become truly development-oriented, capacity building for improved local governance continues to be a invaluable precondition for local governments in South Africa.

4.3 Nicaragua

The institutional framework

The Republic of Nicaragua is divided into 15 departments and two autonomous regions and has a total of 152 municipalities. Although ideologically distinct the country's political leadership was for a long time highly centralist, during both the Somoza dictatorial regime and the Sandinista revolution. Decentralisation of government authority started therefore relatively late. In the Constitution of 1987 municipalities were for the first time considered autonomous political entities. The subsequent Municipal Law[60] of 1988 laid the institutional foundation for the current decentralised system. Municipalities were given a number of responsibilities and obligations, such as the organisation of urban planning and infrastructure, waste management and water drainage, and the keeping of a civil register. Municipal councils were established. The first municipal elections were held in 1990, the same year as the first multi-party democratic elections in the country. The amended 1997 Municipal Law amplified the administrative authority for local governments. Basic services such as the provision of water and electricity, construction, recreational facilities, urban streets and transport were extended and also environmental management[61] and human rights were put on the municipal agenda.

After the Municipal Law had been passed, a series of additional legislation was developed, giving more political and fiscal authority to municipalities (Box 4.4). However, an overall legal framework with respect to decentralisation has never materialised. Although there is agreement that a more efficient and effective public administration system – also in terms of resources – is a major ground to decentralise, decentralisation in Nicaragua is not based on a common belief or unambiguous political vision translated into legislation. In the absence of a Decentralisation Law, and a singular public body that undertakes political leadership and coordination of the process,[62] there are no clearly defined and systematised phases and visions to act upon. The result is a rather patchy and incoherent set of decentralisation legislation and initiatives, and there is a variety of public institutions involved in the subject. This essential missing national strategy for decentralisation not only hinders effective devolution of power and resources, but also the development of a functioning governance system at the local level.

Various authors emphasise that the initiation of the decentralisation process was a result of the Structural Adjustment package of the 1990s which meant a substantial reform of the state, and was imposed under pressure from the international donor community (Pérez Montiel & Barten, 1999; Larson, 2002; Dijkstra, 2004). Induced by donors and with a historically centralist political background, there is a lack of clear intrinsic political will

---

60 Ley de Municipios N°40.

61 For a detailed study on the role of local government in natural resource management in Nicaragua, see Larson (2002).

62 Initially, the local government association INIFOM was recognised as the leading policy-making and coordination institution, but its deviation into financing activities has come at the cost of losing leadership in this respect (World Bank, 2004).

to devolve power to subnational governments. In addition, López Carrión et al. (2004) state there is hardly any interest and knowledge among citizens to be involved in local governance. Central government thus remains the principal decentralisation actor, while local governments and civil society take little initiative. In sum, decentralisation has no clear political vision from 'above', nor is it demanded by civil society from 'below', which makes it a non-organic process.

The lack of a clear vision, and uncoordinated and haphazard efforts to further determine responsibilities and duties of local governments have resulted in an incoherent legal framework. The responsibilities of municipalities set out in the Municipal Law have not been properly specified. Municipalities are expected to 'provide a set of services' and 'to stimulate local development' (Pérez Montiel & Barten, 1999) but specific details remain ambiguous. Leaving a legal void can generate conflicts between government levels or duplications of efforts, as other legislation requires central ministries or other governmental agencies to take up some of the same responsibilities (Gómez Sabaini & Geffner, 2006). Therefore the interrelation and coordination between the various government layers and their assigned tasks and responsibilities is weak; it leaves space for wide interpretation. Also, control is weak and legislation is silent on what happens if a municipality fails to deliver its basic services (World Bank, 2004).

The prime example in the inconsistency of Nicaragua's institutional framework for decentralisation is that while the Municipal Law assigned more responsibilities to local governments, it remained silent about the transfer of financial resources to meet these obligations. At the end of 2002, Nicaragua was the only country in Central America where fiscal transfers to municipalities were not taking place. At that time the share of the national budget transferred to municipalities were already 10% in Guatemala, and 6% in Honduras and El Salvador (FIDEG, 2007). Given the fact that the majority of municipalities in Nicaragua suffer from a complete lack of resources and have insufficient means to raise local revenues, the Municipal Law thus left many municipalities frustrated by the amount of duties without the concomitant resources to fulfil them (Pérez Montiel & Barten, 1999; World Bank, 2004).

Municipalities protested for years against this discrepancy and finally in 2003, a law was adopted regulating national transfers to local government. The passing of the Municipal Transfers Law[63] was the starting point of fiscal decentralisation in Nicaragua. It stipulated that from 2004 an incremental percentage of the national budget be transferred to local governments, from 4% in 2004 to 10% in 2010.[64] The increase must be at least 0.5% annually, provided that GDP grows at least 1%. The adopted law means a substantial increase in the funds available to municipalities. The World Bank (2004) estimated that in 2004, out of 152 municipalities, more than 120 would double their budget.[65] Indeed, total fiscal transfers to municipalities were predicted to be eight times more than in 2003, an increase from 150 million to 1,280 million Córdoba (FIDEG, 2007).

The World Bank (2004) has expressed its concern that the design of the Municipal Transfers Law may lead to a higher fiscal deficit of the country. In order to decentralise

63 Ley de Transferencias Presupuestarias a los Municipios N°466.

64 Before 2004, about 1% of fiscal revenues were annually transferred to municipalities.

65 Before the Municipal Transfers Law, municipalities received funds from national public bodies at the amount of US$105 million, direct transfers mostly financed by foreign donors amounting to $24 million and raised their own revenues for a total of $28 million in 2003 (World Bank, 2004).

Box 4.4 Key legislation regulating local government in Nicaragua

- The Municipal Law,[1] passed in 1988, amended in 1997, is the basic legislation governing municipal activities, rights and duties in Nicaragua.
- The Municipal Transfers Law[2] (2003) mandates that national budget resources be transferred to municipalities, from 4% in 2004 to 10% in 2010. The law regulates total amount of transfers, distribution criteria, limits to the use of the funds, and procedures for disbursement and auditing (World Bank, 2004).
- The Municipal Budgetary System Law[3] (2001) gives direction to the budgeting process of Nicaraguan municipalities, including the drafting, approval and adjustment of the budget. It also regulates control and evaluation of the municipal budget (Gómez Sabaini & Geffner, 2006).
- The Citizen Participation Law[4] (2003) institutionalises public participation in Nicaragua and mandates local governments to consult citizens on planning and budgeting decisions, while at the same time giving rights to citizens to participate in local decision making in various forms. The law calls for the establishment of Municipal Development Committees (CDM) and the organisation of locally held public forums – *cabildos*.

---

1 Ley de los Municipios N°40 and 261.
2 Ley de Transferencias Presupuestarias a los Municipios de Nicaragua N°466.
3 Ley de Régimen Presupuestario Municipal N°376.
4 Ley de Participación Ciudadana N°475.

'responsibly' and to preserve fiscal balance of the national budget, a larger share of central government budget devolved to municipalities needs to be compensated by a cut in other government expenditures. The law is transferring new resources without expanding the responsibilities for local governments. Rather than one comprehensive law regulating funding and expenditure of local governments, two sets of laws have been introduced, one regulating responsibilities (Municipal Law) – ignoring expenditure issues, the other regulating only financing (Municipal Transfers Law), leaving a gap that may undermine fiscal neutrality. Instead of mandating responsibilities to municipalities and supply associated resources at the same time, the transfer of resources came more than six yeas after the unfunded mandate. The Bank concludes (2004, p. 11) that this has "put the oxen behind the cart and now the challenge is to put the cart back behind the oxen."

The developmental role of local government

Like Peru and South Africa, in Nicaragua local governments are not only concerned with basic service delivery, but are increasingly considered key agents in fostering development at the local level. Both Municipal Law and Municipal Transfers Law deal with the role of local government in socio-economic development and poverty alleviation. As discussed above, the Municipal Law is not very explicit and mainly lists responsibilities regarding urban planning and service delivery. Still, López Carrión et al. (2004) provide a range of legal arguments from the Municipal Law which can be interpreted as clear suggestions to the role that local governments, their councils and mayors should take up in this respect. The Municipal Law mandates municipalities to foster socio-economic development, to help meet the needs of the population, including the indigenous population, and also through the more general directive to organise urban development and local infrastructure. The legal framework further makes various references to LED. It should promote local economic initiatives e.g. by distributing business licenses to the private sector, and have proper administration of commercial activities.

The Municipal Transfers Law is believed to bring a new impulse to promote local development in Nicaraguan municipalities. It has the fundamental objectives to promote integral and harmonious development in all territorial areas, to contribute to the reduction of the imbalance between municipal income and expenditures and to facilitate the management and implementation of local development policies and strategies in the fight against poverty (López Carrión et al., 2004; Gómez Sabaini & Geffner, 2006). Total municipal income has increased drastically between 2001-2005 with a total of 124.6% (INIFOM & GTZ, 2007), which provides more opportunities to municipalities to actively take up a role in local development and poverty alleviation.

However, while various references are made towards developmental local government, López Carrión et al. (2004) express their concern that for two reasons the legal framework of decentralisation is too dispersed and incoherent to promote local economic development in a structural manner. First, it has not proved to contribute to a more efficient service delivery. Second, there is no evidence that it brings citizens closer to public administration, as it is a top-down induced process and not demanded by civil society or local communities. Hence there is the risk that decentralisation hence has limited effect on local development.

Another important role of local government that deserves to be explored here is to pursue the generation of local tax revenues more actively. Gómez Sabaini & Geffner (2006) show there is a clear correlation between the level of poverty and the level of own revenues and resources of Nicaraguan municipalities, meaning that the lower the level of own resources of a municipality, the higher poverty level there is to be found under its jurisdiction. It is therefore of crucial importance for local governments to increase their income base in order to adequately tackle poverty and foster local development. A range of tax revenues allows generating own income for municipalities. Own resources are however relatively limited, as municipalities do not possess sufficient capacity or a properly working administrative system to raise local taxes. In 2005, local revenue collection accounted for 43.9%[66] of municipal income, which represented 1.7% of GDP (INIFOM & GTZ, 2007).[67]

As discussed in Chapter 2, fiscal decentralisation often allows for a better geographical redistribution of financial resources. The organisation of municipal finance in Nicaragua provides opportunities in this respect, giving municipalities an important role in manoeuvring national resources to local development and poverty alleviation in their territories, especially to the poorest communities and municipalities. The importance of transfers for the municipal budget has grown tremendously. INIFOM & GTZ (2007) calculated that government transfers

---

66 This does not include non-local fiscal transfers directed to the revenue total.

67 This amount is higher than in previous years but lower than in the early 1990s since tax reforms limited the income generating possibilities for municipalities. Sales tax was reduced in 1997 from 2 to 1% while property tax was raised to compensate the revenue losses. It proved however difficult to raise property tax due to the lack of adequate cadastral systems and administration capacity (World Bank, 2004).

THE CHALLENGE TO STRENGTHEN URBAN GOVERNANCE THROUGH NORTH-SOUTH CITY PARTNERSHIPS

Box 4.5 Pro-poor distribution of transfers in Nicaragua

FISE, an independent public agency, was created in the 1990s by donors to reduce poverty as a way to compensate for the rigid macroeconomic structural adjustments in the country. The role of FISE has been significant for the country's social development:[1] FISE covered 43% of public investment in education and 28% in health in 1999 (Dijkstra, 2004). Before 2004, FISE dominated the budget of many municipalities, accounting for between one-third and half of the total municipal income. By applying pro-poor criteria to municipal transfers and donations, fiscal decentralisation contributes to an allocation of resources and investment in the country that is meant to aid the most deprived areas. This applies to both the fiscal transfers regulated by the Municipal Transfers Law and the FISE funding:

- The total amount of annual fiscal transfers must be distributed among the municipalities according to a formula that takes into account four criteria, i.e. fiscal efficiency, fiscal equity, population, and budgetary execution. The formula intends to guarantee that distribution is prioritised to favour municipalities with low income generating possibilities (World Bank, 2004).
- For the allocation of local investments, FISE makes use of a poverty map which geographically divides the country based on poverty indices. In municipalities of extreme poverty, FISE invested US$93.38 per capita on average between 1991 and 2000, while areas with medium to low poverty rates received an average of US$38.95 (Gómez Sabaini & Geffner, 2006).

---

1   Dijkstra (2004) also concluded that the FISE programme brought additional advantages, including local capacity building programmes to municipalities, increased decision-making power for municipalities on the use of financial resources and a more pro-poor allocation of municipal investments.

represented 26% of the municipal budget in 2005 against 6% in 2000.[68] In addition to the fiscal transfers regulated by the Municipal Transfers Law, municipalities receive additional direct transfers through Nicaragua's local government association INIFOM,[69] the Emergency Social Investment Fund (FISE) or through the Rural Development Institute (IDR), which are central public bodies in charge of local development (Box 4.5). International donors e.g. NGOs or international partner cities also finance municipalities through these agencies, or directly affect municipal budgets. Transfers and financial resources not derived from local revenues still form the largest share of municipal income in the country. It implies that external funding from donors plays a large role in municipal finance in Nicaragua.

Instruments for local governance

With the newly assigned tasks and duties of municipalities and increased budgets, local governments in Nicaragua have a more explicit role in the socio-economic development

---

68   The increase of transfers on the municipal budget has not only improved the municipal financial situation but can also be considered a loss of financial autonomy of the municipalities.

69   Instituto Nicaraguense de Fomento Municipal

of the country. Legislation is explicit in stating that such processes be followed in close coordination with civil society and other stakeholders (See Box 4.4). With regard to the organisation of governance in Nicaraguan municipalities, it is important to outline a number of instruments that are designed to facilitate effective planning and investments, with budgetary accountability in a participatory manner.

In the area of policy making and planning, the Municipal Law requires municipal councils to draw up a Municipal Development Plan (*Plan de Desarrollo Municipal*-**PDM**), and to annually define the objectives and priorities for integrated development. Linked to the PDM is the Multi-annual Municipal Investment Plan (*Plan de Inversiones Municipal Multianual*-**PIMM**) and the Annual Investment Plan *(Plan de Inversiones Anual*-**PIA***)*. The PIMM outlines the investments scheduled by the municipality for a period of three years that need to be made to meet the development objectives of the PDM. It also entails the necessary funding that will be applied for, for example from FISE. The PIA outlines the municipal investments for one year for which resources have been guaranteed. These instruments not only give direction to the policies and investment of the municipality, they also form an important prerequisite for receiving transfers from the national government.

The Municipal Budget is interlinked to the PDM, PIMM and PIA. According to the World Bank (2004), in the absence of clearly defined responsibilities and a general lack of funding, a consistent part of municipal income is spent on personnel costs and goods and services for the public administration, leaving little funding for socio-economic investments. In 2005 the average share of municipal budget spent on personnel costs was 24.6% (INIFOM & GTZ, 2007). It not only shows the limited possibilities of local governments to make investments to improve service delivery, it also may indicate that allocation of local expenditure is dictated more by "political patronage consideration than by efficiency concerns" (World Bank, 2004).

Non-governmental local actors have the right to control and consult on the Budget through two participation mechanisms. Municipal Development Committees (*Comité de Desarrollo Municipal*-**CDM**) are established to consult in the development of plans and policies and the control of budgets. The CDM, presided by the mayor, consists of councillors, local administrators, representatives of public and private institutions, local civil society organisations, the private sector and neighbourhood leaders. Its aim is to promote sustainable socio-economic development through the coordination of action and strategies and to encourage the use of municipal resources in an adequate way (López Carrión et al., 2004). The CDM structure consists of various sectoral committees e.g. production, human and social development and environmental management. A Local Development Office managed by the municipality should help implement the investment projects identified by these committees.

Another key instrument in participatory governance in Nicaragua is the ***cabildo***. Where the CDM has members who form a fixed participatory panel, the *cabildo* is the main mechanism for ordinary citizens, businesses and civil society organisations to exert their opinion and decision making rights. *Cabildos* are public meetings in which interested parties can be informed on municipal issues and decisions, raise questions and concerns and consult on municipal planning. An important function of the *cabildo* is for local government to present the municipal and financial plans to the local community. Cabildos must be held at least twice a year, to approve the annual budget for the upcoming year (PIA) and to take accountability for the expenditures from the previous year. Civil society can also convene *cabildos*. Rather, in practice, *cabildos* often do not take place without pressure from civil society. Howard (2004) shows the example of the municipality of Matagalpa, where needs and priorities put forward by civil society were presented at an extraordinary *cabildo* that was convoked by the community to discuss local development issues.

Challenges to local governance

While local policy making and budgeting is increasingly becoming institutionalised, municipalities continue to deal with a serious lack of resources and capacity to adequately perform their planning and investment obligations. Many municipalities have weak government administrations. With the increased funds available, World Bank (2004) warns for a greater resource-waste potential, especially since auditing and control is weak. As the local revenue base remains very limited, the financial autonomy of municipalities gets reduced. Local capacity building is therefore needed to ensure that the increased funds are spent wisely and to respond to citizens' needs. The donor community has been involved in decentralisation efforts from the start. Many programmes and projects have been set up to provide technical assistance and resources for national government institutions dealing with local government and local development (FISE, INIFOM), municipalities (e.g. the GTZ's PRODELFIS programme) and civil society to be involved in local governance issues. Local governance needs to be strengthened to fulfil the legal mandate to go about in physical and socio-economic development by taking up the competencies set out in the Municipal Law. At the same time, municipalities need to invest their larger budgets responsibly.

The weak and inconsistent juridical framework and the political reality of Nicaragua in which the rule of law is frequently undermined or interpreted ambiguously, causes that the procedures for municipal finance, investment planning and participatory decision-making might turn out to be very different in practice. An example is a new form of citizen participation that was introduced in 2007 by president Ortega of the ruling Sandinista (FSLN) party: the *Concejos del Poder Ciudadano* (CPCs). The initiative, based heavily on Sandinista ideology, was received with much resistance by other political parties. They argued that sufficient participation mechanisms were already in place and they objected the allocation of public resources to non-public entities (such as the CPCs) for the implementation of public investments (Van Bochove, 2008). CPCs operate at the level of the neighbourhood, and community leaders represent their neighbours vis-à-vis local government. The role of CPCs in the already existing CDM has however not been specified, and it appears that one participation structure, put forward by the political agenda of the ruling party, is introduced at the expense of another, although the latter is a result of legislation.[70]

4.4   Local governance in comparative perspective

The previous sections tried to contextualise the current local governance processes that are taking place in the cities under study. This has been done by a general analysis of the decentralisation efforts of the countries Peru, South Africa and Nicaragua, the changing position of local government in public administration and national and local development efforts, and various conditions and instruments that influence local governance including

---

70   Interview with senior official 1, Municipality of León, July 10, 2008.

Table 4.1 Local governance in Peru, South Africa and Nicaragua

	Peru	South Africa	Nicaragua
Institutional framework	• Long and uneven decentralisation process • Fujimori's centralist regime (1990s) delayed decentralisation process • Since 2003 effective legislation on mandate local governments	• Constitutional changes led to a transition phase for all levels of government • Co-operative governance spheres guarantee municipal autonomy and coordinate intergovernmental relations • Induced by Apartheid abolition and subsequent democratic movement	• Separate legislation on LG responsibilities and resources • Fiscal decentralisation 6 years after political decentralisation • Lack of political decentralisation vision • Lack of intergovernmental coordination • Induced by donor community and SAPs
The role of local government in development	• Service delivery • Actor in the nation-wide 'Fight against Poverty' • Pro-poor distribution of transfers • Encourage public participation	• Legally mandated to be 'developmental' • Explicit development role based on community needs • Integrated functions of Planning, LED and service delivery • Encourage public participation	• Legal development role ambiguously defined • Service delivery • Pro-poor redistribution of transfers • Encourage public participation • 2004 legislation promising for increase in municipal financial resource base for development
Instruments for local governance	• PIDC [Concerted Integrated Development Plan] • Participatory budgeting in all phases • Participation through CCL/MCLCP and other (at times duplicating) mechanisms	• IDP [Integrated Development Plan] • Budget based on identified community needs • Participation mainly during joint annual IDP/Budget Review process through *imbizos*	• PDM [Municipal Development Plan] • Budget and investments to be approved by community • Participation through CDM and *cabildos* • Weak legislation
Challenges to local governance	• Human resource capacity needs • Lack of financial resources • Instruments not used adequately • (Limited) donor assistance rather than government assistance	• Human resource capacity needs • Lack of financial resources • Instruments not used adequately • Insufficient government assistance	• Human resource capacity needs • Lack of financial resources • Instruments not used adequately • Donor assistance rather than government assistance

public participation and institutional reform to make local governments more responsive and accountable. The main findings are summarised in Table 4.1.[71]

Changes in the institutional frameworks of the three countries have resulted in new mandates, responsibilities and a stronger financial resource base for their respective municipalities. In Nicaragua and Peru the discourse refers to the term 'decentralisation' while for South Africa it can be said that the changing position of local governments was part of a wider reform of public administration in the country after the change to democracy in the 1990s. The legislative framework of Peru and South Africa appear to be significantly more solid and coherent to stimulate local government reform than the donor-driven weak and inconsistent decentralisation legislation of Nicaragua. While municipalities in all three countries face many institutional and capacity challenges, this poses an additional disadvantage to decentralisation in Nicaragua. Peru's process of decentralisation has been relatively long, since the centralist regime of Fujimori until 2000 negated much of the progress achieved in the years before.

While local governments in all three countries have traditionally dealt with basic service delivery and urban infrastructure, an additional primary concern has become bringing about local development, or to speak in South African terminology, becoming 'developmental'. Indeed, South African municipalities are legally mandated to take a lead role in the development of their area of jurisdiction and their explicit developmental role is based on identified community needs. In Nicaragua and Peru this responsibility is less overt in legislation, but municipalities have a range of means to participate in national development and poverty eradication efforts, for example through their position as local agents in the redistribution of national fiscal and donor transfers based on pro-poor indicators.[72]

Many parallels can be drawn between the countries concerning innovative design of local governance instruments and tools. The legal framework demands local governments to draw up municipal development plans in such a way that public participation is embedded in the whole cycle of urban decision making. This includes the budgeting process, interlinked with the development plans, which are participatory in all three countries to some extent. The example of Peru is most striking in this case, as a large part of the budget drafting is through active participation of citizens, while in South Africa and Nicaragua participation is more related to identifying community needs and approval of annual budgets respectively. Participation is facilitated through a wide range of mechanisms such as local development boards (Peru, Nicaragua) and public forums.

It can be concluded that local governance structures in Peru, South Africa and Nicaragua are legally institutionalised, based on community participation and development-oriented. This is a promising step in strengthening the position of local governments to take an active

---

71 It should be noted that the comparison made here is solely referring to the processes described in this Chapter. The findings here do not correspond to general indicators measuring human development and poverty that would allow for a more general comparison of the state of development in the countries described. Such a comparison goes beyond the scope of this Chapter. Chapter 5 however, discusses the case studies cities and provides a more elaborate comparison of development and poverty dimensions at the urban level.

72 It should be noted that 'pro-poor' is a rather ambiguous concept that more than often reflects (political) rhetoric rather than reality. The meaning here is referred to that in the process of allocating national transfers for municipal investments, the level of poverty and 'most urgent needs' as defined and measured by governments are taken into account.

role in the local development process in their territories. It becomes clear that in all three countries local governance structures provide a foundation on which the interrelations between local government, civil society and local development are brought together.

This foundation however has been severely undermined by the many problems that municipalities are faced with in terms of capacity and resources. The often rapid legislative changes have posed many challenges to local governments, which all seriously keep lacking financial and human resources to perform their tasks adequately. This is obvious from the various examples given on the design, implementation and use of the above mentioned governance instruments, such as participatory budgets, public forums and integrated development plans. Much of this can also be ascribed to a lack financial and technical assistance from central governments, a gap that donors have tried to fill (mainly in Nicaragua). Faced with so many challenges today, the institutional strengthening of local governments in Peru, South Africa and Nicaragua continues to be a major task for the future.

Finally, it should be noted that legislation continues to be weakly controlled – although the degree of this is varying – and the rule of law is sometimes interpreted ambivalently. Especially in highly polarised countries like Nicaragua, new political leaders may ignore legislation that has been approved under previous regimes. The institutional frameworks for developmental local government and local participatory governance that have been discussed in this Chapter may be applied very differently, depending on the local context. Local governance instruments as designed on paper may be employed in a different way in practice. Chapter 5 will therefore turn to the urban level, to provide a more localised account of the cities under study. For example, formulating municipal development plans may be mandatory in Peru's local governments, but how does the municipality of Villa El Salvador implement it as a strategy for local development? How does the IDP in Oudtshoorn function and which development priorities are defined? And does the fact that municipalities in Nicaragua continue to be so dependent on external (donor) funding also apply to the city of León? Understanding the local conditions and implications (Chapter 5) of the national trends with regard to decentralisation, local government and governance instruments (Chapter 4), will subsequently offer insight into the conditions – favourable or disadvantageous – in which C2C initiatives are implemented in the cities in the South.

5 Case study cities and their partnerships: an introduction

This Chapter serves to introduce the four case study partnerships and their cities, in order to meet a number of objectives. First, it is useful to gain more insight into the specific characteristics of the partner cities to better understand the conditions and local situational context in which they operate as international partners through C2C. The Chapter therefore begins with a descriptive review of the cities under study. It should be noted that more attention is given to the partner cities in the South than in the North. This is done deliberately as it is essential to gain insight into local government and socio-economic trends in the cities of the South to say something about the impacts that C2C can have on urban governance strengthening. For the Northern cities some general socio-economic and geographical aspects are considered, which may shed light on some comparative advantages to the municipal role of development partner. It is not attempted to present a systematic comparison of the cases, rather to raise the most relevant issues, which are largely context-dependent and differ from case to case.

Secondly, after the Northern and the Southern cities have been introduced in 5.1 and 5.2 respectively, the Chapter turns to the partnerships themselves. Here the emphasis will be mainly on the historical evolution of these partnerships. It has been observed (Buis, 2009; Van Lindert, 2009; Hoetjes, 2009) that the historical context and path dependency of city partnerships greatly influence policy and practice of C2C today. Section 5.3 reviews these developments over time and concludes with a general overview of trends in C2C and how they apply to the four case studies.

5.1 Local governments in a socio-economic context: partner cities in the North

Amstelveen, The Netherlands

Amstelveen is a middle-sized town with a population of 79,000, located in the shadow of Amsterdam and the national airport Schiphol. It developed in the 17th and 18th century as a wealthy, green suburban area of Amsterdam, a reputation that is still valid today. Annual income per capita in 2005 was 17% above national average (CBS, 2008) and unemployment rates are below 3.5% (2007). In 2003, Amstelveen was selected the most attractive city in the Netherlands to live,[73] based on its accessibility, safety, cultural life and its proximity to Amsterdam. The green surroundings add to the city's attractiveness: with over twenty city parks and the adjacent Amsterdam Forest, Amstelveen was named the second 'greenest city of the Netherlands' in 2006. The town is home to a large expat community. It was estimated that in 2007 'Western' immigrants constitute 17.8% of the Amstelveen population (CBS, 2008) of which one-fourth is Japanese. A number of international companies and an

---

73   Source: Atlas voor Gemeenten, 2003.

international school are based in Amstelveen. The city council has 35 seats, of which the majority (9) is assigned to the Liberal Party (VVD). The labour party (PvdA) and Green Leftist party (GroenLinks) follow with 8 and 5 seats respectively. In total, eight political parties are represented. The municipality has an annual budget of €185 million (2008). Amstelveen maintains official international relations with four partner cities: Villa El Salvador (Peru), Berlin-Tempelhof (Germany), Woking (UK) and Óbuda-Békásmegyer (Hungary).

Utrecht, The Netherlands

Utrecht is the fourth largest city of the Netherlands, with a population of approximately 300,000. The city is centrally located in the country, and forms part of the large urban agglomeration *Randstad* area.[74] Due to its central position, Utrecht is the main hub in the national road and railway network and it hosts a major convention centre ("Jaarbeurs") and a range of trade and event fairs. Although Utrecht has traditionally been an industrial city, today's economy is mainly tertiary-based. Moreover, it has a high profile with regard to the national knowledge economy, as many higher education institutes are based in the city, of which one, Utrecht University, is the largest university in the country. The number of inhabitants has been growing rapidly, and is expected to increase with 36% until the year 2025.[75] Partly to meet the growing housing demand, partly as a cause of this high growth rate, a new large-scale neighbourhood is being built, the largest of the Netherlands. This area, *Leidsche Rijn,* is expected to accommodate 80,000 inhabitants by 2015. Utrecht is subdivided into ten administrative units or neighbourhoods. In each unit inhabitants are represented by neighbourhood councils and Aldermen. The city council has 45 seats. In the current political term (2006-2010) ten political parties are represented, the largest (14 seats) being PvdA. The annual municipal budget in 2008 was €1.5 billion (CBS, 2008). The city maintains international city partnerships with León (Nicaragua) and Brno (Czech Republic).

Treptow-Köpenick, Germany

Treptow-Köpenick is one of the 12 administrative Districts of the City of Berlin. The former Districts of Treptow and Köpenick merged as a result of the 2001 administrative reform which brought the number of Berlin Districts down from 23 to 12. Each District in Berlin is governed by a District council consisting of five councillors and a District Mayor. District administrations have a range of competencies but they are not politically and financially independent and their power is subordinate to the Senate of Berlin. Among Berlin's Districts, Treptow-Köpenick is the largest by area (covering 19% of Berlin) with the lowest population density. The population of 238,000 represents only 7% of Berlin's total population. Located in the South-East corner of Berlin, Treptow-Köpenick is a spacious, green District, covered for 54% by forest and water, a major impulse for tourism in the area. Treptow-Köpenick is located in the former Eastern part of the city, and after unification in 1990 it has dealt with a number of challenges and transformations in functional land use and economic structures. Formerly an industrial area, over 80% of jobs were lost in some parts of the District when factories closed down. It has been estimated that job loss as a result of economic reform

---

74 The Randstad ("Edge City" – referring to a city at the edge of a circle) is an densely populated urban area, consisting of the four largest Dutch cities (Amsterdam, Rotterdam, The Hague and Utrecht) and the surrounding areas. It hosts over 7.5 million inhabitants, half of the country's population.

75 "Randstad groeit, platteland krimpt", NRC Handelsblad, July 8, 2008.

CITIES AS PARTNERS

and the German unification process were larger in Treptow and Köpenick than in any other Berlin District. The total number of jobs fell from 25,000 to 4,000.[76] After 1990, large-scale economic transformation brought new companies, in particular high tech industry, media institutes and science and technology parks. A large number of new houses were built. In recent times (November 2007), unemployment rates in Treptow-Köpenick are with 12.8% below the Berlin average of 14.1%.[77] The District council has 55 seats, divided among eight political parties. The Social Democratic Party (SPD) has 34% of the seats and the Leftist Party (PDS) has a share of 28%. At the last elections of 2006 the extreme right National Democratic Party (NPD) won 5.3% of the votes and now holds three seats in council. The District of Treptow-Köpenick has eleven official partnerships with cities abroad, nine within Europe, and one with the United States and Peru each.

Alphen aan den Rijn, The Netherlands
The city of Alphen aan den Rijn has a slightly smaller population than Amstelveen (71,000). The current area of jurisdiction was formed in 1918 through the merging of the municipalities of Alphen, Aarlanderveen and Oudshoorn. In 1964 the village of Zwammerdam was also included. The city is conveniently located between the four main cities of the Netherlands, in the so-called 'Green Heart', which is the less densely populated core area of the urban *Randstad* agglomeration. Due to its vicinity to Amsterdam, Rotterdam, The Hague and Utrecht, it is a typical commuter city. Similar to Amstelveen, Alphen aan den Rijn was elected the 'greenest city of the Netherlands' (2001). The river *Oude Rijn* flows through the city centre. Agriculture accounted for 62% of land use in 2003.[78] Nine political parties are represented in the city council. The council consists of 35 seats, of which the majority are fairly equally divided between VVD, PvdA and CDA (Christian Democratic Party). In 2008, the municipal administration had an annual budget of €200 million (CBS, 2008). The city of Oudtshoorn in South Africa is the singular international twinning partner of Alphen aan den Rijn.

5.2 Urban policy, development planning and poverty: partner cities in the South

Villa El Salvador, Peru
Villa El Salvador (VES) is the archetype of what has long been called the *pueblos jovenes*, urban areas that emerged as informal settlements at the periphery of Lima by an influx of migrants from the rural regions of Peru. In 1971 some 600 families were mobilised for a land invasion; in several days they built shacks in the desert south of Lima. Such massive mobilisation could hardly be ignored by the authorities, who often even used it as a strategy to facilitate a relatively swift start of formal planning and urbanisation. Some months after the mobilisation, the new settlement called Villa El Salvador became administratively embedded in the municipal District of Villa Maria del Triunfo. In 1983, VES gained autonomy and became one of Lima's District Municipalities. That same year the first municipal elections were held.

---

76 District of Treptow-Köpenick, available online: http://www.berlin.de/ba-treptow-koepenick/
77 Statistisches Jahrbuch Berlin 2007.
78 Annual statistics Municipality Alphen aan den Rijn, 2007, available online: www.alphenaandenrijn.nl

THE CHALLENGE TO STRENGTHEN URBAN GOVERNANCE THROUGH NORTH-SOUTH CITY PARTNERSHIPS

It is widely recognised that the civil culture of organised participation and solidarity have been a major driving force of the development of VES. This organisation and participation of citizens in informal settlements and urban development planning is characteristic to *pueblos jovenes*.[79] Even when formal institutions gained ground in VES, local decision-making continued to be a shared responsibility and included civil stakeholders. Since its origin VES has built a tradition and culture of participatory planning based on constructing a vision for the future (Marulanda, 2002). Many of the instruments and strategies for participatory local governance introduced in Peru's institutional framework as a result of the 2002 legislation (Chapter 4) had already been employed in VES before that time.

Today Villa El Salvador is one of Lima's largest low-income District Municipalities, with over 400,000 inhabitants. The population growth continues at a relatively high rate, making the area more densely populated. This results in a residential occupation of land zoned for agriculture and livestock, and areas that are not fit for settlement (Imparato & Ruster, 2003). Poverty is widespread in VES. In 2001, 54% of the population lived below the poverty line (Marulanda, 2002). A desert community, VES has very limited natural resources. Urban problems are ample and include poverty, insecurity, the lack of economic opportunities and unemployment, lack of basic services, contamination and environmental degradation and poor health and sanitation conditions.

Villa El Salvador, with its commitment to more autonomous forms of local government, is a good example of decentralisation and strengthened local governments in Peru (Zolezzi, 2004). The District has a history of integrated development planning. From 1983 onwards, three consecutive plans have guaranteed the continuation of the local development process which maintained the community's identity (Marulanda, 2002). With the formulation of the *Plan Integral de Desarrollo de Villa El Salvador* (PIDVES), participatory budgeting was introduced under the administration of Mayor Michel Azqueta (1987-1989).

Following 2002 legislation, VES started a two-year participatory process to renew the existing development plan towards an Integrated Development Plan (PIDC – see Chapter 4). A vision, strategic objectives and strategic lines were formulated.[80] Each of the strategic lines has a correlating vision, objectives, programmes and projects. The structure guarantees that all projects and investments undertaken by the municipality correspond to one of the six thematic areas. This applies to various budgets, including the participatory budget, municipal investments funds, local revenues, and funding from Municipal International Cooperation. The plan is also meant as an 'orientation instrument' for other stakeholders in the District and encourages the private sector, (international) NGOs and community organisations to base their activities and investments on the vision and objectives of the Plan (VES Municipality, 2006). Another response to 2002 legislation was the drafting of the Municipality's Institutional Development Plan (PDI MVES) for 2006-2011. It forms the framework for strengthening the institutional capacity of the local administration.[81]

---

79 Informal settlements and the practice of self-help housing in Peru has received ample attention in the literature, especially through the work of Turner (1972).

80 The strategic lines include education and culture; health and environment; economic development; urban planning and infrastructure; safety and security; and citizenship and participatory democracy.

81 Its objectives include improvements in planning, monitoring, and evaluation systems; encouraging learning and innovation; raising local revenues and increasing the financial sustainability of the administration; strengthening the institutional culture and human resource management; and improving the information technology system.

Cajamarca, Peru

The city of Cajamarca, situated 820 kilometres from Lima in the rural Northern Andes mountain range, seats the Regional and Provincial Government of the Department of Cajamarca and is the commercial and industrial heart of the region. The Cajamarca Region is one of the poorest in Peru, with 63.8% of the total population living in extreme poverty (INEI, 2007b). Traditionally, it has been an agricultural area producing mainly dairy and beef products. The annual *Carnaval*, the principal of Peru, held in February, contributes substantially to the local industry and services sector. Cajarmarca's colonial history, marked by the the the city's architecture and the historical event of Inca defeat by the Spanish *conquistadores,* also contribute to modest tourist activity in the region.

In recent years Cajamarca has known drastic demographic, economic, social and cultural changes due to the presence of nearby mining activities of what is said to be the largest mine of South America. The Yanacocha[82] mining zone, with a surface of 251 km², is located 27 km north of the City of Cajamarca. Today the mine, which started operation in 1993, ranks second on the world scale in terms of production volume and the size of the potential extraction area. The export of especially gold (although copper, silver, lead and zinc are also found) is five times higher than in other exploitation areas in the country.

The mining activities have a profound impact on the region. From an economic perspective mining represented more than 40 percent of regional GNP in 2006, and *canon minero* transfers (the redistribution of national mining revenues, profits and taxes to the producer regions, see Chapter 4) allocated to the Provincial Government of Cajamarca has risen from 4 million Nuevos Soles in 2002 to 88 million in 2007 (MEF, 2007). It is estimated that *canon minero* transfers supply more than 80 per cent of the resources available for public investment in the region (Arellano Yanguas, 2008).

The dynamics generated by mining go however beyond economic growth.[83] Cajamarca started to grow rapidly, and its population growth rate ranks among the highest five in the country, totalling the number of inhabitants in the urban area today to 150,000 (INEI, 2007b). This can be largely ascribed to the increase in employment opportunities from the mining activities and the spin-offs to other sectors. As a result, housing and food prices have risen and new social issues have been brought about, including rising crime rates.

Local environmental groups claim that mining leads to environmental degradation, water contamination, air pollution and deforestation which would undermine agricultural activities in the region. Moreover, in recent years Yanacocha has been plagued by various social conflicts with local communities and activists, such as a dispute over mercury contamination allegedly affecting the health of rural populations, social conflicts over water and land, and the loss of security and safety in the city. In 2004 more than 10,000 people protested against the expansion of mining activities onto nearby *Cerro Quilish*, a mountain that supplies water to Cajamarca.

---

82   Yanacocha is a consortium of the United States based Newmont Mining Corporation (51%), the Peruvian Compañía de Minas Buenaventura (44%) and the World Bank's International Finance Corporation (5%).

83   Arellano Yanguas (2008, p. 28) outlines a number of factors that intensify the powerful position of 'new mining' companies in Peru and influence the way in which they interact with their localities: a) they are owned by powerful international companies, b) they are capital intensive, using sophisticated technology, and c) they are located in the mountainous Andes region that is characterised by poverty and has traditionally been neglected by Lima.

The municipality of Cajamarca has thus far responded rather slowly to the mining activities. As a result of the drastic growth of *canon* resources, the current size of the municipal budget of Cajamarca and some of the rural District municipalities around the mine exceeds that of some of the wealthier, densely populated Districts of Lima. This can be considered a reversed development challenge for local politicians and administration: it is not the traditional lack of financial resources, rather the abundance of it that causes new issues in local governance and local development. Today, the main question in the Cajamarca area is how to manage and invest resources wisely to truly foster socio-economic change that brings sustainable improvement of living conditions for all.

León, Nicaragua

León is the second largest city in Nicaragua, after the capital Managua, with a population of 200,000. It is located 18 kilometres from the Pacific Ocean and along the Río Chiquito (*Chiquito River*). León has a Spanish colonial background which is reflected in the historical architecture of the city centre. It has long been the intellectual centre of Nicaragua, hosting a number of universities of which the principal is UNAN (*National Autonomous University of Nicaragua*), founded in 1813. Although León is an important industrial and agricultural centre in the country, it continues to be negatively affected by the sudden decline of cotton production in the 1980s. The León economy heavily depended on cotton mono-cultivation and the decline led to an abrupt crisis, causing unemployment levels to rise rapidly. At the end of the 1990s, they were as high as 60% (Pérez and Barten, 1999) and the economy continues to be relatively depressed.

Natural disasters – of which hurricane Mitch (1998) in particular had a profound impact on the city and its rural surroundings – an unhealthy national economy and the negative socio-economic effects of structural adjustment programmes are other factors that explain the persistent and severe poverty in León: it has been estimated that 60% of the population live in conditions of poverty and 24% in conditions of extreme deprivation (Pérez and Barten, 1999).

The population of León has been growing rapidly as a result of the agricultural exodus that followed after the cotton crisis. Informal settlements and slums emerged on the outskirts of the city. Many of these *asentamientos* lack basic services such as safe water, sanitation, electricity, and refuse and solid waste collection. Today León consists of seven Districts or Sectors which are divided into 124 urban neighbourhoods (*barrios*) and 119 rural communities (*comunidades*). The Municipality has tried to accommodate urban growth with a large-scale urban expansion project in the South-Eastern part of the city with the aim to provide housing for some 20,000 inhabitants by 2020.

Similar to Villa El Salvador, León has a long history of communal and citizen participation. The *Movimiento Comunal* (communal movement), the main form of community-based organisation in Nicaragua, emerged from the struggle against Somoza dictatorship in the days of the Sandinista revolution in the 1970s and 1980s. The movements acted as local authorities in the first years after the revolution. They elected their own Mayors and community leaders and organised the provision of food, shelter, security and health care in many parts of the country, including León. During the first official municipal elections held in Nicaragua in 1990, and the process of establishing municipal councils, the communal movements were also closely consulted and involved. Since 1990 all consecutive Mayors of León have represented the Sandinista FSLN party, reflecting the pro-Sandinista reputation of the city. During the political term of 2004-2008, FSLN had 60% of the seats in council, while the Liberal Party (PLC) had a share of 40%.

Despite a weak financial condition, the municipality is concerned with local development in its area of jurisdiction. From the 1990s strategic and participatory planning processes have resulted in a number of planning instruments, of which the PEDM (Structural Municipal Development Plan, approved in 2004) is the most recent. An organising framework for municipal planning, the PEDM contains a vision for local development that is translated into five strategic lines.[84] The principles of governance, sustainability and gender are incorporated as cross-cutting themes. The municipal strategy serves in both the formulation of new policy plans and the execution of programmes and allocation of investments. Other development planning instruments include sectoral plans (e.g. the Economic Development Plan) and territorial plans (such as the León South-East Urban Expansion Plan).

Oudtshoorn, South Africa

Greater Oudtshoorn Municipality is located in Western Cape Province. Established in 1847 on the banks of the Grobbelaars River, Oudtshoorn became the primary service and commercial centre for the rural Little Karoo area. Oudtshoorn Municipality is part of Eden District Municipality, which is fairly rural compared to the Province's urban image. The area of jurisdiction incorporates Oudtshoorn (comprising the main urban centre and the neighbourhoods of Bridgton and Bongolethu); Dysselsdorp, De Rust and Volmoed as secondary communities, and surrounding rural areas. In 2004 Oudtshoorn had a population of approximately 87,000. The large majority of the population is from coloured background (77%). Afrikaans is by far the dominant language in Oudtshoorn (92%). Xhosa is spoken by 5.5% of the population (Census, 2001).

The economy of Oudtshoorn is characterised as an agri-based regional service and trade centre. The services sector, largely concerned with tourism, contributes about 32% of total production, followed by agriculture (17%) and trade (17%) (OEP, 2005). Approximately 350,000 tourists visit Oudtshoorn annually and the sector is still booming (IDP, 2005).[85] A study by Van der Merwe et al. (2004) shows that economic growth and development potential in the urban area of Oudtshoorn is relatively high, thanks to its strategic position in the region's infrastructural network, good urban infrastructure that can support urban development, and ample opportunity for the spatial expansion of the urban area. The town's popularity as a retirement centre is increasing, and future growth is expected in this sector and in the property market. The study demonstrates however that the rural surrounding areas are among the poorest of the Western Cape Province. Dysselsdorp, De Rust and Volmoed have low development potential and high human needs levels due to a backlog in infrastructure, limited human resources and a weak economic base. Oudtshoorn municipality is thus characterised by vast spatial difference in development potential and quality of life, and is altogether among the most challenged areas of the Province (Van der Merwe et al., 2004).

---

84 The five strategic areas are economy and production; human capital formation; social development; tourism and culture; and natural resources and environment.

85 The annual *Klein Karoo National Arts Festival* is one of the largest and most popular festivals of its kind in the country. Other major tourist attractions include the Cango Caves, and crocodile and ostrich farms. Oudtshoorn has also been called "the ostrich capital of the world".

THE CHALLENGE TO STRENGTHEN URBAN GOVERNANCE THROUGH NORTH-SOUTH CITY PARTNERSHIPS

Not only spatially but also socio-demographically is Oudtshoorn characterised by structural economic inequality. As a result of Apartheid policies of the past, ethnic Whites today are still in significantly better socio-economic conditions than Coloured and Black population groups, measured in terms of income, employment and Human Development Index (HDI).[86] The levels of absolute poverty (people living on less than US$2 a day) have risen. The poverty problem in Oudtshoorn has become more acute since the new Millennium. In 2004, almost 30% of the population was living in poverty compared to 25% in 1998 (OEP, 2005).

The administration of Oudtshoorn municipality is subdivided into three departments: Corporate, Financial and Operational Services. The Municipal Manager is head of administration. The vision of the Integrated Development Plan (IDP) – a broad statement of how council sees the development of Oudtshoorn municipality – is "Peace and Prosperity for All". The Mission statement, which describes the role of the municipality, has a strong focus on providing municipal services and becoming 'developmental' (Chapter 2; 4). IDP development objectives include economic, infrastructural, and social development.[87] For the last several years allocation of the municipal budget has been highly skewed towards physical infrastructure (usually over 50%) with very little attention to the 'softer' key objectives of the IDP, including HIV/AIDS and social development. The municipality acknowledges that the focus of the budget should be restructured and widened in order to increase its developmental position that goes beyond the traditional infrastructural service delivery role of Apartheid days (IDP, 2005). Council has 23 seats which are divided among four political parties.

5.3 Emerging contacts: city partnerships from a historical perspective

While the previous sections have considered the individual cities under study, this section explores the international relationships they maintain. It introduces the four city partnerships under study and discusses their development over time, set against the historical background of municipal international relations presented in Chapter 1. The emergence and history of the partnerships and their influence on current practice, policies and the organisation of city-to-city cooperation are reviewed and compared. Also, a general introduction of contemporary partnership structure, actors and activities is given.

---

86   The racial history of the country largely explains the strong correlation that still exists between poverty and inequality, and ethnic background. The population of South Africa continues to be divided among ethnic lines, also in policy-making. The inequality in Oudtshoorn is striking. While 20% of the Oudtshoorn population is unemployed, the figure for black Africans is 30%, against 3% of Whites (Census, 2001). The HDI rate for Africans and Coloureds living in Oudtshoorn, 0.53 and 0.54 respectively, is in stark contrast to the much higher HDI level of 0.85 for whites. Whites, comprising 15% of the total population, earn 54% of total income, whereas 39% of income is earned by Coloureds (77% of the population). The percentage of black Africans living in poverty in Oudtshoorn is 50%, compared to 33% of Coloureds and 7% of Whites (DBSA, 2005).

87   Oudtshoorn municipality has identified the following seven development objectives: promote economic development; provide appropriate physical infrastructure; provide appropriate community infrastructure; promote and develop HIV/AIDS strategies; provide adequate housing; social development, safety and security.

Amstelveen – Villa El Salvador

The cooperation agreement between the municipalities of Villa El Salvador and Amstelveen goes back to 1997. As with the large majority of Dutch twinnings, first initiatives stemmed from civil society contacts between the two cities and only later the respective local authorities became involved (see Buis, 2009). The initial contacts started in 1987 when the municipality participated in one of the *'Gast aan Tafel'* projects in the Peruvian municipality of Villa El Salvador, organised by the Dutch NGO Novib.[88] Involved Amstelveen citizens then requested the municipality to liaise and to formalise the established relationship by making it a municipal affair. The signing of the cooperation agreement in 1997 institutionalised the partnership. Between 1997 and 2007 Amstelveen and VES cooperated within the framework of various VNG-I programmes.

Over the years, partnership organisation in the North has maintained a parallel structure that is highly characteristic to C2C cooperation: it involves both the local state apparatus and its constituency, the citizens themselves (Chapter 1). The latter maintain a number of people-to-people contacts between Amstelveen and VES with the participation of schools, a neighbourhood committee, the local women's movement and the Rotary. As far as the local administration is concerned, its involvement is most visible in the formal political and technical encounters between mayors, councillors, and officials. Various projects have been executed since 1997, providing both monetary and in-kind contributions. This has resulted in what Hewitt (1999) describes as regular, direct, and on-going contact between municipal officials and technicians, allowing the transfer of technical information and exchange of expertise and best practice. The most recent projects (2004-2007) have aimed at strengthening the local administration of VES with a focus on municipal finance, and environment and waste management (Chapter 9).

Besides the above mentioned aims, awareness-raising and development education for the Amstelveen population has been a key objective in the partnership in Amstelveen. During the first years of the partnership agreement, this task was performed by the regional Centre for Development Cooperation (COS),[89] but since 2003 the municipality itself has taken up this role (see Chapter 7). This move has centralised partnership management and administration: the municipal organisation takes responsibility of all facets and goals of the partnership, including liaising with the public at large to raise awareness and create public support. Up to today, the partnership management and coordination is maintained as such, as the municipality has not found an appropriate civil society organisation that can act as a partner in this respect.

After 2007 Amstelveen could not make use of VNG funding anymore for its partnership with Villa El Salvador, as Peru was no longer a target country under the new LOGO South programme. This has forced the municipality to seek new funding opportunities in order to maintain its institutional capacity building activities in VES. Recently this has led to a somewhat uncertain situation with regard to continuation of municipal participation in the city partnership.

---

88 Now: Oxfam Novib. The Campaign 'Gast aan Tafel' was started in 1963 to stimulate the public to donate the costs of one additional 'guest at the dinner table' to the programme.

89 COS Netherlands is an independent national association of Dutch centres for international cooperation with a head office and 14 regional chapters. It has an awareness-raising and supporting role to citizens and organisations engaged in international development issues.

THE CHALLENGE TO STRENGTHEN URBAN GOVERNANCE THROUGH NORTH-SOUTH CITY PARTNERSHIPS

Treptow-Köpenick – Cajamarca

The relatively young partnership (1998) between the Berlin District Treptow-Köpenick and the Provincial Municipality of Cajamarca is an example of a city link that has been set up as a North-South component in the framework of Local Agenda 21 (Box 5.1). In contrast to the other case studies, this partnership is mainly civil society driven while the municipal role is much more limited. It aims to foster exchanges (of schools, kindergarten teachers), and raise awareness and lobby to draw attention to the social and environmental conflicts and consequences of open pit mining in Peru and in particular Cajamarca. It also facilitates various forms of small-scale development initiatives such as health care projects and fundraising.

Reconstructing the founding process of the partnership is rather slippery. Various developments were taking place simultaneously and ultimately culminated in the signing of a formal partnership agreement in 1998. In 1995 the two Mayors of Köpenick and Cajamarca met at the World Mayors' Conference in Berlin. At that time, the Local Agenda 21 process in Köpenick was one of the first in Germany (see Box 5.1), and from its start one of the practical implementations had been to seek possibilities to link up with a partner city in the South (Liesner, 2006). The then Mayor of Cajamarca, Luís Guerrero Figueroa, put sustainable development high on the political agenda, which made Cajamarca known as the first 'ecological municipality' of Peru. Cajamarca was at that time also involved in a Local Agenda 21 process. The meeting of the Mayors allowed for knowledge and information exchange on the two LA21 experiences and the idea emerged that through a municipal partnership they could be linked and inspired by each other.

At the same time, the Berlin NGO KATE[90] had been running various projects in Cajamarca. KATE is concerned with sustainable development and municipal North-South partnerships and in this respect it had developed a niche for offering assistance to communal development cooperation and to "include North-South aspects in [LA21] agenda processes that are dominated by environmental issues".[91] KATE acted as a broker between the two cities and facilitated the meeting of the two Mayors. When the political contacts between Cajamarca and Köpenick further crystallised, KATE guided Köpenick in the first steps of establishing a city partnership that was embedded in LA21 (1995-1997). KATE later retreated. The lead organisation came in the hands of one of the LA21 Working Groups in Köpenick, 'Staepa'.[92]

According to Staepa, the choice for Cajamarca was based on the experience the latter had gained in implementing some of the LA21 and sustainability guidelines of the 1992 Rio Earth Summit.[93] Köpenick was further interested in the experiences Cajamarca had gained with regard to public participation, in particular the role of the numerous round tables that were active during the term of Guerrero (see Chapter 7).

In May 1998 a formal cooperation agreement was signed in Cajamarca by the two Mayors and by two representatives from the various identified LA21 stakeholder groups in Köpenick (the so called "Pillars" – see Box 5.1). In 2005, the cooperation agreement was renewed during a following visit of the German Mayor to Cajamarca. It was underscored

---

90   *Kontaktstelle für Umwelt und Entwicklung*

91   Website KATE, available online: www.kate-berlin.de.

92   Staepa is an abbreviation of *Städtepartnerschaft*, or city partnership.

93   Website Staepa, available online: www.staepa-cajamarca.de

CITIES AS PARTNERS

Box 5.1 Local Agenda 21 in Treptow-Köpenick

Local Agenda 21 (LA21) is the localised translation of Agenda 21, a programme run by the United Nations to promote sustainability and sustainable development. The programme was adopted by 179 governments at the Rio Earth Summit in 1992. Chapter 28 of Agenda 21 specifically refers to the role local authorities can take to implement the programme at the local level. In Germany the Agenda has inspired many citizens, organisations and local governments, and today over 2,600 communities have adopted a Local Agenda 21. The LA21 process in Köpenick, which started around 1994, was among the first experiences in Germany, and Köpenick was the first District in Berlin to be engaged in Agenda 21. Until today, Treptow-Kopenick's LA21 is considered a key example in the country.

The LA21 process in Treptow-Köpenick seeks to assure a socially just, economically viable and environmentally sound development of the District, based on consultation with a wide range of stakeholders from the public, private and civil spheres. The process is based on 20 objectives, referring to e.g. citizen participation in environmental issues, employment creation, solar energy, and eco-based tourism. A strategy to implement the objectives, various thematic lines and a set of sustainability indicators are formulated to put the process into action.

In order to guarantee widespread participation of all stakeholders, a three-pillar consultation structure is designed in which the local administration, civil society and the church community are represented. Their roles are distinct. The local administration and District council (Pillar 1) are concerned with financial and technical support of LA21 initiatives, as well as incorporating sustainability in urban planning, decision-making and public procurement. Civil society (Pillar 2) is represented in various working groups of the 'Forum Environment and Development' of the District's LA21 Association. This platform brings together citizens, organisations, the private sector and volunteers and promotes their participation in LA21 processes. Pillar 3 consists of the church community in the District, whose mission for "justice, peace and preservation of the Creation" has been a guiding ethical principle in the design of the LA21 programme (LA21TK, 2004).

Objective 3 of the District's LA21 refers to engaging in North-South relations in order to put into practice sustainability thinking and to "support development processes in solidarity". One of the goals is the transfer of technology and know-how by organisations and businesses and the exchange of municipal officials with partner cities (LA21TK, 2004, p. 9). Building on this objective, the partnership with Cajamarca was established. One of the five thematic working groups that constitute the Forum Environment and Development is exclusively concerned with the city partnership and cooperation with the Peruvian municipality.

that it was not the main aim to have technical or political encounters of local administration staff, but to foster exchange of experiences in general and "to get to know each other in all different dimensions".[94] This illustrates the belief that the lead role in C2C should be taken

---

94   Website Staepa.

THE CHALLENGE TO STRENGTHEN URBAN GOVERNANCE THROUGH NORTH-SOUTH CITY PARTNERSHIPS

by civil society rather than the local administration, despite its initiation through a political encounter of Mayors. Staepa – a civil working group – acting as lead organisation, and the modest role of the municipality (Chapter 7) further underline this approach.

Utrecht – León

The start of the partnership between Utrecht and León dates back to 1983. The first contacts resulted from a civil initiative taken in Utrecht to pay a visit to León organised by a member of the Dutch Nicaragua Committee. A Nicaraguan return visit to Utrecht was organised that same year and shortly after, the first schools started to exchange letters. A civil working group was set up in Utrecht, which later led to the establishment of the Foundation Utrecht-León. The ideology of the Sandinistas after the revolution of 1979, perceived among sympathisers in the West as a societal transformation process based on a socialist system with ample education and health care programmes, had raised much international support, also in the Netherlands (Chapter 3). The first years of the partnership were marked by a strong political orientation and especially political debates were organised in Utrecht in the framework of the partnership. Solidarity with the Sandinista revolution was expressed very practically in the organisation of so-called 'building brigades', and numerous *brigadistas* from Utrecht (and other Dutch cities) participated in organised building projects in León and wider Nicaragua. The first project in León took place in the neighbourhood of William Fonseca, where 15 participants from Utrecht helped to construct a community building, and stayed with local host families. The name of the Foundation, *Vriendschapsband,* translates as Friendship Link and clearly reflects the ideological foundation stones of solidarity and friendship on which the partnership was founded.

Alike Amstelveen, civil society – represented by the Foundation – requested the local government to explore the possibilities of a formal municipal partnership. According to the municipal official in charge of this task, "the city partnership between Utrecht and León would never have existed without the Foundation" (VUL newsletter, 2004, p.1). After the mission to León in 1985, six cooperation projects were formulated and accepted by city council.[95] In 1986 a coordinator was appointed within the local administration to establish a network, develop international relations policies, and organise fundraising. The first three municipal projects in León included a self-help housing project (also in William Fonseca), a tree nursery project and a river sanitation project.

The partnership has since then been characterised by participation of both civil society and the local administration in Utrecht. While in the early years the main motive was political solidarity with the revolution and the widespread poverty in Nicaragua, later on both partnership tracks became more project-oriented and increasingly aimed at improving the lives of the Leonese people and contributing to local development in general. Civil society initiatives in Utrecht continue to be coordinated through the Foundation Utrecht – León. Its mission is to execute development projects in León and to raise awareness in Utrecht to create support for the partnership.

Utrecht municipality became involved in technical exchanges and various development projects concerned e.g. with education, river sanitation, and women empowerment.

---

95   Although the then Mayor was not in favour of establishing an international partnership, one of the councillors became engaged and had a strong role in the first years to foster partnership activities (VUL Newsletter, 2004). Local champions and political commitment are key for successful partnerships, as Chapter 6 will demonstrate.

It would be beyond the scope of this section to flesh out all activities and projects that have been developed within the framework of this city link; some examples taken from 25 years of experience will suffice. Having initially started with small-scale, short-term, *ad hoc* projects that created tangible results and responded to immediate needs (e.g. housing), a gradual shift has taken place during the last decade to support larger programmes with long-term objectives such as project management and strategic urban development planning (Rademaker & Van der Veer, 2001; Van Lindert, 2009). A clear example is the long-term assistance Utrecht provided to design a strategic development plan for the Municipality of León (Chapter 9). The shift towards more programme and process oriented activities turned the prime focus to institutional strengthening and capacity building. Many of the early projects gradually evolved into larger-scale and more integrated projects that, with hindsight, indeed have had a structural or even institutional development impact in León. As such, the development of the C2C alliance between Utrecht and León may be described as a typical example of path dependency[96] in decentralised development cooperation.

During the first years, Utrecht's city council decided upon the continuation and the size of the C2C budget on a yearly basis. This led to the formulation of short-term projects that were financially and technically feasible and delivered a number of results in the sphere of urban service delivery and local economic productivity. In the early 1990s, a project was started that would now perhaps be characterised as urban environmental governance. This became the first integrated C2C project and eventually it included more than 20,000 people living in various neighbourhoods bordering the Río Chiquito – at the time nothing more than an open sewer and waste dump. Utrecht took the lead in a consortium that included various European sister cities of León, coordinating a variety of efforts to clean the highly polluted river, including the relocation and technical modernisation of the many tanneries that dumped their poisonous heavy metals into the river. The programme also included participatory dwelling and neighbourhood improvement components for the low-income settlements in the vicinity of the Río Chiquito, resulting in connections to the sewerage system, planting of the riverbanks, sports facilities, etc. Indeed, the project was among the first to match short-term actions with a long-term planning approach, based on community participation.

Since 1998, the Municipality of Utrecht has supported León in its urban expansion ambitions in the south-eastern part of the city. The León Sur Este (LSE) programme entails a planning process that will provide 5,000 plots and infrastructure for low- and medium-income housing. There is ample attention to sustainability in investments, the environment (water and green zones), social development and community participation. A further objective is the institutional strengthening of the municipal organisation in urban planning, policymaking and developing management and leadership skills for municipal directors (Chapter 9).

The specific role and responsibilities of the Friendship Foundation Utrecht-León are quite different from those of the city administration. Its broad spectrum of activities includes the twinning of schools and child care centres; facilitation of Utrecht higher education student internships in León; implementation of concrete development projects in León in the field of primary and environmental education, employment creation and culture; and the

---

96 The path dependence view holds that people make choices that set a specific course of institutional development that is consolidated over time (Boas, 2007).

THE CHALLENGE TO STRENGTHEN URBAN GOVERNANCE THROUGH NORTH-SOUTH CITY PARTNERSHIPS

organisational strengthening of CBOs and micro-finance schemes in the sister city. Over the last decade, the Foundation has moved from executing a range of often uncoordinated and thematically dispersed projects to adopting a policy that prioritises options for cooperation. It has become a more professional partner with institutionalised processes of policy formulation, reporting, and planning, and has developed higher levels of accountability to donors, municipality and partner organisations in León. The Millennium Development Goals have been a guiding framework to policymaking and more recently a specific focus has become MDG-2: to achieve universal primary education.[97]

Alphen aan den Rijn – Oudtshoorn

Alphen aan den Rijn (Alphen in short) signed an official twinning agreement with Oudtshoorn in 2002. From the beginning it has been the aim to establish a two-track partnership with both government and civil interaction between the cities. The relatively young partnership has focused on strengthening institutional performance and fostering community development in Oudtshoorn. The municipality of Alphen has assisted Oudtshoorn in terms of financial and technical resources for the implementation of a Performance Management System, and on municipal policymaking in the fields of HIV/AIDS, gender and social housing. Financial donations have been directed towards tourism development (income and employment creation for women) and the construction of a health care centre for people suffering from HIV/AIDS. A foundation in Alphen coordinates and channels civil society initiatives in the partnership with Oudtshoorn. This has led to small-scale community benefits such as book donations to the Oudtshoorn library, donations of toys and furniture to child care centres and financial contributions to children playgrounds and elderly homes. Another partnership objective has been awareness-raising within the Alphen community about the partner city and the life of its inhabitants. This has been relatively successful thanks to widespread media attention for twinning activities and through various education projects at schools.

Alphen municipality has a thin track record concerning C2C and development cooperation. As the municipal International Cooperation official states: "Alphen hardly has a real history in development cooperation. It never was a city that took a strong stand in certain issues such as the municipalities involved with LOTA" (Local Governments Against Apartheid – see Chapter 3).[98] The first, unofficial contacts between Alphen and Oudtshoorn municipality date back to 1962 but remained an isolated event. Efforts to renew these contacts in the 1980s, driven by a personal interest of one of Alphen's councillors, were held back by the strong political movement against the South African Apartheid system among Dutch local authorities. In 1993 the municipality drafted its first International Cooperation policy with a focus on development cooperation. No clear outcome however resulted from this policy with regard to establishing international twinning relations. Some years later, Oudtshoorn municipality clearly expressed interest in establishing a partnership. Partly as a response, partly due to personal sympathy with South Africa of another councillor in Alphen, Alphen's 1998-2002 *court programme* (see Chapter 6) clearly stated that Alphen

---

97   The activities in the framework of this goal are financially supported by one of the Co-financing Agencies in the Netherlands (Hivos) and by the Dutch Association for Dutch-Nicaraguan Municipal Cooperation (LBSNN) – see Chapter 7.

98   Interview official 1, Alphen Municipality, February 23, 2006.

would actively seek a partner city in South Africa for an international twinning arrangement. In 2000 Alphen became involved in the MMTP training programmes of VNG-I (Chapter 3) and was host to South African local government officials from Umtata, Oudtshoorn and Heldenberg. The Oudtshoorn representative reiterated the city's interest in establishing a partnership. That same year a fact finding mission was conducted by Alphen municipality to the three South African municipalities that were linked with Alphen in the VNG programme, to select an appropriate twinning partner. It was concluded that Oudtshoorn had the greatest possibilities for building sustainable contacts and contributing constructively to local development. On April 6, 2002 an official twinning agreement was signed in Oudtshoorn between the two municipalities. The date, exactly 350 years after the Dutch colonial administrator Jan van Riebeeck set foot in South Africa, added symbolic meaning to the cooperation agreement. In 2003, in addition to ties between the two municipal organisations, a civil wing was formed to shape the civil involvement of the partnership with support from the municipality. The *Platform Stedenband Oudtshoorn* was born, with the former councillor who had expressed interest in Oudtshoorn in the 1980s as chair person and driving force.

Setting up a fact finding mission as an instrument to select an appropriate twinning partner can be regarded as unique and innovative in the context of Dutch-South African twinning relations. While the conclusions of the mission were linked to augur which potential partnership would be most effective in terms of strengthening local governance in South Africa and raising awareness in Alphen, the choice for Oudtshoorn has undoubtedly been fed by the historical ties between Alphen and Oudtshoorn. In 1772 the Baron of Oudshoorn – a village which since 1918 has been situated within the municipal borders of Alphen aan den Rijn (see section 1) – travelled to Cape Town as the successor of the deceased Cape Governor, but he died during the journey. Around 1840 pioneer-*boere* in South Africa built the first church on the site of what today is known as Oudtshoorn, and the wife of one of the community founders of Oudtshoorn was the granddaughter of the deceased Baron. The new community was named after the founder's wife. In 1947 the English governor granted permission to the community to carry the family coat of arms, which the town then was named after (Labordus, 1997). According to the Mayor of Alphen, the historical ties were indeed an important trigger to take the partnership further: "The historical ties were evident. The two towns have some remarkable similarities. The coat of arms of Oudtshoorn, South Africa is a copy of the one here, and street names are similar. For many people this is added value".[99] The shared history was thus merely a trigger to the already existing plans to set up a partnership with a foreign city in the framework of development cooperation. As the Mayor explains: "the relations with Oudtshoorn were relevant because of history. The initial contacts were not aimed to strengthen local governance, but as we wanted to do something – every municipality has twinning partnerships nowadays, so if we do something, let's do it with Oudtshoorn".

In sum, with the historical ties and the various personal relations and repeated interests and invitations from Oudtshoorn Municipality, the twinning started as a cultural exchange which later became utilised as an instrument to implement the 1993 International Cooperation policy. The process was intensified by participation in the VNG training programmes. A growing political awareness to be actively involved in C2C and the

---

99   Interview Mayor of Alphen aan den Rijn, March 15, 2006.

justification to select Oudtshoorn as a partner through the fact finding mission eventually resulted in the establishment of the partnership.

Trends in city-to-city cooperation: The cases compared

This section has discussed how the four partnerships under study have emerged and how they have developed over time. Comparing the four cases, similarities as well as differences can be detected. The partnerships show a wide diversity in age – ranging from 25 years (Utrecht-León) to just six (Alphen-Oudtshoorn). Also, as Table 5.1 shows, the initial motive for cities to start the link, and the lead partner city in the founding process appear to be different for each case. Whereas Utrecht and Amstelveen may have played a unilateral key role in establishing their respective partnerships, based on the pillars of solidarity and charity, in the case of Treptow-Köpenick and Alphen the initiative appears to have been shared with their partners in the South. This could imply a higher potential for shared ownership. Buis (2009) observes that due to the fact that from a historical perspective C2C cooperation has usually been started in the 'North', with Northern cities defining the objectives and contents of cooperation, as a consequence ownership is often lacking for C2C partners in the South. In the German and Alphen examples, parallel processes of Local Agenda 21 and historical linkages have been of influence to taking a shared initiative, respectively.

There are however also some similarities. The cases show that city partnerships do not develop overnight. They have all gone through a process from informal contacts to formalised partnerships. This may be a slow process. The cases show a gap between the year in which initial informal contacts were established and the formalisation of the partnerships. While it took Utrecht-León only two years to become a formal link, Alphen and Oudtshoorn show a 40 year time span between the first contacts and the signing of the official twinning agreement. Thus while it may appear that some of the cases are relatively young, in fact their – unofficial – history may be much longer.

Another similarity is that for all cases, the role of civil society in the start up process is evident. In Utrecht and Amstelveen this is unequivocal and intrinsic to the start up motives of the partnerships, but also in the other cases civil society has played a strong

Table 5.1 Indicators of C2C partnerships' development over time

	Initiative to start was...	Initial motive to start partnership	First (informal) contacts	Formal partnership agreement
Amstelveen – Villa El Salvador	Civil society driven; North	Development cooperation project	1987	1997
Treptow-Köpenick – Cajamarca	Political: North and South; process driven by Berlin NGO	Local Agenda 21	Around 1994	1998
Utrecht – León	Civil society driven; North	International solidarity	1983	1985
Alphen aan den Rijn – Oudtshoorn	Personal; North and South	Historical ties and political global awareness	1962	2002

role. In Treptow-Köpenick, the role of the NGO KATE and the presence of civil society stakeholders at the signing of the cooperation agreement were vital. In the case of Alphen and Oudtshoorn, although the actual formalisation of the partnership was politically kick-started, personal contacts and the sympathy of individuals had shaped the willingness of the local authorities.

5.4 Conclusions

This Chapter has reviewed the socio-economic, demographic and political characteristics of the eight partner cities under study. The processes and situational context provide a useful background to the empirical analysis performed in the following Chapters. Moreover, the developmental needs of the partner cities in the South have been demonstrated, as all struggle with problems of poverty and inequality and deal with a range of challenges with regard to urban service delivery, local conflicts, and municipal development planning.

The discussion of the evolution of city partnerships has moreover been valuable as it partly explains some of the current key characteristics of city partnerships. First, it elucidates the reason why many city partnerships maintain a parallel structure of participation from both the local authority and civil society, which has been mentioned as an element that distinguishes C2C from other types of (decentralised) development cooperation structures. Along the dichotomy of authorities and citizens, a division of objectives and motives is also evident in the North: local government is concerned with technical exchange and institutional strengthening while civil society is involved in charity and fundraising, linked to public awareness of global affairs and development in the partner city. The roles and responsibilities of the various public, civil and private actors in city partnerships, and their interrelations are further analysed in Chapter 7.

Secondly, the historical evolution of C2C is characterised by an increased level of professionalism, with the potential of local authorities and civil society organisations to become professional, full-fledged actors engaged in international development cooperation. Local authorities increasingly comply with the necessary ingredients for successful North-South cooperation, e.g. funding, experienced and skilled staff members and a political mandate. These factors and the extent to which they apply to the cases of this study are further analysed and explained in Chapter 6.

6 Local governments in international cooperation: partnership management and organisation[100]

After a review of theoretical, institutional and policy related aspects of city-to-city cooperation, and an introduction of the in-depth cases of this study, this Chapter marks the beginning of the analysis and presentation of empirical findings. It seeks to examine the conditions under which local governments operate in international development cooperation with regard to existing policies, capacities and political will, and discusses the implications of these factors for the practice of city-to-city cooperation. What are the (political) motives for local governments to be engaged in C2C? How are resources mobilised? What capacities are needed to perform their role? This Chapter aims to respond to these questions that are collectively put forward in research question 2.

As was indicated in Chapter 1, in the discourse on development cooperation through North-South partnerships, there is a lack of knowledge on the conditions for capacity development among *local authorities* and how these partnerships can best be utilised to improve the institutional performance of municipal organisations. Therefore there is a need for understanding the conditions which affect the role of local governments in the North as development agents. The first Section of this Chapter will therefore explore the way local governments in the North participate in international development cooperation. The second section will focus on the South and analyse the conditions of municipalities in the South that may facilitate or obstruct participation in international city partnerships and municipal international cooperation in general. Finally, the Chapter will close with a discussion and conclusion, in which municipal partnership management conditions are summarised and compared, and the implications of such conditions (or their lack thereof) for the practice and outcomes of city partnerships.

6.1 Local governments in the North: four critical conditions for municipal participation in development cooperation

This section aims to explain the political and organisational factors that shape the position and potential impact of local governments in the North as partners in international development cooperation through C2C partnerships. If local governments want to act successfully as development agents, they need to comply with some necessary preconditions. Development cooperation is not a core task of municipalities and lack of expertise may undermine good intentions. As Chapter 1 pointed out, partnerships are doomed to fail when

---

100 Parts of this Chapter have been published elsewhere in adapted version (Bontenbal, 2008; Bontenbal & Van Lindert, 2008b; Bontenbal, 2009a).

THE CHALLENGE TO STRENGTHEN URBAN GOVERNANCE THROUGH NORTH-SOUTH CITY PARTNERSHIPS

Table 6.1 Four critical conditions for the participation of Northern municipalities in international cooperation

Factor	Empirical findings
The extent to which C2C partnerships are politically embedded in municipal international cooperation policies	• Municipal political programmes and policies rather than a legal framework shape the scope of international cooperation • C2C is part of wider international policy frameworks • C2C serves a range of municipal objectives • The absence of a political mandate makes partnership activities vulnerable
The availability and quality of human resources in the local administration for C2C	• Organisation-wide formalised consultation structures allow to tap necessary expertise • Key roles in partnership management are various and complementary • Selection criteria to match staff expertise with partnership needs are important
The availability of financial resources and the capacity to tap from external funding	• Municipal resources are modest; C2C competes with other municipal international activities • Departmental and personal contributions add to resources available and reflect staff commitment • External funding is dominant. Municipalities therefore decentralise and multiply development aid, but are also in a more dependent position.
The level of political and administrative support for C2C	• Champion role of political leaders is crucial • Local parties' political programmes reflect political interest in international cooperation • C2C is a tool for human resource management • Political and administrative support remains passive

Northern partners wrongly assume they have all the necessary experience and knowledge to engage in development cooperation. Drawing on empirical evidence from four North-South city partnerships, and taking an institutional perspective from the North – i.e. local governments as development agents, four critical conditions are discussed that have been found to influence the role of local governments in development cooperation through the practice of C2C. The factors and their main implications – which are the result of the empirical analysis performed in this study – are summarised in Table 6.1.

6.1.1. Municipal international cooperation policies

Perhaps the greatest difference between local administrations and mainstream, traditional decentralised development actors such as NGOs and charity organisations is that international cooperation (IC) is not a core task of local administrations. In the Netherlands and Germany, municipal IC is not required by law. While it is heavily promoted by Local Government Associations and (inter)national support institutions (Chapter 3), local governments are not formally mandated to invest in IC or establish policies. Hence, municipal IC efforts are voluntary. In this light, and given the fact that municipalities are political institutions, a first critical factor is the political orientation of the municipal council and of the leading local political parties. In the absence of a guiding legal framework, political programmes (*court programmes*)[101] and supporting IC policies shape and outline the international vision and

---

101 In the Netherlands, the court programme *(collegeprogramma)* is a four-year political programme which entails the political vision and main policy objectives established by the Court of Mayor and Aldermen and approved by

> **Box 6.1** The notion of International Cooperation in Dutch municipal court programmes (2006-2010): three examples
>
> The appearance of what has been called an 'international paragraph' in the court programme can be considered a political determinant of municipal international cooperation. How do Utrecht, Alphen and Amstelveen justify their international activities?[1]
>
> **Utrecht**
> "...Utrecht municipality is intertwined with the world (...). We continue International Cooperation with the aim to stimulate global awareness and to implement the UN Millennium Development Goals."
> "...In addition to the city partnerships with Brno and León and cooperation in the European context (...), the cooperation with migrant countries (such as Morocco where many Utrecht citizens have their roots) is further shaped through cooperation projects with various cities and organisations in these countries. The current budget (2006) for International Cooperation is sustained."
>
> **Alphen aan den Rijn**
> "...Knowledge exchange with the South African municipality Oudtshoorn will be continued."
> "...Key issues [of democratic functioning of Alphen municipality] include an effective and efficient administration aiming at its core objectives, reducing the local tax burden, maintaining a distinct position in the region and contributing to strengthen local governance in Oudtshoorn, the twinning partner."
>
> **Amstelveen**
> "...Amstelveen takes accountability for its international orientation and dimension which is expressed in the diversity of its population, the presence of international businesses and international partnerships. This means on the one hand to sustain existing contacts and city partnerships from the viewpoint of solidarity, and on the other hand to broaden the vision on international cooperation through an integral approach to international affairs aimed at knowledge and innovation, idealistic contacts and economic cooperation."
>
> ---
>
> 1 Sources: The respective court programmes "Utrecht voor elkaar" (Utrecht), "Samenleven in de complete stad" (Alphen aan den Rijn) and "Samen werken aan kwaliteit voor Amstelveen" (Amstelveen).

strategy of municipalities. Moreover, formalised IC policies guarantee a stable availability of financial resources as it secures IC as a fixed item on the municipal budget. The political programmes of the three Dutch cities under study do contain an item on international cooperation and they reflect part of the motives for and initiatives taken in municipal international cooperation (Box 6.1).

Council at the start of a political term.

THE CHALLENGE TO STRENGTHEN URBAN GOVERNANCE THROUGH NORTH-SOUTH CITY PARTNERSHIPS

C2C partnerships are often embedded in a general IC policy that serves a range of objectives. IC policies show great variety regarding geographical orientation (e.g. European vs. North-South), instruments (long term partnerships, international city networks, projects) and activities (knowledge exchange, granting subsidies). North-South city partnerships may be just one aspect of a municipality's international cooperation strategy (e.g. Utrecht), or it may be the singular IC activity performed (Alphen). Diversity in policy objectives is evident: they may be economical and trade oriented (Amstelveen and Utrecht), include EU affairs, such as subsidies and legislation (Utrecht and Treptow-Köpenick), or aim to foster international exchange and city networking (Treptow-Köpenick, Utrecht, Amstelveen). The North-South partnerships of this study contribute to a fourth objective, i.e. international solidarity and taking up a role in development cooperation. The Dutch cases show a dual strategy in this respect: on the one hand contributing to strengthening local governance and local democracy in the South, on the other hand awareness-raising and education of citizens on development issues.[102]

The case of Amstelveen will be used here to illustrate how C2C partnerships are embedded in a more general IC policy framework, whereas in Box 6.2 the cases of Alphen and Utrecht are further illustrated. The partnership agreement with Villa El Salvador fits into the wider 'international orientation' programme which forms the political mandate that gives guidance to all international activities of Amstelveen. It is based on three main motives to engage in international cooperation:

1. The exchange of knowledge, innovation and 'best practice' of municipal affairs
2. Economic motives in attracting foreign investments
3. Ideological motives, i.e. raise global awareness, and "contribute to local democracy and governance elsewhere through the provision of in-house municipal expertise" (Amstelveen Municipality, 2006, p. 3).

The latter provides the framework for cooperation with Villa El Salvador. VES is considered the principal partner city; an estimated 70% of the budget reserved for the four international city partnerships of Amstelveen is allocated to VES.[103] Also, political, administrative and community involvement is predominantly aimed at VES rather than at other international activities.[104]

In contrast to the Dutch examples, the Berlin District of Treptow-Köpenick has no official political IC vision or policy. One of the reasons is related to the administrative status of Treptow-Köpenick as one of the 12 Districts of Berlin (Chapter 5). While the Berlin Senate has its own IC policies and city partnerships, the majority of the Districts maintain their own international relations in addition. For the latter, however, IC is not an official administrative competency. Accordingly Districts, being non-autonomous, do not get any financial or technical means for IC from Senate. Treptow-Köpenick thus has very limited resources for international cooperation and this has been a major limitation for the international relations of the District.[105] Despite the absence of a formal IC policy, the local administration is engaged in international affairs. The focus is mainly on the European Union e.g. attracting

---

102 This duality is also expressed in the organisation of finance and in the relations between the local administration and civil society as city partnership actors, as will be discussed in Chapter 7.

103 Interview official 1 Amstelveen Municipality, January 18, 2007.

104 Interview official 2 Amstelveen Municipality, July 5, 2007.

105 Interview official 1 Treptow-Köpenick Municipality, January 10, 2007.

Box 6.2 The international orientation of Utrecht and Alphen

Utrecht has a diverse and extensive IC policy framework with a budget of over €565,000 in 2007. First, it has a a strong focus on Europe, expressed in the participation in European networks for European fundraising and knowledge exchange, and a shared lobby office in Brussels with the three largest Dutch cities (G4), e.g. for attracting European funds and acquiring information on European (municipal) legislation. The city partnership with Brno, Czech Republic (since 1993) is linked to this objective. Utrecht's second focus is on IC directed to developing countries and the countries of origin of the main migrant groups in Utrecht. The city partnership with León and the granting of subsidies for civil society development initiatives are instruments to this objective. Recently, the Millennium Development Goals have become an organising framework for international (development) cooperation. Utrecht has become a so called 'Millennium Municipality' and as such it expresses its commitment to attaining the MDGs (Chapter 3). In practice however, this has not drastically changed IC policies. While the international scope of Utrecht has become substantial and very diverse today, the partnership with León was among the first international aspirations of the municipality. León continues to be a key issue: Not only is a substantial amount of the IC budget allocated to León (23%, compared to 10% for Brno and 15% for EU affairs), as Figure 6.1 indicates, it is also based on broad participation within the local administration thanks to a decentralised consultation structure (see 6.1.2).

In Alphen, the partnership with Oudtshoorn is the singular IC activity. The dual motive to engage in IC is expressed in the 1993 IC municipal policy. It intends to raise awareness of international responsibility and dependency relations and strengthen local governance and democracy in other parts of the world (VNG & COS, 2005). The municipality allocates a considerable share of its IC awareness-raising subsidies to the partnership with Oudtshoorn.

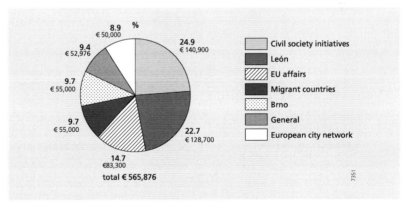

Figure 6.1 Budget International Affairs, Utrecht Municipality, 2007 - Source: Utrecht Municipality, 2007

EU funds and projects, and engaging citizens in European affairs and exchanges. In addition, the administration is concerned with an impressive number of 11 city partnerships, Cajamarca being the only partner in the South. A large number of these partnerships are however inactive.[106]

Some observations can be made from comparing the cases. First, lack of a political mandate such as in the German case makes the involvement of the administration voluntary which may undermine the stability and continuity of municipal engagement in C2C. The role of political will and in particular personal commitment of the Mayor becomes crucial in this respect. However, secondly, it must be noted that the Treptow-Köpenick – Cajamarca partnership is largely civil society driven, in which the local administration only has a modest role through providing political support, and some funding. There are for example no direct exchanges between municipality staff. The consequences of the absence of a municipal IC policy should in this respect not be exaggerated. Thirdly, alternative instruments can provide guidelines to shape the international cooperation strategy and activities (De Villiers, 2009). In the German case this is the partnership agreement signed by the two cities and the Local Agenda 21 process in Treptow-Köpenick.

The examples show that North-South city partnerships are not activities on their own; rather they fit into a wider municipal IC policy framework. For local administrations, city partnerships are instruments to serve a range of objectives, including contribution to global awareness-raising, facilitating civil society initiatives and showing solidarity by strengthening partner municipalities and local governance conditions in the South.

6.1.2. Local government human resources for C2C

A second factor affecting the performance of municipalities in development cooperation refers to the availability of human resources for IC activities. The existence of organisation-wide consultation structures and the definition of key roles in the organisation determine whether a pool of experienced and skilled staff is available for C2C activities. Individual capacities (both technical and partnership capacities to interact with the partner, such as language, cultural understanding and knowledge of the partner country) as well as the mechanisms to select staff for projects are underlying factors. The availability of human resources is particularly relevant as local governments are not core development experts and questions have been raised about the suitability and knowledgeability of local governments to act as partners in the international development arena.

A first point of attention is the positioning of IC in the organisation, the subsequent staff time available for IC, and how participation and decision-making are organised. In Amstelveen municipality, the administrative responsibility for IC lies with the Policy Department, with twenty hours available per week. The number of individuals involved can be regarded as limited and fixed. There is no formalised consultation structure such as a working group or task force that brings together partnership participants. In Treptow-

---

106 According to an official, the partnership with Cajamarca is distinct, since it is Treptow-Köpenick's most active international relationship. Moreover, it is embedded in the District's Local Agenda 21 structure (Chapter 5) which is mainly sustained by civil society (Chapter 7). A discrepancy can be detected that while Cajamarca is considered the most relevant city partnership by both the local administration and the community, at the same time the administration's IC affairs are mainly geared towards Europe.

Köpenick, IC is administratively embedded in the Mayor's Office. The full-time position is officially for EU affairs only, and due to the absence of a clear C2C mandate, partnership activities are not formally administered. No additional municipal staff is involved in the partnership as there is no institutional exchange relationship with Cajamarca. In the Alphen administration, the four to six hours dedicated per week for IC can be regarded as very limited.[107] Similar to Amstelveen, while a relatively limited but permanent group of officials is involved in the partnership, there is no formalised consultation structure within the local administration. Part of this is due to the unfortunate position of IC in the organisation. IC is embedded in the Department of Welfare and Education, which covers more than 30 policy topics and where IC is an odd one out.[108] The administration has considered shifting IC to the Municipal Manager's office. Such a position would not only permit more integral project planning and corresponding participation from the various Departments, it would also enhance the possibilities to make IC more visible and exert influence directly to Departments.

In Utrecht, the administrative responsibility of the partnership lies with the Department of Governmental and International Affairs, concerned with a wide range of international issues (Box 6.2). In addition, a decentralised consultation structure is set up within the organisation to manage the León South East (LSE) project, which has been the key focus of cooperation between Utrecht and León since 1998. The structure brings together various line Departments, staff, external advisors and an external consultant, who acts as project coordinator. A multi-disciplinary team of urban planners, architects, and social policy advisors, thus contributes to the integral approach the LSE project seeks to take. It also facilitates and coordinates the division of labour in accordance to the needs expressed by León municipality. The project group meets every six weeks. Four to six work visits are paid to León by one or two members annually.[109] The decentralised structure allows for broad consultation within the Utrecht administration. Not only do the involved officials deliver technical expertise, each line Department also contributes financially to the LSE project. An integral project structure can be considered a positive factor with regard to generating wide administrative support and additional funding for the partnership and facilitating in matching existing expertise with the partner city's needs.

A second remark that can be made with regard to human resources is that various key roles can be detected in municipal partnership management, with different functions on partnership level (political, coordinating, representative) and on project level (e.g. technical

---

107   As an official notes, with the time investment of one work visit to Oudtshoorn per year alone, the amount of time is easily exceeded, leaving very little room for policymaking and other activities (Interview official 1, Alphen Municipality, February 23, 2006).

108   It was noticed that the various thematic foci of the partnership with Oudtshoorn (e.g. performance management, social housing) do not always relate well with the thematic framework of the Department. Moreover, the current IC decision making chain is inefficient as the Welfare & Education Department can only indirectly liaise with other Departments through higher management levels (Interview official 1 Alphen Municipality, October 23, 2007).

109   Having an external coordinator has been mentioned as a success factor of the consultation structure (LSE evaluation, 2005). The consultant, solely concerned with the LSE project and not with other partnership activities, coordinates the work and visits of the Utrecht officials to León and brings together relevant technical expertise from the various Departments.

Box 6.3 Key roles in partnership management in the North

In local administrations in the North, who are involved in partnership activities and what is their role? Key positions and roles roughly comprise of three categories.

1. Creating support and accountability: Political key roles. Local political leaders take both key political and representative roles in the partnerships. Usually, the political responsibility for International Cooperation lies with the Mayor.[1] Political leaders have the capacity to increase and sustain political support for the partnership within council and to assist in approaching potential actors to participate in partnership activities.[2]

2. Exercising control: Decision-making and evaluative roles. A second role is concerned with decision-making, and inspection and evaluation of partnership project implementation, usually performed by senior officials. Alphen's Municipal Manager has represented his organisation on a high administrative level on work visits to Oudtshoorn and was therefore in the position to take key decisions on-site.[3] In Amstelveen, the role of the Head of the Policy Department and the Municipal Manager are of an evaluative nature, to assess the results of the projects jointly implemented by VES and Amstelveen staff.

3. Implementing partnership activities: Executive roles. In the four cities in the North, there is one official appointed as coordinator of the partnership. Roles include budgeting and developing IC policies, maintaining correspondence with the partner city, organising delegation visits, liaising with partnership stakeholders from civil society, and organising awareness-raising activities. In Utrecht, until 2005, a permanent Dutch representative employed by Utrecht municipality was posted in León. This role is now performed by a local NGO.[4]

---

1   This is the case for Alphen, Amstelveen and Treptow-Köpenick, whereas in Utrecht, an Alderman is the political representative of international affairs.

2   Councillors also participate in partnership affairs. Politicians may be part of capacity building activities, which occurred in Amstelveen (Aldermen of Environment and Finance) and Alphen (Alderman of Finance).

3   Says an Alphen official: "I can go [to Oudtshoorn] and say 'we are going to work on infrastructure' but who am I? (...) Sometimes you get stuck and then it is good to have the highest chief to take decisions (Interview official 2 Alphen Municipality, March 7, 2006).

4   Utrecht municipality therefore is now only engaged with local partners in the partner city, a fact that can be considered a precondition to more ownership in the South (Chapter 8).

vs. policymaking). These are illustrated in Box 6.3. Also within project cycles various roles are performed by different staff (e.g. executive vs. evaluative). In Amstelveen the number of individuals involved can be regarded as limited (3) and fixed. In Alphen such a modest group is also present (3) however there has been additional staff engaged on a more flexible basis (5), contributing their specific expertise. In Utrecht, finally, the LSE work group is varied and dynamic as some Departments and officials have left and others have joined. It brings together over 12 members from a range of Departments.

Finally, various mechanisms are in place for the selection of project participants. In Amstelveen and Alphen it has been attempted to match staff positions with the technical requirements of partnership projects.[110] In Utrecht, the selection of participants in the LSE project group is based on interviews and CVs. Not only technical expertise but also knowledge of the Spanish language and experience with working in developing countries are considered, as well as the ability to understand the way of working of the Southern partner. Such criteria are important to take into account if local governments seek a professional approach to development cooperation, not only to maximise project performance but also to prevent the involvement of staff that merely seek the opportunity to travel or that may be very eager to participate but lack the necessary technical or cultural skills to cooperate effectively with the partner organisation.

6.1.3 Financial resources and the capacity to tap from external funding

A third factor is concerned with the financial resources that municipalities make available for their North-South partnership. As municipal IC is voluntary, the availability of capital may be vulnerable. In the examples used here, part of the municipal budget is allocated on a structural basis to international cooperation and the partnerships in particular. Table 6.2 provides an overview of the main annual financial figures:[111]

1. The four cities spend an average of 31% of their general IC budget[112] (LA21 budget for Treptow-Köpenick) on North-South city partnerships.[113]

2. The figure is relatively low for Amstelveen, where a large bulk of the IC budget is absorbed by economic development and trade activities. Seventy per cent of the budget allocated to international partnerships is dedicated to the Peruvian partner city.

3. In Utrecht, €70,000 is reserved for municipal projects while €58,700 (46%) of the budget for the León partnership is transferred to the Foundation Utrecht-León (Chapter 7).

4. The figures for Alphen are rather surprising as Oudtshoorn is considered the single instrument for International Cooperation in Alphen. Apparently a large share of the IC budget is also allotted to civil society initiatives. The amount of €35,000 is based on the rule of thumb that 1 former Dutch guilder per capita is dedicated to municipal international solidarity.

5. As the partnership with Cajamarca is an element of Treptow-Köpenick's LA21 process, the figures show IC as a share of the municipal contribution to LA21 activities. In 2006, the municipality allocated for the first time a structural budget of €30,000 per annum

---

110 For example, in Amstelveen's environment project, two Amstelveen officials provided their individual expertise: one from a policy-making perspective and one from a more technical viewpoint.

111 The figures only reflect structural contributions. In addition, municipal councils may decide on occasional donations. Examples include a project by Amstelveen for disabled people and donations for reconstruction after a fire in 2003 in VES, and emergency relief by Alphen (e.g. for the 2005 Asia tsunami, and for the humanitarian crisis in Darfur). The amount of these ad-hoc donations have ranged from €1,000 to €25,000.

112 The overall IC budget relates to all IC activities. The figures are derived from an analysis of municipal budgets and IC policy and work programmes and from personal communication.

113 When the overall IC budget is compared to the municipalities' general annual budget, none of the Northern partners allocate more than 0.1% to International Cooperation. This is less than the UN-norm of 0.7% that is set for national government budgets, and to which the Dutch national government is committed. The figures show that municipalities invest a negligible share of their annual budgets in IC.

Table 6.2 Annual municipal budgets for C2C and International Cooperation (€)

	Municipal budget for C2C partnership	Municipal budget for international cooperation*	Share of C2C partnership in the IC budget (%)
Amstelveen (2007)	30,000	146,000	21
Treptow-Köpenick (2006)	10,400	30,000	35
Utrecht (2007)	128,700	565,876	23
Alphen (2006)	15,000	35,000	43

* For Treptow-Köpenick: Municipal budget for Local Agenda 21

to LA21. This helps overcome the vulnerable financial position of the partnership, as the municipality does not have a structural budget for IC.[114]

The budgets in Table 6.2 refer to the financial resources available at municipal level. In addition, there are various examples where on organisational and even individual level, financial contributions are made. A very clear example of the former is the decentralised financial contribution that the line Departments of Utrecht municipality make as member of the León South East Working Group. Six line Departments contribute €13,000 each to the project annually. The aggregate amount of €78,000 is an addition to the central municipal LSE budget[115] and accounts for over 50% of the project budget made available by the municipality annually.[116]

Donations from municipal staff have also been reported. Examples include fundraising activities during Christmas or at social staff gatherings (Alphen, Utrecht), charity events such as the collection of second hand toys (Alphen), donations of departing Councillors (Amstelveen) and officials (Utrecht) and the donation of Christmas bonuses. These contributions can be considered as very modest. However, rather than providing a substantial financial contribution for partnership activities, more important is their added value in awareness-raising and creating support for the partnership among staff.

Municipalities in the North are usually heavily limited in their international aspirations due to restricted financial resources. In particular medium and small-sized cities do not have large budgets for international cooperation. Municipalities therefore turn to external funding sources that have increasingly become available by national and supranational organisations. In the case of Amstelveen, the main external funding has been provided by the Dutch local government association VNG (Chapter 3). It contributed 78.5% of the project aid invested by Amstelveen in VES during the years 2004-2007, with a total of

---

114   According to an official, "…either we seek funding opportunities from Senate – if you are lucky – or from the EU. In addition, the Mayor has a small budget for 'representation'. But it is relatively limited. Previously the partnership activities were financed with this budget. This is not much. And it really depends on the commitment of the Mayor. If she thinks 'no, we don't need so many partnership activities' then she will also not provide the resources" (Interview official 1 Treptow-Köpenick Municipality, January 10, 2007).

115   Departments invest their share individually, or donate it to the general LSE project budget. In 2004 for example, activities that were funded by decentralised budgets included a housing market survey in León and a management course for political leaders and senior officials of León municipality.

116   Interview LSE working group coordinator, May 10, 2005.

CITIES AS PARTNERS

€274,000. In addition, the municipality has also been able to obtain resources from the Province of Noord-Holland to which the city pertains, and from a local housing association (Chapter 7). The financial contributions from the local administration itself are very modest in comparison to external sources. Own resources are mainly provided on in-kind basis, i.e. the hours invested by local officials providing their knowledge and expertise. While it was estimated that in 2004 and 2005 a total of over €500,000 was invested in the partnership from external funding (Amstelveen Municipality, 2006), the contribution of the municipality itself was approximately €60,000 in that same period.[117]

VNG has also been a major source of additional funding to Utrecht and Alphen. In Utrecht, VNG funding accounts for 40-50% of the annual budget for the LSE project. In Alphen, virtually all technical exchanges and work visits are financed by VNG subsidies. In recent years Utrecht has further attracted resources from a range of NGOs and other partners.[118] It was estimated that in 2007 €70,000 was allocated to León from the municipal budget against €502,000 from external sources (Utrecht Municipality, 2007). Also, both Amstelveen and Utrecht have been very successful in getting donors and other partner cities of VES and León respectively on board their partnership projects, which generated further financial assistance.

Hence for three of the four partnerships under study, external funding is important. With the exception of Treptow-Köpenick, where no additional external funding has been observed, the majority of financial aid has derived from external sources. At least two observations can be made in this respect:
- The cities in the North have caused a multiplier effect of financial resources channelled to their partner cities in the South. Through using C2C partnerships as development cooperation strategy, various flows of Dutch national and subnational funding sources are directed towards the local level in the South, allowing Dutch financial development assistance to become decentralised.
- It should be noted that while additional funding is often crucial to the financial viability of C2C partnerships, there is also a danger for local administration in becoming too dependent on external funds. As will be shown in more detail in Chapter 8, the criteria to gain access to external funding may have a strong impact on partnership agendas and may impose limitations to tapping the full potential of municipal expertise. It can also undermine the continuity of partnerships when subsidies are withdrawn.

6.1.4 Political and administrative support for C2C

A fourth condition is the political and administrative support that is needed to sustain C2C efforts. Hafteck (2003) considers it an advantage that international cooperation is not a core competency of municipalities, as they are not dependent on it for their existence. It however also puts forward one of the main vulnerabilities of IC: it is highly dependent on the political will and administrative support to make it a municipal affair. Will and commitment are relevant on both the political level, to bring about a political mandate that justifies IC activities, and on the administrative level, as for the large majority of local officials, IC is not a core responsibility and staff are involved on a voluntary basis.

---

117 Interview official 2 Amstelveen Municipality.

118 E.g. LBSNN, Kiwanis, Cordaid, private companies and the Czech partner city Brno. The latter example shows how individual city partnerships may become part of a wider city network with new functional relationships.

THE CHALLENGE TO STRENGTHEN URBAN GOVERNANCE THROUGH NORTH-SOUTH CITY PARTNERSHIPS

As was noted in Box 6.3, local political leaders take both key political and representative roles in C2C partnerships. Mayors play a significant role and are often involved in work visits and other activities. It has been found that the representation and ceremonial aspects of international cooperation are perceived to be highly valued, especially by municipalities in the South. This is illustrated by the signing of cooperation agreements which has been done by Mayors in all examples, or official Mayoral visits to the partner city.

In Treptow-Köpenick, in absence of a formal IC policy, the role of the Mayor and the need for political commitment are significant. In Alphen, political engagement in IC can be regarded as very limited, despite the fact that IC is politically mandated and financially secured, and the Mayor is strongly in favour of strengthening local governance in the partner city Oudtshoorn.[119] Weak political support makes partnerships vulnerable, which became clear in 2004 when, in the context of municipal expenditure cuts, Alphen Council proposed to remove IC from the muncipal budget. The case of Amstelveen shows similarities. While there is Council support for IC, the city partnerships are rarely an agenda item for Council meetings and cannot be considered a relevant political issue.[120] In the case of Alphen and Amstelveen, we can therefore speak of 'passive political support', in which council approves and tolerates International Cooperation rather than being pro-actively involved and politically interested.

The presence or absence of political concern is also reflected in the appearance of IC as an issue in election programmes of local political parties. From a review of election programmes of the various local political parties in Alphen and Utrecht presented during the municipal elections of March 2006, mixed evidence is found regarding the importance of municipal international cooperation to local political parties. While the election programmes in Alphen reveal that local political parties hardly acknowledge the potential role local governments could take up in international cooperation,[121] the political parties in Utrecht are

---

119   According to the Mayor of Alphen: "The political vision [on IC] in Alphen is quite weak (...). Some municipalties choose very fundamentally (...) to provide assistance or to strengthen local democracy in cities elsewhere. This does not really apply to our Municipal Council. Formally it is properly organised but if you look into the hearts of the people, it is really not of interest to them". The Mayor furthermore observes that the lack of interest in international affairs stems from a general inward focus of Alphen's municipal Council: "This Council (...) is concerned with the town itself, less with neighbouring towns and even less with municpalities far away (...) they are also not interested in Europe, (...) they strongly feel we are local representatives, we are concerned only with the Municipality of Alphen aan den Rijn (Interview Mayor of Alphen aan den Rijn, March 15, 2006).

120   Interview official 2 Amstelveen Municipality.

121   In Alphen, out of 11 political parties that participated in the 2006 municipal elections, only three have a clear viewpoint on IC as expressed in the election programmes and only one is among the dominant political parties (PvdA). The leading parties VVD and CDA do not mention IC in their programmes. The PvdA programme acknowledges the role of Alphen municipality in "fostering global awareness" through its cooperation agreement with Oudtshoorn and other (not specified) activities (PvdA Partijprogramma 2006-2010 "Rozen voor Alphen", p. 5). The programme of the social-liberal party D66 mentions IC by stressing the relationship with Oudtshoorn, and the dual responsibility of the municipality of facilitating civil initiatives on the one hand and fostering municipal knowledge exchange on the other. The Christian party ChristenUnie finally sees awareness-raising among citizens with regard to their 'position in the world' as a local government responsibility and believes the twinning partnership with Oudtshoorn provides opportunities to encourage civil involvement in global affairs.

in general much more aware of the international position of the municipality.[122] With some exceptions, the frequent appearance of IC as an item of municipal election programmes shows that local political visions do contain an international dimension in Utrecht.

In addition to political will, support among administration staff for C2C activities has been found to be of similar importance. Although participants are believed to reap benefits from engaging in international relations and are usually strongly committed, overall administrative support was generally found to be rather passive. The majority of staff are not involved in partnership activities.[123] Municipal administrations have attempted to increase and justify involvement from staff to promote partnership participation as an element of their human resource management policies. The opportunity to participate in partnership activities can be regarded as fringe benefits for local government officials: it fosters employees' satisfaction and motivation while at the same time it strengthens the capacity of the local administration. For example, the Mayor of Amstelveen stresses that participation in the partnership enriches his staff, empowering and inspiring them in their work. A senior manager points out that the partnership has offered staff that have been in the organisation for many years a "completely new point of view".[124] Partnership participation is seen as a relatively radical but vital way to put daily work into perspective.[125] The international experience through partnership participation is thus regarded an opportunity for human resource development. In Amstelveen therefore, it is currently discussed whether the partnership activities can become a more integral part of HR policies as a fringe benefit.

In the light of the trends portrayed here that both political will and staff engagement and support for C2C activities are not always secured and are relatively vulnerable and passive, the role of local champions acting as ambassadors to the partnership in their organisation and beyond, appears crucial. Moreover Mayors, as 'committed political agents' (Heller,

---

122 In Utrecht the large majority of political parties do have an item on IC in their election programmes, with the exception of *Leefbaar Utrecht*, which was the leading party in Utrecht in the previous term (2002-2006). The programmes refer to continuation of the partnerships with León and Brno, although it is mentioned that León should become less dependent on Utrecht and mutuality and equality should be encouraged (Leefbaar Utrecht, PvdA), and that regular evaluations should be performed (CDA). Several parties envisage an increased focus on partnerships with migrant countries (Groen Links, PvdA, SP). PvdA and CDA stress that IC should be exempted from future budget cuts. In contrast, the liberal VVD party argues that the partnerships with León and Brno should be terminated: "Municipalities should focus on their core tasks and IC is not one of them. [City partnerships] are not something the municipality should deal with. Therefore the long-term partnerships [with León and Brno] will be phased out carefully" (Election Programme VVD "Doe mee® met Utrecht", 2006-2010, p. 14).

123 In Amstelveen for example, various attempts have been made to broaden participation and to inform officials on partnership affairs. Through Intranet messages, lunch meetings and staff journal articles, various instruments are applied to widen administrative support. Nevertheless, participation is "limited and vulnerable" (Interview Mayor of Amstelveen, July 5, 2007). Informative meetings on the partnership are not well attended, and reports on work visits in VES are hardly read by municipal staff.

124 Interview official 1 Amstelveen municipality.

125 Another senior official notes: "It is a wonderful method to help develop your staff. It is also a trend now at [HR] training institutes to offer international experience. People joke about this – 'you are going to Italy to reflect on your career' – but I believe the gains are much higher than when you read management books for a whole year" (Interview official 3 Amstelveen Municipality, January 18, 2006).

Table 6.3 The champion role of political leaders in C2C partnerships

Amstelveen	• Leadership for campaiging and fundraising after a 2003 fire that caused damage in the partner city • Mayor lobbied within council to create political support during the 2006 Municipal Elections • Mayor lobbied in Dutch parliament and VNG for C2C and Peru
Treptow-Köpenick	• Ceremonial openings of partnership exhibition by Mayor • Mayoral work visits to Cajamarca • Mayor allocates municipality's 'representation budget' or 'token money' to C2C
Utrecht	• Regular Mayoral visits to León • Chairing city-wide consultation meetings on C2C with León
Alphen	• Technical project started thanks to personal contact between Mayor and counterpart in South Africa • Mayor has IC track record and has had a key advisory position in international VNG activities • Mayor pleaded succesfully to include an international paragraph in the municipal programme and budget (2002-2006) • Mayor seeks public relations opportunities with interviews in staff journal and local newspapers to promote C2C

2003) have proved to be vital in creating such support. Table 6.3 provides an overview of Mayoral actions that are illustrative to the champion role performed.

6.2 Municipal partnership management in the South: C2C cooperation as strategic alliance to meet municipal development objectives?

While the previous section has reviewed partnership management conditions in cities in the North, the Chapter now turns towards the South. It will be demonstrated that comparable C2C partnership management and capacity conditions apply in North and South, but that their implications differ, as the partner cities operate in dissimilar financial, organisational and political realities. Rather than exploring whether partner cities are fit to take up a role in development cooperation, which was a relevant question for the partner cities in the North, the main question of this section is of a different nature. It concerns the extent to which partner cities in the South manage their international relations as a strategic tool to perform their municipal responsibilities and meet their development objectives, and which capacities and conditions promote or hamper this potential.

The section starts with a general introduction of the international orientation of municipalities in the South. It then discusses organisational and financial partnership management conditions, followed by an analysis of political support as critical factor for partnership success or failure. Finally, the section examines to what extent C2C and IC are strategically employed by local governments in the South to meet municipal development objectives.

6.2.1 The international orientation of municipalities in the South

León's sister cities are of vital importance to the economic survival of the municipality. It was estimated that in 2007, 77% of municipal investments were financed by international cooperation: sister cities, development projects and direct donor support (Box 6.4). The strong dependency on external assistance reflects the international orientation and concomitant organisational infrastructure the municipality needs to have in order to maintain relationships with its numerous sister cities and donors. A municipal Department called 'Cooperación Externa' (external cooperation) is dedicated to specifically manage these liaisons.

The figures of León are exceptional compared to other cities in the South. Oudtshoorn is hardly involved in any other international activities,[126] although the municipality is increasingly focused on bringing foreign investors and tourists to the Oudtshoorn area to promote local economic development. At this moment, also Cajamarca's international orientation is restricted. In addition to the partnership with Treptow-Köpenick, a partnership agreement was signed in 2007 with Taxco de Alarcón in Mexico.[127] In the past however, the international scope of the municipality used to be much wider. During the terms of office of Mayor Luis Guerrero in the 1990s, the municipality participated in various internationally funded development projects. The international and environmental orientation of the Mayor[128] connected the City of Cajamarca to a range of international organisations and initiatives, such as the UN- Habitat conference in Istanbul (1996), IULA, ICLEI and the Dutch NGO SNV.[129]

With its long tradition of international cooperation, Villa El Salvador has some commonalities with León. Its history of struggle and its culture of participation and solidarity have raised much sympathy in the rest of Peru and abroad. This has resulted in a vast amount of continuous financial, humanitarian and technical support to various community initiatives. One of these initiatives was the Women's Federation whose president María Elena Moyano was assassinated in 1992 by the Shining Path. This fact drew even more international attention to VES.[130] In Villa El Salvador, there is a wide presence of internationally funded NGOs in the local governance arena. Furthermore, the participation structure of VES has been subject to a number of international case studies and pilot projects (World Bank, 1998; Cities Alliance, 2001; Marulanda & Calderón, 2001). The municipal organisation itself is also internationally oriented. The municipal development

---

126 In addition to Alphen aan den Rijn, Oudtshoorn has a twinning partnership with Hualien, Taiwan. The relationship has however been dormant since the early 1990s. It was initiated by the Taiwanese consulate in Cape Town to foster trade between the two countries. Oudtshoorn saw a number of opportunities, given the economic isolation during the Apartheid regime, in terms of gaining know-how and production, and trade investments. The partnership however only resulted in two delegation visits to both cities with no concrete outcomes.

127 Cajamarca and Taxco de Alarcón have a number of features in common, such as tourism, cultural heritage, and jewellery production.

128 Luis Guerrero was secretary of IULA Latin America (1997-98) and member of the board of ICLEI World (1997-98).

129 The decrease of international orientation could also be a reflection of a general trend in Cajamarca that NGOs are leaving. Due to the massive income generation resulting from the mining industry through the *canon minero* (Chapter 5), Cajamarca may no longer be viewed as poor and in need of development assistance – at least in terms of financial resources (Interview Municipal Manager Cajamarca Municipality, March 8, 2007).

130 The visit of Pope John Paul II in 1985 has also put the community of Villa El Salvador into the international spotlights.

Box 6.4 The economic dependence of León on foreign assistance

The case of León illustrates the economic relevance city partnerships potentially offer to local governments in the South. León has an impressive number of nine sister cities, all from North America and Europe. Their financial assistance contributes heavily to the implementation of municipal projects in León: in 2007, of the 221 million córdoba invested in municipal projects, 169 million córdoba (77%) was financed by International Cooperation. Figure 6.2 shows that León's own resources only cover 13% of public investments, while central government transfers account for 10%. Part of the dominance of international resources is explained by the absence of national government financial transfers to municipalities. Nicaragua is among the last countries in Latin America to decentralise. As was explained in Chapter 4, while more responsibilities to local governments are assigned, the corresponding transfer of financial resources to meet these obligations has been lagging behind. In addition, the majority of municipalities in Nicaragua suffer from a complete lack of resources and have insufficient means to raise local revenues. Cities like León thus continue to be overly dependent on foreign assistance to carry out public investments. Critics argue that the excessive role of international cooperation sustains the status quo of aid dependency of Nicaragua and its municipalities in particular (e.g. Van Wijland, 2003; Schat, 2005) – see also Chapter 8.

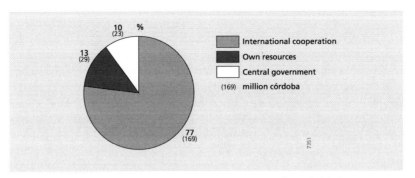

Figure 6.2 Sources of municipal investments León, 2007 (in million Córdoba) - Source: PIA, 2007

plan refers to Agenda 21 and sustainable development of the 1992 Rio Earth Summit and the Human Development concept of UNDP as the main logic behind the planning focus. More importantly, the municipality has recently established the International Cooperation Department. Its responsibilities include managing international aid and cooperation, liaising with international actors and donors and managing the partnerships with the four sister cities of VES: Amstelveen (the Netherlands), Santa Coloma de Gramenet (Spain), Rezé (France) and Tübingen (Germany).

6.2.2 Partnership management structures: policies, departments and resources

The international orientation of municipalities in the South may not only become visible in the number of sister cities and participation in international projects (which is further explained below), another indicator is the existence of a *municipal policy* or plan with regard to international cooperation and foreign relations, or in other words, the extent to which C2C partnerships are politically embedded in municipal international cooperation policies. An outlined strategy for international affairs, which is common among partner cities in the North should give guidance to maintaining partnerships, defining objectives for new activities and seeking new partners and projects with an international scope. It is striking to note that in all four cities, even León, such a policy is lacking. It may be a reflection of the general absence of policymaking and policies in municipalities in the South, which often struggle with capacity needs and may be more concerned with implementation of investments (Box 6.6). Moreover, alternative structures appear to be in place that shape the form and direction of international activities and serve to provide a policy framework to international cooperation. Joint twinning agreements with partner cities are examples (Chapter 8). In León, the annual operational plan defines in more detail the tasks and responsibilities of the External Cooperation department. Still, a general lack of C2C policies raises questions about the ownership of Southern municipalities in C2C agenda and decision-making processes.

Another reflection of having a structure for international cooperation in place are the previously mentioned International or External Cooperation *Departments*, which are full-fledged subdivisions in the municipal organisations of VES and León. In Vila El Salvador, the Department of International Cooperation, established in January 2006, serves to coordinate and promote the various international partnerships and projects of the local administration. It is in charge of the formulation of cooperation projects and programmes that are in line with municipal policies. Municipal departments can provide input and propose projects eligible for international assistance. In addition, the Department's duties include observing the various international cooperation agreements and seeking new opportunities to expand international cooperation initiatives. During delegation visits it takes care of logistical and organisational aspects.

In León 'Cooperación Externa' (CE) is a subdivision of the Department of Planning and External Cooperation. It is concerned with public participation, e.g. organising the Municipal Development Committee (Chapter 4) and other *cabildos* to validate annual investment plans with citizens. With regard to the municipality's international relations, the Department serves a number of goals. Given the high dependency of León on foreign assistance (Box 6.4), the Department's position is crucial. Its mandate is formally to develop thematic cooperation lines based on the municipality's priorities set out in the Strategic Development Plan (PEDM) and based on input from other Municipal departments regarding capacity and investments needs. At the same time, it should liaise with Leon's international partners on the formulation and implementation of projects and inform and report on the disbursement of project investments made by donors. The Department thus serves as a bridge between the municipal organisation and its international partners. Activities include the organisation of monthly meetings with representatives of *hermanamientos* (city partnerships) and other international organisations to exchange information on projects and future plans, and to coordinate efforts. Moreover, the Department seeks to find new funding sources for technical assistance e.g. from foreign embassies in Nicaragua. After a reorganisation in

2005 the competencies of Planning and CE have been brought together in one Department. The logic behind this is to close the project cycle, i.e. to bring together project formulation (CE) and implementation (Planning).[131] It poses however also challenges to the capacity of the department to manage such distinct and heavy-weight municipal responsibilities in an integrated way and to execute projects and report on progress on time, taking into regard that the number of staff in the CE subdivision is limited to five.

The municipalities of Cajamarca and Oudtshoorn do not have full-fledged international cooperation departments.[132] In Cajamarca, partnership management falls officially under the Planning and Technical Cooperation Office, a subdivision of the Planning Department, as outlined in the partnership's cooperation agreement. At the time of research however, there had not been any participation of the municipality in partnership affairs for a number of years. The municipal organisation had experienced a high level of staff turnover, and the previous liaison officer responsible for Treptow-Köpenick had left without leaving behind an archive of partnership documentation. The result was that not only did the partnership lack a municipal representative for the remainder of the political term: at the start of the next term (in 2007), the new official in charge lacked the necessary information, e.g. contact details in Germany, content and objectives of the partnership, and relevant partnership stakeholders in Cajamarca's civil society. This example shows first the danger of political regime change to the continuity of partnerships: when a new Mayor enters, many staff are reshuffled and replaced, leaving a void of knowledge and experience in the municipal organisation. Secondly, it demonstrates the lack of sustainability when partnership responsibility lies with one person only, and the need to maintain a partnership information system.[133] Much of these vulnerabilities can be ascribed to the lack of capacity of local government in general and the characteristics that are typical to local political systems in the South (Box 6.6).

Finally, which *financial resources* do partner cities in the South invest in international cooperation? Here, there is evidently a great contrast with partnership management in the municipalities in the North: municipalities in the South make very little money available for international activities. In the examples used here, overseas missions are always financed by the Northern city, also when representatives from the partner cities travel. Such a discrepancy in financial contribution to international cooperation is one of the main persistent inequalities in North-South partnerships, also in a municipal context. Chapter 8 explores the implications of such imbalances.

6.2.3 Political support to C2C in the South

While financial resources and international relations policies may thus be factors that are predominantly present in municipalities in the North, in the South there is usually an

---

131   It was however also suggested by one of the respondents that the merger was the result of the personal preference of the acting Director of Planning to place CE under his responsibility; Liaising with foreign partners is considered status-enhancing.

132   The Municipal Manager is responsible for international relations in Oudtshoorn. For practical and logistic al matters and day-to-day communication, a *liaison officer* is appointed. Previously this used to be the Head of Planning, but recently it has been the IDP manager.

133   In Cajamarca, this has been especially the case because there have not been any municipal projects in recent years, which could have guaranteed a wider involvement of municipal staff and possibly a number of champions that kept the partnership alive.

abundance of political and administrative support for C2C. This is not surprising given the fact that twinning often brings financial and technical gains for organisations in the South, which – as the example of León shows – may be in painful need for external resources. In León, Oudtshoorn and VES all local political parties support the twinning partnership unambiguously (Box 6.5).

The case of Cajamarca however tells a different story, which demonstrates that political will for C2C partnerships in the South is not as obvious as one may expect at first sight. It has been found that after the term of office of Luís Guerrero, initiator and political champion of the partnership with Germany, the Municipality has been criticised for a lack of knowledge and political interest towards the twinning partnership, despite the fact that an official partnership agreement was signed. It was during the term of Hoyos Rubio (1999-2002), that the last municipal technical exchanges took place. Since then, municipal interaction has been slack, with the exception of a ceremonial visit of Treptow-Köpenick Mayor Ulbricht in 2005. At the time of research there was no political representative in Cajamarca for the partnership, which could generally be considered a key indicator of political will. During Ulbricht's visit, the Mayor of Cajamarca showed little interest in partnership affairs[134] and was frowned upon for not properly hosting his counterpart. Also, when the new Mayor of Treptow-Köpenick boarded the plane to visit the partner city for the partnership's 10th anniversary (May 2008), she had not received an official invitation from the Municipality of Cajamarca and it was unclear whether she would meet her counterpart Mayor. These are exceptional circumstances in official city twinning, which is usually strongly embedded in ceremonial customs. The lack of a formalised municipal-to-municipal invitation potentially undermines official diplomatic relations and would be unthinkable in bilateral relations at country level.

What could cause such a (perceived) disinterest from political leaders in the South for international city partnerships? While it is difficult to provide clear-cut answers, some observations can be made:

- The city partnership was perceived as the creation of former Mayor Guerrero. The contacts with Germany and the framework of Local Agenda 21 have therefore been identified as 'political tools' of Guerrero. Subsequently, his successors did not want to be identified with the partnership. While the civil society wing of the partnership continued to propagate the partnership as an LA21 affair, the latter was no longer a municipal issue. Environmental management lost momentum as a local government priority and in municipal jargon new buzzwords emerged, such as 'local governance' and 'democratic transition'.[135]
- Given the nature of local politics in the South with a strong tendency to break down old policies and investment plans and build up new ones after a regime change, including the replacement of key staff within the municipality (Box 6.6), there is danger of a lack of sustainability. This has affected partnership management, as was explained above.
- The civil society wing of the city partnership was weakly organised and lacked institutionalisation, i.e. financial resources, a juridical position and proper infrastructure.

---

134   One respondent mentioned that the Cajamarca Mayor lacked vision and preferred to "take the German mayor to the birthday party of the Regional President rather than showing him the partnership activities and projects" (Interview NGO representative Cajamarca 1, March 16, 2007).

135   Interview official 1 Cajamarca Municipality, March 13, 2007.

THE CHALLENGE TO STRENGTHEN URBAN GOVERNANCE THROUGH NORTH-SOUTH CITY PARTNERSHIPS

> **Box 6.5** Politicians' views on city-to-city cooperation in the South
>
> - "International Cooperation has always existed in Villa El Salvador and has been very important, because it has not only been economic cooperation, but also technical exchange. And exchange is mutual, it means getting to know different places, countries, cultures, customs. And also that they learn about our reality, that means a lot to us. It is [a form of] cooperation that is much more human, more horizontal." *Mayor Jaime Zea, Villa El Salvador, February 2007.*
> - "León would not go forward or develop if it hadn't been for External Cooperation (…). Thanks to city partnerships we delivered houses, streets, sewerage. We could work on issues of environment and leadership capacity building." *Councillor Vielka Gutierrez, León, November 2005.*
> - "We have a gift, [the partnership] is a gift. I am not expecting the world to turn around because Alphen and Oudtshoorn have a twinning, but we can greatly benefit here and there." *Speaker Pierre Nel, Oudtshoorn, April 2006.*
> - "The city partnerships have a fundamental role in the development of León. In times of emergency but also in development. The municipal strategic plan is for example a product of External Cooperation." *Mayor Tránsito Téllez, León, November 2005.*
> - "Alphen supports us, like with performance management, this is very positive. We are a council in a rural district; we haven't got all the money. It takes a heavy weight from our tax payers to support us in that way. And eventually we will have a more efficient service delivery". *Councillor Pieter Luiters, Oudtshoorn, April 2006.*
> - "[The partnership] does not only bring cooperation for the city's development, linking with cities in better economic conditions also brings solidarity and exchange of culture, knowledge and friendship." *Councillor Luz Castro, VES, April 2007.*

Its position vis-à-vis the municipality in putting the partnership on the political agenda was therefore weak (Chapter 7).

- Contrary to the other cities of this study, there were no direct financial benefits for the municipality from the relations with Germany. Also, municipal exchanges are not taking place. Critics have argued that municipal staff and politicians are only interested in the opportunity to travel, especially since they have observed that civil society initiatives do involve missions to Germany.

While political support in the South may thus at first sight be obvious because of the very concrete economic and capacity benefits offered, the reality is often much more complex. Municipalities in the North have for example observed that political support expressed by partners in the South is lip service rather than real interest. Participants from Alphen perceived that councillors in Oudtshoorn showed very little interest in the joint project on Performance Management (Chapter 8). Also, when a group of Alphen students visited Oudtshoorn to work in a community project in 2007, councillors did not show up on site to demonstrate political support. Politicians in the South may also question the allocation of investments, which is often subject to donor decision-making. In León for example questions

Box 6.6 Characterising local government in the South

The cities in the South that are examined in this study show strong commonalities in characteristics that are typical for local government in the South (Chapter 1, 2) and that are mutually reinforcing: high political volatility and low administration capacity. This affects the role of municipalities in international city partnerships and shapes the political-organisational context in which municipal international cooperation takes place.

- **Regime change** Changes in political power after municipal elections often cause a drastic transformation in policies and plans, and also in the staff composition of the administration. This especially occurs in highly polarised countries, such as Nicaragua. It is not unusual that new Mayors replace a large part of staff of the previous administration. The turnover of officials is a threat to the administration's institutional memory and the continuation and sustainability of municipal planning and projects, including C2C activities and maintaining international contacts. City partnerships may be considered part of the legacy of the old regime, which may cause lack of political interest in the new government (e.g. Cajamarca).

- **Political turmoil** Political instability and internal politics may paralyse the decision-making capacity of municipal councils. This in turn may negatively affect administrative competence. In 2006 and 2007 the Municipality of Oudtshoorn went through a severe political and administrative crisis, marked by corruption, mismanagement, political turmoil, and personal fights. As a result, the decision-making powers of Council and the Municipal Manager were revoked and the organisation was placed under administration of Provincial Government. The activities with Alphen were therefore put on hold and it proved difficult to sustain the results of previous C2C projects.

- **Centralist decision-making** Decision-making power may be excessively concentrated in one person. In Latin America this is the Mayor, in South Africa it may be the Municipal Manager. A centralised power structure may slow down decision-making. Especially in Latin America, citizens traditionally see the Mayor as someone to solve their personal (financial) problems. Mayors may be more occupied with addressing citizens' needs than setting out visionary long-term strategies, not in the least to strengthen their electoral position.

- **Shortage of staff** The size of the local administration in the South is very small compared to Northern standards. For example: Utrecht and León are cities of comparable size in terms of inhabitants. However, the Municipality of Utrecht has around 4,000 staff, compared to 700 in León. The scarce positions in the South are allocated to either management tasks or tasks concerned with the implementation of projects, while policymaking staff – necessary for a long-term planning vision – is often lacking.

- **Administrative mismanagement and internal distrust** These are important factors that affect a healthy administrative work culture. The lack of job security causes a culture of fear, which may lead to decision-making based on strengthening the position of oneself rather than the interest of the municipality. In South African local government moreover, suspicious attitudes towards others with a different racial background are persistent. In the case of Oudtshoorn, this was further intensified by the attempts of the Municipal Manager to eliminate the entire – White – senior management staff based on accusations of fraud and non-performance. For about a year all three municipal departments were not managed properly and the uncertainty and hostile atmosphere that came with it, put much of the municipality's duties to a halt – including twinning projects.

- **Lack of competent staff** Officials in local governments may lack the necessary skills, knowledge and experience to properly fulfil their position. Staff are sometimes appointed on the merit of patronage relations rather than of their qualifications. Also, local governments seriously lack financial resources. Due to relatively low salary levels in public administration competent staff may be lost at the expense of the private sector. Frequent staff turnover caused by political change undermines consolidation of capacities. In South Africa it has been noted that due to 'affirmative action measures',[1] the appointing of staff is increasingly based on quota rather than on qualifications. This may lead to incompetent persons in key positions.[2]

- **Lack of information and knowledge sharing** Municipal departments often work in isolation, and little interdepartmental consultation and coordination takes place. The work culture is counterproductive to teamwork, communication and cooperation. Moreover, many administrations lack proper information systems and records of projects and policies, hampering continuity when staff turnover occurs. The abovementioned culture of fear may further cause a lack of openness and transparency and the willingness of staff to share information. C2C projects are affected by this: it may be difficult to link projects with Departments that do not express their capacity needs. Projects become isolated events due to lack of coordination, and a general disharmony among C2C activities may occur.

---

1   The traditional White staff of public administration – a legacy of Apartheid – should transform into a more mixed composition that represents all population groups proportionally. The Employment Equity Act promotes equal opportunity and fair treatment in employment, and "implements affirmative action measures to redress the disadvantages in employment experienced by designated groups". Designated group refers to black Africans, women or people with disabilities. Municipalities need to draft an employment equity plan, "to ensure their equitable representation in all occupational categories and levels in the workforce" (Employment Equity Act, 1998).

2   In Oudtshoorn, it was however also noted that while the influx of new staff poses capacity challenges, a new staff generation also brings a positive attitude towards the ongoing reform process of local government in South Africa. The traditional staff in Oudtshoorn, although skilled and experienced, holds a very conservative attitude towards change and learning. Among the new staff there is a lack of capacity but a greater willingness to reform and incorporate new legislation (Interview HR Manager Oudtshoorn Municipality, May 5, 2006).

were raised in council on the focus on León South East in the cooperation with Utrecht, as it excludes many other poor districts of León. Also in León, some councillors criticised the dependency of León on international assistance. As was noted in Box 6.4, critics from both North and South have argued that city partnerships, despite their perceived potential

Table 6.4 International funding to VES municipality 2004-2006 (US$)

	2004	2005	2006	Total
The Netherlands [Amstelveen municipality, VNG, Woongroep Holland, Province Noord Holland, Rotary Clubs]	98,831	287,675	232,410	618,916
Spain [Catalan Fund, Princedom of Asturias]		45,178	14,888	60,066
France [City of Rezé]	14,209	13,762	13,961	41,932
Total hermanamientos				720,914
Italy [Italian Peruvian Fund]			538,858	538,858
European Union [Propoli, Urbal]		16,468	67,278	83,746
United Nations [UNIFEM, UNICEF]		13,736	1,539	15,275
Total other sources				637,879
Total	**113,040**	**376,819**	**868,934**	**1,358,793**

Source: VES Municipality International Cooperation Department. Original figures in Peruvian Nuevos Soles. Exchange rate set at an average of 3.30 Soles = 1 US$.

for mutuality and horizontal exchange, may also lead to aid dependency of Southern counterparts. This is further discussed in Chapter 8.

The example of Cajamarca moreover illustrates that also in the South, political leaders have a crucial champion role in municipal partnerships. Since decision-making is traditionally centralised in local administrations in the South, the influence that Mayors exercise on a wide range of municipal issues is generally high. Partners in the North follow closely the municipal elections in their sister city, as the newly elected Mayor may make or break continuation of the partnership. In León as well as in VES, there have been Mayors in the past whose attitude towards international cooperation undermined the partnerships with Utrecht and Amstelveen: a general lack of interest, lack of vision on how IC may contribute to local development and institutional strengthening, poor management and leadership which causes administrative capacity (to implement projects and manage international cooperation) to deteriorate, etc. It demonstrates the vulnerability of city partnerships since they always operate in a political context. Local politics – and the orientation and capacities of the local administration – are therefore an important determinant to C2C partnership success or failure.

6.2.4 City partnerships as strategic alliances: Linking international cooperation to municipal development objectives?

Now that the capacity conditions for municipal international cooperation in the South have been reviewed, a number of issues are raised that relate to the main question of this section, i.e. the extent to which partner cities in the South employ international relations as a strategic tool to perform municipal responsibilities and meet development objectives. Do international cooperation activities correspond to existing municipal policy-making and planning? In addition to the organisational and political capacities and conditions discussed above, which instruments and mechanisms are in place to match international cooperation to local municipal (development) priorities? This last section deals with these questions. It

THE CHALLENGE TO STRENGTHEN URBAN GOVERNANCE THROUGH NORTH-SOUTH CITY PARTNERSHIPS

draws on the experiences of Villa El Salvador and León in particular, as the scope and extent of their international cooperation position imply a more full-fledged strategy than the rather anecdotal international activities of Oudtshoorn and Cajamarca. First, an overview of international funding sources of the municipalities is presented, further reflecting on the economic relevance of international cooperation for the two organisations. Then the extent to which international funding sources are harmonised through joint donor coordination and collaboration is reviewed. Finally, the section returns to the main question of how municipalities in the South can link international cooperation strategically to attain municipal development objectives.

Villa El Salvador maintains four formal municipal partnerships with cities in Europe. For the municipality, these *hermanamientos* are the principal form of international cooperation. Table 6.4 shows the main international funding sources in the years 2004-2006 which totalled US$1.36 million. The Netherlands are the largest contributor covering 46% of total international financial resources, investing more than US$ 600,000 in VES municipality. This is a considerable amount compared to the contribution of other sister cities from Santa Coloma de Gramenet ($60,000) and Rezé ($42,000). The economic importance of the *hermanamientos* for VES municipality is evident as the three European partner cities[136] together provide more than half of the international assistance. In addition to the city partnerships, VES municipality participates in various international (donor) programmes, including the EU (URB-al, PROPOLI[137]) and the United Nations (UNIFEM, UNICEF[138]). The Table further shows that while the partner municipalities contribute their own resources to some extent, e.g. in the case of Rezé that invested in the construction and equipment of youth homes, the largest amount is provided indirectly by external funds. As explained in 6.1, Amstelveen has been successful in attracting additional resources for VES. This also applies to Coloma de Gramenet that arranged additional funding from the regional Catalan Fund.

As Box 6.4 already showed, León municipality has a range of city partnerships. Municipal international cooperation has been vital for León's municipal management and public investments. On its website, it lists 18 direct international partners, 9 are partner cities. The United States account for three sister cities, Europe has six, of which two

---

136   The figures do not include the fourth partner city, Tübingen, as the partnership with VES was only formalised in September 2006.

137   URB-AL is a decentralised cooperation programme of the European Commission. It brings together local communities from Europe and Latin America in thematic networks on a range of urban issues. Participating local governments and civil society organisations mutually exchange experiences and best practices through e.g. seminars, and joint projects. Villa El Salvador participated in thematic network 9 on Local Finance and Participatory Budgeting, coordinated by Porto Alegre. URB-al facilitated an amount of US$16,624 in VES that was invested in a project to link participatory budgeting and economic development through inclusive public-private partnerships. PROPOLI (*'Programa de Lucha Contra la Pobreza en Lima Metropolitana'*) is a EU funded programme to fight poverty in ten Districts that are classified as marginal urban areas in Metropolitan Lima. Promoting local economic development and the empowerment of marginal groups, it implemented a number of projects with the Municipality of VES, investing a total of US$67,000 in 2005 and 2006. The projects concentrated on promoting business development, waste management, and youth.

138   UNIFEM ran a project on municipal development plans, participatory budgeting and gender. UNICEF organised a district workshop on working with adolescents.

CITIES AS PARTNERS

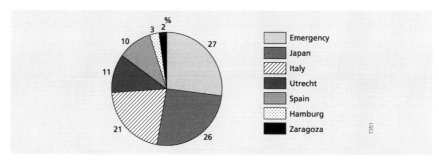

Figure 6.3 International funding to public investments León, 2007 (tot. 169 million Córdobas) - Source: PIA, 2007

from Spain.[139] Together with NGOs (e.g. Mercy Ship, Ecodes), they form the category of 'Decentralised Cooperation'. Other types of international partners that the Municipality of León distinguishes are 'Official Cooperation' i.e. direct funding from national donors, such as Japan and Spain, and 'Multilateral Cooperation', such as the European Union, who recently supported the construction of the municipality's website. Figure 6.3 provides an overview of the international sources that together account for 77% of public investments in León in 2007. First, the figure shows that only three sister cities directly contribute to municipal investments,[140] Utrecht leading with 11% of the total international contribution.[141] The remaining sister cities may be considered formal partners of León municipality, they cooperate however with civil society counterparts rather than the local administration. Their financial resources are therefore not administered by the municipality. Secondly, Official Cooperation with Spain, Japan and Italy represent a higher share than the city partnerships. Further international resources were provided via a national emergency fund that facilitated the construction of a Medical Centre for maternal and child health care. It can thus be concluded that while in Villa El Salvador the majority of funding was derived from sister

Table 6.5 Share of international cooperation in public investments León (1997-2002)

Year	Total public investments (C$)	Funding from External Cooperation (C$)	Share of External Cooperation (%)
1997	19,556,720	11,450,075	59
1998	25,883,716	18,769,103	73
1999	79,581,538	54,713,633	69
2000	116,736,829	66,624,481	57
2001	86,987,240	40,911,401	47
2002	57,225,628	41,422,762	72

Source: Department of Local Development, León Municipality

139   León's city partnerships are with Utrecht (Netherlands), Zaragoza (Spain), Hamburg (Germany), the Basque Country (Spain), Lund (Sweden), Salzburg (Austria), New Haven (USA), Oxford (UK), and the Italian region of Tuscany.

140   In 2007 Basque Country was the fourth partner city that contributed, the amount was however too insignificant to be included in the figure. Other funding sources in 2007 included the NGO Ecodes and Cesta.

141   Eight projects financed by Utrecht are administered. Zaragoza financed two projects, Hamburg twelve.

THE CHALLENGE TO STRENGTHEN URBAN GOVERNANCE THROUGH NORTH-SOUTH CITY PARTNERSHIPS

Table 6.6 Key characteristics of International Cooperation in León (2007) and Villa El Salvador (2006)

	León	Villa El Salvador
Number of sister cities	9	4
Annual municipal budget	$15,855,637[a]	$10,431,065[c]
Contribution from international cooperation	$9,406,314[b]	$896,119[d]
Share of IC in annual municipal budget	59%	8.6%
Approximate population	200,000	400,000
International municipal funding per capita	$ 47	$ 2

a) Year: 2007. Original figures in Nicaraguan Córdobas (1 US$=18 Córdoba). Source: Ejecución presupuestaria 2007, Alcaldía de León, Dirección Económica; b) Year: 2007. Source: Plan de Inversión Anual 2007, Alcaldía de León; c) Year: 2006. Original figures in Peruvian Nuevos Soles (1 US$=3.20 Soles). Source: Presupuesto Institucional de apertura 2006, Municipalidad de Villa El Salvador; d) Year: 2006. Source: VES Municipality International Cooperation Department.

cities contributions, in León this share accounts for 16% whereas the individual contributions by national donors are much higher. The outcome has a number of implications. Although it remains unambiguous that León is heavily dependent on international cooperation, the fact that the bulk is derived from national donors (official cooperation) challenges the perception that the sister cities of León can principally be accounted for the international financial support to León. The amounts that partner cities can make available are only a small component compared to these national programmes. Moreover, as national donors provide a major share of External Cooperation resources, the total of international funding may fluctuate considerably from year to year, depending on their participation. Indeed, in 2005, international funding accounted for 'only' 48% of public investments compared to 77% in 2007. The figures for the years 1997-2002 however reveal that also in the past the share of international funding has been within the range of 50 to 70% (Table 6.5), indicating a pattern of constant, significant international cooperation with León municipality.

How do León and Villa El Salvador compare with regard to international assistance to the municipalities' financial situation? To make a comparison it is necessary to calculate the contribution of international funding as share of the total municipal budget, as the difference in project investment administration between the two organisations does not allow a comparison on public investment level. Table 6.6 puts the two municipalities into perspective. It points out a striking difference: In 2007, 59% of León municipal budget was financed by International Cooperation, while in VES, in 2006 the contributions of international cooperation was 8.6% of the municipal budget. In VES, the financial role of international cooperation and in particular city partnerships is evident, albeit on a more modest scale compared to León. While León may be considered a success story with regard to attracting foreign assistance, it also shows its financial vulnerability and aid dependency, especially when compared to the more moderate share of international assistance in the municipal budget of Villa El Salvador: International municipal funding in León is almost US$50 per capita, against only US$2 in VES.

Municipal donor coordination?

León and Villa El Salvador are examples of municipal administrations that have established a large network of international partners that provide a considerable amount of funding to the municipal organisations. Given the wide variety of partners, ranging from bilateral municipal partners (sister cities) to international donor programmes and decentralised cooperation funded directly by national development programmes, the question rises to what extent these multifarious efforts are coordinated and international partners collaborate to deliver development assistance in a joint fashion. This would for example not only allow the pooling of funding, it would also facilitate León and Villa El Salvador to put forward a set of policy priorities to which international cooperation can be linked and coordinated thematically.

To some extent, international partners active in León try to coordinate their development efforts. León and its partner cities come together every two or three years in one of the cities that constitute León's partner city network. The most recent sister cities conference was held in Zaragoza in March 2007. Over 80 delegates from municipal and civil society wings of each city or region discussed the main challenges ahead for León. Such an event provides an opportunity to León Municipality to link the efforts of its international partners to existing municipal priorities to meet urban development objectives, especially since Leon has the PEDM in place which can serve as a guiding framework for coherent C2C cooperation. It was observed however, that León's representatives did not arrive at the conference with specific project proposals geared to the municipal development plan (Van de Ven, 2007). They therefore fell short of exercising ownership in setting out priorities. Moreover, donor coordination may be hampered by the fact that each partnership has different focus areas that have developed throughout the longstanding cooperation.[142] In addition, as was noted above, most partner cities do not liaise directly with the Municipality of León, but have their direct counterparts in León's civil society, which limits the coordinating role of the local administration. Finally, for the international partner cities of León, it may be difficult to influence national donor programmes, whose agendas are often rigid and strongly shaped by national development cooperation policies.

In Villa El Salvador, donors have to some extent coordinated their efforts and have worked together in various projects, albeit on an *ad hoc* basis. The European Union for example linked up to Amstelveen's environmental management project by financing a waste separation station in the framework of PROPOLI. VES also lobbied successfully for additional funding from the Italian Peruvian fund when it turned out that the funds from the Province of Noord-Holland proved insufficient to execute a sanitation water project. Similar to the tradition of sister cities conferences in the case of León, representatives from Amstelveen, Santa Caloma and Rezé came together for a three day conference in VES in 2004. Although the conference did result in a financial commitment from the three European cities for investments in security and environment, the great divergence in approach, objectives, and expectations of the different sister cities prevented real implementation of collective projects. The perspectives and expectations of the participants differed so much that no agreements could be made with regard to designing more concrete projects. While

---

142   Take for example the partners shown in Figure 6.3: Zaragoza's projects relate to environment and rain water drainage infrastructure, whereas Hamburg's projects range from tourism promoting and renewable energy to capacity building projects for youth and nurses, and the institutional strengthening of the municipality's CE Department. Japan donated resources for a project on road maintenance, Spain financed projects relating to promotion and restoration of cultural heritage sites and local tourism, and Italy's project concerned the construction of a blood donation centre.

THE CHALLENGE TO STRENGTHEN URBAN GOVERNANCE THROUGH NORTH-SOUTH CITY PARTNERSHIPS

Amstelveen emphasised the need for institutional strengthening, Santa Coloma and Rezé were focused on VES' civil society. Hence, also among sister cities, it proves difficult to organise coordinated action that go beyond the mere pooling of funding.

The cases of León and VES suggest that coordination of foreign assistance in a municipal context is difficult to achieve. It raises questions about the leadership role of the recipient municipality in setting out development priorities and the willingness of donors to adapt to these priorities in their projects in a demand-driven way. Strengthening donor policy coherence that is driven by local development needs and expressed in e.g. a municipal development plan could increase the effectiveness and coordination of individual C2C aid efforts.

Linking C2C cooperation to municipal policy and development objectives

Financial assistance of city-to-city cooperation is evident in León and Villa El Salvador, but how is it used to improve urban governance and the developmental role of the municipal organisations? To what extent do the partner cities in the South employ their international relations as a strategic tool to perform municipal competencies and meet development objectives? Drawing on the case of León in particular, a number of critical factors can be outlined that increase the potential of city-to-city cooperation making partner municipalities in the South more developmental.

A first condition relates in how far municipal planning and development objectives match with investment decisions made by international partners. Municipal Plans are an important tool in this respect. They provide a thematic framework for international cooperation. International Cooperation Departments should function as brokers between the municipality's demand, expressed in policies and preferences of municipal departments, and the 'supply' of international assistance. Hence an important underlying factor is the presence, role and capacity of International Cooperation Departments to facilitate, promote and sustain international relations as a full-fledged municipal responsibility.

It has been observed that León Municipality has had difficulties in reaping the benefits of international funding and using its international partner network in a strategic way. One underlying reason is the persistent lack of capacity of the CE Department. It has been noted that León does not always adequately report to Utrecht on the implementation of projects. It also falls short in putting forward new project proposals and it should take a more pro-active position vis-à-vis Utrecht (Van de Ven, 2007). Representatives of partner cities in León noted that the monthly meetings organised by CE to inform on municipal projects and development objectives were very frequently cancelled. Moreover, real strategies to be developed jointly and problems to be tackled were not discussed.[143] Donors agree that there is a need to cooperate more closely, but also stress that the municipality should take up a stronger role in facilitating donor coordination, and should specify its priorities for cooperation in a more pro-active manner.[144] At the same time partner cities have recognised that improving the performance of the Department is imperative; both Utrecht and Hamburg have implemented projects that aim to strengthen the CE Department.

The CE Department acknowledges its capacity needs and stresses that an attitude change is needed to get out of its dependency situation: "We would like to strengthen our

---

143   Interview city partnership representative 1, November 4, 2005.

144   Personal communication research dissemination workshop, León, July 9, 2008.

work, to be more proactive because often it is [donors] that identify [projects] and make proposals. This is not bad but we think that it is [our municipality] that should take the lead. (…) We need more capacity to propose [projects]. We have had difficulties, delays in reporting, even to execute projects when funding has arrived".[145] The CE Department is trying to redefine the role of the municipality in order to increase the effectiveness of international aid. This includes moving away from cooperation that is merely dealing with alleviating poverty and emergency relief, towards a focus on development.

Various donors emphasise that the Municipality insufficiently employs its international relations in a strategic way. One city partnership representative who had worked with the Municipality for over six years, remarks: "The municipality (…) lacks a development vision. The departments function too much in isolation, there is no general vision. CE needs to capitalise more on projects and increase the benefits of its resources. It needs to open its eyes more".[146] Better information management is needed to improve the role of the CE Department to act as broker between Departmental needs, and funding and capacity building opportunities. Another respondent questions the real impact of international cooperation and whether "this gold mine is used in a sustainable way".[147] The lack of strategy and constant political regime changes are mentioned as key factors. This view is underlined by a representative of the Association of Nicaraguan Municipalities (AMUNIC), who states that "the municipality of León does not have a modern vision of local governance. Therefore they do not reap the benefits as much as they could from the high amount of international aid".[148]

Of similar importance to the role of the recipient municipality in matching the organisation's needs to international funding opportunities is the position and attitude of donors. A second condition therefore deals with the role and position of donors in international cooperation. Do international partners take into account municipal objectives and existing needs and priorities, or are investments shaped by their own agenda? Do demand and supply of investments match?[149]

The AMUNIC representative observes a mismatch between the structure of the León administration and the design of international aid: "international projects become islands, with their own logic and dynamics, they don't integrate with the Municipality" which strongly reduces the resources' impact. The mismatch is embedded in problems of cultural differences, poor communication, and little interest to work together: "If there is no synergy, and the *hermamanientos* have to disburse their money, they make their own plans without communicating. They only need the signature of the Mayor. Harmonising their efforts with the municipality is rather uncommon." In order to increase the impact of international aid in León, donors thus also must redefine their way of working. Donors have the tendency to make their own choices (Van de Ven, 2005). Indeed, they specialise thematically, have a range of funding criteria that recipient partners need to meet, and may have a preference to

---

145   Interview Director CE Department, November 2, 2005.

146   Interview city partnership representative 2, November 8, 2005.

147   Interview local government expert León, November 8, 2005.

148   Interview AMUNIC representative, November 21, 2005.

149   As was discussed in Chapter 1, demand-driven cooperation is often more rhetoric than reality, especially when donors need to meet disbursement criteria set in the North. Donors have their own thematic preferences which influence agenda setting. Chapter 8 examines the implications for city-to-city cooperation.

THE CHALLENGE TO STRENGTHEN URBAN GOVERNANCE THROUGH NORTH-SOUTH CITY PARTNERSHIPS

work in a particular geographical area of the city. Although city partnership representatives agree there is room for improvement, they also observe that the development objectives and priorities of the municipality may not always be based on formal existing plans and strategies. They would rather reflect the personal preferences of individuals, in particular the Mayor, and many *hermanamientos* do not always identify with the preferences of local politicians.

A third issue is raised here. In addition to the capacity of the Municipality to strategically allocate international funding, and the policy coherence of donors' activities and municipal priorities, it is important to take into account the way municipal decision-making on the allocation of public investments is shaped. Municipal (strategic) development plans (the 'PIDC' in Villa El Salvador and the 'PEDM' in León) set out the strategies and thematic lines that the municipalities pursue and define objectives for various policy areas (Chapter 4, 5). As pointed out in Chapter 4, these plans function as governance instruments for the municipalities to play a developmental role in the area of their jurisdiction. Hence, in order to meet the objectives defined in municipal development plans, the decision-making on the allocation of municipal investments should first and foremost be based on municipal planning. This also applies to the municipal investments made possible by international cooperation.

León Municipality has been criticised for not applying the Municipal Development Plan as the agenda for cooperation. This can partly be ascribed to a more general trend that the PEDM has received little political interest in recent years and its purpose of strategic planning tool has been diminished and replaced by more *ad hoc* decision-making.[150] The poor performance of the Municipality of León in defining a carefully considered CE strategy is hence not only a problem of limited organisational capacity available in the CE department, but also -particularly − a political-institutional issue. If the Municipal Development Plan fails to function as a strategic planning instrument, it will therefore also be insufficiently employed to define a strategy for international cooperation.

Although it is risky to make any comparisons in this respect, it seems that Villa El Salvador is much better able to link the assistance provided by international cooperation with its development agenda set out in the PIDC. At least three observations support the argument:

1. Villa El Salvador has a relatively modest international portfolio to manage, compared to the numerous sister cities and donors León has to liaise with. According to a senior official of the CE Department in León, the day-to-day communication with donors, reporting on projects, meeting information requests from donors and receiving delegation missions is a heavy burden on the Departments capacity, which leaves very little time for strategy and planning.[151]
2. In Villa El Salvador, the municipal development plan PIDC has a significantly more powerful position as guiding framework to urban planning than the PEDM in León. It is strongly promoted and supported by politicians, backed up by national legislation − which is more commanding than in Nicaragua − and presented to donors as the principal agenda for cooperation. The PIDC has thus more institutional authority power than the PEDM in León, which also provides a stronger negotiating position for the

---

150   Personal communication local government expert León, July 9, 2008.

151   Interview with senior official CE Department, July 9, 2008.

municipality of Villa El Salvador vis-à-vis municipal Departments who want to see their projects financed by IC and vis-à-vis international counterparts in C2C agenda setting and decision-making.

3. In municipal projects in which Amstelveen has cooperated, the large majority of the investments were financed by Villa El Salvador itself. The contributions of Amstelveen accounted for only one-third of the total of €1,045,000 invested in the financial management and environmental projects that were executed jointly. The large share of own resources invested by VES, which is virtually absent in investment allocations in León, demonstrates the ownership of VES municipality in these projects and consequently the interest it has in putting these particular thematic priorities on the cooperation agenda.

6.3 Conclusions and discussion: issues in C2C partnership management and organisation

This Chapter has reviewed the organisational and political preconditions that local governments need to meet in order to engage successfully in C2C partnerships. The Chapter has taken the perspectives of both North and South. As partner cities in North and South operate in distinct organisational, financial and political contexts, the Chapter has dealt with two main questions that are relevant with regard to these respective contexts.

A first question was concerned with the position and role of local governments in the North to act as partners in development cooperation through C2C partnerships. The main difference between local governments and other, traditional, actors in international cooperation is that for local governments, development cooperation is not their *raison d'être*. Their existence is not dependent on it, nor are municipalities legally mandated to engage in C2C. Hence, municipal international cooperation is an entirely voluntary activity of local governments. The voluntary nature makes participation in C2C vulnerable and subject to political changes. As a result, municipalities that want to be engaged in North-South city-to-city cooperation and sustain their partnership activities need to meet a number of criteria, principally connected to aspects of 'interest and infrastructure', which have been reviewed extensively in 6.1:

- In the absence of a legal framework, political programmes and policies need to be in place to shape the scope of municipal international cooperation and define the objectives of C2C. These are found to range from expressing solidarity and awareness-raising to facilitating civil society initiatives and strengthening local governance and local democracy in the South.

- As Northern local governments are no development organisations, their staff do not automatically possess the necessary skills and expertise to engage in international cooperation with the South. In order to tap from the human capital available in municipal organisations, it is important to acknowledge the various, complementary key roles in C2C (political, decision-making/evaluative and executive). Moreover, it was found that participatory structures that enable broad consultation of staff within the local administration and appropriate selection mechanisms to identify staff to participate according to the merits of their skills, knowledge and experience, allow a sensible match of the human resources available in the North with the capacity and know-how needs in the South.

- The voluntary nature of C2C implies that municipalities generally have little financial resources available for their international activities. The extent to which municipalities are successful in attracting external funding is therefore another crucial factor. External funding generally exceeds partner cities' own contributions, and as such, local governments in the North cause a multiplier effect of funding channelled to partner cities. It implies that through C2C, various forms of national and even international funding sources become decentralised and targeted directly towards the local level in the South.
- The voluntary status of C2C as municipal responsibility makes partnership activities vulnerable, and partnership continuation depends much on the interest and will of politicians, and volunteer support of staff. The champion role of political leaders, mainly Mayors, have been found to be crucial in this respect. When C2C and the opportunity to participate in international exchanges and missions are promoted as human resource development instrument, support among staff may become intensified. Generally, however, political and staff support remain quite passive. C2C is tolerated and approved rather than being driven by pro-active involvement and political interest. As local governments are by definition political institutions with a cyclic nature, the extent to which C2C is practiced and supported financially and institutionally is always subject to regime changes and political volatility.

In the partner municipalities in the South, (political) 'interest and infrastructure' are also important conditions that need to be met for successful participation in C2C. However, an additional factor is critical in local governments in the South, which is intimately connected to the second question posed in this Chapter: to what extent to municipalities in the South employ their C2C partnerships as strategic instruments to meet municipal development and planning objectives?

With regard to organisational capacities, the existence of municipal International Cooperation Departments, that can facilitate, sustain and promote C2C as a full-fledged municipal responsibility and that can act as a broker to match the capacity and investments needs of the organisation, with the corresponding know-how and resources offered by partner cities, was found to be important. The infrastructure that such Departments can provide, including maintaining information systems, may also reduce the risk of partnerships becoming too dependent on one person – which is essential because of the cyclic nature of public institutions and the concomitant frequent staff turnover that is common practice in the South. Political interest in the South for C2C appears obvious given the economic and financial benefits that are often offered. However, the case of Cajamarca illustrates that the reality is much more complex, and political will may turn out to be lip service rather than real interest.

The analysis of the example of León also revealed that, despite the facts that: 1) the municipality is assisted enormously by international funding for its public investments, 2) political support for C2C is evident and 3) a full-fledged international cooperation Department is in place to manage IC, municipalities may not be very successful in reaping the full benefits of C2C in order to become more developmental. It proves difficult to guarantee that international projects are linked to development objectives set out in Municipal Development Plans. Such plans could form the basis of a clear, locally owned development intervention strategy and may provide a framework for municipal donor coordination and attract potential new donors. The example of León shows that the underlying reasons why

C2C is insufficiently linked to urgent issues in urban governance and the developmental role of local governments in the South are a matter of:

- Organisational capacity: lack of resources and skills to develop strategies and propose projects for cooperation, and a time-consuming abundance of international partners to liaise with
- Political interest: Personal preferences dominate over institutionally defined development objectives in political decision-making, including the allocation of international investments. This may be especially the case when political decision-making power is highly centralised
- Institutional concern: The weak authoritative power of the Municipal Development Plan as instrument for urban planning results in a lack of strategy and vision to allocate international cooperation funds for development planning.

Although the key factors for C2C partnership management and organisation appear to be fairly comparable in both North and South, their meaning and significance differ in both contexts. The difference in financial resources invested by the partner municipalities can be considered the main discrepancy – virtually all C2C activities are financed by the North. Also, the existence of international relations policies that provide a clear political-institutional mandate for IC are a predominantly Northern issue. In the South however, international cooperation is usually a more important municipal affair than in the North, given its significance as source of income for municipal investments and its central position it may claim in the organisation and staff allocation. Part of the differences can be explained by the distinct roles municipalities take up in North-South C2C partnerships, which can arguably be seen as 'donor' versus 'recipient' positions.

Chapter 8 will deal in greater detail with the debate whether partner cities in C2C can indeed be considered donors and recipients or whether they deserve a more equal status. First however, we will move beyond local institutions in the next Chapter and consider the various actors from private, public and civil spheres that are involved in city-to-city cooperation and together constitute urban C2C networks in partner cities.

7 Cooperation and conflict in municipal C2C partnership networks[152]

The previous Chapter discussed the role of local administrations in C2C cooperation. C2C is however not confined to local authority involvement. Municipal organisations do not operate on their own in North-South partnerships. As discussed before, a major characteristic of city partnerships, distinguishing them from other forms of decentralised cooperation, is the wide diversity of urban stakeholders engaged. These actors have various roles and responsibilities. Moreover, the interrelations among them are diverse. It is relevant to study these characteristics and explore in greater detail how municipal networks of C2C partners, actors and stakeholders are constructed and how they operate. This Chapter is related to research question 3 and as such seeks to provide answers to some of the following issues: Which actors are involved in partner cities in C2C? What are their roles and how are they related? How do local government and civil society actors cooperate in their C2C efforts? Are strategic alliances built for mutual benefit or may participation of certain actors in C2C partnerships also cause conflict and frustration within the partner cities?

Following the structure used in Chapter 6, the analysis in this Chapter will first focus on municipal partnership networks in the North, where most actors are engaged as 'development partners' to provide some form of resources (financial, know-how, people) in order to facilitate C2C projects in the partner city in the South. In particular, the interrelation between the local administration and the main civil society body engaged in the partnership will receive attention. This interrelation is in many cases based on mutual dependency. In the next section the various actors engaged in C2C in the South are examined, as well as their mutual relationships. Finally, in section 7.3, comparisons are made and conclusions are drawn with regard to actors and their networks in partner cities engaged in North-South city-to-city cooperation.

7.1 Municipal partnership networks in the North

Figures 7.1 through 7.4 display the actors and their interrelations of the four cities under study in the North. From the figures, six main categories of C2C actors can be distinguished. Section 7.1.1 discusses the various actors and roles, while 7.1.2 focuses on the (mutual) relations between the actors and the C2C partnership network they construct.[153]

---

152 Part of this Chapter has been published elsewhere in adapted version (Bontenbal & Van Lindert, 2008b).

153 The use of 'actors' and 'networks' in this Chapter has been inspired by social network analysis, which aims to connote complex sets and structures of social relationships between e.g. individuals or organisations. The social network approach is used here as a metaphor to differentiate between 'nodes' (C2C actors) and 'ties' (their relationships) rather than a tool for analysis.

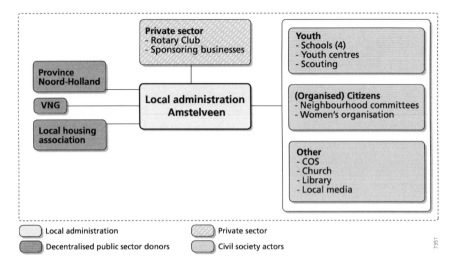

Figure 7.1 Municipal C2C network Amstelveen

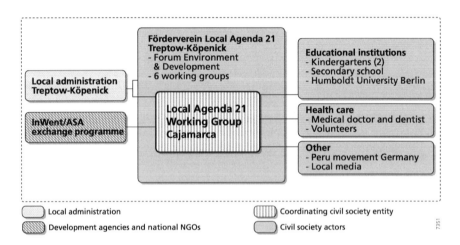

Figure 7.2 Municipal C2C network Cajamarca

7.1.1 The actor perspective: roles and responsibilities

A. The local administration

The local administration as an actor has been the focus of attention in Chapter 6. In all cases, local administrations are present in the partnership network, with a dominating position in the Dutch cities. In Utrecht and Alphen a parallel position of local administration and the coordinating civil society initiative is displayed. While in Amstelveen the latter is absent, it takes centre stage in Treptow-Köpenick where the local administration has a more peripheral position (7.1.2).

It should be noted here that in addition to the network that local administrations maintain in the framework of C2C partnerships, municipalities may have more extensive

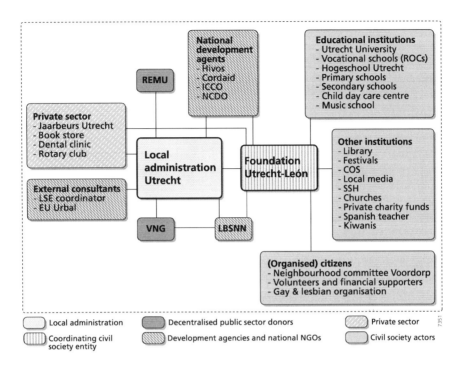

Figure 7.3 Municipal C2C network Utrecht

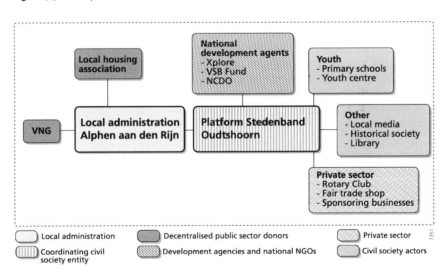

Figure 7.4 Municipal C2C network Alphen aan den Rijn

THE CHALLENGE TO STRENGTHEN URBAN GOVERNANCE THROUGH NORTH-SOUTH CITY PARTNERSHIPS

networks to implement other International Cooperation (IC) policies and objectives. In Utrecht for example the municipality offers subsidies to civil society initiatives and organisations active in international cooperation through two organisations – SISU[154] and COS. Also since 2006, Utrecht has worked with cities in countries of origin of the main migrant groups in Utrecht. Another development has been the establishment in 2005 of the network 'Utrecht International' with the Utrecht Chamber of Commerce, aiming to bring together businesses, institutions and organisations concerned with international issues, partly for economic motives such as attracting international investments.[155]

B. Coordinating civil society entity

Coordinating civil society entities (CCSEs) can be defined as non-governmental organisations that have been established to carry out activities in the framework of the C2C partnership. They have a distinctive position in the partnership network in the sense that their existence is based primarily on the partnership, while C2C in most of the cases is not a core issue for the other network actors. Coordinating entities are often funded by local administrations, to put into practice awareness-raising and development education. For other actors, it has a coordinating and facilitating role in the various collaborations and projects executed in the partner city. These interrelations between coordinating entity, local administration and civil society actors are further discussed in 7.1.2.

As Figure 7.1 shows, in Amstelveen there is no single CCSE. This used to be different in the past. In the first years of the partnership the objectives of awareness-raising and education of the Amstelveen population were performed by the regional Centre for Development Cooperation (COS). COS had received structural funding since the beginning of the 1990s for awareness-raising and providing general support to the various partnership activities between Amstelveen and Villa El Salvador. In 2003 however, the municipal council expressed its intention to draft a new international cooperation policy. One of the consequences of the policy was to halt the subsidies granted to COS. The reason was the lack of financial transparency and the lack of information COS delivered about achieved results. The organisation was found to be 'insufficiently effective and professional' (Amstelveens Nieuwsblad, 2004).

In Treptow-Köpenick, civil society takes a central position in the municipal C2C network, as shown in Figure 7.2. The coordinating entity is the Working Group Cajamarca, which is one of the six thematic subdivisions of the Local Agenda 21 association in the District (Chapter 5). The Working Group consists of about a dozen members of volunteers and representatives of schools, kindergartens, and the District administration. The group meets several times a year to discuss projects and prospective activities. It receives

---

154 The *Stichting Internationale Solidariteit Utrecht* (Foundation International Solidarity Utrecht), founded in 1979, has an advisory role towards the municipality on IC and manages financial resources available to civil society initiatives. Previously it fell under the administration's responsibility however together with COS it became independent in 2005.

155 Although it should not be neglected that IC network structures that do not directly relate to C2C partnerships still may be of influence to the latter – especially in the light of future interweaving of the various strands of IC policy making, which is the case for Amstelveen – these elements will not be discussed here in order to maintain clarity in the analysis.

modest funding through the general subsidies provided by the District administration to the LA21 association. The working group can be seen as a rather informal and loose structure; projects are formulated on an ad hoc basis; clear policies, annual work plans or monitoring and evaluation mechanisms for C2C partnership management are not properly defined, which somewhat hampers the transparency of the group, its activities and financial accountability. Rather, the working group provides a platform for citizens and volunteers who seek to be involved with Cajamarca and has an awareness-raising role towards the District administration and the inhabitants of Treptow-Köpenick. The group maintains a website and publishes newsletters on a regular basis.

In Utrecht, as explained in Chapter 5, initiatives from civil society to support León are channelled through the Foundation Utrecht-León. The foundation facilitates twinning of schools and child care centres in both cities, sets up development projects in León in the field of education, employment creation and culture, and aims at the organisational strengthening of Leonese NGOs and micro-finance schemes. Over the years it has developed into a professional local organisation, with a board of directors (5), an Advisory Committee, a remunerated Coordinator and two part-time staff, and a group of approximately 20 volunteers. Between 2001 and 2007, the Foundation employed a Dutch coordinator in León, who was then replaced by a Leonese representative. Objectives are defined annually, and revolve around four major activities:

1. Provide financial assistance to projects run by Leonese civil society organisations and groups to improve the living conditions of the Leonese population and the emancipation of marginal groups
2. Contribute to public participation, institutional development and capacity building in León
3. Raise awareness and educate citizens about León, Nicaragua, and North-South issues (Box 7.1)
4. Facilitate twinning contacts between organisations in Utrecht and León and promote the exchange of knowledge and culture.

The foundation is funded by the municipality to cover administration costs. In addition financial resources are generated through fundraising and donations from citizens, organisations and external funds, which resulted in a yearly amount of some €50,000 in recent years.

Civil society in Alphen aan den Rijn is represented in the partnership through the *Platform Stedenband Oudtshoorn*, which started in February 2003. The Platform, a foundation with five Board Members, has the objective to foster international contacts between citizens of both communities. Both cities underline these contacts as an important element of the twinning agreement. Platform activities include campaigning, awareness-raising, and providing education projects for schools. The Platform organises several meetings per year, reaching out to the various organisations involved or interested in the partnership and Oudtshoorn. The Chair of the Board who as a Municipal Councillor initiated contacts between Oudtshoorn and Alphen (Chapter 5) is the driving force behind the Platform. The role of the Platform is facilitating rather than maintaining all the civil contacts between the two communities. Says the Chairperson: "…If people are interested in contacts with Oudtshoorn, they have to do it themselves. I want to help them and show them the way and also knock on the door, but when the door opens they have to say what they want."[156] A database was created where organisations and civil initiatives can present themselves. They are posted on-line to reach out to counterparts in the partner city. The Platform has encouraged the establishment of a mirror organisation in Oudtshoorn. Although the activities of the Platform and their outreach to media and local organisations has been significant, the establishment of a coordinating civil society entity in Oudtshoorn has thus far not materialised, which has held back further twinning efforts (section 7.2).

C. Decentralised public sector

Various public institutions (government or semi-government) at sub-national level also participate in partnership activities. There are some similarities among the four cities. The role of *VNG* in the Netherlands has been discussed in Chapter 3 and on case level in Chapter 6. VNG-I has provided both financial resources and to a lesser extent technical capacity to the three Dutch cities. In Alphen and Amstelveen, *local housing associations* have been an actor in the partnership. In the latter, the association 'Woongroep Holland' has provided external funding to set up a municipal technical support office in Villa El Salvador to advise VES citizens on housing construction and gaining access to government housing subsidies and construction licenses. In Alphen the municipality has discussed the possibilities to get financial and technical assistance from the 'Wonen Centraal' association for a project in Oudtshoorn on social housing. Other decentralised public sector actors include the *Province* of Noord-Holland, to which the city of Amstelveen pertains. The Province has provided funding to install a water and sanitation system in one of the younger neighbourhoods of VES. In Utrecht, the local electricity company REMU facilitated the installation of solar energy panels in the rural development project in Clarisa Cárdenas outside León. In Treptow-Köpenick, no actors of this category are part of the C2C partnership network.

---

156   Interview Chairman CCSE Alphen, February 23, 2006.

D. National NGOs and external development agents

This category refers to actors that bring in external resources to the partnership network, either financial or know-how related. These include various national subsidy schemes aimed at decentralised development cooperation, and subcontracted technical project consultants. Examples of the former include NCDO, which has funded awareness-raising activities (Utrecht, Alphen). In Utrecht, various Dutch NGOs (MFOs)[157] have contributed to partnership activities (ICCO, Novib, Cordaid and Hivos). These MFOs also finance awareness-raising projects. Moreover they have contributed to existing projects through national funding schemes that double the investments made, such as KPA.[158] In Utrecht finally, an important actor is LBSNN, of which the majority of Dutch cities with a partner city in Nicaragua are a member (Chapter 3). LBSNN is both linked to the municipality through Utrecht's participation in VNG's LOGO South programme and to the Foundation Utrecht-León in a national network to strengthen civil society in Nicaragua, of which the MFO Hivos is also partner. Treptow-Köpenick has been able to invite a number of officials and students from Cajamarca on a three month professional environment-related internship in Germany, financed by the ASA programme.[159]

Utrecht municipality used external consultants, bringing in development expertise and know-how that were not available in the local administration. These include the LSE project coordinator (Chapter 6) and a transport consultant who managed the EU/URB-al financed bicycle promotion project.[160]

E. The private sector

The role of the private sector in C2C is limited. Business participation is often channelled through local charity wings of business associations such as Rotary clubs representing the business sector rather than local businesses themselves. In the Dutch cities, Rotary clubs have been active actors in C2C, donating money and running charity projects. Some individual businesses have been found that donate directly on an ad hoc basis (Alphen, Amstelveen, Utrecht). In Alphen, the local Fair Trade shop sells products made by a small-scale handicraft business in Oudtshoorn.

A recent project in the city partnership between Utrecht and León is the establishment of an international trade fair in León. Existing fairs within León's sister cities Utrecht and Zaragoza support feasibility studies for an international fair in León, which is envisaged to be built in León South East and is considered a potential catalyst to local entrepreneurship and economic development. The project will not only bring more private sector involvement to

---

157 10% of the national government budget for Dutch development cooperation is disbursed annually through the *medefinancieringsorganisaties* (MFOs) or co-financing organisations. These NGOs cooperate with local partner organisations in the South and include, amongst others, Oxfam/Novib and Cordaid.

158 The KPA programme for small-scale local activities managed by NCDO (in the case of Nicaragua by LBSNN) increases fundraising activities aimed at developing countries with a maximum contribution of 50% of the total amount, provided that awareness-raising activities are included.

159 The ASA programme is a network for 'learning in the field of development policy' and offers three month internships in Germany to young professionals and students from developing countries.

160 Utrecht and León have participated in the thematic URB-al programme on urban mobility. A project was launched by the Utrecht based International Bicycle Consultancy to promote and integrate the use of bicycles in urban transport systems.

the C2C partnership, but will also lead to new local public-private cooperation arrangements, also in Utrecht. The municipality and *Jaarbeurs*, the principal fair in the Netherlands, will deliver joint expertise, the former on organisational matters, the latter on developing and managing such a fair. This example stands out in the four cases as it has added the private sector as a more mature category in Utrecht's municipal C2C partnership network. Its participation is based on structural, technical capacity-oriented involvement rather than the anecdotal participation of businesses in the other cases, which mainly concerns fundraising.

F. Civil society actors

The category of civil society actors is the most diverse. In all cities, this group of actors is present, although there is divergence among the cases in terms of amount and diversity of participating institutions, organisations and citizens. Some trends can be detected. First, educational institutions and youth are well represented. Local schools have been found to participate in all four cities. These include primary and secondary schools, kindergartens, vocational schools and universities. There are also youth centres (Amstelveen, Alphen) and other institutions offering extracurricular activities (Amstelveen, Utrecht). These actors are involved through fundraising and awareness-raising activities, organised exchanges with the partner city through visits, emails, drawings and letters and educational activities to inform about the partner country and city. A second category of civil society actors are citizens, either individuals (project volunteers, sponsors) or organised groups. The latter may be neighbourhood committees (Amstelveen, Utrecht) or women's organisations (Amstelveen). Citizen groups run their own partnership projects and organise fundraising activities. Finally there is a large and highly diverse group of civil society actors that do not apply to the above. Churches, libraries, local COS chapters, private charity funds, and a historical society are just a few examples. These actors run projects or sponsor them, engage in exchanges with twinning partners in the South, or organise educational and awareness-raising activities.

7.1.2 The network perspective: interrelations between actors

Relationships according to function

The categories of actors described above are interlinked through a set of relations, that are visualised in the Figures 7.1-4. At least six types of relations can be distinguished, that are expressed in the role of actors and their respective position in C2C partnership networks.

1. Financial flows

Financial relations are diverse and the majority of flows are directed to the local administration and the CCSE. National subsidies and third party decentralised public institutions are the main providers of funding, and to some extent the private sector, albeit on a more ad-hoc and modest scale. Other financial flows of importance are resources provided by the local administration to the CCSE, or in the case of Amstelveen, directly to civil society actors. Local administration subsidises the coordinating entity and in return the CCSE gives expression to the municipal objective of awareness-raising and education. Fundraising activities are organised by civil society, which may be implemented in partnership projects managed by the CCSE.

2. *Raising awareness*

The link between local administration and the CCSE is evident in city partnership networks in the North. Awareness-raising is a political objective for the local administration and usually a *raison d'être* for CCSEs, especially when it is dependent on municipal funding. Awareness-raising relations however also occur between civil society and the CCSE, e.g. running parallel with civil society fundraising activities to facilitate CCSE partnership projects which also generate publicity. Vice versa, CCSEs offer awareness-raising products that may be used by civil society actors such as thematic teaching packages for primary schools, documentaries and other materials on the partner country and city.

3. *Delivery of know-how and expertise*

Similar to financial flows, these relations are mainly directed to the local administration and the CCSE. It has been mentioned above that decentralised public sector actors in addition to financial resources also offer technical expertise to assist with partnership projects. Local housing associations and VNG are examples. Furthermore the category of national donors and external agents is a clear example of actors delivering know-how and expertise, such as LBSNN and the external consultants contracted by Utrecht. There are very few flows from business and civil society sectors, although the participation of the *Jaarbeurs Utrecht* in the LSE projects seems promising in this respect.

4. *Creating support to sustain C2C partnerships*

Relationships between C2C actors may further function to create support among politicians, local administration staff and citizens alike. The awareness-raising responsibilities of CCSEs for example have been geared towards municipal council (e.g. Utrecht, Alphen) in order to inform local politicians and strengthen political support to sustain C2C partnerships. Civil society actors may furthermore generate publicity for CCSEs, e.g. when schools or churches organise fundraising activities that support the activities of the latter. The role of champions in these relationships is evident in all cities.

5. *Providing a window to developing countries and development cooperation*

In return to the delivery of financial resources and expertise, local administrations and CCSE offer a window to the developing world. They provide an opportunity to a wide range of national and local actors to be involved in development cooperation. Citizens find a way to express their global involvement. Schools find a destination for their annual fundraising fair, and churches for their collection of donations. The twinning of local institutions and establishing contacts with the South is facilitated by CCSEs. For the private sector and decentralised public sector actors, participation in city partnerships is a means to give expression to their *corporate social responsibility* agenda and public image building.

6. *Implementing projects and twinning/exchanges with the South*

Finally, relations are aimed at implementing C2C partnership projects. These relations may imply a joint project implementation by several actors, such as the above mentioned VNG-LBSNN-Hivos partnership with Dutch cities and their Nicaraguan counterparts. The ASA programme has facilitated North-South exchanges between Cajamarca and Germany. Civil society actors may implement development projects initiated by the CCSE in the partner city while CCSEs in return make twinning and exchange activities possible for civil society actors.

For example: schools participate in projects set up by CCSEs, or ask CCSEs to facilitate contacts with the partner city when they want to do a twinning project. In the case of Amstelveen, direct relations exist between the local administration and civil society in the implementation of projects. Interesting to mention here is the example of Alphen, where a relationship between CCSE and private sector consists for project implementation in which the CCSE arranges the sale of Oudtshoorn souvenirs in the local Fair Trade shop in Alphen aan den Rijn.

Relationships according to actors: Local administration – CCSE relations
The actor-network can further be typified as a set of relations according to actors. The focus of attention will be here on the linkages between local administration and coordinating civil society entities, as their dominance in the network has been clearly demonstrated.[161] The dual role of C2C partnerships was explained in Chapter 6. It refers to strengthening local democracy and governance in the South (performed by the local administration) and awareness-raising and development education in the North e.g. through promoting contacts between different population groups (under responsibility of civil society). This dichotomy partly explains the network structures and the relations between local administrations and civil society. The latter is in many cases represented by CCSEs. The relationships between local administrations and CCSEs in the cities in the North are discussed in more detail below.

Amstelveen
The current absence of a functioning CCSE in Amstelveen emerged when the local administration froze the subsidies to COS (the then CCSE) due to ineffective performance and lack of transparency regarding finances and results achieved. The local administration took over the role of COS in awareness-raising and publicity. As a consequence, partnership management and administration has become more centralised. The municipal organisation takes responsibility for all facets and objectives of the partnership. Until today partnership management and coordination is maintained as such, as the municipality has not found an appropriate civil society organisation to take up the responsibilities of awareness-raising and publicity. Instead, the subsidies that used to be allocated to COS are now managed internally in the local administration as part of the international cooperation budget.

As a result, the local administration takes up responsibilities that in the other cities are performed by civil society. For example, Utrecht municipality and the Utrecht-León Friendship Foundation coordinate while having well-defined, complementary responsibilities in which the latter is concerned with awareness-raising. In Amstelveen, however, it was the local administration that organised a festival to celebrate the tenth anniversary of the partnership with Villa El Salvador. On work visits to Peru, local government officials act as civil society bridge builders and ambassadors for Amstelveen civil society by paying visits to

---

161 It should be noted from the Figures that all relations include either the local administration or the CCSE, being the central actors in the network. There is one exception – the joint project implementation of VNG, LBSNN and Hivos in the management of Dutch Nicaraguan city partnerships, bringing together decentralised public institutions and national NGOs. Moreover, the Figures reveal that decentralised public sector actors cooperate with local administrations only and not directly with civil society.

schools and evaluating projects supported by Amstelveen organisations. They also report to the latter upon return.

The role of local administration in orchestrating citizen's actions has been criticised as not relating well with "…the way Dutch government normally deals with civil society initiatives: government facilitates and merely provides a framework for activities" (Amstelveens Weekblad, 2003). The perception has risen in both Amstelveen and Villa El Salvador that the partnership has become more technocratic and a local administrative affair, with an emphasis on technical exchanges, rather than a partnership owned by the community. There is a risk in the perception that civil society participation has become of minor importance, as it reduces public support and commitment. It has been noted that this has led to the withdrawal of at least one civil society group as actor in the partnership network.[162]

In both VES and Amstelveen, voices are raised to make the partnership more community driven. In the opinion of an Amstelveen Alderman, municipal IC policies have been too bureaucratic, managed in the rigid framework of VNG project criteria.[163] Instead, there is a need to stimulate civil society participation, and part of the municipal budget for C2C should be managed by civil society to implement projects, especially to foster youth exchanges. This would also increase public support for the partnership.

Treptow-Köpenick

The dichotomy of C2C partnerships of local governance strengthening vs. awareness-raising does not fully apply to Treptow-Köpenick, as the District administration is not directly engaged in North-South twinning with the partner municipality in Cajamarca. Rather, the partnership focuses on establishing contacts between the two communities, putting civil society centre stage while the administration takes up a rather modest role that is merely related to providing support to civil society initiatives. This is done in a direct and an indirect way.

Indirectly, the partnership with Cajamarca receives support as an element of the Local Agenda 21 process in Treptow-Köpenick. The administration has officially endorsed the LA21 process. The political mandate offered is illustrated by the fact that the operational costs of running the LA21 office are covered by the municipality. Since 2007, the District municipality has made financial resources available for the implementation of LA21 projects, part of which is allocated to the partnership with Cajamarca (Chapter 6). Thus, the embedding of the partnership in LA21 guarantees political and financial support from the local administration.

A direct relation between the CCSE and local administration exists as the responsible IC official is a member of the Cajamarca working group, which facilitates the exchange of information and coordination between the two actors. Also, work visits to Cajamarca have been a joint operation. The Mayor has furthermore funded a number of C2C activities on an ad hoc basis. However, it can be concluded that there is no structural funding provided to the partnership. Funding for LA21 projects is very limited and partnership projects compete with other LA21 projects and are dependent on external decision-making on budget allocation. Furthermore, the political mandate for the partnership is only expressed indirectly (the LA21 process) while there is no formal International Cooperation policy established.

---

162 Interview official 2 Amstelveen, May 22, 2007.

163 Interview Councillor Amstelveen, July 10, 2007.

Political support for the CCSE finally is highly dependent on the personal commitment of the Mayor. This was already discussed in Chapter 6.

The relationship between the CCSE and the local administration can be regarded as very informal. The work group has few accountability and transparency mechanisms such as publishing annual reports, work plans, and financial reporting. Also, there is no reporting on how partnership activities organised by the CCSE meet the objectives set out in the formal partnership agreement between the authorities of Treptow-Köpenick and Cajamarca. The culture of informality not only makes the partnership less visible towards the District administration, it also impedes transparency towards citizens of community money spent. Moreover, there is a risk that the personal agendas of individual working group members prevail over the collective partnership interest in the allocation of the budget.

With modest funding, lack of municipal international cooperation policy, vulnerable political support largely based on the champions role of the Mayor and weak reporting and control mechanisms, the partnership structure in Treptow-Köpenick can be regarded as little formalised. The implications will be further discussed in Chapter 8.

Utrecht

In Utrecht, the functional relations between the local authority and the Foundation Utrecht-León are multifarious, complex and professional. It is, as noted above, based on the reciprocal relationship in which local government financially supports and thus 'subcontracts' the CCSE to meet one of its international cooperation objectives; this is to inform the Utrecht population about developing countries and global poverty, and foster contacts between citizens in Utrecht and León. Almost 50% of the municipal budget for the partnership with León is dedicated to this objective, and the Foundation Utrecht-León receives some €60,000 annually from the municipality to cover administrative costs, e.g. the remuneration of staff and office expenses.

In addition to a financial relationship, the organisations also liaise to organise joint activities. When staff from León Municipality visit Utrecht for a technical exchange, an event with the Foundation is always included in the programme so that volunteers and interested citizens can meet the León representatives. Also, the Foundation and municipality have worked together on projects related to sports and youth in León South East. In general however, both organisations seek to keep a distinct geographic and thematic profile in the partner city – the municipality is concerned with the long-term urban expansion and technical capacity building project in León South East, and the Foundation has focused specifically on the indigenous quarter of Subtiava in León with small-scale community projects.

In Utrecht, the "Municipal Working Group Utrecht – León" is a city-wide consultation structure that brings together local administration and civil actors to coordinate and inform on all activities pursued. The working group meets twice a year and is presided by the Alderman of International Cooperation. In addition, the coordinator of the Foundation and responsible municipal official meet every other month to share information and discuss issues raised. It can thus be concluded that the financial and thematic relations between local administration and CCSE in Utrecht are to a large extent institutionalised and consolidated.

Box 7.2 Public relations instruments used in Northern cities to promote C2C

A range of public relations strategies are used by various actors in the municipal partnership network to generate publicity for C2C partnerships. They include:

- Municipal websites, which contain an international page (Utrecht, Amstelveen, Treptow-Köpenick), or refer to the partnership and the partner city (Alphen). Websites and (online) newsletters of civil society coordinating entities (Treptow-Köpenick, Alphen, Utrecht) are also used.
- Weblogs of Mayors and Aldermen involved in the partnership (Amstelveen, Utrecht, Alphen) report on partnership activities.
- Articles and interviews in various national and international journals. Especially Utrecht has been successful in this respect, with publications for Eurocities, in the Dutch public administration magazine *Binnenlands Bestuur*, and a Best Practice study for UN-Habitat.[1]
- Also the local media and civil society initiatives are used for public relations purposes. Alphen in particular has had a strong outreach to the community through the local media. A visit by an Alphen journalist and photographer to Oudtshoorn in 2004 resulted in a series of articles about Alphen's sister city in the local newspaper. In the other Northern cities there has been reporting on partnerships in the media as well.
- Anniversaries of partnerships can be considered ceremonial instruments that generate public awareness and give publicity to the partnership. Amstelveen and VES celebrated their 10th Anniversary in June 2007 with a festival held at the town square in Amstelveen. In 2008, Utrecht and León had their 25th Anniversary while Treptow-Köpenick and Cajamarca celebrated their 10th.
- Another tool is participation in local Fairs or meetings with an information stand, such as the Platform in Alphen at the Annual City Fair and the Working Group in Treptow-Köpenick at the welcome reception organised for the new Mayor (2007).

---

1   Published by UN-Habitat as the first Best Practice case study on city-to-city cooperation under the UN-Habitat Best Practices and Local Leadership Programme.

Alphen

With the establishment of an official *Platform* in 2003 to represent and channel civil initiatives with Oudtshoorn, Alphen municipality has followed a two track line with strengthening governance as a responsibility of the municipality while the social and civil initiatives are the responsibility of the Platform. The Platform functions independently, but it maintains strong ties with the administration. Says the chairman of the Platform: "the link administration-Platform is important (…). I need the municipality to drive the process further; otherwise it will become very difficult." The municipality supports the Platform financially mainly to cover operational costs – like in Utrecht – rather than financing partnership projects. Municipal funding is directly aimed at awareness-raising and education which should eventually create more initiatives from citizen groups in Alphen itself, as well

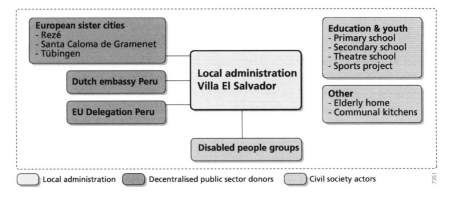

Figure 7.5 Municipal C2C network Villa El Salvador

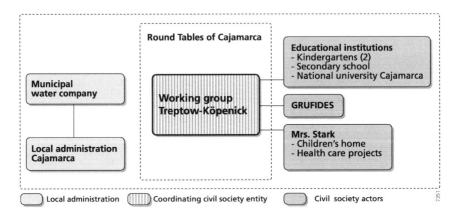

Figure 7.6 Municipal C2C network Treptow-Köpenick

as linkages with citizens in Oudtshoorn.[164] The financial support of the local government to the CCSE thus facilitates a mutually supportive role for Alphen citizens: while they are encouraged to set up partnership projects and activities, then once created, these activities could in return be supported and facilitated by the Platform.

Awareness-raising activities of the Platform are not aimed solely at civil society. Also, local political parties and municipal Council are targeted, e.g. by sending out newsletters (see Box 7.2). It is remarkable that while it is a formal municipal policy objective to raise international awareness among Alphen civil society, the latter approaches local politicians in return with the same motives. It can be regarded a consequence of the passive and weak political support for the partnership discussed in Chapter 6.

According to the Platform chairperson, the link with the municipality is not very intensive, rather it is meant to inform one another and on occasion taking joint action in delegation visits in Oudtshoorn or Alphen. An example is that the technical assistance organised by the Alphen administration can benefit from the Platform's network, for example in the case of

---

164   Interview Chairman CCSE Alphen, February 23, 2006.

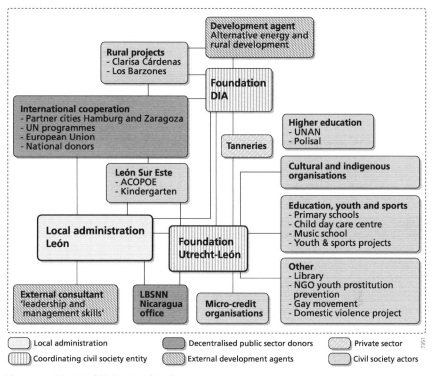

Figure 7.7 Municipal C2C network León

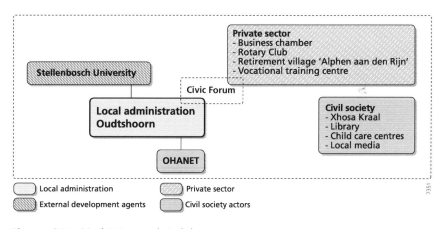

Figure 7.8 Municipal C2C network Oudtshoorn

"…health, HIV/AIDS. If this leads to [municipal] contacts with a hospital [in Alphen], why shouldn't the Platform be involved in that? It makes it only stronger".[165]

---

165 Interview Chairman CCSE Alphen. The link is intensified by the fact that one of the key staff engaged in the municipal partnership is also board member of the Platform.

THE CHALLENGE TO STRENGTHEN URBAN GOVERNANCE THROUGH NORTH-SOUTH CITY PARTNERSHIPS

7.2 Municipal partnership networks in the South

This second section considers how municipal C2C partnership networks are constructed in the South and which actors take up principal or peripheral roles. Figure 7.5 through 7.8 display the actors and their relationships in the four cities under study in the South. Six main categories of actors can be distilled from the Figures.

7.2.1 The actor perspective: roles and responsibilities

A. The local administration

The role of local administrations and what characterises them as partners in development has been discussed in-depth in the previous Chapter. From the Figures it becomes clear that local administrations do not always have a principal position in C2C partnerships. In the case of Cajamarca, as was noted above, civil society has a lead role in the partnership, whereas the local administration has a more marginal position. Also, Figure 7.6 demonstrates that there are no direct relationships between local administration and civil society in partnership management. This will be further discussed in 7.2.2. In the networks in Oudtshoorn and Villa El Salvador, the respective local governments have a key position. In León, this position is shared with the CCSE, which reveals that both local administration and civil society participation in C2C are well developed and mature.

B. Coordinating civil society entity

In Cajamarca and León, coordinating civil society entities play a key role in municipal C2C networks, whereas in Oudtshoorn and Villa El Salvador, CCSEs are absent.

Similar to its partner city Amstelveen, there is no CCSE active in VES to coordinate civil society initiatives and liaise with the local authority wing of the partnership. Its absence reflects the rather technocratic approach to C2C in this city link, in which the role of civil society is less significant, which has been already discussed above. Instead, VES municipality partly acts as a substitute to perform such duties. It has for example facilitated a project financed by Amstelveen to work with disabled persons and increase their employment opportunities. At the same time, Figure 7.5 demonstrates that lack of a CCSE causes other civil society initiatives to remain isolated activities, that have no direct relationship with other C2C actors.

Also in Oudtshoorn, a CCSE is not in place in the C2C network. Despite encouragement from Alphen and several initiatives taken in Oudtshoorn in the past, a mirror organisation to the civil Platform in Alphen was never sustained. When the twinning agreement was signed in 2002, first steps were taken to establish a *Gespreksforum* (consultative forum) in Oudtshoorn, representing local businesses, schools, churches, community organisations and local media. Two years later, Oudtshoorn Municipality approved the set-up of the Forum, with the objective to involve the community in the city partnership with Alphen. A chairman was appointed and ten sub-committees were formed, in which stakeholders could cooperate on different thematic issues, such as culture and history, education and youth, health and religion. A coordinator was assigned to each subcommittee. After several meetings however, the Forum lost momentum. It never materialised into an institutionalised organisation with appropriate organisational infrastructure and independent legal status. Lack of resources and a local champion to drive the process, and strict regulation and control exercised by the local administration which discouraged civil and business participation in the Forum, were underlying causes. This is further illustrated in 7.2.2. As a result local administration, together with the private sector, takes up a central position in Figure 7.8. Recently, these actors have tried to boost coordination of twinning activities to some extent through Oudtshoorn's Civic Forum, which may possibly replace the role of the *Gespreksforum* as CCSE in the near future (see 7.2.2.).

The entity that coordinates civil society initiatives in Cajamarca is the "Working Group C2C Partnership Treptow-Köpenick". It is a loosely defined group of about twenty volunteers and civil stakeholders, and has no legal or official status. The working group came into existence when Treptow-Köpenick sought to strengthen its partnership with Cajamarca by getting on board new cooperation partners after Luís Guerrero left office as Mayor of Cajamarca, and the municipal wing of the partnership slowly came to a halt. The group is led by three volunteers who have participated in technical exchanges in the German partner city in the past. It has a coordinating and liaising role for civil society participants in Germany and Cajamarca. Moreover, it aims to promote and mainstream the ideology of Local Agenda 21 on which the C2C partnership was founded in 1998, in all activities undertaken by civil society actors in the partnership. Although the working group takes up a central position in Figure 7.6, it should be noted that its influence in partnership affairs is rather weak. At the time of research, it was not connected to Cajamarca Municipality, falling short on bridging public and community spheres in the C2C network. Moreover, it was observed that the coordinating role of the Group was undermined, since the various civil society actors often directly liaise with their counterparts in Germany, rather than through the mechanism of the Working Group. For example, when a representative of the Humboldt University in Berlin visited the National University in Cajamarca to discuss cooperation opportunities, the Group was not informed on the visit.

Figure 7.7 finally shows the pivotal position of the CCSE Foundation Utrecht-León in the ample and diverse C2C partnership network in León. The Foundation acts as the local representation of the Friendship Foundation in Utrecht. In the past, a paid Dutch coordinator was stationed in León. Since 2006 the position has been assigned to a Leonese representative, who is employed by the Foundation for 24 hours per week. Utrecht-León is thus the only example in this study where CCSEs supersede their often amateurish character and where legal entities are in place with staff on the payroll and resources available for proper organisational infrastructure. The Foundation liaises with the counterpart in Utrecht and with local organisations to match local needs with the priorities and policies of the Friendship Foundation in Utrecht, and vice versa to link local partners and beneficiaries to fundraising activities in the Netherlands. Moreover, it facilitates communication between twinning partners, such as schools and child care centres in Utrecht and León. Also, it offers expertise to local organisations for proposal writing when they seek funding, and provides news and information on León to the Foundation in Utrecht for awareness-raising activities in the latter. In sum, it has a key role in supervising the implementation of projects funded by Utrecht civil society.

The position of the "Foundation DIA" in the Figure also deserves clarification. Whereas the Foundation Utrecht-León is linked to the Foundation in Utrecht, DIA acts as the local representative of the Municipality of Utrecht. It replaces a Dutch municipal official who was stationed permanently in León as local coordinator for Utrecht Municipality until 2005.

As coordinator between the local authorities of Utrecht and León, DIA manages funding, liaises with programme managers, facilitates inter-municipal communication, arranges and accompanies delegation visits from Utrecht officials and politicians and supervises project reporting. Moreover, it was responsible for the implementation of some projects funded by Utrecht Municipality that did not directly relate to the local administration, such as the integrated rural development projects in the areas of Clarisa Cárdenas and Los Barzones outside León, and a project to upgrade the local tanneries and strengthen the Cooperative of local tanners in León. Foundation DIA and Foundation Utrecht-León also cooperate and coordinate in the implementation of projects, for example when specific fundraising activities organised by civil society in Utrecht were allocated to projects in León Sur Este (the local kindergarten) or the tannery cooperative.

C. (Decentralised) public sector donors

Public sector donors are direct development cooperation partners of the local administration. In the Figures, only those donors are presented that are part of the specific C2C networks under study. For example, Chapter 6 showed that León has many international cooperation partners, however only donors that have worked with Utrecht in joint projects are represented. Hamburg, Zaragoza and Utrecht have collaborated in the past in various instances, also in the Utrecht-led León Sur Este project.[166] Moreover, UN-Habitat and UNDP sponsored programmes have linked with activities undertaken by Utrecht in cooperation with León municipality. The European Union has contributed to one of the rural development projects in which Utrecht participated. The local chapter of LBSNN in Nicaragua, officially called the "National Council of Dutch-Nicaraguan Municipal Partnerships" is also displayed as public sector donor in León's municipal C2C network. Financially sponsored by LBSNN in the Netherlands, it has a coordinating role in Nicaragua for partner municipalities of Dutch cities. In the past it has for example run exchange projects in which participating local governments exchanged knowledge on municipal cadastral systems and local revenue raising. Moreover, the National Council seeks to strengthen civil society organisations in Nicaraguan cities to foster local development through civil empowerment. As such it cooperates directly with the Foundation Utrecht-León, which acts as local counterpart in the network.[167] Chapter 6 already demonstrated that León and Villa El Salvador are two examples of cities with a wide and diverse international cooperation network. It also discussed VES' partner cities, that cooperate on joint municipal development projects with Amstelveen and VES municipality, albeit modestly and hesitantly. In addition, Figure 7.5 shows that the Dutch embassy and the European Union's Delegation in Peru are also included as partners in the network. The EU has for example sponsored en element of the environmental project facilitated by Amstelveen. The Dutch embassy does not participate financially or technically in joint efforts between Amstelveen and VES, rather it provides moral support and facilitates communication and delegation visits where necessary.

---

166 Other efforts of sister cities in collaborating with Utrecht in León Southeast have been aimed at infrastructure and micro-credit (Oxford), and sewerage systems (Basque Country).

167 The FODEL network ("Federation of organisations for local development") promotes local development in its 11 participating municipalities through the strengthening of local civil society organisations. Activities include organisational and institutional strengthening and exchange of best practices. Governance and public participation are key principles.

D. External development agents

External development agents take up similar roles as national NGOs and development agents in the networks in the North, by bringing in external resources to support municipal partnership projects. There are however differences between North and South in responsibilities and positions. First, in the examples of this study in which their presence has been identified (León and Oudtshoorn), external development agents were subcontracted and financed by the Northern cities and not by their partners in the South. Secondly, the development agents as such did not deliver additional financial resources, they rather provided local expertise and know-how that was needed for a successful implementation of C2C projects. Utrecht subcontracted a local consultant from Managua to build capacity in the fields of organisational skills, leadership and time management. Training sessions were organised for the Mayor, Directors and Head of Departments of León municipality. It was estimated that the costs to locally deliver this capacity building trajectory of six months equalled the costs of one mission from an Utrecht official.[168] Subcontracting local expertise is thus cost-efficient, and moreover there are no language and cultural barriers, so that a high level of mutual understanding can be achieved. The latter may be especially important when capacity building is aimed at organisational change, which at times may be a highly controversial exercise.

In the joint project of Alphen aan den Rijn and Oudtshoorn to implement a Performance Management System in the local administration of the latter, a third party from South Africa was subcontracted by Alphen to implement the project. Consultants from the School of Public Management and Planning of the University of Stellenbosch trained councillors and local government staff and guided the various steps to meet legal requirements on Municipal Performance Management in South Africa, to define performance indicators and evaluate progress. It is interesting to note that the role of Alphen, as the partner from the North, was largely confined to funding, while the content of the project – legislative knowledge and technical capacities – as well as the guidance in the learning process for implementation was delivered by the Stellenbosch consultants. The involvement of local external development partners in C2C cooperation caused a number of advantages, i.e. the spatial proximity which enables the meeting on a regular basis, a shared language and the specific knowledge of South Africa's legislation and public administration system.

E. The private sector

Similar to the North, the role of the private sector in municipal C2C networks in the South is relatively insignificant. Only in Oudtshoorn, the private sector is a well-represented actor, and this example demonstrates well the various ways in which the sector can be involved in C2C. First, the local Business Chamber was engaged in the city link with Alphen. After it proved unsuccessful to establish a CCSE in Oudtshoorn, the Business Chamber wanted to express its commitment to Alphen and demonstrate that Oudtshoorn was willing to make the partnership work, despite the negative experiences of the failing CCSE. In 2004 a group of six Chamber members visited Alphen. Although at first sight the visit appeared to be a trade mission, in which contacts between Dutch and South African businesses were established and trade opportunities were explored, the real objective of the visit was "…to touch base. To find out what was going on. At that time, the municipality and businesses

---

168   Interview LSE working group coordinator Utrecht, May 10, 2005.

Box 7.3 The "Alphen aan den Rijn" retirement village in Oudtshoorn: city twinning as marketing tool?

In the desert just outside Oudtshoorn, a new property development scheme is planned that may become one of the most visible and explicit reflections of the twinning relationship between Oudtshoorn and Alphen aan den Rijn. Signs on the roadside draw attention to the possibility to "find time to live" and "find time to breathe" in Alphen aan den Rijn. The advertisements do not refer to the partner city in the Netherlands, but to a "lifestyle village for 40 plus buyers" carrying the partner city's name. The gated community of over 6 hectares with health care facilities, shopping mall, hotel, sports club and church, has many references to the Dutch city. The names of the streets are in Dutch and refer to existing streets in Alphen, such as *Jaagpad* and *Cornelis de Vlamingstraat*. The artificial river crossing the Village is called *De Oude Rijn* and is connected to the *Zwammerdam* pond. The church is named after the Sionskerk in Alphen, and the medical centre will carry the name of the son of one of the Platform board members in Alphen. Even the community's logo is based on Alphen's coat of arms, although the star in the centre of the emblem has been replaced by ostrich feathers. The project developer claims that the Alphen aan den Rijn Village offers a "revival of Alphen in Oudtshoorn", given the shared history between the two cities (Chapter 5): "This is how we [Oudtshoorn] return historical value to the Netherlands (…) we give this area back to Alphen" (Algemeen Dagblad, 2007). Of more importance for the property developers are probably the commercial gains that are made by naming the Village after an exotic, far away place. Moreover, given the context of Dutch-South African relations, the Netherlands are associated with historical roots for many (white) South Africans, which may further appeal to the white, middle-class market segment at which the developers seem to aim. Is the Alphen retirement village a homage to Oudtshoorn's sister city or is its name employed merely as a marketing tool to attract potential buyers?

Figure 7.9 Find time…to live in Alphen aan den Rijn retirement village, Oudtshoorn

CITIES AS PARTNERS

[in Oudtshoorn] had a very bad relationship so the municipality was not informing us [the Business Chamber] on anything. All contacts had to go through the municipality. We wanted to see with our own eyes so we decided to go [to Alphen] ourselves".[169] Upon return, a number of events were organised to share experiences with business and community members. Also, the Chamber was able to link to the partnership with Alphen when it started a vocational training centre to train local unemployed youth in technical skills. In the summer of 2007, 41 students from Alphen spent several weeks in Oudtshoorn to work on community projects. They had raised €41,000 to upgrade the building in which the training centre was to be opened. Secondly, Oudtshoorn's Rotary club has been involved in partnership projects. It has coordinated the distribution of wheelchairs that were collected and donated by the Rotary in Alphen aan den Rijn, and it has acted as counterpart to the Alphen community to select beneficiaries in a project to donate playgrounds to primary schools. Hence, both the Business Chamber and the Rotary perform roles in the municipal partnership network that in other cities are assigned to CCSEs: the coordination of aid and the supervision of project implementation. It appears that the private sector in Oudtshoorn is the most reliable and stable cooperation partner for Alphen initiatives, since civil society coordination has been lacking to a large extent and the municipality has gone through a severe political and bureaucratic crisis (Chapter 6). Thirdly, the twinning with Alphen has inspired property developers to name a retirement village to be built in Oudtshoorn after the partner city in the Netherlands. As such, it appears that city twinning has been employed as a marketing tool to business initiatives (Box 7.3).

F. Civil society actors
Like in the cities in the North, the presence of civil society actors in municipal C2C partnership networks is diverse and frequent. They include educational institutes, organisations for disabled, elderly or indigenous people, youth groups, NGOs, CBOs and micro-credit schemes. Roughly, three types of civil society actors can be distinguished:
1. Beneficiaries – organisations or projects that are financially supported by the partner city in the North, such as the sports project in VES, the home for disabled children in Cajamarca and several child care centres in Oudtshoorn.
2. Twinning or exchange partners – actors that are involved in twinning activities with partner organisations in the North, e.g. schools and universities, the gay movement in León, and kindergartens in Cajamarca.
3. Non-governmental project partners – Rather than being beneficiaries of sponsored activities in the North, these actors have a role in the implementation of projects, e.g. the NGO OHANET in Oudtshoorn, counterpart in Alphen's HIV/AIDS project, and the NGO GRUFIDES[170] in Cajamarca which is an important source of information and counterpart to the Cajamarca Working Group in Treptow-Köpenick with regard to its lobby activities on sustainable mining in Peru.

The Figures show that various civil society actors have no direct relationship with other actors in the C2C network. This means they only have a direct twinning or beneficiary link with the partner city in the North and actually do not form part of the C2C network in their own municipality. This is especially the case in cities where a CCSE is lacking. It demonstrates

---

169 Interview Oudtshoorn Business Chamber member, April 25, 2006.

170 GRUFIDES – Grupo de formación e intervención para el desarrollo sostenible.

once more the role and relevance of CCSEs in collectively organising and coordinating civil society participation in C2C. Moreover, isolated actors in C2C networks may be a sign of weak coordination between the public, private and civil spheres in intra-municipal C2C cooperation. Indeed, it has been found that in some of the cities a persistent gap between these spheres keeps existing, undermining the potential for joint cooperation in C2C vis-à-vis the partner city. The next section will examine the extent to which network actors cooperate in partnership activities, and how lack of coordination and conflict among actors can be explained.

7.2.2 The network perspective: interrelations between actors

Which functional relationships can be detected between the various actors in municipal C2C networks in the South? The case of León reveals that many different and complex relationship structures may exist. The purpose of these linkages are partly inherent to the role of the actors discussed above and are therefore not considered in-depth here. Examples include the bilateral delivery of financial assistance (by public sector donors) or technical expertise (by external development agents) to local administrations, and the coordinating role of CCSEs in the implementation of civil society projects. In Chapter 6 the various international cooperation relations of local governments have already been reviewed extensively, as well as the extent to which local government donors coordinate their programmes and projects. Instead, a number of issues are discussed here that come to the forefront when analysing Figures 7.5-7.8. These are relevant to better understand how C2C networks function and to comprehend to what extent and in what way the coordination and cooperation of actors in joint C2C activities can and should be promoted.

A first issue relates to the potential of C2C actors to establish strategic alliances or relationships with other partners to sustain their efforts and meet their objectives. As was already demonstrated in Chapter 6 and section 7.1, local governments in the North are successful in attracting external funding for C2C activities and as such they generate a multiplier effect in the transfer of resources to the partner city. These efforts are however not confined to municipal and national partners in the North (see 7.1). In the partner cities in the South, Northern local governments are also actively engaged, often in close cooperation with their Southern partners, to attract additional funding and assistance. The previously mentioned financial contribution by the European Commission Delegation in Lima in a joint environmental project of Amstelveen and Villa El Salvador is an example, as well as the role of the various public sector donors and other partner cities in León that contribute to Utrecht-led projects in León (see 7.2.1). It has been found that especially the role of Northern municipal lobby has been important to build strategic alliances in the Southern cities between municipalities and donors. The importance of the leverage function to attract additional donors and funding has been stressed by e.g. the Mayors of Alphen aan den Rijn and Amstelveen. Moreover, cities in the North act as a quality label that Southern municipalities can put forward when they lobby to find new international cooperation partners. Amstelveen officials state that the fact that the Mayor of Villa El Salvador was able to demonstrate to have cooperated successfully with reliable and accountable partners such as European local governments, made it is easier for VES to approach larger supranational donor programmes including Cities Alliance, UCLG and the European Union.[171]

---

171   Interviews with various officials Amstelveen Municipality, July 5 & 10, 2007.

Secondly, the functional relationships that are linked to the role of actors in coordinating C2C activities and project implementation deserve some more attention here. Whereas CCSEs perform this role with respect to civil society wings of C2C partnerships, Chapter 6 demonstrated that local governments have a coordination position in relation to public sector donors that may be hampered by the limited capacity of the local administration to fulfil this role. When CCSEs are absent, civil society projects are sometimes implemented in isolation and may have little connection to wider C2C partnership processes, as is the case in Oudtshoorn. At the same time the example of Cajamarca shows that when C2C networks do contain a CCSE, coordination of civil society actors may still be weak. The majority of civil society actors in Cajamarca operate independently and directly with partners in Germany. An example is Mrs. Stark, a German lady with a wide fundraising network in her home country, who runs a home for disabled children in Cajamarca. The twinning relationships between the Anne Frank school in Treptow-Köpenick and the St. Vicente de Paúl school in Otuzco outside Cajamarca, as well as the contacts between the previously mentioned universities are bi-lateral and are not necessarily coordinated by the respective CCSEs. Comparing the case of Cajamarca with León, it becomes clear that the role and position of CCSEs in municipal C2C networks may vary drastically.

A third issue is whether municipal C2C networks are embedded in already existing city-wide consultation structures or whether they make use of such structures to strengthen the relationships among actors and employ them to meet joint C2C objectives. Oudtshoorn and Cajamarca provide some evidence to this question. In Oudtshoorn recent efforts have been made by the private sector in particular to establish a city-wide Civic Forum in which stakeholders from the public sector, civil society and businesses can meet. The Forum would go beyond existing forms of community participation in Oudtshoorn. Usually community participation is organised in geographical lines (through wards) and in sectoral lines of particular interest groups (e.g. the Businesses Forum and the Safety and Security Forum).[172] The Civic Forum provides a space where local government and civil society can interact, and municipal representatives are invited to Forum meetings. Although the Forum has been established recently and its potential to act as city-wide consultation structure remains yet to be demonstrated, the idea has been launched that the Forum might perform the role of mirror organisation of the *Platform* in Alphen and as such reactivate a coordinating mechanism in Oudtshoorn's C2C network. It would prevent the duplication of coordinating mechanisms, and twinning activities could be easily aligned with issues identified by the community through the Forum.

Cajamarca has known a tradition and culture of consultation and *concertation* (Chapter 4) that was instigated in the 1990s under Mayor Guerrero and became known as the Roundtables of Cajamarca (Box 7.4). As the partnership with Treptow-Köpenick was also a product of Guerrero's policy, linked to the city's Local Agenda 21 and participatory sustainable planning process through the Roundtables, it was by definition embedded in existing consultation structures. The Roundtables flourished as institutionally autonomous participation mechanisms through which shared political decision-making was facilitated and Cajamarca's reputation of the 'first ecological municipality of Peru' (Soberón, 1995) was promoted. In 2006 over a decade after the first thematic subdivisions were established, the Working Group Treptow-Köpenick formed the 7th thematic axis, and the C2C partnership

---

172   The various mechanisms are used for e.g. the consultation process of the annual IDP cycle (Chapter 4).

THE CHALLENGE TO STRENGTHEN URBAN GOVERNANCE THROUGH NORTH-SOUTH CITY PARTNERSHIPS

Box 7.4 The Roundtables of Cajamarca

The Roundtables of Cajamarca are a well-known example of urban governance structures in Peru which allow for shared decision-making and inclusive consultation of urban stakeholders in local sustainable development.[1] The Roundtables presented a unique model of a participatory approach to planning, one which defined sustainability and environmental protection as central objectives (Irigoyen & Machuca, 1997). During the 1990s, the system of Roundtables (*mesas de concertación*) put NGOs and civil society in a strong position with regard to political decision-making. Throughout the years, the Tables developed as key instrument to province-wide coordinated planning. The process started in 1992 when several NGOs in Cajamarca formed the "inter-institutional consortium for regional development" to work collectively on ecology and sustainability issues with local authorities. One of the first results of this Roundtable was the Provincial Development Plan, which was formalised by local government as official municipal development policy. At a later stage, the Roundtable was decentralised and each of the 12 urban Districts and 35 rural centres in the Province started its own Roundtable. It brought about an effective participation and consultation mechanism that was accessible to everyone. The Roundtables had six thematic subdivisions: urban environment; natural resources and agriculture; production and employment; cultural patrimony and tourism; education; and food, health and population. The municipality facilitated the process by providing technical assistance, and over 60 agreements between the municipality and the Roundtables guaranteed the legal institutionalisation of the latter. In the long-term, the Tables aimed to collectively draw up a Sustainable Development Plan for the region. Short-term activities were focused on the coordination of development initiatives and project formulation. On average more than 60 civil society and public institutions were engaged. In the heyday of the process (1995), 98 actors were counted (Soberón, 1995).

---

1   According to Soberón (1995, p. 77) the example of Cajamarca stands out for five reasons: recognition of the need of an integrated approach to planning, active citizen participation in the formulation and implementation of development planning, cooperation with local authorities, ecological vision and the perspective of sustainable development.

Roundtable was formalised in the Roundtable structure. The step was taken to increase the institutional authority of the Working Group. At the same time however, the Roundtable process had grown quite dormant. It had lost the momentum of the 1990s and more importantly, the new political regimes were not eager to continue the participatory and open approach to urban planning and political decision-making that Guerrero had initiated. With a weak institutional role today, the Roundtable system does not appear to provide the political mandate, technical infrastructure and institutional authority the Working Group sought to gain by embedding their activities in the former.[173]

---

173   It should be noted that as the consultation mechanisms in Cajamarca and Oudtshoorn discussed here were not properly in place during the time of research, they have been visualised in Figure 7.6 and 7.8 in dotted lines.

When comparing the Figures of the South, a final issue that emerges is that only in León a direct relationship exists between the local administration and the coordinating civil society entity. The link proves relevant to bridge the gap between local government and civil society, which is not only an important precondition to 'good' urban governance (Chapter 2), it is also a key relation to bring together the two wings on which C2C is generally based and thus to allow broad participation and consultation in municipalities on joint C2C activities. The absence of this relationship in Cajamarca, Villa El Salvador and Oudtshoorn suggest that instead of cooperation, there may also be conflict among C2C actors which undermines the performance of municipal C2C networks. The next paragraph examines this in more detail.

Coordination versus conflict among actors in municipal C2C networks

The examples of Oudtshoorn and Cajamarca are applied here to demonstrate that the relationships between local government and civil society in municipal C2C networks may be weak or absent, and may even be characterised as negative and inimical. The cases are interesting because they provide insight into the underlying causes of disconnection and exclusion in municipal C2C networks. The causes have been found to be very dissimilar.

As was observed above, Oudtshoorn entrepreneurs organised a visit to Alphen aan den Rijn as they felt excluded from partnership activities. Since the early days of the twinning agreement, Oudtshoorn Municipality has taken up a key role in partnership management. In the beginning it was agreed with Alphen that Oudtshoorn municipality would initiate and facilitate the establishment of the civil wing of the partnership, the *Gespreksforum*. As such, it provided the necessary infrastructure (use of computers and meeting rooms in town hall) and one of the councillors was appointed to lead and guide the process. In return, however, the Municipality requested that all civil society projects be approved by municipal council, exercising strong control over civil participation in the partnership. Alphen protested and attempted to convince Oudtshoorn Municipality that local government participation (technical exchanges financed by VNG) and civil society participation (direct twinning with organisations in the Alphen community) should function independently.[174] Until today however there has been a weak understanding of the distinction between these two forms of participation in Oudtshoorn. This has caused frustration, mistrust and resentment among all actors. When officials of Alphen municipality visit Oudtshoorn for technical exchanges, they are approached by CBOs and NGOs who seek funding for their civil projects. When community members in Oudtshoorn received *Platform* representatives from Alphen, they were warned by Oudtshoorn municipality that they had disturbed the international relations between the cities, because they had not officially involved the municipality. At the same time Oudtshoorn citizens feel left out in partnership affairs and perceive that it is only the municipality that benefits from cooperation with Alphen, when they read in the local media about the technical projects carried out with VNG subsidies. The private sector and community organisations stayed away from the *Gespreksforum* as they did not want to be controlled by the municipality in their activities with Alphen. The Municipality of Oudtshoorn demanded that all donations for the Oudtshoorn community be approved and administered by the local administration, and is not pleased to see that the Alphen community has

---

174   Source: Letter from the Mayor of Alphen aan den Rijn to the Municipal Manager of Oudtshoorn, March 4, 2005.

increasingly made use of alternative channels (such as the Rotary and the Business Chamber) to organise its C2C activities and find a destination for its fundraising activities.

The increased hostility in Oudtshoorn between the municipal and civil society wings in the partnership further deteriorated joint cooperation and coordination of C2C activities. As civil society was weakly organised, it was not able to take up a strong negotiation position towards the municipality and was therefore no longer informed about how the twinning with Alphen should be arranged and managed. Instead, civil participation imploded. Many other underlying reasons can be given for the fact that an independent mirror organisation to the Alphen platform never materialised: lack of infrastructure and resources, lack of leadership of local champions to drive the process, persistent social conflicts and racial segregation among interested parties that prevented cooperation and the drafting of a common agenda, lack of visibility and means of public relations, lack of a feeling of responsibility towards Alphen, and lack of a culture of volunteerism to be involved on a non-paid basis.

At the same time it appears that Oudtshoorn municipality has not learned its lessons from the past. Local politicians have argued that the civil C2C wings should be reactivated through ward structures instead of the Civic Forum.[175] The area of jurisdiction is divided into 12 wards. Citizens are represented by a ward committee, and each ward is represented in council by a ward councillor. The wards, as the level of government closest to citizens, are increasingly considered a key instrument in the developmental role of local government and participatory governance in South Africa. Critics argue however that civil participation organised through wards will become heavily politicised and as such local politics and municipal control will continue to exercise influence on community involvement in C2C affairs.

In Cajamarca, a similar gap between local administration and civil society in C2C involvement has been observed, although it is not caused by the aggressive approach to maintain a monopoly in partnership management and control exercised by the municipality, but the lack of local government interest to sustain a relationship with Treptow-Köpenick. It was shown in Chapter 6 that the poor political will in Cajamarca was an important factor of the absence of local government participation in partnership affairs with Germany. It has been found however that the lack of political interest has also undermined the position of civil society in the partnership and the coordination between municipal and civil C2C participation. At the same time, the vulnerable position of the working group has prevented the civil society wing from exercising strong influence to get the municipality involved again.

The decrease of political interest in partnership affairs in Cajamarca has already been explained in Chapter 6. The partnership, as well as the Local Agenda 21 process and the Roundtables were considered a legacy of the political term of office of Mayor Guerrero, and the following political regimes wanting to bring about political change, were not concerned with these issues. The twinning agreement between the German and Peruvian city however, was never terminated and the District administration in Treptow-Köpenick continued to express its interest in partnering with Cajamarca. The Mayoral visits in 2005 and 2008 to Cajamarca illustrate this. But neither the partner city nor the C2C working group in Cajamarca have been successful in increasing the involvement of Cajamarca Municipality.

---

175   Personal communication research dissemination workshop, Oudtshoorn, February 18, 2008.

According to several members of the working group in Cajamarca, the lack of political support for C2C activities is the main cause for the current weak performance of the C2C partnership.[176] They feel the municipality should take its political responsibility in respect of the existing twinning agreement. Political support would give the necessary authority and organisational infrastructure to the Working Group to take up a stronger role in partnership management. Working group members fear that the municipality would only become interested to engage more in the partnership if financial gains can be made or if it provides the opportunity to staff and politicians to travel.[177] Some argue the municipality feels resentment towards the Working Group since kindergarten teachers are invited to Treptow-Köpenick while politicians are not.

Overall it can be concluded that in Cajamarca coordination of C2C affairs between local government and civil society has been absent for several years now. By a lack of political support the Working Group is in a weak position, without an office, communication tools, remunerated staff, and resources to implement projects. At the same time, by its vulnerable organisation, the Group has only weak negotiating power, which hampers fruitful interaction with local government to stimulate participation of the latter.

7.3 Conclusions and discussion

This Chapter dealt with the actors involved in city-to-city cooperation, how these actors relate and how their relationships promote or hamper city-wide international cooperation efforts. In partner cities in North and South, C2C goes beyond the participation of local government, and includes actors from civil society, the private sector, public donors and development agencies.

Especially in the North the relationships of local governments with other C2C participants have been found to be ample and diverse. Coordinating civil society entities (CCSEs) are a central element of the municipal C2C partnership architecture. They have a unique position in the sense that their existence is based primarily on the C2C partnership, while the partnership in most of the cases is not a core issue for other participating actors, including local government. The coordinating entities are often funded by local administrations to put into practice the objective of awareness-raising and education. For other civil society actors involved in C2C partnerships, it has a coordinating and facilitating role in the various collaborations and projects executed in the partner city. The participation of the private sector in C2C activities can be regarded as very limited.

The awareness-raising role of CCSEs can be regarded relevant in the light of the literature discussed in Chapter 1, which put forward that public support is of crucial importance to sustain local government participation in C2C. It is beyond the scope of this research to measure the extent of public support for municipal international cooperation and to examine the linkages between awareness-raising, public support and partnership performance. It is appropriate however to reflect briefly on the issue here. In general it appears that the public is not very well informed on C2C partnerships and public involvement is based on passive rather than active support. In Amstelveen for example, the technocratic approach to C2C and the dominant position of technical exchanges and participation of local officials

---

176   Interviews with various working group members Cajamarca, March 12 & 16, 2007.

177   Interview NGO representative Cajamarca 1, March 16, 2007.

in partnership affairs may have resulted in a rather weak public support. The public festival that was organised to celebrate the 10th anniversary between VES and Amstelveen hardly attracted any visitors. On the other hand the Mayor never receives any complaint letters from citizens about the international partnerships of Amstelveen and the allocation of municipal resources to C2C. According to the Mayor, the public generally supports the partnership with Villa El Salvador, but no concrete actions emerge from that support, and citizens are indifferent towards C2C.[178]

Although the general tendency is thus a rather passive attitude of the community towards municipal participation in international cooperation, critical questions are sometimes raised. Criticism mostly revolves around the question whether tax payers' money should be spent on overseas missions. How do international partnerships advantage local communities? What are the costs of sending councillors and officials on trips abroad (the so-called junkets and jollies)? Should municipalities take up a role in development cooperation or is that something that should be confined to national government? At times, such opinions are articulated publicly, e.g. in the local media.[179]

Having reviewed and compared municipal C2C partnership networks, it can be concluded that various differences exist between the networks in North and South. It appears that in the examples discussed, the relationships within the Northern networks are more formalised and coordination between actors is more harmonised and crystallised. In the South, on the contrary, relationships are more informal, less obvious and visible, and not all actors are linked to the network. The inclusion of these isolated actors in the Figures is based on their direct cooperation with Northern counterparts rather than their coordination and liaison with other C2C actors in their own community. Network relationships in the North can be generally characterised as mutually supportive and complementary: actors benefit from each other's presence and participation in C2C. In the South however sometimes conflict instead of cooperation within partnership networks prevails. In several cases the gap between civil society and local government is especially evident.

The analysis further detected some of the underlying factors that determine the participation of actors beyond local government, in particular those of civil society. It became clear that if civil society in the South seeks to be more than beneficiaries of C2C projects and be actively involved actors rather than mere aid recipients, they need a certain level of institutionalisation. This includes the availability of some resources and the provision of organisational infrastructure. The case of Cajamarca also showed that political backing from local government for civil society involvement in C2C is important, although in the example of Oudtshoorn it was found that too much political and municipal involvement is only counterproductive. The relevance of resources and infrastructure is demonstrated in León, where the civil wing of the partnership with Utrecht is flourishing thanks to a strong organisational position of the CCSE. In Oudtshoorn it seems that the private sector (with sufficient resources and existing organisational infrastructure such as the Rotary and Business Chamber) has been more capable to perform the role of coordinating civil society entity than the forum that was initially set up for that reason. The case of Cajamarca shows

---

178   Interview Mayor of Amstelveen, July 5, 2007.

179   See, for example a column by J. Bos in the *Amstelveens Nieuwsblad* (May 7, 2003), and "Barrow dreig belasting terug te hou" in the Oudtshoorn newspaper *Die Hoorn* (February 23, 2007).

CITIES AS PARTNERS

that the very lack of resources and infrastructure is one of the key explanatory factors to the weak position of the Working Group.

Another implication deserves attention here. The fact that León is the only city in the South where civil society participation in the C2C partnership is really thriving, suggests that the capacity of civil society to participate is largely dependent on financial assistance from the North. The financial and technical support from both the Municipality and the Foundation in Utrecht, including remuneration of coordinators in León, are key to the strong position of the CCSEs in León. The important role of Amstelveen and Utrecht in attracting additional donors and external development partners to their respective partner municipalities illustrates also the influence that Northern partners exercise on the municipal C2C partnership networks and relationships in their partner cities in the South. It thus seems that in the South the potential of the range of actors and stakeholders to establish strategic alliances or relationships with other partners to sustain their efforts, depends to some extent on the role and position of the cities in the North.

This Chapter and the previous one have tried to provide a better understanding of how partnerships are organised in the partner cities, within local administrations as well as from a city-wide perspective. C2C partnerships are not only the international contacts of local authorities, but may consist of and be supported by entire local networks that may even have an international dimension. Chapter 6 and 7 have moreover demonstrated that various commonalities and differences exist between North and South with regard to (political) motives for cooperation, resources available, and participation of actors. How do these commonalities and differences influence cooperation *between* partner cities? In the next Chapter the analysis shifts from partner cities to the partnerships between them, and concentrates on the challenges inherent to North-South partnerships in a municipal context.

THE CHALLENGE TO STRENGTHEN URBAN GOVERNANCE THROUGH NORTH-SOUTH CITY PARTNERSHIPS

8   The partnership challenge[180]

As was pointed out in Chapter 1 there is a lack of knowledge on the conditions to good partnering for capacity development by local authorities. There is a need to understand how these partnerships can be used best to reach a maximum potential to improve the performance of participants and municipal organisations. This Chapter seeks to elucidate which conditions are of influence to the application of C2C partnerships as mechanisms for capacity development and knowledge exchange.

It has been assumed that if partnerships function successfully, they will be a more powerful instrument to achieve sustainable results in C2C. In the definition of success in C2C partnering, ownership, demand-driven cooperation and the sustainability of capacity building are important issues. Relevant in this respect is to try to understand whether city twinning can overcome some pitfalls of working in North-South aid relationships. These relationships are believed to be inherently unequal. Chapter 6 demonstrated that in municipal partnerships, such persistent (financial and technological) differences between North and South exist indeed. What are the implications of such asymmetries for working in partnerships? City twinning is often celebrated for its high level of mutuality with regard to learning benefits. But to what extent can mutuality exist in North-South relationships? Which challenges arise?

In this Chapter, rather than discussing the various project outcomes (which will receive more attention in the next Chapter), the focus is explicitly on the factors and conditions under which urban governance strengthening is pursued. The Chapter links to the literature reviewed in section 1.4 on various concepts and trends with regard to partnerships in international cooperation. It relates to research question 4, which is geared towards understanding the extent to which C2C partnerships function effectively as capacity development mechanism for urban governance strengthening. Five sub-themes are explored:

1. Ownership and decision-making power
2. Mechanisms for sustainable capacity development
3. Individual and organisational learning
4. Mutuality in C2C partnerships
5. The added value of the C2C partnership modality.

Evidence is presented from a survey held among local government staff who have participated in exchange missions and other partnership activities.[181] A number of case examples illustrate in more detail the implications of the general processes and dynamics presented.

---

180   Part of this Chapter has been published elsewhere in adapted version (Bontenbal, 2009a).

181   Surveyed local government staff are referred to in this Chapter as 'respondents' and 'participants'. No survey data was gathered in Cajamarca and Treptow-Köpenick, since municipal technical exchanges have not systematically taken place. For more details on survey design and output, see Annex I.

8.1 Setting the agenda: decision-making in partnership arrangements

A first partnership challenge that is examined relates to the question to what extent the processes of capacity development and the formulation of partnership projects are demand-driven. Demand-driven cooperation implies that it is based on existing needs and a desire to change and improve, and that the strategy for intervention to meet these needs is mainly designed and 'owned' by the 'recipient' partner. As the literature in Chapter 1 shows, demand-driven cooperation is believed to be more sustainable. It will generate better results that are embedded in existing organisational structures. Thus the process of agenda-setting and decision-making between the two cooperation partners in C2C partnerships is crucial, as it largely defines whether projects and programmes are based on ownership. Ownership means here that cooperation is tailored according to existing capacity, expressed needs and a locally owned strategy of the organisation in the South. This section explores this by comparing the opinions of participants in various C2C partnerships. In 8.1.1, two case studies shed further light on ownership and decision-making in city-to-city cooperation.

Comparing Utrecht-León, Amstelveen-Villa El Salvador and Alphen aan den Rijn-Oudtshoorn, it becomes clear that the extent to which ownership is claimed by the Southern partner cities in setting the agenda and defining the needs for cooperation differs considerably from case to case. Whereas respondents in the Dutch-Peruvian and Dutch-Nicaraguan partnerships indicated that ideas for cooperation are the result of coordination and consensus and mostly based on the needs identified by the partner cities in the South, the Dutch-South African example clearly shows that it is the North who sets the agenda for cooperation.[182]

Participants in Amstelveen and VES agreed that decision-making in the partnership was always done in coordination. Generally officials from VES put forward priorities, whereas Amstelveen assisted in translating ideas into formal project plans and realistic and measurable objectives. This complementary approach is further illustrated in 8.1.1. As a result, participants in VES felt comfortable with the way cooperation projects were tailored to the needs of the organisation. Respondents indicated that the thematic focus on environmental management and financial administration was relevant and useful, as the Municipal Development Plan defined a 'clean and green city' and a 'modern administration' that operates efficiently, as key priorities.

In León and Utrecht participants sensed also that the agenda for cooperation was based on dialogue and consensus building. As the León South East project is a long-term, integrated cooperation programme in which various Departments of both municipalities engage, the general lines of cooperation are drawn by the project manager of LSE in León and the coordinator of the LSE working group in Utrecht. They define needs and priorities, which form the basis of the content and objectives of exchange missions and the selection of participants from both cities. Some respondents in León, who had been involved on a long-term basis in the joint LSE project, observed that the delegation visits had become much more structured over the years, and that objectives and results to be achieved are defined more clearly today than in the past. Throughout the years the process of agenda

---

182   It should be noted that in each of the cases, respondents in North and South shared the same opinion, and their perception in this regard did not differ much. For example, in both Alphen and Oudtshoorn participants agreed that it is Alphen who has to a large extent defined the scope and priorities for cooperation.

setting for partnership activities has indeed become more formalised, e.g. through the use of Terms of References (ToRs) in exchange missions. ToRs are to be drawn up by León, which guarantees more ownership. This is further discussed in 8.2.

The example of Oudtshoorn and Alphen tells a very different story. In Oudtshoorn all respondents remarked that it was Alphen and VNG who took the initiative for exchanges and partnership projects. One participant stated that "everything was started in Alphen with support from VNG".[183] Also in Alphen it was observed that the ideas and initiatives for cooperation originated in the North. One participant declared: "The plans are made here. What is more, they are made by VNG. Everything is stipulated, and we have very little influence". The case is thus an example of little ownership in partnership cooperation for the Southern counterpart, while the parameters for cooperation (e.g. scope and objectives) are largely defined in the North, especially by the funding criteria of VNG subsidies. In 8.1.1 this is discussed in detail.

A danger to ownership and demand-driven cooperation is that some participants in the South (Oudtshoorn, León) stated that they became a partner in exchange missions and joint projects without having been properly informed on their role and responsibilities.[184] There lurks a danger when officials are imposed to engage rather than that participation is founded on a personal ambition to learn and to exchange knowledge: the latter offers more prospects with regard to the implementation of skills obtained and lessons learned into daily work and existing routines (cf. Johnson & Thomas, 2007).

In sum, it appears that partners generally seek to cooperate in a demand-driven way, although in reality there is always a tension between the 'demand' expressed by the recipient organisation and the 'supply' provided by the partner city, which more than often needs to operate within the parameters set by funding opportunities and its own (political) objectives. As an Utrecht official concludes: "In an ideal situation León defines its needs and we deliver expertise. But there is always a tension in this. We exercise control over finances, which eventually frames the scope of cooperation".

8.1.1 Two examples of ownership in agenda-setting and decision-making

A. Ownership in the South: Villa El Salvador – Amstelveen

Key persons and participants in the partnership and projects of Amstelveen and Villa El Salvador alike agreed that the input and initiative to develop projects on financial management and environment originated in Villa El Salvador. The environment project was put on the agenda by the current Mayor, Jaime Zea. Previously, under his wing as councillor, waste collection became a municipal service, which eventually resulted in a full-fledged Environmental Services Department in the local administration. The financial management

---

183   Moreover, one official observed that he "was sent to Alphen by the municipal manager on invitation of VNG". Others expressed that "…we have not taken any initiative to organise something here. The Netherlands are more serious than us when it comes to the implementation of the partnership agreement".

184   As an Oudtshoorn official said: "I was just invited but I was not informed why. They said, do you want to go to the Netherlands? Yes of course I want to go. But there was no preparation, no information. Only later we learned about the purpose of the visit."

project, which started in 2004 after a request of VES officials,[185] came right after the 2002 Peru legislation that put great pressure on municipalities to reform (Chapter 4). According to VES municipality, the project has assisted the organisation to comply with the newly assigned responsibilities. It was "…right on this moment, [that] Amstelveen came on board. While they initially did a project to provide equipment [for information technology], the new legal framework shaped the project, it became more of an institutional development project."

A strong advantage for ownership on the side of VES is the presence of the Municipal Development Plan (PIDC), which is seen, in the words of a VES official, as "the basis of all international cooperation projects of the municipality". This holds also true for the Institutional Development Plan (PDI) (Chapter 5). Respondents observed that these plans have been an important guiding framework for cooperation and shape future partnership activities. VES participants agreed that municipal priorities are reflected in the cooperation's focus.[186] The viewpoint of Amstelveen is in line with the opinion of VES that the ideas for project themes and activities originate with the latter. The perception of Amstelveen's role however is more prominent in the project formulation phase, translating the organisational needs and demands of VES into operational and suitable project parameters.[187]

In sum, institutional strengthening is largely based on the needs defined by VES, putting forward the umbrella project themes of environment and municipal finance. Also, on the project level, the agenda setting of specific project objectives and activities was largely driven by VES. Amstelveen's participation is seen as rather facilitating, taking more leadership in transforming ideas and needs into a functional project cycle.

B. In the back seat of the car: Oudtshoorn – Alphen aan den Rijn

Alphen aan den Rijn has participated in VNG sponsored C2C programmes since 1997, first under the GSO programme, later in the framework of LOGO South (Chapter 3). The municipal technical exchanges with Oudtshoorn rely heavily on the financial contribution of these programmes and according to the Mayor of Alphen the partnership would significantly slow down without VNG support.[188] The municipality fears the consequences of the tightening LOGO South criteria in their twinning arrangement. The Country Programme prescribes that social housing be a key focus area in cooperation between Dutch and South African municipalities. In contrast to other Dutch-South African agreements, the partnership between Alphen and Oudtshoorn does not primarily focus on social housing and would thus require a shift in approach and activities.[189] In the first place Alphen municipality may not

---

185 During the environment project, VES officials expressed their interest in learning about the financial organisation and management of the Dutch municipality.

186 It was observed that "…the initiative lies with us. We present a series of ideas, and they look which is the best. But it is always based on our needs". Another added: "[the Amstelveen officials] ask critical questions and we have discussions which strengthen our ideas".

187 An Amstelveen official explained: "Usually, we [Amstelveen] define the project objectives and expected output, perhaps due to a cultural difference; we are used to plan more ahead". A colleague confirmed: "The expressed needs are clear, we only help them to make it more concrete".

188 Interview Mayor of Alphen aan den Rijn, March 15, 2006.

189 Says an official: "LOGO South seems more restrictive. It may be an impoverishment to our twinning partnership."

have the capacity and willingness to take up social housing as twinning objective. The Dutch housing context differs greatly from the South African context. Dutch municipalities have no active role in social housing; rather it is the responsibility of social housing foundations that to a large extent work independently from the local administration. Housing projects would thus largely depend on the willingness of Alphen's social housing foundation to work with Oudtshoorn, which up till now remains uncertain. Secondly, the capacity and priorities of Oudtshoorn municipality towards social housing are disputed. Alphen municipality feels there is a lack of both human and financial capacity which will inhibit to obtain good results in a social housing programme. Indeed, a study by Van der Veen (2008) shows that Oudtshoorn's housing department is greatly understaffed, a functional housing policy is lacking, and the position of Director of Department became vacant in 2007. Moreover, although housing is one of the seven Key Focus Areas of the Integrated Development Plan (IDP, 2005), it has hitherto not been a real priority for the municipal council. Alphen municipality prefers to focus first on getting a proper administrative system in place, e.g. through the project to implement a Performance Management System (Chapter 9), before starting to work in a thematic field of which the priorities and structures are not (yet) crystallised: "If [social housing] is not supported politically in Oudtshoorn, we will need to invest much time and effort to take it further. (...) Before we enter with a new project such as social housing, could we please first assess where we are standing now?"[190]

The needs and priorities for cooperation expressed by Oudtshoorn are rather different from the key themes put forward by VNG. The South African municipality has indicated to prefer to gain more expertise in the fields of social development and local economic development. Boosting the local economy is considered a critical imperative to overcome poverty in the area and to foster local development. Social development is a fairly new responsibility under municipal law in South Africa and as such it is also included as a key area of the IDP. But the municipality does not have the necessary experience and knowledge within the organisation to develop policies and formulate projects on social issues: "Our budget is more geared towards physical infrastructure than to social issues. We need assistance in terms of social development, that may be one of the roles that Alphen can play. For example, maybe [Alphen] is more structured in terms of youth [development] and they can assist us with that".[191]

Nevertheless, since Alphen aan den Rijn is heavily dependent on VNG subsidies to organise technical exchange projects with Oudtshoorn, it proves difficult for Oudtshoorn to exercise ownership in setting the agenda for cooperation. It appears that Oudtshoorn is put in the back seat of the car and Alphen upfront, although it is VNG which is really behind the wheel. This implies that the greatest needs of the Oudtshoorn administration are possibly not attended to. C2C projects therefore run the risk that sustainable results are not achieved if they are not fully supported by Oudtshoorn in terms of political interest, organisational capacity and development priorities.

---

190   Interview official 1 Alphen, February 23, 2006.
191   Interview official 1 Oudtshoorn, May 16, 2006.

THE CHALLENGE TO STRENGTHEN URBAN GOVERNANCE THROUGH NORTH-SOUTH CITY PARTNERSHIPS

Box 8.1 Typology of exchange and learning mechanisms in C2C partnerships

Based on the experiences of the cities under study, a typology of exchange and learning mechanisms in C2C partnerships is presented here. This Chapter refers to 'missions' or '(delegation) visits' when local government staff and representatives visit the partner city with the purpose to work collectively on partnership projects and to exchange municipal expertise with staff in the partner administration. Generally, delegations consist of two to six members, and the majority of visits have a duration of two weeks. Visits take place to both cities.[1] What activities take place during missions?

1. **Peer-to-peer exchange.** Participants liaise with counterparts on a colleague-to-colleague basis and exchange information on the subject of interest, e.g. housing, urban planning, environment, solid waste management, human resources, municipal management and financial administration. This type of exchange is usually organised in the offices of local administrations (sharing and gaining 'on-the-job' experience).

2. **Meetings and workshops.** Group sessions are held, in particular when project formulation, monitoring and evaluation are conducted. Delegation members and their counterparts hold presentations and discuss jointly the issues at stake. Also, missions are frequently wrapped up with a presentation to council or to other staff to share conclusions.

3. **Field visits to places and organisations of thematic interest.** Examples include visits to health clinics and municipal HIV/AIDS projects in Oudtshoorn and the Municipal Health Services in Alphen in the framework of a formulated HIV/AIDS project; visits in León to the León South East expansion area, to meet with neighbourhood organisations and inhabitants, and to study infrastructure, housing and social services. In Utrecht León officials have visited the Utrecht urban expansion area *Leidsche Rijn* (Chapter 5). In Amstelveen waste recycling companies were visited in the framework of the environmental project.

4. **Attending conferences and other events organised by third parties.** Some Oudtshoorn officials have participated in national conferences organised by VNG and SALGA[2] in the framework of LOGO South. These events, which took place in South Africa, brought together officials from Dutch and South African municipalities, thus allowing not only for North-South exchange and interaction, but also for the dissemination and sharing of municipal practice among South African municipalities (South-South exchange).

5. **Training courses.** Under VNG's GSO programme, various municipal training programmes were organised in the Netherlands. These MMTPs (Chapter 3) involved group training for local government staff in the South. For South African

---

1   In the example of Amstelveen and VES, in recent years one work visit was paid to Amstelveen by VES officials, and one visit to VES by Amstelveen officials took place annually. Utrecht and Alphen officials tend to visit the partner city more frequently than vice versa. A visit by León municipal representatives to Utrecht occurs once a year.

2   South African Local Government Association.

officials, including participants from Oudtshoorn, e.g. training courses were organised on Integrated Development Planning. External consultants have also provided training courses to local government staff in the South, e.g. the PMS project in Oudtshoorn and organisational skills development in León (Chapter 7).

8.2 Designing the mechanisms for exchange and interaction: sustaining partnership efforts and results

This section examines the main mechanisms for exchange and interaction in C2C partnerships and how participation of local government staff is organised. It explores a second challenge in C2C partnering, i.e. the extent to which the design of capacity building and exchange activities is based on a process approach which includes existing knowledge, capacity and practice. The literature in Chapter 1 suggested that the long-standing relationships that C2C partnerships generally intend to be, are an important success factor to generating sustainable results. Hence, the various sub-themes reviewed in this section all reflect on the question how partnership efforts of city-to-city cooperation may be sustained, so that capacity development and knowledge exchange can induce real change. The main mechanisms for exchange and interaction of municipal officials and politicians in C2C partnerships are summarised in Box 8.1. After a general analysis of findings two examples of regarding capacity as a process are discussed in more detail, in 8.2.1. In 8.2.2 finally, a number of instruments used in C2C partnerships to sustain cooperation efforts are reviewed and compared.

At least two conditions are relevant in how sustainability and continuity in C2C partnerships can be understood and promoted. These conditions are linked to the findings from the literature review in Chapter 1: First, it was concluded that due to the volatile nature of local politics and municipal organisations, especially in the South, there is a danger in C2C that staff is substituted, which may interrupt relationships. Staff turnover may result in the loss of skills and knowledge that were acquired through capacity development in the framework of C2C. A first issue relating to seeing capacity development as a process concerns therefore the importance to have continuity in the composition of the project working groups and exchange mission participants. A second critical success factor that was identified is the potential of C2C to build sustainable relations between partner organisations and their staff, and the long-term character of these contacts, based on the principles of friendship and trust. In how far do these conditions apply to the cities under study and how do they affect sustainability and continuity of partnership affairs?

Relating to the first issue, although literature suggests that staff turnover is high in public administration in the South, the survey findings do not support this. Whereas respondents in the cities in the North had been employed in the municipality for 10.5 years on average, their counterparts in the South had been working for 11.5 years on average in their respective administrations.[192] Both figures imply that C2C participants maintain rather

---

[192] The majority (20 respondents or 56%) had worked between 4 and 7 years in the local administration at the time of research, 6 respondents between 8 and 10 years, 5 between 11 and 20 years and 5 had worked for more than 20 years in the organisation.

THE CHALLENGE TO STRENGTHEN URBAN GOVERNANCE THROUGH NORTH-SOUTH CITY PARTNERSHIPS

constant positions in local authorities, and the findings do not point at high risks of losing acquired skills and knowledge after participation in partnership activities.[193]

An ongoing discussion is whether continuity is guaranteed by engaging a wide variety of participants, which generates broad support among staff and allows for a greater diffusion of knowledge within the organisation, or rather by investing in a limited number of key participants who engage on a long-term basis, with the corresponding benefits of potential trust building, consolidation of knowledge, and building experience in working with partners and the local context of the partner city.[194] Local administration staff are confronted with this dilemma, and they generally respond to it in diverse ways. In Utrecht and León there is generally a broad participation of staff. One respondent in Utrecht mentioned that recently there has been more diversity of Utrecht staff participating in exchanges than several years ago, although participation is generally confined to members of the LSE working group. Staff selection depends on the expertise and capacities of officials and how these correspond with the contents and thematic focus of particular technical exchanges. It was noted that such an approach prevents participation of staff that is merely based on the desire to travel. In Amstelveen, a relatively fixed group of staff has been engaged in the projects carried out in the last years (see 8.2.1). This brought continuity in the projects. In the partner city in Peru however, although several officials were engaged on a more permanent basis, the Mayor sought to engage as much key staff as possible in technical exchange missions.[195] Respondents in other cities also acknowledge the value of providing exposure and learning opportunities to a wide range of people, so that the partnership is owned by the entire organisation and not just by a number of individuals.

With respect to the second issue brought forward above, continuity is – besides staff retention – also expressed in the ongoing contacts that are maintained between the two organisations and their staff *in-between* visits. It was found that very little long-distance exchange takes place (e.g. by email or telephone) and cooperation and interaction is mainly confined to periods when one of the partners goes on mission to the partner city. The large majority of respondents do not keep in touch upon return, neither on a personal basis nor for professional or technical purposes. Reasons that are mentioned include: participants are absorbed by other responsibilities and daily work after missions, the use of email is not practiced by everyone or emails are not responded to, and language barriers prevent partners to interact directly without the help of an interpreter. In the case of VES-Amstelveen for example, all contacts are maintained between the international cooperation coordinators of the respective municipalities. In sum, long-term direct contacts between officials and politicians with counterparts in the sister city are scarce. The friendship that is often emphasised in partnership relations should not thus be considered as an aggregate of

---

193 It should be noted here that there may be a strong bias in the findings, since the selection process of survey respondents may have excluded staff who no longer work in the municipality. Although it was attempted to also include former staff in the survey, this was not always possible due to the difficult access to this group of respondents.

194 The survey reveals that staff in the North participate on average 3 times in exchange missions, against an average of 2 times of staff in the Southern municipalities.

195 One VES respondent noted: "The Mayor wants broad participation. For each mission to Amstelveen, he selects different participants. This is good, because many different people benefit in this way and get the opportunity to be exposed to [the practice and experiences of] Amstelveen Municipality".

individual relations, but as a rather symbolical connection between two institutions or cities. In reality the actual contacts are fostered and maintained by professionals (partnership coordinators, liaison officers) who are officially mandated to do so. The risk of a lack of maintaining contacts in-between missions is, that visits become rather isolated one-time events, and if monitoring is not exercised properly, progress may be lost and subsequent missions may not build on the findings and results of previous visits. As a result, the process approach to capacity building may be undermined and the momentum that long-term partnership projects seek to have may never be reached.

Now that several underlying conditions for sustainable partnership mechanisms have been discussed, the next paragraph turns to a number of examples of how sustainability and continuity is promoted or hampered in partnerships.

8.2.1 Two examples of 'capacity as a process'

A. The case of Amstelveen-Villa El Salvador
In Amstelveen's view the financial management project proved more successful than the environment project. One reason was the high turnover of participants in the latter. In VES, three out of four officials, including the Head of the Environmental Services Department, were replaced during the project. The two officials in Amstelveen only became involved when the project was already up and running. They considered it a disadvantage not having been able to participate in the project formulation phase: "This made it difficult to understand what our exact role was. When goals are jointly formulated, it is easier to monitor later on and ask the right questions."[196]

Seeing capacity as a process also implies that capacity development builds on existing knowledge, resources and practice. Two examples, one positive and one negative, are used here to illustrate. When the environment project took off, the idea to introduce the *Bono Verde* system had already been raised in VES. The *Bono Verde* is an incentive system that encourages citizens to separate their waste, and was implemented with assistance from Amstelveen (see Chapter 9). At first, the *Bono Verde* concept appeared illogical to the Amstelveen officials.[197] Still, Amstelveen took the role of assisting in developing the existing plans rather than introducing new ideas or approaches.[198] An example of unsustainability proved to be the donation of a water basin by Amstelveen in an earlier environment project (2001-2003) to recycle and store waste water for irrigation. When the basin was implemented, there was no operational plan in place. The basin was not guarded and citizens tapped the waste water for personal use. The water had to be chlorinated to prevent the spread of diseases and a permanent guard had to be hired.[199] Rather than embedding the project in existing capacity and structure to build upon, the water basin only resulted in higher, unanticipated operational costs for VES municipality. These examples demonstrate

---

196 Interview officials 4 and 5 Amstelveen, January 18, 2007.

197 An official stated: "During our first visit [to VES] we tried to understand why it was so important for them to separate their waste. We thought, why not first try to get it off the streets?"

198 This again reflects the ownership practices by VES in its partnership with Amstelveen (see 8.1.1). An official explained: "*Bono Verde* was their own idea. We assist, with know-how. We offer them our reflection, more than wanting to steer or propose ideas."

199 Interview NGO representative 1 Lima, February 8, 2007.

that for future cooperation it proves of critical importance that the Municipal Development Plan (PIDC) and the Institutional Development Plan be further institutionalised to serve as 'locally owned' frameworks to build on systematically from a capacity development perspective.[200]

B. Contrasting outcomes: León versus Oudtshoorn

The examples of Oudtshoorn and León provide a contrast which clearly illustrates how the long-term character of C2C partnerships can best be employed to generate sustainable results. As Chapter 5 already indicated, the partnership between Utrecht and León is characterised by a shift from small-scale, short-term, *ad hoc* projects towards a more programme and process oriented approach expressed in the design of long-term cooperation activities that build on previous cooperation outcomes and existing structures. The most evident examples in this respect are the long-term assistance to the design of strategic planning instruments which ran between 1994 and 2004, and the LSE project, which is still ongoing after ten years.[201] The joint urban planning exercise entailed assistance from Utrecht to León in the design of a range of strategic municipal development plans, each of them building on previous plans and results. The long-term planning process not only made León the first municipality in the country to operate on the principles of integrated, strategic development planning, it also brought about sustainable change in the municipal organisation. The LSE project has similar characteristics. Using an integrated, programmatic planning approach, Utrecht has assisted León for over ten years in planning a new neighbourhood area. Issues of housing, infrastructure, social development and social cohesion, and environment are tackled simultaneously. Sub-projects in these respective fields always link to the overall planning strategy of the project. The coordinator of the project in León can be regarded as a key driving force in securing the progress made and sustaining the long-term vision.

In the case of Alphen-Oudtshoorn, the young history of technical exchanges has been very diverse and volatile. In less than four years, exchange missions and projects have been formulated and implemented in a wide range of subjects, including Integrated Development Planning, gender, public participation, HIV/AIDS, and performance management (PMS). The diversity was largely a reflection of the supply of thematic exchanges and training programmes offered by VNG. In the years reviewed here, the funding criteria of VNG altered considerably, as the GSO programme was terminated and replaced by LOGO South (Chapter 3). Consequently, new areas of cooperation had to be included, making it difficult for Oudtshoorn and Alphen to define a long-term strategy that could build on previous results and that guaranteed that results achieved were sustained. Moreover, the partnership was only established recently in 2002, and the cities still had to find common ground regarding thematic focus and methodologies. It was noted that after several technical missions and exchange activities, cooperation declined and few concrete outcomes e.g. in policy-making, organisational capacity building or service delivery could be observed. The only exception

---

200 This is especially relevant as VES municipality has expressed its concern that, although the PIDC has been approved and is currently met by ample political support, there is great uncertainty as to how policies should be put into practice due to organisational capacity constraints, and how the organisation can meet the growing capacity demands in the future.

201 The two examples are examined in more detail in Chapter 9.

was the PMS project (see Chapter 9). Partly as a result of volatility in partnership focus which led to many single one-time events, partly due to a lacking vision and leadership of Oudtshoorn municipality in defining its own objectives in partnership activities and exchanges, it proved difficult to build momentum and induce real change.

8.2.2 Instruments to sustain partnership efforts

A final point of concern in the discussion on how partnership efforts can be sustained is the use of instruments to facilitate exchange and interaction that could affect the sustainability of activities. These include instruments to outline the objectives and activities of partnerships (mainly cooperation agreements, memorandums of understanding and terms of references), and instruments to monitor and evaluate partnership objectives, activities and results.

A. Instruments to shape partnership content

The partnerships under study are all shaped and supported by an official, bi-lateral cooperation agreement. Agreements, usually signed in a ceremonial setting by Mayors, are found to have a highly symbolic meaning (Mamadouh, 2002). In the case of Alphen and Oudtshoorn for example a date was chosen for the signing of the agreement that marked a historical event in Dutch-South African relations (see Chapter 5). The agreements generally outline a mutual recognition of the cities as official partners, and include formulated partnerships objectives. It may also contain an ideology or umbrella theme on which cooperation is based. In the case of Treptow-Köpenick and Cajamarca for example the cooperation agreement builds on the principles of Local Agenda 21, while Utrecht and León have organised their agreement around the concept of sustainability.[202] Cooperation agreements may be renewed after some years, which may be a forceful sign to reiterate the willingness to be a partner and to show political support.[203]

While cooperation agreements offer a framework that shapes C2C partnerships in general, separate agreements may be drafted and signed when specific projects and exchange activities such as technical missions and delegation visits are organised. Amstelveen and Villa El Salvador for example, make use of so-called 'Declarations of Intention'. Alphen and Oudtshoorn sign Memorandums of Understanding (MoUs) at the end of each work visit to summarise the main outcomes and agree on subsequent action to

---

202   A cooperation agreement is different from international relations policies of the partner municipalities in at least three ways. First, international relations policies usually entail more than the partnership alone (e.g. European affairs, economic issues) while the agreement is tailored to the partnership *per se*. Secondly, ideally a cooperation agreement is a product of two partner cities, reflecting the intentions of both North and South, while international relations policy are confined to one municipal organisation. Thirdly, municipal IC policies are a product of council decisions and local politics, and thus imply that policy implementation should be accountable to political decisions made. In contrast, cooperation agreements can be considered a mutual accountability mechanism, in which partner cities are accountable to one another. The latter type of accountability may be organised much more informally, as partner cities have little means and instruments to push their partners to comply with the agreements made. The case of Cajamarca and Treptow-Köpenick is a good example in this respect. Although a cooperation agreement was signed and even renewed between the two cities, in practice both partners fall short in meeting the objectives set and exercising their responsibilities and obligations.

203   Treptow-Köpenick and Cajamarca renewed their agreement after five years. Utrecht and León signed sustainability agreements in 2001, 2003 and 2007.

be taken. Utrecht and León make use of Terms of References (ToRs) drafted in preparation of a work visit that outline the objectives, activities and expected output of a mission. Not only do these instruments allow the definition of clear work plans and objectives that may lead to a more sustainable approach to organising capacity development, they are also a reflection of the extent to which cooperation is demand-driven and based on existing needs and capacity. The mentioned example of the use of ToRs in León applies here: through Terms of References constituted by León and approved by Utrecht, the relevant needs are signalled, priorities are set and the budget for cooperation is appointed accordingly, which allows greater ownership for León.

B. Instruments to assess and account for partnership results
The above mentioned instruments (e.g. ToRs and MoUs) are also useful for monitoring and evaluating partnership activities and events. Other instruments include annual plans (Utrecht, Alphen), annual reports (Utrecht), mission reports (all cases) and internal or external evaluations. The Dutch cities in this study all have evaluated their international relations policies, partnerships or specific elements (such as the LSE project in Utrecht). Evaluations are used to review and adapt international relations policies if necessary, which was the case for Alphen (an external evaluation done by VNG and COS in 2005 (VNG & COS, 2005), and in Amstelveen (2002). In Utrecht an external evaluation in 1997 was followed by interval evaluations every four years, which form the basis of decision-making for the municipal council on whether or not to continue the partnership with León.[204]

The use of these instruments is important to justify international cooperation activities vis-à-vis local political leaders and constituents. They also facilitate coordination of activities and participants' involvement. For example, ToRs and written reports of work visits are shared in Utrecht's LSE working group, so that participants are informed on the progress made and the conclusions of technical missions performed by their colleagues. These instruments may also be important to lift individual learning and experiences to a higher organisational level. This will be discussed in the next section. Monitoring and evaluation mechanisms are furthermore helpful to make C2C partnerships and the activities and overseas travels inherent to them more transparent and accountable. Partnership agreements alone may not be valuable when the objectives set and activities specified are not regularly assessed against the results obtained. Moreover, evaluation helps to overcome the undesirable image and (perceived) practice of C2C exchange as an opportunity for participants to travel and gain personal benefits.[205]

---

204 In the early days of the partnership, municipal involvement was intended to be short-term, with a duration of two years upon which a decision would be made about prolongation (Chapter 5). Although the local administration valued the role in awareness-raising with regard to 'developing countries' for the Utrecht population, questions were also raised on the effectiveness of employing only one 'long-term permanent partnership with one country' to perform this role (Van Zanen, 1993). Later, the assessments and evaluations became more dispersed which resulted in the current practice of evaluations done every four years.

205 This was for example observed in Cajamarca. A civil society representative stated: "This partnership does not obligate us to anything. What do the ones that travel to Germany bring back to the community? What is the impact of their visits? We need to have some terms of reference so that these persons take their responsibility to draft a plan, present it and inform us on what they did. I know of many people in Cajamarca who went to Germany. They had their tourism trip, and some now have higher salaries and better job opportunities. But

8.3 Implementing change: individual and organisational learning

This section explores the learning that occurs in North-South partnerships in both partner cities. There are three relevant questions are. First (8.3.1), who is generally engaged in exchange activities and missions, and hence, who is exposed to learning opportunities? Secondly (8.3.2), what is learned by participants on a personal level and in a professional sense? Thirdly (8.3.3), has it been possible to move beyond individual learning and induce organisational change as a result of partnership activities and which mechanisms are present to foster this transition from the individual to the organisational level?

8.3.1 Who learns? Characteristics of exchange participants

Who is involved in international twinning relations within municipal organisations,? The number of municipal participants in partnership activities varies widely among the cities under study and is strongly related to the scope and content of the projects executed. The number of staff is generally smaller in municipalities in the South than in the North which makes it more likely for staff in the South to somehow become involved.[206] In projects that specifically focus on strengthening a particular department (e.g. Environmental Services in VES) or a specific municipal competency (e.g. urban planning in León, human resources in Oudtshoorn), the number of participants is limited: between 1 and 10. Projects related to organisational strengthening in the South usually have a much wider target group in the municipal administration. In VES for example, 188 staff were trained on software use in the framework of the financial administration project. In Oudtshoorn, 30 staff and 40 councillors received training on the new Performance Management System. And in León, all political leaders and administrative directors followed workshops on leadership skills, time management and decision-making (Chapter 9).[207]

In total, 36 respondents from local government that participated in exchange activities were surveyed.[208] Sixteen participants (44%) were local administrators. This category includes a range of staff positions, such as policy officers, policy advisors, project managers and project assistants, coordinators and technical staff. Another 18 participants (50%) were local administrators with a leadership or senior management position in the municipal organisation: this group is classified as having positions in which they manage people in subdivisions of the administration, such as Heads of Departments. Participants in key strategic positions (e.g. Municipal Managers) are also part of this category. Only two respondents were political representatives (councillors).

---

we didn't hear from their experiences. We need more monitoring and accountability" (Interview civil society representative Cajamarca, March 20, 2007).

206 A distinction can be observed between departments' and officials' involvement in the *management* of the partnership (as an objective per se) versus those involved as *participants* and beneficiaries of partnership activities, especially with regard to capacity building. Officials involved in partnership management include for example the staff of the IC Departments of VES and León discussed in Chapter 6.

207 Such organisation-wide capacity development activities allow a large number of staff to participate, which increases support among municipal staff for the city partnership, while at the same time it enhances learning opportunities in an organisational context.

208 Fourteen respondents were from the North and 22 from the South.

The large majority of participants exposed to learning opportunities and skills development are thus the administrative staff of local governments. Moreover, many have a managerial or influential position, providing opportunities to act as 'change agents' to enhance organisational learning, as argued by Johnson & Thomas (2007). With regard to councillors' participation, some respondents questioned the value of sending councillors on missions, as they are perceived to be replaced at every political regime change. A few officials also fear that some councillors participate for personal or political gain, rather than for the benefit of the community. It may be difficult to justify towards constituents participation of political representatives in overseas travels. On the other hand, it was found that in order to create and foster buy-in from political leaders, engaging councillors in exchange missions proved to be a valuable tool.[209] Participants in exchange missions are generally highly educated. In the South, the large majority of respondents (19 out of 22, or 86%) had a university degree. In the North, the percentage is 71% (10 out of 14). Seventeen respondents are female, nineteen male.

Thematic expertise of participants is diverse, and obviously depends partly on the thematic focus of technical projects. In Oudtshoorn for example, participants were reported to work in housing (social housing), human resources (gender), auditing (performance management) and health (HIV/AIDS). In León, the majority of respondents worked at the Urban Development Department, and participated in joint projects with Utrecht for several consecutive years. Capacity building occurred at LSE project office which initially functioned relatively independently from the municipal structure. Recently, the office has been integrated into the Department of Urban Development, creating capacity spill-over to other subdivisions and departments. Also, the LSE project has become more interdisciplinary, involving and strengthening other municipal departments, dealing with e.g. social development and environment. In Villa El Salvador, most respondents represented either the Environmental Services Department, or were involved in financial administration and institutional development, such as the Head of Local Revenues Administration, Head of Planning and Budgeting, and Head of one of the Municipal Agencies (Chapter 9).

8.3.2 Individual learning experiences in North and South

Personal learning in the North
Respondents in Amstelveen, Alphen and Utrecht listed a wide range of personal learning experiences gained from participation in C2C partnership exchange activities. These experiences can be roughly categorised in five learning dimensions. First, and most frequently, participants noted that they had become more aware of inequality in living and work conditions in the world, and that the wealth and opportunities in their own country should not be taken for granted. They learned to put their own situation into perspective, and many participants responded that they considered it a privilege to get in touch with different cultures.[210] A second point is that officials in the North not only learned to reflect

---

209   For example, in 2005, five council members from three political parties in Utrecht (they were not among the survey respondents) visited León. They participated on their own account and covered their own expenses, as they felt a trip paid by tax money was not appropriate, and would moreover not be approved by council.

210   Officials noted: "I experienced we are in a fortunate position here", "I am thankful to be born here", "It was an eye opener. We are so bothered about small things, but life is good here". One Alphen official reflected on

CITIES AS PARTNERS

on their own situation, but also took inspiration from the attitude (towards life and work) of their colleagues in the South.[211] Thirdly, learning about different countries, poverty, and culture was mentioned as an important learning experience. Experiencing inequality in developing countries, the effects of globalisation, and racism are examples. One councillor noted she learned to look at poverty in a different way.[212] Some officials also noted that they also learned more about international development cooperation and its benefits.[213] A fourth dimension of personal learning in the North is related to personal skills development, although it applied to only a few respondents: "Being overseas challenges you to operate and function in a setting that you are not familiar with".[214] A final dimension is not so much related to learning, rather to overall personal benefits. Many participants in the North said emphatically they had truly enjoyed themselves in exchanges and missions. Occasionally, the personal contacts and friendships made were also put forward as personal gains.

Personal learning in the South
The personal learning benefits of participants of Villa El Salvador, Oudtshoorn and León show similarities with the North, but they also differ in some aspects. Learning experiences can be grouped in four main dimensions. First, the most frequent observation was that C2C partnerships offer the opportunity to get to know different countries and cultures, which was considered "rewarding", "exciting", and "instructive". Participants said to learn about the differences in the quality of life and lifestyles, and the characteristics of the Dutch. Secondly, learning also emerged from comparing conditions in North and South, and some respondents mentioned how the differences observed could explain the 'level of development' the Netherlands had reached.[215] Similar to the North, respondents observed that difference in life and work conditions triggered a change of perspective: "Getting in touch with other paradigms helps to revise your focus and vision". Thirdly, personal skills development was mentioned, albeit sporadically in the South. A female León official said

behaviour in the North: "We are spoiled people. We have moved very far away from the basic things in life. They [South Africans] should not copy our situation, we consume too much." Getting in touch with different cultures has been "…enriching to see their optimism and how they get things done. My outlook on life has become more optimistic".

211 An Amstelveen official observed: "They give me courage. They talk with enthusiasm and pride about their work". Another adds: "I took their warmth and energy home, it is very constructive". Others esteemed that "much can be achieved with very little resources" in the South, and the positive attitude despite the many problems encountered.

212 "At first sight it appears they are dependent, they live in poor conditions. But when I was there, I sensed a great cultural wealth. And solidarity among people is huge"

213 One Amstelveen official stated: "I saw how useful our cooperation with Villa El Salvador is. It is beautiful and humane. I have also experienced how valuable personal relations are. [The Mayor of VES] talks often about friendship. Now I understand what he means. And he is right".

214 One Alphen official explains: "I was young, I flew on my own to South Africa and spent two days alone in Johannesburg. It made me more independent". Personal growth was also observed by an Utrecht official: "I realised I could employ my personality to achieve results. I learned the value of building strong personal relations."

215 A VES official stated: "I learned that in order to advance, you need good education systems". A colleague added: "I was able to study how and why the Netherlands were so developed. I compared it with Peru."

for example that she had gained a more confident work attitude.[216] Finally, the dimension of building friendship and sharing interests and social exchange was mentioned more frequently in the South than in the North. Especially in VES and León, friendships built were repeatedly valued.

Professional learning in the North

The most common type of professional learning, i.e. the learning that corresponded to professional skills and occupation, was the acquirement of skills that are needed for problem solving and functioning in a different social, financial and cultural context. As an Utrecht official put it, participation in technical exchanges was like "…a training course in creative thinking, how to achieve something with very little resources".[217] Learning to be flexible was often mentioned as well.[218] Furthermore, a range of practical but essential work skills were said to have improved through engagement in C2C, such as advisory skills. This includes the "capacity to translate your own expertise to a different context and make it applicable", "taking into account different visions even when they are not yours", and "learning to formulate objectives in capacity building". Also, networking, communication and negotiation skills were mentioned as important learning outcomes.

Another dimension of professional learning in the North that was perceived, was that visits to partner municipalities were instructive to put own work conditions into perspective by reflecting on them. As one Utrecht official put it: "A mission challenges you to look very critically at the organisation there [in León]. Automatically you will reflect on your own organisation and functioning as well".[219]

Public participation and the (perceived) closer relationship between citizens and local government in the South was in general an important and frequent point of observation mentioned by respondents in the North. An Amstelveen official was interested in the interactive decision-making processes taking place in Villa El Salvador, but at the same time concluded that such processes are not easily applicable in Amstelveen.[220] Learning about

---

216 "I came straight from university and I didn't dare to do anything [in my work]. There is a lot of *machismo* here and women are not always taken seriously. They don't think highly of themselves. [My Dutch counterpart] said I should just try. I learned that I was capable. I learned to be more self-assertive."

217 Another adds: "you learn how to deal with constraints. When there is no electricity, you cannot give a powerpoint presentation. You cannot make photo copies when there is no paper. So you find solutions".

218 One Amstelveen participants confirmed: "You need to let go of the Dutch way of working, and be flexible to deviate from your standards. You need to be open to take a different road in order to get there".

219 Also in Amstelveen an official observed that she had become more aware of how the local administration operates: "Our projects with VES on financial administration and environment were connected. It taught me that financial control is important, which helps me to understand my own organisation better". An Utrecht official noted that she took a new perspective on the interaction between citizens and local government: "In my position I work very directly with citizens in Utrecht. They complain although we have little problems here. They complain about unlevelled street pavements. The image of the municipality is not so positive here. But there, government is more untrustworthy, and corrupt. It has less to offer to its constituents, and still citizens are more open to cooperate. I find that inspiring".

220 "Public participation and participatory budgeting are very interesting phenomena, it puts citizens centre stage. But a municipal mission formulated in citizens' own words would never work here, it becomes inefficient. For us, this is too democratic. But it makes you think about your own way of governing".

CITIES AS PARTNERS

Box 8.2 The return of the caravels? Bringing participatory processes from VES to Amstelveen

The example of introducing participatory decision-making processes in urban service delivery in Amstelveen correlates strongly to the concept discussed in Chapter 1 of the adoption in the North of innovative practices of democratic and participatory governance that have sprung up in cities in the South. This trend, also dubbed 'the return of the caravels' (e.g. Allegretti & Herzberg, 2004) has been observed in recent years in Europe. It implies that the experience of Southern municipalities, in particular in Latin America, to apply urban governance instruments such as participatory budgeting and participatory municipal planning are increasingly exported to and used by municipalities in the North. The case of Villa El Salvador-Amstelveen offers an interesting example in this respect, as the tradition of community participation and shared decision-making have made VES an archetype of innovative participatory planning approaches in Peru and beyond.

Amstelveen municipality has showed considerable interest in the experiences of VES. It has moreover attempted to reproduce the participatory approach in its own delivery of services. The Amstelveen waste management Department was seeking new ways to deal with solid waste collection. After several work visits to VES in the framework of the environment project (Chapter 9), one official decided to involve citizens in the selection of new forms of waste collection. Citizens were asked how they preferred their solid waste to be collected. They could either opt for house to house waste collection once a week, or they could opt to take their waste to central waste collection containers in their neighbourhood. The participatory approach started with an announcement in the local newspaper, to invite a group of citizens to join actively in the decision-making process. They were informed on the legal requirements municipalities have to meet in terms of solid waste, and they were taken to a municipal waste disposal plant. Four meetings were organised in which they could express their preferences. In addition, an internet poll was set up to reach a larger group of citizens, who could vote on-line for the collection method of their preference. Finally, a meeting was held to round up the participatory process and to share the results and choices made with other interested parties.

Although Amstelveen did eventually base its new form of solid waste collection on the outcomes of the participatory decision-making process, it acknowledges at the same time that the process was not very successful. Which underlying reasons can be ascribed to the failure of participatory decision-making in urban service delivery in Amstelveen? The lack of tradition in participation and the lack of interest among citizens to be involved is a first factor mentioned. The newspaper announcement yielded only 14 citizens that were willing to engage in the process. A change in waste management is perceived as relatively irrelevant, as quality of life is high and citizens' livelihoods are not significantly affected by municipal waste services and how they are organised. The need among citizens to fight for better service delivery and make their voices heard is simply not as great in the North as it is for the poor in the South. Secondly, although Amstelveen has shown interest in the democratic governance processes in VES, at the same time officials and political representatives alike have argued that the approach is not readily applicable to municipalities in the Netherlands. The processes in VES are seen as 'too democratic' for the Dutch context, which result in inefficient, costly and lengthy service delivery planning and implementation. The responsible official in this example agreed that the involvement of citizens in waste collection had cost "…much time, money and energy, while very little came out of it". Also the Mayor of Amstelveen noted that "the ideas about public participation are not relevant in our context". The only advantage that was noted by the responsible official was "…when citizens now complain about the waste collection services of the municipality, we can say that it is based on their own wishes and preferences".

other aspects of local government in the South was also commonly mentioned, such as the role of the Mayor, the interaction between politicians and local administration, and the effects of political regime changes on the composition of local administration staff in the partner city.

Finally, technical learning, or applying technical or organisational lessons learned in daily work, was mentioned only sporadically. Two Amstelveen officials attempted to apply the participatory approach in decision-making and implementation of municipal projects practiced in Villa El Salvador in their own context. One explained: "I am not afraid to involve others when I need to take decisions. I see the value of participation, and I apply it. It is the most important lesson I have taken home". Her colleague set up a project to directly engage citizens in a decision-making trajectory on the collection of solid waste in the city, following the principles of participatory decision-making in Villa El Salvador. Box 8.2 describes this concrete example of professional learning in the North through C2C in more detail, including the constraints and limitations encountered.

Professional learning in the South

The concrete learning outcomes on the technical level turned out to be much more ample and explicit in the South than in the North. Learning about one's own field of expertise was the most frequently mentioned professional learning dimension in Oudtshoorn, VES and León. Some respondents said to have gained a better understanding about their own specialisation.[221] Others were exposed for the first time to new policy fields, especially in Oudtshoorn,[222] where it was moreover noted that by seeing how public service delivery is organised in Alphen would help Oudtshoorn to improve its services.[223] In León, most professional learning took place in the field of urban planning.[224] Respondents mentioned that they not only deepened their knowledge, but also widened it: "I am a civil engineer and not an urban planner. But I learned a lot about planning and housing, and I have developed

---

221   "I now really understand what is meant by social work and social development", "I have gained an understanding of how sports should be administered, and how my Department operates."

222   "I learned for the first time about social housing, how it is organised in the Netherlands". Also Oudtshoorn officials said to have learned in the fields of police and security, and infrastructure and public transport systems.

223   "The Netherlands are technologically advanced. They have cleaning machines for waste removal. We can learn from that, to make use of more advanced methods for public services".

224   One respondent noted: "I have seen how cities are built and organised in Europe".

a greater interest for these issues".[225] In Villa El Salvador, participants said to have learned particularly from institutional arrangements, financial planning and municipal management in Amstelveen. One official explains: "We learned how the municipal organisation is run. The municipality [of Amstelveen] as an institution is more viable, more rapid, more business-style. We have the knowledge but not the experience in this field."[226] Having an adequate local revenues information system and a municipal cadastral system in place were observed as critical preconditions to improve the financial administration in VES. Other VES officials mentioned human resources, staff engagement, process management, internal communication systems and the delegation of tasks within the local administration as important aspects in learning from the Amstelveen administration.

The latter relates intimately to another professional learning dimension among participants in the South, i.e. learning about the organisational culture and values in the partner city. Discipline, planning, responsibility and punctuality were virtues often ascribed to Dutch organisations and their staff, and respondents noted the advantages deriving from these virtues.[227] In Villa El Salvador several respondents mentioned that officials in Amstelveen interact more and team work is more often practiced than in VES: "You see it in the design of the city hall. There were many meeting rooms, which reflects team work. Officials work in an open office, there is transparency".

Finally, some officials observed that they had acquired specific work skills thanks to cooperation in the context of C2C. In line with the last observation on team work in Amstelveen, a VES official said: "I have learned that municipal management is stronger when you work together." Although Amstelveen officials said to have learned similar skills from the participatory nature of local government in VES, negotiation and consensus building were thus also incorporated as stronger approaches to decision-making in VES. Other skills obtained included learning to formulate projects and run a project cycle.

8.3.3 From individual learning to organisational change

To what extent have these individual learning experiences and C2C partnerships in general had wider impact and influence on the partner organisations? The literature from Chapter 1 suggested that real learning only occurs when knowledge is practically applied in existing work structures. This implies in the first place that the individual learning outcomes

---

225 Another added: "I have learned that urban expansion is much more complex than only physical expansion. It entails financial management, participation…In Utrecht I learned about bicycle use, public transport; I have developed many new ideas".

226 The Head of Planning and Budgeting explained the advantages of municipal budgeting in Amstelveen but also observed that the context of Villa El Salvador is very different. Whereas budgeting is participatory in VES, it is more technocratic in Amstelveen. Planning in Amstelveen is long-term, as the municipality is able to calculate very precisely the amount of local revenues for prospective years. In Villa El Salvador, there is a culture of non-payment of taxes, which undermines the long-term budgeting capacity of the municipality. This makes a direct application of the Amstelveen system not applicable.

227 Says one Oudtshoorn official: "I can't deny it, it is very well organised over there. Everyone is on time, they have a good infrastructure. They have clean offices, no files lying around on the desks. Everyone knows exactly what to do and where to go". A colleague mentioned the better opportunities for female staff in local government: "Women have higher positions there. They are more liberated in expressing their ideas. Especially here in Oudtshoorn that is very different".

described above are only valuable to achieve individual and organisational change when they have altered the behaviour of participants and whether there were opportunities to apply acquired skills and knowledge into daily work practice. Secondly, in order to make learning opportunities more organisation-wide, knowledge that is acquired individually needs to be disseminated and shared with colleagues. In order to examine these issues, the survey included a number of questions that were related to the implementation of acquired knowledge and (organised) information sharing after partnership activities. The findings on these two issues are discussed in consecutive order below.

Implementing acquired knowledge in daily work practice

Although participants of C2C exchange activities in the North indicated to have learned in many different ways as well on a personal as a professional level, application of acquired knowledge and skills to daily work practice was found to be less evident. Few respondents were able to clearly demonstrate the positive effects of participating in C2C in this respect. Two officials expressed their awareness in using the skills obtained though C2C.[228] The large majority of respondents however stated that they had not implemented any new insights, technical knowledge or skills into daily work practice. As one Utrecht official observed: "I have many years of policymaking experience. But policymaking is new in León, so there is no specific knowledge or skills that I can use here". A colleague added that applicable, technical learning in the North is not really a reality: "Regarding technical learning, it is an absolute one-way direction. You see how things work over there but you cannot apply it here. You give more than you receive. There is relatively little to learn that you can apply here."

The findings in the South are in stark contrast to the outcomes in the North. Especially in Villa El Salvador and León, respondents noted a wide range of changes at the organisational level that were the result of C2C exchanges and the individual learning of participants. Moreover, overall they noted that project objectives are usually met and projects are generally implemented successfully. In Oudtshoorn, concrete examples of implemented change was less notable as respondents perceived that it was too early to see clear results.[229] The question of organisational change in the South touches upon the issue of urban governance strengthening, as Chapter 2 indicated that both individual learning (human resource development) and organisational strengthening are important elements of capacity building in the public sector in the South (Grindle, 1997). The next Chapter discusses

---

228 One stated: "I have definitely changed my way of working. I am more open and flexible now". Another said: "As a policy advisor, having interpersonal skills is very important. I was able to apply that from my experience in missions" An official from Amstelveen moreover provided a very practical example of municipal expertise that was directly transferred to the partner city, i.e. a project on youth participation that was strongly based on lessons learned from Villa El Salvador: "A clear example of what we could apply from VES is the concept of a youth ambassador. We are currently formulating a project for youth participation and we will use the idea of having a youth ambassador for this group".

229 Especially in the field of social housing, exposure and learning from the Dutch context had not yet led to concrete action. One official observed that projects had to be formulated first, and that very little capacity was available to perform this task: "There are currently only two staff in the housing department. Who is going to write a proposal? We are really understaffed here". Others also stressed that the South African context was very different from the Dutch which complicated the implementation of lessons learned.

CITIES AS PARTNERS

the question to what extent organisational and institutional change has taken place in local government in the South in greater detail. Respondents' reflections on organisational change are included in the analysis of Chapter 9 and will therefore not be discussed here. Instead, we will look below at the degree in which mechanisms are in place that enable knowledge dissemination. For it is spreading knowledge that allows wider organisational learning beyond the individual experience of participants of exchange missions.

Knowledge dissemination and application in the wider organisation

How are knowledge and skills acquired through participation in C2C partnership events shared and disseminated in the institutional setting of participants? Do participants of exchange activities and delegation visits inform their colleagues on partnership experiences? Who are informed and how is knowledge shared? How did colleagues respond to the information available?

In local administrations in North and South, participants generally organise dissemination activities to share their findings and experiences with staff and politicians. Various mechanisms are used. In Amstelveen, delegation members reported about their experiences on the organisation's intranet, arranged a presentation open to all staff during a lunch meeting and held various presentations in their respective Departments. A councillor made a video report of her visit to VES that was shown in council. One official said he always keeps a diary when on mission and upon return the diary is distributed to colleagues, mission members, municipal manager and Mayor, to "…demonstrate we were not on holiday. I take responsibility for my absence and explain what we have done." Being accountable and reporting to politicians was frequently mentioned as key reason for information sharing also in Utrecht, rather than the objective of dissemination *per se*.

In Utrecht, thanks to the organisation-wide consultation structure in which various line Departments are represented in the LSE working group, the findings of missions and exchanges are structurally shared with colleagues. Each mission member presents a written report upon return and communicates verbally in working group meetings on outcomes and progress made.[230] In addition, mission members share their experiences during organised lunch meetings, Department meetings, publications in the staff magazine and in more informal ways with colleagues directly.

In the South, formal mechanisms to disseminate experiences and conclusions with the wider organisation have mainly occurred in Villa El Salvador, and to a lesser extent in León and Oudtshoorn. In the latter, dissemination is random and depends on the willingness of mission members to report upon return. There are hence no formalised and structured mechanisms that guarantee information sharing in the wider organisation. In VES, managers report to their respective Departments on exchange experiences. They also transfer information to other Departments through interdepartmental management meetings. Still, one official noted that in order to achieve and sustain organisation-wide change, more

---

230 One official observed that disseminating her experiences in the working group proved not only informative, but it also allowed her to stress the value of social issues in the integrated LSE project: "I took the chance to demonstrate with my visit the importance of social development in the project, which has been traditionally very focused on physical development. So I achieved to bring in the social dimension more. Social services should not be something that only I contribute to the project, it should be integrated in all facets of planning".

people should be directly involved in exchange activities.[231] This observation implies that capacity building is less effective when it is based on the learning experiences from others, rather than direct exposure to and participation in concrete partnership activities.

Although creating spill-over of information and lessons learned is thus done by many participants, it was also observed, especially in the North, that the reaction of colleagues generally hardly moves beyond taking notice and showing interest. As one Utrecht official put it: "My colleagues are interested in my exotic stories, but they are not inspired. They have not done anything with the information".[232] This confirms the findings of Chapter 6, where it was demonstrated that support among administrative staff for C2C activities is rather passive: C2C is tolerated and approved rather than being sustained by pro-active involvement of the entire organisation. Moreover, some respondents observed rather negative sentiments among colleagues, who questioned the purpose and contents of C2C missions.[233] Overall, it can be said that while participants in C2C activities generally seek to share their findings with other staff members and politicians, the transfer of knowledge and lessons learned is restricted, either because it is not considered applicable in the own organisational context, or because colleagues do not take an active and open approach to getting informed.

Utrecht shows that organisational structures are important to create a more structural approach to knowledge dissemination. As was already found in Chapter 6, the LSE working group offers a consultation structure which allows for the exchange of experiences and findings on partnership affairs between various Departments. Utrecht officials valued the opportunity the working group offers to share information when they return from missions. It allows for a more systematic diffusion of knowledge which is not only useful for participants but also to sustain the LSE project and its progress made. The relevance and need for such knowledge spill-over mechanisms was at times felt in other cities. In Oudtshoorn, one official observed that the "...knowledge stays with the people who are involved in exchanges. There is no mechanism to report back". As such, she sensed that although the content and purpose of exchange missions were good, they could be more valuable when there were "systems in place to share".[234]

In sum, a number of conclusions with regard to learning in North and South can be drawn:

1. Personal learning has various dimensions and has been widely observed in both North and South
2. Professional learning in the North is perceived as limited and is mainly linked to acquiring and improving work skills and reflecting on one's own work. Learning is triggered by being exposed to different (cultural) organisational contexts. In contrast,

---

231 "In order to build more capacity, more people should visit Amstelveen. Only then we can convince them we should work according to these [administrative] methods".

232 This view was confirmed by officials from Amstelveen: "They take notice, they show their interest, but the information is not used by others. This does not stimulate active involvement".

233 As one Amstelveen official explained: "They said, did you enjoy your holiday? People think my visit to VES was a leisure trip, they don't see the value for our organisation".

234 Also in Villa El Salvador, several respondents mentioned that there is a need for a more institutionalised "learning mechanism" that enables a more sustainable distribution and sharing of knowledge in the wider organisation. The idea was raised that the HR department could play a role in this respect.

Table 8.1 Learning and knowledge application in local administrations in North and South

	North	**South**
Dimensions of learning	Mainly through exposure to different organisational contexts	Mainly technical knowledge in specific field of expertise
Application of knowledge into existing work structures	Weak	Strong
Potential to generate organisational change	Weak	Strong

professional learning is more often experienced in the South, and is largely based on gaining technical knowledge in the specific field of expertise of participants.

3. In the South, C2C projects have generally generated results beyond the individual sphere, as will be demonstrated in the next Chapter. Particularly the cases of VES and León reveal a successful transformation of individual learning experiences into real organisational change. In the North however, while respondents pointed out diverse learning benefits, their observations revealed that the knowledge and skills obtained was not evidently implemented into daily work practice.

8.4 Mutuality in C2C partnerships

Observing the findings presented above, it can be concluded that there is a discrepancy between the learning benefits in the Northern and the Southern partner cities. Difference is expressed in the dimensions of learning, the extent to which new knowledge is applied into existing work structures, and the potential to move beyond individual learning experiences and generate organisational change (Table 8.1). The findings suggest that there is no equality or resemblance between North and South with regard to opportunities for learning and the applicability of learning outcomes.

At the same time, this does not necessarily mean there is no mutuality in learning. As was noted in Chapter 1 (e.g. Johnson & Wilson, 2006; Brinkerhoff, 2002) mutuality is based on complementary roles and flourishes on the merits of difference between partners, which triggers opportunities for e.g. learning. Before any conclusions on the extent to which North-South city partnerships are mutual can be drawn, it is moreover necessary to move beyond the aspect of learning alone and delve deeper into the various dimensions of mutuality.

Approaching the concept of mutuality in a way other than mere learning and knowledge acquisition is especially relevant for cities in the North, where it was found that local governments do not put the improvement of organisational performance or the enhancement of staff knowledge and skills as central objectives in C2C. Instead, the purpose of their involvement is of a very different nature. The Utrecht official who stated above that the partnership with León is 'more give than take', explained: "We are not equal partners. Nicaragua is a developing country. It is alright that we are in this kind of relationship".[235] Others confirmed the viewpoint that technical learning in the North is not a necessary

---

235 He moreover mentioned that the relationship with the Czech sister city Brno is very different in this respect, and Utrecht can for example clearly "…learn from how Brno has organised its infrastructure and public transport."

Box 8.3 "We can do this": perceptions on strengthening local governance in the South

While the international cooperation policy objectives outlined in section 6.1.1 refer to the *approach* local governments in the North take regarding international affairs, this Box reflects on the underlying municipal *motives* to engage in IC, in particular with regard to cooperation with a partner city in the South. The Mayors of Alphen and Amstelveen both underline the potential of Dutch municipalities to be a partner in development cooperation. The Alphen mayor is strongly convinced that local authorities, as experts in local governance, have a role in the development of other cities in the world. "We live in a part of the world where democracy is valued and cherished, and we are convinced this is the right way. (...) If we truly believe [in local decision-making], then we owe it to ourselves (...) to cooperate with places where things aren't right yet. Not to preach our faith like missionairies, but if you see local governance isn't functioning properly – that corruption is widespread, that health care and education aren't properly in place, that poverty is not tackled adequately – we can contribute significantly at the local level simply because we are experts."[1] This view is shared by the Mayor of Amstelveen, who states: "We can do this. We know how to run a municipal organisation".[2] In addition he stresses the potential role of municipalities in generating financial resources for the partner city. Especially in Amstelveen, the multiplier effect that has been generated by the municipality to increase additional financial assistance for Villa El Salvador has been significant (Chapter 6; 7).

1   Interview Mayor of Alphen aan den Rijn, March 15, 2006.
2   Interview Mayor of Amstelveen.

component of 'good' North-South partnering. As another Utrecht official observes: "Mutuality is a noble cause, but it is a fact that we [Utrecht] have more resources, more means. Plus we are insufficiently open to learning from their experiences. Most of us here see [the partnership with León] as pure development assistance, in a one-way direction. We talk about cooperation but it is really altruism. We are apparently not prepared to learn from them." This observation thus implies that the principal reason for the North to engage in C2C is to deliver development assistance, and learning from the South is not really an objective. As a result, C2C is not 'conceptualised as potential source for learning' in the North (*cf.* Johnson & Wilson, 2006), and learning may remain unintentional, and thus unrecognised (*cf.* Devers-Kanoglu, 2009; Mündel & Schugurensky, 2005).

Chapter 6 indeed demonstrated that engagement of Northern local governments in North-South partnerships is mainly solidarity-driven at the political level. Mayors strongly believe in the value of exporting municipal expertise to strengthen local government and urban governance in other parts of the world (Box 8.3). As the Mayor of Amstelveen puts it: "The political viewpoint of Amstelveen is that municipal international cooperation is important as a form of development assistance. The learning benefits for our own organisation are negligible. I experience that C2C contributes to local development elsewhere. That is our key motivation".[236]

236   Interview Mayor of Amstelveen, July 5, 2007.

Hence, it has been stressed by both staff and politicians in the North that local governments are engaged to contribute to urban governance strengthening and local development in the partner city, rather than to benefit in a technical or organisational sense from their participation. If learning in the North is not an objective, it implies that the question whether mutuality of learning is evident in C2C is not relevant, at least not from a policy perspective. Several benefits have been identified in the North though that have accrued to Departments and the wider administration, but are not directly learning and knowledge related. They may offer stronger opportunities for mutuality in C2C partnerships:

- One official explained that her long-term participation in a C2C project had made her a more loyal employee: "I was committed to complete the project. I have had several job offers but the [C2C] project was one of the main reasons to stay. It has made my work more interesting and therefore I am more loyal to the organisation now."

- Officials in Amstelveen, Utrecht and Alphen alike agreed that participation was highly motivating, which made them better employees. Some also observed that "working together for a good cause" offers team building opportunities to local government staff. The findings confirm the outcomes of Chapter 6, where it was already observed that participation in C2C can serve as a fringe benefit to employees to foster motivation and satisfaction in the workplace.

- One official observed moreover that the partnership with León is good publicity for the city of Utrecht: "The LSE project puts Utrecht in a favourable light. It is known as a best practice in C2C, also by UN-Habitat. This is good publicity for Utrecht Municipality".

- In Alphen and Utrecht it was stressed that having a twinning relationship is important for awareness-raising inside and outside the local administration. Also, "with C2C, you not only show your solidarity with poor areas in the world, but as local government you also set an example to your constituents. The municipality builds a more social image". Officials also noted that C2C offers opportunities for citizens and their organisations to become involved in development cooperation.

How do respondents in the South perceive the question of mutuality in C2C partnerships? Do they perceive their partners in the North benefit from C2C, despite the fact that projects are generally aimed at capacity building in the South and 100% of the financial resources in C2C partnerships are provided by the North, as Chapter 6 demonstrated? The perceptions and opinions differ greatly in this respect. A first opinion that was frequently expressed among Southern respondents is that they feel their organisation and city benefit more from C2C partnerships than their partner cities, as a result of inequality in technology and equipment, resources and capacities. This was especially felt in Oudtshoorn.[237] A second general opinion in the South has a more positive outlook on mutual benefits in C2C partnerships. Especially in Villa El Salvador it was stressed that the rich culture of Peru and the strong tradition and experience with public participation in local decision-making could

---

237 As one official observed: "When you look at the poverty situation and the history of South Africa, you'll understand we don't support Alphen financially and technically like they support us. The Netherlands are a first world country. We are in the third world. There is nothing that they can learn from us. If we were experts ourselves, we wouldn't need them". A colleague estimated that the distribution of the partnership benefits were 90% for Oudtshoorn and 10% for Alphen. At the same time, the sustainability of such a distribution was questioned: "this is not good. We have a mutual agreement. If only one partner benefits, Alphen may think, why should we extend the agreement?"

be of inspiration to Amstelveen participants.[238] Also in Oudtshoorn, some officials observed that the exposure and opportunities to gain new experiences are beneficial to participants in both North and South: "Twinning is benchmarking. We can both benefit from comparing our municipal organisational systems."[239]

8.4.1 Some examples: food for thought for the mutuality debate

This second part of this section aims to provide more anecdotal evidence of mutuality issues in C2C partnerships. By presenting two different scenarios and examples found in this study, a better understanding of the concept is offered, which could be useful in the light of the patchy and at times contradicting perceptions and viewpoints of survey respondents presented above.

A. Utrecht-León: new opportunities for mutuality?

The partnership between Utrecht and León is a typically solidarity-driven twinning relationship. The key motivation for participation in Utrecht is to contribute to local development and institutional strengthening in León. This view is supported by politicians and staff engaged in capacity building missions alike. As the findings discussed above reveal, professional learning and improving the organisational and technical capacity of Utrecht municipality is not an objective of Utrecht's partnership with León. Such an approach to twinning implies that mutuality of learning and knowledge and skills development will be unlikely, because on the Utrecht side of the linkage these aims are not pursued. Moreover, as some respondents indicated, the learning potential for the organisation and individual participants may not be sufficiently accepted and valued. As such, learning will not be made explicit and intentional in the North.

A lack of mutuality however may undermine the partnership in the long run. In Chapter 6 it was already noted that questions have been raised among critics and politicians about the serious dependency of León on foreign aid. It has been argued that development aid may deepen rather than eradicate poverty: while Nicaragua received US$ 20 billion of aid between 1980 and 1999, its poverty situation has only worsened. Critics have argued that the unlimited availability of aid assistance has led to a mentality of passive waiting for external aid rather than finding solutions 'from within' (Slutsky, 2003). Also in Utrecht it has been noted that the twinning between Utrecht and León is one of the factors that can be held accountable for sustaining the vicious circle of aid, dependency and poverty in the latter. Reporting on a partnership mission in 2005, an Utrecht councillor concluded: "The enormous budget dependency of León Municipality on foreign aid is troublesome. If aid is easily available, there is little incentive to generate own revenues. The Utrecht willingness to help is so great that with each demand for assistance the question is raised how it can

---

238 As one VES official put it: "Their advantage is that they have financial resources. Our advantage is we have strong community participation". It was observed that Amstelveen could learn from the "community participation, consultation mechanisms and the solidarity focus we have here. We maintain a permanent communication with our citizens to listen to their needs and involve them in the developmental process of the city". In terms of Peruvian culture, the diversity in food, dance and music was put forward as an advantage in twinning, especially to involve the Amstelveen population and schools.

239 Another official observed: "perhaps we gain more economically, but in terms of experience we both win". One official however stressed that Alphen officials "can learn, but they have to be interested in our context".

be financed, rather than first assessing the usefulness and relevance of aid" (Schat, 2005, p. 10). In León the viewpoint was confirmed that both the municipality and the population have become used to seeking external solutions and support rather than finding internal alternatives.[240]

The concept of mutuality may help to partly overcome the (financial) dependency relationship that has built up between Utrecht and León over the years. It challenges Utrecht to consider alternative ways to meet its political objectives to contribute to poverty alleviation and raise awareness on development and inequality issues. The recent approach Utrecht has taken in international cooperation to meet the Millennium Development Goals (Chapter 3, 6) offer new opportunities in this respect. Although first steps have only been taken very recently (2008) and it is too early to draw any conclusions on the effects, it appears that new forms of activities are slowly getting attention. These new forms stress the role of the own municipality to contribute to sustainable development and e.g. to prevent climate change. For example, Utrecht has drafted a sustainable procurement and environmental policy to use more fair trade products and to reduce energy consumption in the municipal organisation. Also, a new project has been formulated to compensate the organisation's CO_2 emission with a reforestation scheme in the vicinity of León. As such, Utrecht might play a complementary role in overcoming global inequality and dependency relations, which offers a new approach to mutuality in C2C partnerships.

B. Alphen-Oudtshoorn: The linkage between 'ownership' and 'mutuality'

Mutuality in C2C partnerships cannot only be considered in the light of learning opportunities or the benefits that accrue for partners, but also in the motivation and investments (in terms of time and commitment) made. The latter dimension of mutuality is closely connected to the concept of 'ownership' discussed earlier in this Chapter. When partners are not actively engaged in shared decision-making, lack of a sense of ownership may result in a general passive attitude towards partnering. Consequently, it affects the extent to which mutual relations between partners in terms of dedicating time and showing commitment are maintained. The case of Alphen-Oudtshoorn illustrates this aspect of mutuality. In Chapter 7 it was demonstrated that civil society participation in the twinning with Alphen is weakly organised in Oudtshoorn. Section 8.1 showed that ownership in municipal projects has been at risk and projects are not always formulated from an intrinsic demand, structure and capacities. The combination of these factors has put Oudtshoorn in a rather reactive position towards partnership commitment and activities. Officials in Oudtshoorn observed that Oudtshoorn "should do more to make the partnership work. We have been a heavy burden for Alphen. They present plans, communicate, send letters, but we haven't achieved anything here. It must be frustrating for them".[241] Officials suggested a dedicated officer be

---

240 Interview city partnership representative 2, November 8, 2005; Interview Director CE Department, November 2, 2005.

241 A colleague noted: "The guys from the Netherlands do their best to keep things going. But politics and circumstances are not helping us here to complete the [PMS] project". An Oudtshoorn councillor stated that part of the problem lies with the poor communication from Oudtshoorn side: "There has been a lack of communication between Alphen and Oudtshoorn municipalities. We cannot blame Alphen, our officials do not answer to their requests. If we would lose this twinning, the town would lose a lot. We have to show that we are eager and show appreciation of what Alphen is trying to do for us."

appointed to act as partnership coordinator and to liaise directly with Alphen to improve communication.

Alphen officials share the opinion that it has indeed been frustrating to get little feedback and response from their South African counterparts. One official explained it has discouraged her to the extent that she no longer wants to be involved in technical exchange with the municipality: "I have invested so much time in numerous phone calls and emails and I don't get any response. They are adults, we should not patronise. So when they don't respond, then it's finished for me".

In the Oudtshoorn business community, the lack of 'mutuality of input' in the relationship with Alphen has also been sensed. It was one of the main motivations for a group of Business Chamber members to organise a visit to Alphen aan den Rijn (Chapter 7). They felt that more commitment should be shown and that Oudtshoorn needed to give "something in return".[242] At the same time, the sustainability of the partnership was questioned when mutual feedback and input from both partners is lacking. A business representative explained: "You cannot have a relationship that is one-way traffic only. Think about a marriage. If one person is only giving and the other person is only taking, it does not work."

8.5 The city-to-city cooperation modality: added value?

A final theme discussed in this Chapter relates to the question whether city-to-city cooperation, as a form of development cooperation which puts local governments and municipal expertise centre stage, has a comparative advantage over other aid modalities. This question is tricky to examine and it may prove useful to break it down into two related viewpoints. The first viewpoint argues that not the municipal expertise, but the financial assistance offered is perceived by the South as the greatest benefit of engaging in North-South C2C partnership. Such a viewpoint – reducing the role of C2C partnerships to mere channels of funding – would undermine the unique position of municipalities as partners in international cooperation. The second point of view ascribes more added value to C2C, and holds that municipalities in the North provide a niche in the sense that they offer much needed expertise in municipal service delivery and management.

8.5.1 "At the end of the day, it is money that matters most..."
The first view challenges the belief that municipalities – as public institutions with specific local government expertise and experience – have an additional advantage as partners in international cooperation. This approach sees the role of municipalities and C2C partnerships as rather conventional within the spectrum of development assistance, i.e. as donors and donor-recipient relationships that provide mere financial assistance to the South. The belief is based on some of the sentiments and perceptions felt both within and outside local administrations, principally in the North.

Several respondents from Alphen and Amstelveen in particular observed that while they sought to exchange knowledge, and transfer skills and expertise in their respective C2C

---

242 A business representative elaborated on their visit: "We have never been so embarrassed in our lives. The goodwill on their side was unbelievable compared to the nonsense going on on this side. Alphen was willing to invest energy, send money, emails and so on. From this side, so little was happening."

partnership arrangements, they strongly sensed that the main interest of the partner city in the South was only to get financial resources and operational equipment. An Alphen official explained: "They [the Oudtshoorn administration] see us as someone who brings a big bag of money. We wanted to learn from each other and assist them with their [municipal policy] planning. But they reiterated that with money, we could serve them best."[243] In Amstelveen, officials at times questioned the value they could offer with their municipal knowledge and expertise. To implement the Institutional Development Plan, Villa El Salvador needs an efficient information and communication system, software and corresponding staff training. The administration has clearly assessed its capacity needs in this respect, and the expertise and knowledge offered by Amstelveen may not necessarily be the most appropriate form to meet these demands. VES municipality would rather receive financial resources from Amstelveen to organise the capacity building according to their own preferences. An Amstelveen official mentioned: "We strongly feel that at the end of the day, it is money that matters most to them. The differences between us get smaller, and the need for our knowledge [in VES] is less evident. Would it be better to just donate money? Have we made ourselves redundant?"[244]

In additional to financial resources, partner cities in the South have expressed a great need and interest for receiving technical and operational equipment. Examples include the donation of vehicles, computers, and software. In Alphen it was noticed that Oudtshoorn at times articulated that it desired to receive hardware and software rather than the numerous training courses organised for staff and councillors on performance management. A Utrecht official mentioned that when the Mayor of León put forward his vision on international cooperation at a sister city conference in Zaragoza in 2007 (Chapter 6), he requested the donation of fire trucks instead of capacity building initiatives or strategic organisational contributions from donors. These examples demonstrate that at times operational equipment is valued more by the South than capacity building.

8.5.2 Perceptions on municipal vs. NGO assistance

The second view acknowledges the added value of institutional strengthening through city-to-city cooperation compared to some of the mainstream development cooperation schemes provided e.g. by NGOs. The question what this added value implies is a relevant one, in particular in the cases of Villa El Salvador and León, where international aid is so ubiquitous and many stakeholders are concerned with urban development and often

---

243 The (now former) Municipal Manager of Oudtshoorn stated that not only the technical exchanges were relevant to his organisation, but that Oudtshoorn would greatly benefit when more financial resources would be donated by Alphen: "Two years ago there were two [community] projects that Alphen municipality financed (…). But I think it is still not enough. If they really want to make an impact or a difference in the livelihoods of the community in Oudtshoorn, I think they can invest a bit more".

244 A colleagues confirmed: "[VES] is doing fine. They know where they want to go and what they need. What they want are resources to meet their needs, whereas we want to exchange knowledge. Is our way of working patronising? What is our value added?" A colleague added: Other Amstelveen officials shared the opinion that their knowledge and expertise was not always sufficiently valued in Peru: "I noticed we are no longer of great importance to them. Our counterparts in VES show less interest; our last visit was not a priority to them. They had lost interest in discussing the project and exchanging knowledge".

compete.[245] An NGO representative in VES observes that C2C partnerships are perceived as relations between authorities that share a mutual understanding and a common base: "These [partners] are both municipal authorities, have municipal resources, are community leaders, and face similar problems (…). They feel more equal. NGOs are seen as institutions that consult from a distance. They are perceived as unable to understand municipal affairs since they are not municipalities themselves."[246]

In this respect, various respondents in VES municipality underlined the advantages of C2C over working with NGOs. The Mayor states that if development intervention targets the municipal administration directly, the results will be more sustainable and more in line with the integral development vision of the city. While NGOs are perceived as inducing little real change, C2C projects are considered to be more institutional: "NGOs do not necessarily coordinate with local government and the city's development priorities. They get their money, implement, and leave. There is no sustainability. We [the municipality] somehow do have sustainability (…). We have resources from the State and some revenues. The *hermanamientos* enable us to cooperate in a direct way, in an institutional way."[247]

This is also the view of a VES Councillor, who adds: "International cooperation is NGO oriented. We believe it should be more intimately connected with municipal development plans and therefore with the local government. Certainly, NGOs play an important role. But here we have a lot of NGOs. There is duplicity of projects, and resource allocation is not always optimised."[248] She also mentioned that C2C partnerships bring cities closer together through solidarity and cultural exchange. The exchange of mutual knowledge and friendship "opens our views and broadens our horizons".

Also in León it was considered an advantage that organisations and sister cities that liaise directly with the municipality can play a stronger role in the developmental process of the city. When their projects and activities link to the development objectives set by local government, it allows León to orchestrate the various local development initiatives in a strategic and integrated way. An official observes: "It happens that [donor] organisations want to invest without studying the demands. We want to direct their projects more towards the needs of our area. Since we have official cooperation agreements with *hermanamientos*, we can exercise more control in what they do, and where and how they operate. This is different from the organisations that arrive like parachutes and don't know where they land".

At the same time, municipalities in the South understand their weaknesses with regard to being an attractive partner to international NGOs. These include perceptions on political instability, corruption, and the lack of capacity in local governments in the South. In Peru it was noted that local authorities lose credibility from international partners, due to the lengthy bureaucratic process exercised on public income and expenditures.[249] This causes

---

245 There is a wide presence of internationally funded NGOs in Villa El Salvador and León. This has been demonstrated above and in previous Chapters. Both cities receive a vast amount of continuous financial, humanitarian and technical development support.

246 Interview NGO representative Lima 2, February 22, 2007.

247 Interview Mayor of Villa El Salvador, February 9, 2007.

248 Interview Councillor 1 VES, February, 2007.

249 Peruvian municipalities need to report on all international funding sources, which have to pass through various administrative regulations concerning budgeting and audit controls, public tendering procedures, and the

the delay of the execution of municipal projects, which the public at large (and donors) perceive as local government being incompetent and slow. The example of León further underlines this weakness. Only three of the nine sister cities of León cooperate with the León municipality directly in the execution of projects and investments of funds. A study by Van Bochove (2008) confirms the perception of many decentralised donors that working directly with the municipality slows down disbursement and project implementation in León.[250]

These two scenarios presented pose contrasting perspectives on the added value of city-to-city cooperation. The first can be seen as rather sceptical, reducing the role of partner cities in the North to mere providers of financial assistance and equipment. It questions the value of the potential of C2C partnerships as instruments for knowledge exchange and the transfer of municipal technical knowledge through joint capacity building activities, often based on peer-to-peer cooperation. Therefore the assistance and resources provided by the North to municipalities in the South would not necessarily need to be confined to sister cities and municipal administrations, but could be also delivered by other types of donors and partners, such as NGOs or through national state-led decentralised development cooperation programmes. The second viewpoint however illustrates clearly that Northern municipalities can fill a niche by strengthening their Southern counterparts who are sometimes left out of international assistance, due to the relatively negative perception on local public institutions in the South. Moreover, C2C is seen as a modality that links institutions of the same kind. Connecting municipalities that have relatively similar characteristics, activities and roles in communities, C2C partnerships have been perceived to reach a rather high level of mutual understanding (e.g. the mutual interaction to define existing needs) and share common ground.

8.6 Conclusions

This Chapter discussed the various challenges C2C partnerships are faced with as instruments for North-South capacity development and exchange of municipal knowledge and expertise. A number of concepts have served as guiding principles in the analysis, and have been found to be strongly interrelated. They include ownership; sustainability and continuity; individual and organisational learning; and mutuality. Further, the Chapter has reviewed the perceptions and viewpoints with regard to the added value of city-to-city cooperation in comparison to other forms of (decentralised) development cooperation. With regard to the latter, two different views, that may even exist in parallel in one municipality, have been put forward.

It was found that in the partnerships under study, partners generally seek to cooperate in a demand-driven way through dialogue and consensus building. Agenda setting and decision-making is mainly pursued by partner cities in the South, which offers a greater potential for cooperation tailored towards the existing capacity and needs of the organisations in the South, based on a locally owned municipal development strategy. At the same time however, it was found that a tension exists between the ambition to enhance ownership in the South and the reality that financial control is exercised by the North, which

---

necessity to comply with the legal framework.

250   This view was also put forward in interviews with several NGO representatives in León.

to a considerable extent shapes the conditions for cooperation. The example of Alphen-Oudtshoorn in particular illustrates how ownership may be undermined by the restricting of funding and the setting of project criteria by the North.

Various mechanisms for exchange and interaction exist in C2C arrangements, but the majority is confined to short-time work visits to partner cities. The rather isolated nature of these mechanisms implies that the continuity in the composition of C2C project and mission participant groups and the extent to which ongoing contacts are maintained in between visits, are factors contributing to making capacity development a sustainable process. Staff retention was found to be rather high, despite the volatile nature of local politics and public administration. This enables capacity building results to be sustained in the organisation. At the same time, the process approach to capacity building may be undermined by the fact that little interaction takes place in between missions. Missions therefore have the risk to become isolated one-time events, and momentum in long-term partnership arrangements may be lost. Monitoring and evaluation mechanisms are important tools to sustain progress made, and signal relevant future needs.

With regard to the potential for learning in C2C partnerships, a number of conclusions can be drawn. First, personal learning has various dimensions and has been widely observed in both North and South. Examples include personal (skills) development; learning about different cultures, poverty and development challenges; viewing different attitudes to life and work. There were no great disparities detected between the personal learning in North and South. Secondly, professional learning in the North is mainly linked to acquiring and improving work skills and reflecting on one's own work. Learning is triggered by exposure to different cultural and organisational contexts. In contrast, professional learning in the South is largely based on gaining technical knowledge in the specific field of expertise of participants. In terms of professional learning, considerable differences between North and South are thus found. Thirdly, C2C projects in the South have generally generated results beyond the individual sphere. Particularly Villa El Salvador and León reveal a successful transformation of individual learning experiences into real organisational change. In the North however, while respondents pointed out diverse learning benefits, their observations revealed that the knowledge and skills obtained were not evidently implemented into daily work practice.

The discrepancy in learning between North and South is important in understanding the implications for mutuality in C2C partnerships. At the same time, it was found that partner cities in the North do not regard the improvement of their own organisational performance or enhancement of staff knowledge and skills as necessary components of good partnering. Rather, objectives in the North – both political and individual – can be seen as rather altruistic and strongly related to delivering development assistance to the South. If learning in the North is not an objective, it implies that the question whether mutuality in learning is evident in C2C is not relevant, at least not from a policy perspective. Instead of learning, stronger opportunities for mutuality in C2C may be offered by the benefits that may accrue to Northern municipalities from a strategic political and organisational perspective, e.g. fostering staff loyalty and motivation, creating awareness-raising inside and outside the local administration, and generating good publicity for the municipality. The findings suggest that mutuality in C2C is not necessarily related to seeking to generate identical benefits for North and South. Rather it is strongly linked to the extent to which results achieved correspond with the political and strategic partnership objectives set. Since these objectives are different in North and South, the understanding of mutuality in C2C partnerships needs to move beyond learning alone and should include political and strategic organisational outcomes as well.

What do these findings mean with regard to the potential of city-to-city cooperation as capacity development mechanism? Can the process of knowledge exchange be considered effective? Although it remains to be studied how C2C compares to other modalities of decentralised development assistance in terms of cost effectiveness, a number of factors can be outlined which make city-to-city cooperation advantageous as a form of development intervention and a mechanism of exchange and capacity building. First, the findings reveal a high potential for ownership, thanks to high levels of mutual agreement and understanding of needs. As such, interventions can be linked to existing municipal policy frameworks and to development objectives defined by the South. To foster ownership, and make capacity building a sustainable process, municipalities in the South need a thorough understanding of their strategic development needs, while funding criteria should not be too restricting and volatile. Secondly, as municipalities in North and South are institutions of the same kind, with relatively similar characteristics, activities and roles in communities, they have been perceived to reach a rather high level of mutual understanding (e.g. the mutual interaction to define existing needs) and share a common base. This further enables C2C to at least partly overcome the usual inequality of North-South cooperation and foster a greater comprehension of issues arising and how to tackle them. Thirdly, although partnerships are in particular learning sites for the South rather than the North, there is little risk that a lack of mutuality harms the effectiveness of capacity and skills exchange. If learning and capacity development is achieved in the South and the political and strategic organisational objectives of engaging in C2C are met by the North, C2C offers benefits and opportunities to both North and South. As such, the need for mutuality, e.g. to make partnerships and commitment more enduring (Brinkerhoff, 2002; Johnson & Wilson, 2006) is met, which sustains partnership structures. Finally, Northern municipalities can fill a niche by strengthening their Southern counterparts who are sometimes left out of international assistance, due to the relatively negative perception on working with local public institutions in the South.

9 Strengthening urban governance in the South through North-South city partnerships[251]

While the previous Chapters have served to provide insight into context, conditions and capacities that affect city-to-city cooperation, the analysis will now shift towards the actual (development) practice, programmes and projects. This Chapter examines to what extent C2C has contributed to strengthening urban governance in the partner cities in the South. It refers back to Chapter 2 in which the analysis of urban governance strengthening through North-South city partnerships was discussed. It takes the perspective of building both a strong local state and a strong civil society. How does C2C perform in these spheres? To what extent and in what way can the external forces of city linkages function as an intermediary to bridge gaps and enhance responsibility and responsiveness of all urban stakeholders? In order to assess the impact of city-to-city cooperation in urban governance, the Chapter first explores how C2C strengthens municipal administrations and public service delivery. Secondly, city partnership effects are identified in the conditions that foster citizen participation in processes of local decision-making and local development. Finally, the analysis will reveal that it is appropriate to include a third category of impact, which requires the adjustment of the analytical framework of urban governance strengthening through C2C as presented in Chapter 2.

Based on the four case study partnerships a number of C2C interventions will provide empirical evidence to the questions posed here. Urban governance strengthening is unravelled, aided by the analytical framework presented in Chapter 2. Trends that will be detected show in which way partnerships perform well and which areas are hardly affected by partnership activities. Taking an inductive approach, several steps are taken to achieve this goal. First, a number of interventions are discussed that have been selected from the four partnerships. These examples can be typified as the principal partnership activities in recent years.[252] They serve as revealing illustrations of what has been taking place in North-South C2C practice in terms of urban governance strengthening in municipalities in the South, with the intention to cover the full scope of potential intervention outcomes. Secondly, the evidence of the cases is categorised, taking into account the dual perspective of building strong local states and strong civil societies at the same time. Thirdly, the categorised empirical results are then applied to conceptualise urban governance strengthening through

---

251   Parts of this Chapter have been published elsewhere in adapted version (Bontenbal & Van Lindert, 2008b; Bontenbal, 2009b).

252   It should be noted that it is not intended to be exhaustive in this respect and to cover the full range of projects, activities and other interventions undertaken during the total time span of existence of the partnerships as was presented in Table 5.1.

C2C. In this step the analytical framework is adapted and transformed into the form of an optimal scenario, indicating all the potential ways for an impact of C2C on urban governance processes in cities in the South.

9.1 Evidence of urban governance strengthening through C2C

Case A. Improving financial and environmental management in the municipality of Villa El Salvador

In recent years, a series of municipal staff exchanges and overseas missions have taken place between the Municipalities of Amstelveen and Villa El Salvador. They occurred in the context of several projects to strengthen the municipality of VES of which the two most recent and principal are presented briefly here. The first project (2004-2006) was concerned with improving the financial administration of VES municipality. Financial reform had been put forward by VES as one of the main priorities, as the weak financial administration hindered adequate policy-making and decision-making on the allocation of investments based on financially sound planning. In a series of work visits in Amstelveen and VES, exchange of knowledge and experience took place with regard to the reform process of the local administration, decentralised budget management, audit and information technology systems, implementation of municipal legislative changes, raising municipal taxes, municipal financial regulations, and human resource management. In addition, the project delivered hardware and software needed to support the financial reorganisation and provided training to 188 staff to guarantee a proper application and implementation of the financial management system. Some of the results that were found include the provision of up-to-date financial information readily available to all municipal departments, so that it is made easier to perform audits. This has not only resulted in more realistic investment planning and decision-making, it has also improved the conditions for a better service delivery to citizens and for the increase of municipal revenues from local taxes on property and services. A concrete project example of institutional strengthening is the upgrading of the various decentralised municipal agencies that are dispersed in the neighbourhoods of VES. For a large number of citizens these agencies perform the functions and services of the municipality, due to the long distance to the Town Hall and long queues.[253] Previously, the agencies were struggling to provide adequate financial information to citizens who came to pay their municipal taxes. This caused frustration and mistrust and increased the citizens' unwillingness to contribute. A network system was set up connecting the agencies with the Town Hall which allowed integration into the financial administration and direct data access and processing. Citizens who pay their contributions at the municipal agencies, now instantly receive a confirmation. This increases customer satisfaction, while at the same time the municipality has a more reliable budget overview on which it can base financial planning. Overall, it can be said that the conditions for better service delivery and local revenue raising have improved and that municipal transparency has been boosted thanks to

---

253 In general, the municipal agencies have three objectives: geographical dispersion of the local administration, bringing the municipality closer to citizens physically; facilitating revenue collection by raising awareness among citizens and changing the culture of non-payment of taxes; and involving citizens in municipal planning, by promoting the practice of participatory budgeting and *concertated* municipal development planning (Interview municipal agency manager, VES, February 19, 2007).

the provision of adequate and up-to-date financial information. The reform of the financial administration is seen as an important precondition to further strengthen the institutional performance in the context of the municipality's Institutional Development Plan (Chapter 5).

The financial management project has been largely paralleled by an environmental management project that took place between 2004 and 2007. It built on a previous cooperation between Amstelveen and VES (1998-2000) that facilitated the start of waste collection as a municipal service. Based on an integral approach, the environment project aimed at strengthening the new Environmental Services Department. An environmental management plan was designed, which was approved by the Provincial authorities of Greater Lima and integrated in the PIDC, to structure waste management services. Concrete project results include improvements in waste collection, including the introduction of waste recycling and separated waste collection, surface increase of green zones in the municipal area and a supporting irrigation system where use is made of treated waste water instead of the scarcely available tap water in the arid environment of VES. It also resulted in the first operating station for separation of solid recyclable waste in Peru, with co-finance from the European Commission (Chapter 6). A remarkable innovation has been the introduction of the *Bono Verde* (Green Ticket), which is an incentive-based system that gives citizens a discount on their municipal waste service fee for separating solid waste. The advantages of the *Bono Verde* system that have been mentioned are numerous. The service fee discount provides an incentive to citizens to separate their waste and raises awareness on environmental issues. Separated waste collection facilitates the work of private local waste collectors and enables them to generate an income from the sale of recyclable waste to wholesale buyers. At the same time the municipality benefits from reduced service costs by outsourcing part of the waste collection to the private sector and it contributes to one of its objectives (set out in the PIDC) to make the city a more healthy place to live.

The two projects were mutually supportive. Strengthening the financial organisation allowed the results achieved in the field of environment and waste collection to become more sustainable, based on realistic financial planning. It has further promoted the introduction of service fees for waste collection. At the same time, the environment project served as a show case to underline the relevance of financial reform. Says an Amstelveen official: "Environment and waste is easily quantifiable in terms of production and performance (...) You can show where the money comes from and where it goes by calculating the tonnages of waste collection (...) The environment project demonstrated the effects of good financial planning."[254]

Case B. Introducing a municipal performance management system in Oudtshoorn

The municipality of Oudtshoorn was assisted by the partner municipality Alphen aan den Rijn with the implementation of a Performance Management System (PMS) in the municipal organisation. Having a PMS in place is a legal requirement for all South African municipalities under the Municipal Systems Act of 2000. In the framework of the country's White Paper on Local Government objective to make local government developmental (Chapter 4), performance management can be viewed as a management instrument embedded in the annual cycle of municipal Integrated Development Planning (IDP) and the municipal

---

254   Interview official 6 Amstelveen, January 18, 2007.

THE CHALLENGE TO STRENGTHEN URBAN GOVERNANCE THROUGH NORTH-SOUTH CITY PARTNERSHIPS

budget.[255] PMS is considered a tool to measure and review the performance of the local administration and its staff, and consequently to assess "[local] government's commitment to good governance and service delivery" (SALGA, 2005). As a new element of public administration in South Africa, many municipalities, including Oudtshoorn, did not have a functioning PMS at the time it became legally mandated. The efforts of Alphen aan den Rijn were geared to ensuring that Oudtshoorn Municipality became able to fulfil its legal obligations in this respect. For Alphen, the project linked well with its partnership objectives to 'strengthen local governance' in the partner city (Chapter 6), since PMS is a mechanism for monitoring the implementation of the IDP and hence for enhancing the role of the municipality as community developer.

The objectives of the two-year project facilitated by Alphen, which started in 2005, entailed implementation of a functioning performance management system ("comprehensive, effective, efficient and practical") and empowering all stakeholders in Oudtshoorn to sustain the PMS through the transfer of knowledge, skills and competencies.[256] Alphen has effectively made use of external expertise to implement the PMS project by subcontracting a consultancy firm from Stellenbosch to guide the process in Oudtshoorn Municipality (Chapter 7). Their role was to train councillors, management, and officials on the system's legal requirements and rationale. Also, the consultants assisted very practically with setting objectives and targets and defining key performance indicators for municipal projects, which resulted in numerous work shops and training sessions for councillors and local government staff. Responsibilities were defined and a performance measurement framework, including targets and dates, was created, as well as a performance auditing mechanism and reporting and reviewing cycles. Altogether, about 30 staff and 40 councillors were trained during the project.

The project was concluded with a seminar organised by Alphen and the Provincial government of Western Cape. The seminar brought together some 70 representatives from some 20 municipalities located in Western Cape Province, facilitating South-South exchange and creating knowledge spill-over on performance management and the experiences and lessons learned from Oudtshoorn municipality.

Case C. Towards strategic planning in León

From the early 1990s, Utrecht and León started to work together on strategic urban development planning in tackling some of the most stressing bottlenecks – economic decline and lack of adequate housing, which in combination with an explosive population growth led to uncontrolled urban expansion and illegal land occupation (Bredenoord, 2005). With technical assistance from Utrecht municipality and financially sponsored by the Dutch Ministry of Foreign Affairs, a two-year planning process took place which started in 1994 and eventually led to the creation of the *Plan Maestro*.[257] It was approved by León's

---

255   The PMS system is founded on key performance indicators that are used as a yardstick for measuring performance relating to municipal development priorities and IDP objectives. Whereas IDPs fulfil the planning stage of performance management, PMS fulfils the implementation management, monitoring and evaluation of the IDP process.

256   Source: Memorandum of Agreement between Oudtshoorn Municipality, Alphen aan den Rijn and Unistel Consultus (Proprietary) Limited, May 25th, 2005.

257   Plan Maestro Estructural de León, 1996.

municipal council in 1996. The plan set out a vision for future urban development of the municipal territory (including the surrounding rural areas) with a corresponding zoning plan and defined control measures (Bredenoord, 2005). The planning process included surveys to identify the main priorities, the definition of development objectives in both urban and rural zones with regard to urban expansion, housing, and economic activities. The planning process resulted in a set of defined strategies, such as the upgrading of the historical-colonial city centre, the improving of rural infrastructure and the promotion of tourism as an economic activity. It also included the León South East (LSE) urban expansion project, which some years later became the prime focus of cooperation between Utrecht and León (see below). A monitoring mechanism was defined to secure integration of ongoing developments and regular upgrading of the Master Plan.

The *Plan Maestro* became a starting point for a consultative process assisted by Utrecht which led to the approval of the Strategic Plan of León in 1999. It meant that the element of public participation was introduced, with various community organisations and neighbourhood representatives participating in the planning process. A next step was to integrate both existing plans into one strategic municipal development plan. From 2004, this PEDM[258] has been the organising framework for municipal planning. It serves as an instrument to bring together municipality, civil society and private sector stakeholders to achieve an integrated and consultative development process and a participatory allocation of investments and project implementation.

The results of the Utrecht-León joint cooperation, that lasted over a decade, have thus materialised in a number of long-term strategic municipal urban planning instruments. In addition, the numerous work visits and technical exchanges between Utrecht and León officials strengthened the organisational and technical capacity of the municipal planning team of the Department of Physical Planning. Since the early 1990s, technical exchanges between Utrecht and León municipal staff have been common practice. Many officials from León have also come to the Netherlands to participate in the so-called Municipal Management Training courses offered by VNG (Chapter 3) and pay work visits to Utrecht municipality.

The wider impact of the planning process to which Utrecht contributed on the development of León is mixed. While it has contributed to setting planning priorities and implementing a number of them (such as the LSE project), economic development and the access to land for economic activities have been lagging behind. Also, as was shown in Chapter 6, the political will and institutional capacity to employ the PEDM has gone down in recent years. Still, it can be concluded that the cooperation has led to the introduction of a new – integrative – planning strategy, a monitoring system and a more 'professional' way of working[259] at the municipal planning department (Bredenoord, 2005). The municipal Plans have also been praised as being the first of its kind in Nicaragua, granting León a pioneer role in municipal strategic planning in the country. This is underscored by the fact that the

---

258   Plan Estratégico de Desarrollo Municipal – see Chapter 5.

259   Examples include the increased access to available, existing data; setting and managing priorities; seeking to establish public private partnerships; and increased level of know-how and skills. Pitfalls include the absence of clear responsibilities within the municipal planning department, and weak overall management and steering of the process (Bredenoord, 2005)

Plans existed long before changes in legislation required all Nicaraguan municipalities to draft municipal development plans.

Case D. Urban environmental capacity building in Treptow-Köpenick

One of the strategies and practices of *communal development cooperation* (Chapter 3) in Germany is providing learning opportunities to professionals working in local governments and communities in the South. German cities have the opportunity to invite representatives from their partner cities working in urban development and environmental management to follow capacity building programmes in Germany. Treptow-Köpenick has made use of these subsidy schemes and arranged for a number of professionals from its partner city Cajamarca to attend workshops and do on-the-job training in German companies and organisations in the framework of Local Agenda 21. The C2C working group in Treptow-Köpenick facilitated a number of internships in and around the District, mainly in the field of water and sanitation.

One of the programmes (sponsored by InWent (see Chapter 3) and the Federal Ministry for Economic Cooperation and Development) was a one-year capacity building track in 2003 for 19 urban professionals from Latin America on the themes Local Agenda 21 and urban infrastructure. The programme consisted of courses and workshops on the scope and rationale of LA21, ecological efficiency, sustainable development, public participation and consensus building. The participants not only gained insight into related processes in Germany, they also exchanged experiences from their home country. This facilitated mutual learning from different local contexts. Three professionals from Cajamarca participated: two from the Municipality and one from the municipal water company SEDACAJ. The local internships negotiated by Treptow-Köpenick were performed in Berlin's water treatment plant, the District administration and in an open air learning centre for nature and environment in the District's vicinity. An implicit objective of the capacity building initiative was for the C2C partnership to intensify the link between LA21 oriented processes in both cities in Germany and Peru.

In addition to LA21 and urban infrastructure, the exchange of knowledge on water and waste water management has been a focal point of the partnership. In 2000 the District organised a conference on water and waste water management in which six *Cajamarquinos* participated from SEDACAJ, local NGOs and the municipality, to exchange German and Peruvian experiences. During the years, several staff members from SEDACAJ were interns at the Berlin municipal water company. The emphasis in the various capacity building programmes was mainly on technological and operational issues.[260] The theme of water management is closely connected to the environmental and social problems caused by mining activities around Cajamarca (Chapter 5), which is a key focus area of the partnership. In that light, the partnership also facilitated a three-month internship in Germany in 2005 for a representative of its main counterpart NGO in Cajamarca, GRUFIDES, which is concerned with environmental degradation and social conflict due to the mining activities in Cajamarca area.

---

260 Personal journals by participants reveal the focus on technical innovation. For example, one participant noted the practice of locating clogs in water tubes through sensors displayed on small monitors.

Case E. Urban expansion in León South East

Since 1998 the municipality of Utrecht has supported León in its urban expansion ambitions in the South East of the city. It is one of the key strategies of the Plan Maestro. A long-term partnership project, called *León Sur Este* (LSE), has been concerned with the development of 5,000[261] parcels and 15,000 dwellings, physical and social infrastructure for low and medium income households. It should be completed by 2020. A rotating fund, kick-started by Utrecht, facilitates municipal land acquisition and provides a loan scheme to households for self-built housing. The project not only responds to the large housing demand in León, it also intends to prevent illegal land occupation on the urban fringe.

During the first years of the LSE support programme, assistance was mainly technical and on an individual basis. Urban planners and engineers from Utrecht assisted their peers in León by means of field visits, coaching and developing products together. Topics ranged from urban planning issues including legal advice on land acquisition and the allotment of land to designing the lay-out of the new urban area and planning infrastructure. Later, the planning approach became multidimensional, including social cohesion and community participation, environmental management and the provision of social services. Utrecht municipality has also directly targeted the inhabitants of León South East. The community organisation ACOPOE was supported in strengthening its role in liaising with the community and promoting citizen participation in the area's planning process. A community building was constructed, providing a physical space where municipal representatives and citizens discuss future plans and projects. The project management in Utrecht is embedded in the inter-departmental LSE working group as described in 6.1.2. This allows for a multi-disciplinary and integrated approach to planning support, meeting in a better way the variety of capacity needs of León municipality.

Overall, increased attention has been paid in the LSE project to institutional strengthening of the municipal organisation in León, and the skills and competencies of its staff in the sphere of urban planning, policy-making and developing management and leadership skills for municipal directors. Utrecht officials assisted in the drafting of policy plans in a range of municipal themes. An example is the social policy plan, setting out the strategies for social development as part of León's *social programme* which also focuses on sport, recreation and citizen participation. Assistance in policy-making not only allows the León administration to set objectives and define implementation strategies, it also promotes a *culture* of policy-making and long-term planning, which used to be a weak point in the administration. In 2004 León expressed interest to improve the organisational capacity of the local authority. Utrecht subcontracted a local consultant (Chapter 7) to provide courses on leadership skills, time management and decision-making for political leaders and administrative directors in León.

Utrecht applies the practice of capacity building moving towards a more integrated approach and the shift away from providing technical solutions to process and organisational support. But Utrecht's role is also changing to prepare León for independent continuation of the project. An important step was the integration of the LSE project office, founded in 1998 as an independent entity of the León administration, into the Department of Urban Development. This merged the project's institutional setting and existing policy and planning

---

261   As of 2006, some 2,300 lots had been delivered and sold. In February 2008, 56% of the lots sold were built upon (personal communication Head of Project LSE, León municipality, July 4, 2008).

instruments with the wider urban planning structure of the municipality. In 2010 Utrecht will retreat from the project, closing an era of capacity building activities that have contributed to the efficiency of León's institutional reorganisation and planning expertise.

9.2 Unravelling impact on urban governance strengthening

In the previous section five city partnership interventions in the framework of North-South city-to-city cooperation were presented. The examples provide relevant insight into the practice of C2C and the potentials and opportunities offered with regard to affecting urban governance mechanisms in the partner cities in the South. A next step is now to compare the examples: which commonalities and differences can be detected? How can the outcomes discussed here be categorised in order to analyse types of effects – in terms of local government strengthening and building community capacity? Table 9.1 provides an overview of the cases' findings, broken down into two categories: local government strengthening and civil society capacity building.

The cases show a strong commonality in the richness and diversity of outcomes of the first category of local government strengthening. It demonstrates the impact city-to-city cooperation can have on the effectiveness of local governments in the South. Although 'effectiveness' is slippery to analyse empirically, the outcomes reinforce the assumption that city-to-city cooperation is specifically valuable in terms of exchanging municipal expertise: something regular development agents such as NGOs can hardly compete with. It also underscores Hafteck's view (2003) that local authorities are at the core of C2C, both as actors and – at least directly – as beneficiaries. Based on the three areas of local government capacity building as presented by Grindle (1997) in Chapter 2, the effectiveness outcomes (relating to the role of local government as 'service provider'), can be further categorised. The five empirical examples have elements of all areas, and in most cases target simultaneously at all levels. At the individual level of *human resources and capital*, the training of staff is an element found in all cases, provided through workshops, internships, technical exchanges and training courses. It ranges from general skills development with regard to management, organisation and leadership (León, Villa El Salvador) to building more specific technical expertise such as water management and infrastructure (Cajamarca), planning expertise (León), performance management (Oudtshoorn) and financial administration (VES). With regard to *organisational strengthening*, the examples of VES, Oudtshoorn and León (strategic planning) provide substantial evidence. The interventions may contribute in terms of technical upgrading and the introduction of new instruments and tools, such as the delivery of IT systems, hardware and software (VES), implementing tools to measure organisational performance (Oudtshoorn) and developing strategic plans as instruments to long-term planning (León). Organisational strengthening is further expressed as aligning and improving internal processes, such as the financial administration in VES (budget management, financial planning, tax raising). Then, the cases show that the city partnerships have also generated results at the level of *institutional change*. In León, the integration of the León South East project office into the municipal administration that took place in the framework of the LSE project with Utrecht, shows the effects of institutional reorganisation, while the assistance delivered for policy design (e.g. in the field of social development) broadened the institutional scope of the administration. This is also the case for Villa El Salvador, where the establishment of an Environmental Services Department

Table 9.1 Case study evidence of local government and civil society strengthening through C2C

	Local government strengthening	Civil society strengthening
Financial and environmental management – Villa El Salvador	• Improved financial administration: e.g. budget management, financial planning, tax raising • Technical upgrading: IT, hardware, software • Staff training financial management • Set-up Dept. Environmental Services • Policy-making • Introducing new services – waste collection/green zones	• Training environmental neighbourhood committees
Introducing Performance Management – Oudtshoorn	• Meet municipal legislation requirements • Tool to increase organisational performance, service delivery and development planning • Training of municipal staff and council	N/A
Towards strategic planning in León	• Designing a long-term planning instrument • Building municipal planning expertise (urban development vision and strategies; zoning plan; monitoring and control mechanisms)	N/A
Urban environment capacity building in Germany	• Capacity building – training courses and internships – for municipal and municipal water company staff on urban infrastructure, LA21 and water management	• Capacity building – training courses and internships – for NGO staff on urban infrastructure, LA21 and water management
Urban expansion in León South East	• Developing management and leadership skills • Institutional reorganisation administration • Policy making	• Supporting neighbourhood committee ACOPOE

introduced a new area of service delivery to the municipal administration, with new policies, implementation instruments and responsibilities towards the Provincial Government of Lima. The performance management project in Oudtshoorn is strongly linked to supporting the widening institutional role of local government in South Africa, that is legally mandated to be developmental and to base service delivery on community needs. It also touches upon the wider sense of municipalities' roles as 'community developers' set out in Chapter 2.

The evidence of C2C interventions' impact on civil society capacity building is considerably more mixed. The projects of strategic planning in León and performance management in Oudtshoorn do not show any *direct* involvement of the community. However, indirect effects can be observed as both processes are participatory; this will be discussed below. In the other cases, some examples are noteworthy. In VES, the training of numerous environmental neighbourhood committees to participate in environmental management indirectly enhanced community participation, although lack of institutionalisation undermined the sustainability of citizens' involvement in the service delivery structure.[262] The León South East project led to the birth of the neighbourhood committee ACOPOE and its partaking in municipal planning.

In these municipal C2C projects, community participation was thus a key component. Participation has traditionally been a feature of local planning in both León and VES (see Hordijk, 2005). The projects not only acknowledged the long-term experience of citizens as 'makers and shapers' rather than 'users and choosers' (Cornwall & Gaventa, 2000), they also created favourable conditions to further encourage citizen engagement. Furthermore, the capacity building for professionals from Cajamarca in Treptow-Köpenick can not only be considered a form of local government strengthening, but also of building civil society capacity: some of the participants represented NGOs and CBOs of Cajamarca. Their organisations may benefit from the knowledge acquired in terms of operational capacity and negotiation power in collective urban decision-making processes on environmental affairs.

Now that the previous steps have been taken of presenting empirical evidence of C2C interventions and categorising the evidence into local government and civil society strengthening effects respectively, it becomes clear that it is appropriate and even essential to add a third category of impact. This category considers the reinforcement of local government-civil society relations, which is not only a direct result of C2C interventions, but stems from a indirect effect of the respective inventions that aim to strengthen local government and civil society. Table 9.2 shows the results of the impact of C2C on reinforcing these local government-civil society relations. This heterogeneous category entails the concepts of participation, responsiveness and accountability as mechanisms to bridge the gap between local administration and non-public actors (citizens, the private sector, CBOs and NGOs) of the partner cities in the South.

Apart from the German case, which is confined to capacity building activities of selected individuals with little direct impact on the intra-urban dynamics of Cajamarca, the cases show some interesting findings. A first issue concerns building multi-sectoral partnerships, leading to higher responsiveness and participation. The case of Villa El Salvador shows how public-private partnerships are set up through the *Bono Verde* project, by outsourcing municipal waste collection to private waste collectors. The example of the financial project in VES resulting in a more efficient financial administration demonstrates how institutional strengthening has indirectly led to increased government responsiveness and accountability by improving customer care to local taxpayers and transparency of financial records. In Oudtshoorn, the PMS project brings about opportunities to increase accountability on municipal organisational and project performance, since it aids the design of performance indicators and targets which makes government objectives more explicit and transparent – and thus easier to control and monitor for both insiders and outsiders of the local administration. The case of León shows how the partnership with Utrecht has fostered a participatory approach to municipal planning, both at neighbourhood level (the LSE project), and at city level (strategic plans). It calls for increased citizen participation which can further trigger marginalised and poor groups to raise their voice and express their needs. At the same time – in the case of the LSE project – the administration appears to

---

262   It was noted however that this aspect was considered the weakest link in the project. The environment committees were heavily supported by an NGO and after it retreated, much of the committees' work imploded (personal communication with official Amstelveen Municipality, May 22, 2007).

Table 9.2 Case study evidence of reinforcing local government – civil society relations through C2C

Financial and environmental management – Villa El Salvador	• Public-private partnerships (Bono Verde) • Increased financial transparency and accountability (financial administration) • Increased responsiveness (decentralised municipal agencies)
Introducing Performance Management – Oudtshoorn	• Increased bureaucratic accountability on organisational and project output performance
Towards strategic planning in León	• Planning process becomes participatory (responsive) • Strategic planning calls for increased participation
Urban environment capacity building in Germany	N/A
Urban expansion in León South East	• Building municipal expertise on social cohesion, community participation etc. • Introducing a participatory approach to neighbourhood planning

take up its role as 'community developer' and becomes more responsive to such processes, which is demonstrated by the introduction of new policy fields including social cohesion and community participation.

9.3 Conclusions: adjusting the analytical framework

Adding this third category of impact of urban governance strengthening through C2C, which takes a more dynamical approach and specifically accommodates the interactions and relations between the two spheres of urban governance, implies that the analytical framework that was derived from the review of literature in Chapter 2 needs to be adjusted. Table 9.3 brings together the findings summarised in Tables 9.1. and 9.2. As such, Table 9.3 provides the basis to this adjustment and the transformation of the analytical framework into an optimal scenario undertaken in the next step.

Before turning to the analytical framework that can be derived from Table 9.3, some remarks need to be made. The cases discussed here show that the role of civil society as actors in North and South are underrepresented. This is possibly due to the selection of cases, which may be biased towards interventions involving local government. However, as the examples have been selected as the most prominent of the city partnerships under study, it also suggests that civil society involvement in C2C does not always lead to clear-cut outcomes. Efforts have been found to be *ad hoc* and isolated. There is little evidence of civil society initiatives in the partner cities in the North that have empowered the position of citizens overseas. These initiatives are known to be hindered by lack of structural funding and lack of professional knowledge on working with partners in the South and understanding the development needs. This sometimes lead to amateurish aid efforts. Moreover, projects are usually small-scale and directed at improving the immediate living conditions in the partner city, rather than working on more abstract issues of citizenship and participation. This may further explain the sometimes weak results of civil society capacity building in Table 9.3.

Table 9.3 Case study evidence of urban governance strengthening through C2C

	Local government strengthening	Civil society strengthening	Reinforcing local government-civil society relations
Financial and environmental management – Villa El Salvador	• Improved financial administration: e.g. budget management, financial planning, tax raising • Technical upgrading: IT, hardware, software • Staff training financial management • Set-up Dept. Environmental Services • Policymaking • Introducing new services – waste collection/green zones	• Training environmental neighbourhood committees	• Public-private partnerships (*Bono Verde*) • Increased financial transparency and accountability (financial administration) • Increased responsiveness (decentralised municipal agencies)
Introducing Performance Management – Oudtshoorn	• Meet municipal legislation requirements • Tool to increase organisational performance, service delivery and development planning • Training of municipal staff and council	N/A	• Increased bureaucratic accountability on organisational and project output performance
Towards strategic planning in León	• Designing a long-term planning instrument • Building municipal planning expertise (urban development vision and strategies; zoning plan; monitoring and control mechanisms)	N/A	• Planning process becomes participatory (responsive) • Strategic planning calls for increased participation
Urban environment capacity building in Germany	• Capacity building – training courses and internships – for municipal and municipal water company staff on urban infrastructure, LA21 and water management	• Capacity building – training courses and internships – for NGO staff on urban infrastructure, LA21 and water management	N/A
Urban expansion in León South East	Developing management and leadership skills • Institutional reorganisation administration • Policymaking	• Supporting neighbourhood committee ACOPOE	• Building municipal expertise on social cohesion, community participation etc. • Introducing a participatory approach to neighbourhood planning

An exception to this trend, used here for illustration, is the Friendship Foundation Utrecht-León. As Chapter 5 and 7 pointed out, the Foundation coordinates all civil initiatives in Utrecht related to the partnership with León. Over the years, it has assisted various

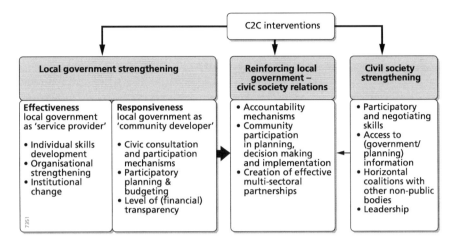

Figure 9.1 Assessing C2C contributions to urban governance strengthening in the South: the optimal scenario

CBOs in León in building management and organisational skills, such as writing business plans, getting a financially sound administration, formulating strategies and actions, and developing proposal-writing skills to apply for external funding. Examples include micro-credit associations, an organisation dealing with the prevention of youth prostitution and a CBO concerned with the promotion of sport and the prevention of crime. Organisational strengthening can be considered a precondition for having more negotiation power and a stronger voice in local decision-making processes. The Foundation has also been involved in capacity strengthening of community participants of the Municipal Development Committee (CDM) in León, a community-wide structure introduced with the administrative decentralisation legislation in Nicaragua[263] to function as a permanent, external advisor to municipal development planning (Chapter 4).

While such – anecdotal – support from *civil* actors do to some extent contribute to civil society strengthening in the partner cities in the South, it appears that the way in which *municipal* C2C interventions are executed is of more importance in opening up space for participatory and responsive urban governance processes. The participatory nature of municipal C2C projects, the indirect effects on responsiveness and transparency, and the objectives of building municipal expertise on community participation and participatory planning are examples.

How can urban governance be systematised to analyse the impact of city-to-city cooperation? Which indicators and issues need to be taken into account when we seek to understand the relationship between C2C intervention and the effects with regard to building strong local states and civil societies? Which outcomes deserve attention and why are they relevant? In Figure 9.1, based on the case studies discussed above, an attempt is made to present the analytical framework of urban governance interventions through C2C. It takes an optimal scenario, indicating all the potential ways for an impact of C2C on urban governance processes in cities in the South. It shows first that C2C can have a direct

---

263   Ley de Participación Ciudadana N°475 (2003).

impact on local government, civil society capacity building and reinforcing their mutual relations. Secondly, it reveals some indirect effects that may occur, due to e.g. increased local government responsiveness on the one hand and improved participatory skills of civil society on the other. They are not only an end to C2C interventions, they are also a means to further enhance the interaction and accountability between different urban actors and promote collective planning.

10 Conclusions: shifts in North-South cooperation, shifts in governance?

This study has addressed the interface between city-to-city cooperation (C2C) and urban governance. Aim of the study was to gain a better understanding of the relevance of cities' participation in development cooperation and the opportunities municipal partnerships may offer with regard to strengthening urban governance in cities in the South. Moreover, it was intended to gain insight into the underlying factors affecting C2C decision-making and potential impact. A number of recent policy and development trends provided an important rationale for putting these objectives central in the study. As a result of ongoing decentralisation and public reform processes, local government in the South has become increasingly mandated to be a key driver of local development planning. Local administrations therefore need to become more effective organisations and need to be more responsive to community needs. At the same time, several trends have resulted in a greater interconnectedness of local governments and communities world-wide: more recognition of local government as partners in development cooperation, the increased importance of the role of institutions and 'good governance' in urban development thinking, and the rise of international city networks and city-to-city cooperation. To what extent and in what way have these translocal linkages between the global North and South contributed to get stronger local states and civil societies in communities of developing countries?

This concluding Chapter starts with a short summary of the study and its main components, doing justice to the various conceptual, policy and empirical perspectives laid out in this research. Then, the main research findings are presented by addressing the research questions asked in the Introduction. Subsequently, the Chapter considers what these conclusions imply for the discussion on city-to-city cooperation and urban governance strengthening.

10.1 Summary

This research has drawn on a comparative study of four North-South city partnerships involving cities in Peru, Nicaragua, South Africa, the Netherlands and Germany. In all cities (four in the North and four in the South), a structured research strategy was followed, allowing for cross-case comparison. Research was conducted between 2005 and 2008 by means of qualitative methods. The main criteria for the selection of the partnerships included a) actors involved represented and targeted both local institutions and civil society in the partner cities, b) the institutional context of the cities in the South was shaped by a process of recent decentralisation or public sector reform, bringing about new challenges and responsibilities to local state and citizens alike and c) the objectives of the partnerships were linked to institutional strengthening or local (sustainable) development.

Two concepts were at the core of this study. The first concept is city-to-city cooperation. Chapter 1 pointed out that from an evolutionary perspective of international municipal relations, C2C partnerships specifically targeting development are a relatively new but growing phenomenon. City-to-city cooperation is aimed at supporting municipalities in institutional capacity building and the improvement of urban governance issues such as service delivery, creating an enabling legal and institutional environment, and fostering partnerships with key local public, private and community actors. Cities set up and support projects, and provide knowledge and expertise through capacity development in their partner cities, often organised in a peer-to-peer setting for local government officials and technicians. A review of documented case studies of North-South city twinning programmes in Chapter 1 offered a literature-based synthesis of the perceived benefits, strengths and weaknesses of C2C cooperation, which provided insight into the question which factors affect C2C partnerships as instruments to achieve the developmental objectives of municipal cooperation. These factors included the level of institutionalisation of the partnership in the municipal partner organisations and the quality of the partnership as vehicle for decentralised development cooperation. Key issues identified in the literature included moreover the notion of 'partnership' in North-South cooperation; the political dynamics inherent to capacity building in the public sector; and mechanisms of learning, knowledge exchange and mutuality in North-South partnerships.

Urban governance was a second key concept of this study. Chapter 2 illustrated that the growing attention to urban governance is largely fed by the reshaping of public administration in the South, which has resulted in a more prominent role for local government. An underlying rationale is that bringing government closer to the people will make it more responsive to the needs of 'ordinary citizens'. Decentralisation brings government and civil society closer together and introduces participation and responsiveness into the debate. The concept of urban governance recognises that decision-making power exists both inside and outside local government institutions, diminishing the distinction between the public and private spheres. Literature suggests that in order to achieve good, participatory local governance, people and institutions need to be brought together, and both a strong local government and citizenry are therefore needed. Chapter 2 concluded with the presentation of a theoretically grounded analytical framework to serve in the empirical (qualitative) assessment of urban governance strengthening in this study.

After reviewing the existing knowledge base on C2C and urban governance, the study turned towards the institutional and policy frameworks in which these concepts can be placed. Chapter 2 and 3 examined the policy context that supports and encourages cities and their local authorities in establishing and sustaining C2C relations. The rise of city-to-city cooperation as a mechanism for development assistance was explained by a number of trends. The increased acknowledgment of local governments as stakeholders in global governance and development is witnessed by an impressive array of international programmes that support municipal international cooperation. Chapter 3 moreover introduced the Dutch and German policy context for C2C, to serve as a background for the empirical analysis of the cases, and provided a policy evaluation of Dutch C2C funding programmes that aim to strengthen urban governance in South African municipalities.

Whereas Chapter 3 focused on policies that support municipalities in the 'North' to engage in C2C, Chapter 4 considered the institutional frameworks in which cities in the 'South' operate, with regard to municipal and decentralisation legislation and urban governance instruments and practice. A comparison was made between Peru, South Africa and Nicaragua. The Chapter revealed that in the three countries under study, recent and considerable changes have taken place with regard to decentralisation, the (developmental) mandate of municipalities and the scope of municipal competencies and responsibilities local governments now need to meet. As such, the analysis not only provided a relevant institutional context for the empirical analysis, it moreover was a tool to justify the methodology with regard to the selection of case studies, as the rapid legal and institutional changes in these countries have led to a significant capacity imperative within local government to respond to these changes.

The empirical part of this study was introduced by a review of the cities under study in Chapter 5, which included their socio-economic and institutional dynamics. Also, the C2C partnerships maintained by these cities were presented, in particular their origin and evolution over time. The Chapter served as a background to the empirical analysis conducted in the following Chapters.

Taking the perspective of both North and South, Chapter 6 examined the organisational and political preconditions that local governments ought to meet in order to successfully engage in C2C partnerships. Issues relevant to the context of municipalities in the North included the various organisational, political, and financial conditions that are essential to act as partners or donors in international development cooperation. The issues of municipalities in the South were related to comparable conditions, however of additional importance in the analysis was the question to what extent C2C partnerships are employed as strategic instruments to meet municipal development and planning objectives. The Chapter moreover shed light on the economic relevance of decentralised cooperation for municipal investments and the practice of donor harmonisation at the urban level in the South.

In addition to the unique feature that local governments are the protagonists in development cooperation discussed in Chapter 6, a second distinguishing feature of C2C was explored in Chapter 7. C2C is not confined to the participation of local governments, but also includes a range of urban actors from the civil and private spheres. As such, entire local networks may be engaged in international municipal cooperation. The presence or absence, as well as the roles and interrelations of these municipal C2C actors were discussed for the eight cities under study. Together, Chapter 6 and 7 provided a better understanding how partnerships are organised in the partner cities in North and South, both within local administrations and from a city-wide perspective.

In Chapter 8, the analysis shifted from partner cities to the partnerships between them, and concentrated on the challenges inherent to North-South partnerships in a municipal context. Conditions were examined that are of influence to the application of C2C partnerships as a mechanism for capacity development and knowledge exchange. A number of concepts have served as guiding principles in the analysis, which moreover were found to be strongly interrelated. They included ownership; sustainability and continuity; individual and organisational learning; and mutuality. Furthermore, the Chapter reviewed the perceptions and viewpoints with regard to the added value of city-to-city cooperation in comparison to other forms of (decentralised) development cooperation.

Finally, Chapter 9 touched upon the core of the research by bringing together the two key concepts of C2C and urban governance. It addressed to what extent and in what way the city partnerships under study have contributed to strengthening urban governance in

THE CHALLENGE TO STRENGTHEN URBAN GOVERNANCE THROUGH NORTH-SOUTH CITY PARTNERSHIPS

the partner cities in the South. The link between urban governance strengthening and city-to-city cooperation was identified as multifarious and complex. The potential impact that city partnerships can have on urban governance was presented in the form of an optimal scenario, indicating all the potential ways for an impact of C2C on governance processes in cities in the South. The analysis built on the conceptualisation of the two-fold precondition for good governance put forward in the theoretical framework. It first assessed how C2C has led to the strengthening of municipal administrations and their services. Secondly, it focused on the effects of C2C on the conditions that foster citizen participation in processes of shared local decision-making. Moreover, the empirically grounded analysis called for an adjustment of the theory-driven framework, to include a more dynamical approach to accommodate more explicitly the mutual local government-civil society relations that were found to be potentially reinforced through city-to-city cooperation.

10.2 Findings

Having summarised the content of this study, while reiterating the aim and rationale of the research, the principal research findings, reflecting on the research questions posed in the Introduction, are presented below.

1. *Which national and supranational institutional and policy conditions shape the role of local governments in international cooperation and local development processes?*

Two – at first sight – independent developments, relating to (donor) development policy on the one hand and decentralisation policies and the changing institutional framework of local governments in the South on the other hand, explain the rationale and growing recognition for city-to-city cooperation.

The first development concerns the growing significance of the position of local government in international cooperation, as Northern cities have become more and more engaged in the international development cooperation arena. Three trends were identified that clarify the growing role of municipalities as development partners. First, there has been increased recognition from supranational donors, national and local governments alike for local government as partners in development cooperation. It reflects a more general trend that the international donor community has become more receptive to incorporating non-conventional donors including NGOs, civil society, local authorities and communities. Secondly, development thinking and planning has more and more embraced the importance of institutions and good governance, also at the local level. An increased understanding that urban development requires strong local governments has emerged. The rapid urbanisation of poverty and the growing belief that tomorrow's solutions to poverty and underdevelopment are to be found in cities, has re-intensified the need for local government capacity building and improving urban governance. Thirdly, it was demonstrated that there has been a sharp rise in the number of international city networks and a growing importance of 'partnerships' in international cooperation. Fostered by ongoing globalisation, cities increasingly seek to learn from their (transnational) peers through networking, exchange of knowledge and seeking best practices elsewhere to find solutions to their urban challenges. The growing recognition for C2C and the role of local governments in development is reflected by a plethora of donor policy and support programmes at supra-national and national levels, that provide financial assistance and technical capacity to municipalities engaged in development cooperation, and facilitate networking among cities.

The example of Dutch C2C policy revealed in more detail how policy instruments are shaped and how they are applied to affect C2C practice. Dutch decentralised development aid is aimed at the institutional development of municipalities in the South in terms of service delivery, organisational and financial management and policy making. While policy instruments increasingly attempt to incorporate local context, knowledge and experience and pay more attention to ownership in the South, it was found that Dutch C2C policy has not always focused on the most pressing urban needs and municipal priorities in the target countries. Moreover, local governments in The Netherlands risk the danger to become overly dependent on national funding for their C2C activities, which may lead to the (unfavourable) situation that project objectives are defined by funding criteria rather than the needs expressed by partner institutions in the South.

The second institutional development that explains the rationale for C2C relates to the capacity imperative for local government in the South that has resulted from ongoing decentralisation and public sector reform. Local governments and local communities have rapidly become more autonomous and proactive agents of development, with growing responsibilities regarding service delivery, poverty alleviation and improving the quality of urban life. Changes in the institutional frameworks of Peru, South Africa and Nicaragua have brought about new mandates, responsibilities and a stronger financial resource base for their respective municipalities. It was demonstrated that local governance structures in these countries are legally institutionalised and based on community participation, which potentially allows local governments to become more responsive, accountable and development-oriented. At the same time, however, the often rapid legislative changes have posed many challenges to local governments, which uniformly continue to seriously lack from financial and human resources to perform their tasks adequately. The institutional framework explains the need for capacity building, which could be achieved through C2C, and in addition shapes current urban governance processes in the partner cities in the South. It can be concluded that not only from a theoretical but also from a policy-oriented perspective, the assessment of C2C initiatives and their results should take into account the (desired) participatory, developmental and inclusive nature of urban decision-making.

2. *Under which local political and institutional conditions do local governments operate in international cooperation and what are the implications for the practice of city-to-city cooperation?*

As partner cities in North and South operate in distinct organisational, financial and political contexts, the second research question was subdivided into two sub-questions. A first sub-question was concerned with the position and role of local governments in the North to act as partners in development cooperation through C2C partnerships. Development cooperation is not the *raison d'être* for local governments: their existence is not dependent on it, and they are not legally mandated to engage in C2C. international relations are thus an entirely voluntary activity of municipalities. The voluntary nature makes participation in C2C vulnerable and subject to political (regime) changes. As a result, municipalities need to meet a number of criteria that are connected to aspects of 'interest and infrastructure'. Four political and institutional conditions have been found to be of particular importance in the North:

1. In the absence of a legal mandate, municipal policies and political programmes need to be in place to shape the scope and objectives of C2C. Objectives were found to be predominantly related to global awareness-raising in the own city and strengthening local governance in the South.

2. As local governments are not development organisations, their staff do not automatically possess the necessary skills and expertise to engage in C2C. In order to tap from the human capital available, it was found that key roles need to be properly defined and broad consultation should be promoted. Selection mechanisms are relevant to identify staff to participate on the merits of their skills, knowledge, and experience to respond sensibly to the capacity needs in the South.

3. A third crucial factor is the extent to which municipalities are successful in attracting external funding. It was found that external funding generally exceeds the partner cities' own contributions, which are limited due to the voluntary nature of C2C. Local governments in the North cause a multiplier effect of funding, which implies that through C2C, (inter)national resources are decentralised and targeted directly towards the local level in the South.

4. The voluntary status makes C2C vulnerable as municipal task, and as such political interest and will are crucial factors. Moreover, support from staff may benefit from promoting C2C as human resource development instrument. Generally, however, political and staff support remain quite passive, in which C2C is tolerated and approved rather than being driven by pro-active involvement and political interest.

The second sub-question did not only consider the political and institutional conditions for municipalities in the South to engage successfully in C2C, it also addressed to what extent they employ their C2C partnerships as strategic instruments to meet municipal development and planning objectives. The presence of municipal International Cooperation Departments was found to be important to facilitate and sustain C2C as a mature municipal responsibility, act as a broker to match the capacity and investments needs of the organisation with the available know-how and resources from partner cities, and reduce the risk that partnerships are too dependent on one person. Political interest in the South appears obvious given the economic and financial benefits. However, it was also illustrated that political will may turn out to be lip service rather than real interest.

Having international relations and the necessary organisational conditions available in the South does not solve municipal capacity challenges *per se,* rather the extent to which C2C projects are employed to meet municipal development objectives is crucial. It was found that municipalities were not always successful in this respect. The example of León showed that the underlying reasons why C2C is insufficiently linked to urgent issues in urban governance and the developmental role of local governments in the South are a matter of organisational capacity (lack of resources and skills to develop strategies for C2C), political interest (personal -mayoral- preferences dominate over institutionally defined development objectives in political decision-making and allocation of (international) investments) and institutional concern (weak authoritative power of Municipal Development Plans as instrument for urban planning and allocation of international funds).

3. *Which actors constitute municipal C2C networks in partner cities, what are their roles and responsibilities and which interrelations can be found among them?*

In partner cities in North and South, C2C goes beyond the participation of local government only, and includes other actors. The participation of actors has been found to be ample and diverse. The main categories recognised were local administrations, coordinating civil society entities (CCSEs), (decentralised) public sector donors, external or national development agents, the private sector, and civil society actors. CCSEs have been identified as taking a unique position as their existence is based primarily on the C2C partnership, while the partnership is generally not a core issue for other actors involved. Local governments and CCSEs are usually the key elements of the municipal C2C partnership architecture, although their presence is not found to be significant in all cases. It can be said that the group of civil society actors is the most diverse, whereas the private sector is generally underrepresented.

Municipal C2C networks in partner cities are the result of the interrelations among these actors. Moreover, these relations define to a large extent the actors' roles and responsibilities. Six types of functional relationships were distinguished for C2C networks in the North, serving financial flows, awareness-raising, delivery of know-how and expertise, creating support to sustain C2C partnerships, providing a window to developing countries and development cooperation, and implementing projects and twinning with the South. Especially the relationships between local governments and CCSEs have been found to be diverse and complex. The two-folded objective of C2C that is often pursued in the North (local governance strengthening in the South and awareness-raising in the North) is an underlying explanation for the network structures found. Where present in the network, local governments 'outsource' the second objective to CCSEs, providing financial assistance to the latter. CCSEs in return undertake activities to raise awareness and create public support to sustain C2C partnerships.

Various differences exist between the networks in North and South. The relationships within the Northern networks appear to be more formalised, and cooperation and coordination between actors is more harmonised and crystallised. In the South relationships are more informal, less obvious and visible, and not all actors are linked to the network. Moreover, whereas network relationships in the North can be generally characterised as mutually supportive and complementary, in which actors benefit from each other's presence and participation in C2C, it has been observed that in the South. Sometimes conflict instead of cooperation arises within partnership networks. In particular the gap between civil society and local government is evident in several cases.

The analysis has further shown underlying factors which determine the participation of actors beyond local government, especially in the South. If civil society in the South seeks to be actively involved actors rather than mere aid recipients, they need a certain level of institutionalisation, i.e. resources and organisational infrastructure. Cajamarca showed moreover that political backing from local government for civil society participation in C2C is important, although in the example of Oudtshoorn it was found that too much political and municipal involvement may only be counterproductive. The relevance of resources and infrastructure is demonstrated in León, where the civil wing of the partnership with Utrecht flourishes thanks to a strong organisational position of the CCSE. The case of León however also suggested that the capacity of civil society in the South to participate in C2C is partly dependent on financial assistance from the North. The fact that the North attracts additional

THE CHALLENGE TO STRENGTHEN URBAN GOVERNANCE THROUGH NORTH-SOUTH CITY PARTNERSHIPS

funding for partner municipalities illustrates moreover the influence (through lobby and funding) that Northern partners exercise on municipal C2C partnership networks in the South. It thus seems that in the South the potential of actors engaged in C2C to establish strategic alliances to sustain their efforts depends to some extent on the supportive role and position of partner cities in the North.

Overall, although a causal relationship is difficult to demonstrate, it appears that a balanced participation of local government and civil society provides the most favourable conditions to sustain city-to-city cooperation. Without local government participation, C2C may be undermined by lack of political support, resources, infrastructure and mechanisms to account for spending public resources. The absence of civil society participation on the other hand poses the risk of technocratic, isolated cooperation with little public support.

4. *Under which conditions and to what extent do C2C partnerships function as mechanism for capacity development and knowledge exchange?*

Who decides and sets the agenda in C2C partnerships? It was found that partners in C2C arrangements generally seek to cooperate in a demand-driven way through dialogue and consensus building. Decision-making is in the main pursued by partner cities in the South, which offers a greater potential for cooperation tailored towards the existing capacity and needs of 'recipient' organisations. At the same time however, it was found that a tension exists between the ambition to foster ownership and the reality that financial control is exercised by the North. The example of Alphen-Oudtshoorn in particular illustrated how ownership may be undermined by restricting (external) funding and project criteria set in the North.

What mechanisms are employed for exchange and interaction? The majority is confined to short-time work visits to partner cities. The process approach, precondition to sustainable capacity development, may be undermined by the fact that little interaction takes place in between missions. Missions therefore have the risk to become isolated one-time events, and momentum in long-term partnership arrangements may be lost. Monitoring and evaluation mechanisms are important tools to sustain progress made, and signal relevant future needs.

What is the potential for learning in C2C partnerships? A number of conclusions can be drawn. First, personal learning has various dimensions and was observed in both North and South. Examples include personal (skills) development; learning about different cultures and poverty; and viewing different attitudes to life and work. Secondly, professional learning in the North is mainly linked to acquiring and improving work skills and reflecting on one's own work. Learning is triggered by being exposed to different (cultural) organisational contexts. In contrast, professional learning in the South is largely based on gaining technical knowledge in the specific field of expertise of participants. Thirdly, in the South, C2C projects have generally generated results beyond the individual sphere. Particularly the cases of VES and León reveal the effects C2C may have on organisational change. In the North however, while diverse learning benefits were identified, it was also found that the knowledge and skills obtained were not evidently implemented into daily work practice.

A fourth condition, mutuality, was found to be present in North-South city partnerships, but it was not confined to the dimension of learning. Cities in the North do not regard the improvement of their own organisational performance or enhancement of staff knowledge and skills through learning as necessary components of 'good' partnering.

Instead, objectives in the North – both politically and individually – can be seen as rather altruistic and strongly related to delivering development assistance to the South. If learning in the North is not an objective, it implies that the question whether mutuality in learning is evident in C2C is not relevant, at least not from a policy perspective. Instead of learning, stronger opportunities for mutuality in C2C may be offered by the benefits that may accrue to Northern municipalities from a strategic political and organisational perspective, e.g. fostering staff loyalty and motivation, creating global awareness inside and outside the local administration, and generating good publicity and a social image for the municipality.

Although it remains to be studied how C2C compares to other modalities of decentralised development assistance in terms of cost effectiveness, it can overall be concluded that city-to-city cooperation holds several advantages as a mechanism of capacity development. The findings reveal a high potential for ownership, thanks to high levels of mutual agreement and understanding of needs. To foster ownership, and make capacity building a sustainable process, municipalities in the South need a thorough understanding of their strategic development needs, while funding criteria in the North should not be too restricting and volatile. As municipalities in North and South are institutions of the same kind, with relatively similar characteristics, activities and roles in communities, they have been perceived to reach a rather high level of mutual understanding and share a common base. This fosters a greater comprehension of issues arising and how to tackle them. Next, although partnerships are in particular sites for learning for the South rather than the North, there is little risk that a lack of mutuality harms the effectiveness of capacity and skills exchange. When learning and capacity development is achieved in the South and the political and strategic organisational objectives of engaging in C2C are met by the North, C2C offers benefits and opportunities to both North and South. As such, the need for mutuality, e.g. to make partnerships and commitment more enduring (Brinkerhoff, 2002; Johnson & Wilson, 2006) is met, which sustains partnership structures. A final advantage is that Northern municipalities can fill a niche by strengthening their Southern counterparts who are sometimes left out of international assistance, due to the relatively negative perception on working with local public institutions in the South.

5. *To what extent and in what way do C2C partnerships contribute to strengthening urban governance in the South?*

In the first category of urban governance strengthening, that deals with local government capacity, a rich diversity of outcomes was found. It demonstrates the impact C2C can have on the effectiveness of local governments in the South, underlining the assumption that city-to-city cooperation is specifically valuable in terms of exchanging municipal expertise, which is something that regular development agents such as NGOs can hardly compete with. It also underscores Hafteck's view (2003) that local authorities are at the core of C2C, both as actors and – at least directly – as beneficiaries. Based on the three areas of local government capacity building (Grindle, 1997), the effectiveness outcomes (relating to the role of local government as 'service provider'), were further categorised. At the individual level of *human resources and capital*, the training of staff is an element found in all examples, ranging from general skills development to building more specific technical expertise. With regard to *organisational strengthening*, substantial evidence was also found, e.g. technical upgrading and the introduction of new instruments and tools, and aligning and improving internal processes. Results at the level of *institutional change* were also identified, referring to processes of institutional reorganisation, and broadening the institutional scope of administrations e.g. through the introduction of new areas of policymaking and service delivery. The latter also touched upon the wider sense of municipalities' roles as 'community developers'.

With respect to the second category of urban governance strengthening, i.e. C2C interventions' impact on civil society capacity building, the evidence is considerably more mixed and rather weak. With some exceptions, C2C interventions in general show little *direct* effects on community strengthening. There is little evidence of civil society initiatives in the partner cities in the North that have empowered the position of citizens overseas. Civil society involvement in C2C does not always lead to clear-cut outcomes, with projects characterised as small-scale and directed at improving very practically the living conditions in the partner city, rather than working on more abstract issues of citizenship and participation.

Instead, it was found that civil society strengthening occurs mainly as a result of the participatory nature of C2C projects that are in the first place concentrated on strengthening local governments. These projects not only acknowledged the long-term experience of citizens as 'makers and shapers' rather than 'users and choosers' (Cornwall & Gaventa, 2000) in especially León and Villa El Salvador, they also created favourable conditions to further encourage citizen engagement. Therefore, it can be concluded that not only the direct impact of C2C on the two (the public and civil) spheres of urban governance is of importance, but also the *indirect* effects these interventions may have on reinforcing mutual local government-civil society relations.

As a result, a third category of impact was added to the framework of analysis, that justifies this more dynamical approach to evaluating C2C effects. This category included the emergence of multi-sectoral partnerships, offering opportunities for participation; increased government responsiveness and accountability, e.g. by improving customer care to local taxpayers and increased fiscal transparency; improved opportunities for controlling and monitoring local government performance for both insiders and outsiders of the local administration; a more participatory approach to municipal planning, calling for increased citizen participation which can further trigger marginalised and poor groups to raise their voice and express their needs; and the introduction of new policy fields including social cohesion and community participation which challenges local administrations to take its role as 'community developer' more seriously.

In sum, it can be said that C2C appears to be especially applicable to improve the effectiveness of local administrations in the South, whereas direct civil society strengthening is more limited. Instead, the way in which *municipal* C2C interventions are executed is of more importance in opening up space for participatory and responsive urban governance processes. The participatory nature of municipal C2C projects, the indirect effects on responsiveness and transparency, and the objectives of building municipal expertise on community participation and participatory planning are examples. In the analysis of urban governance strengthening through C2C, it is therefore useful to not only consider the direct impact of these interventions. The *indirect* impacts, which result from increased local government responsiveness on the one hand and improved participatory skills of civil society on the other are vital to take into account. They are not only an end to C2C interventions, they are also a means to further enhance the interaction and accountability between different urban actors and promote collective planning.

10.3 Discussion

10.3.1 Putting the findings into perspective

This study has provided different perspectives on the role of international city partnerships and networking in improving urban governance and opportunities for local development in countries in the global South. As such, it has aimed to further feed, structure and systematise the existing body of knowledge on city-to-city cooperation. Although it has grown rapidly in recent years, the empirical knowledge base can still be characterised as rather patchy, isolated and anecdotal. Not only has this study attempted to bring together existing knowledge in a more systematised way, it has also expanded it, providing new insights based on empirical findings. Of particular relevance might be the set of factors that was unravelled as influential in how international cooperation between cities is shaped and how it performs with regard to the objectives it seeks to meet. These include institutional, legal and policy contexts at a national and supranational level (*cf.* Hafteck, 2003; Keiner & Kim, 2007; Buis, 2009), political and organisational conditions at the level of the local administration (*cf.* Un-Habitat, 2003; Hewitt, 1999), actors engaged in municipal partnership networks at city-level (*cf.* Rademaker & Van der Veer, 2001; Van Lindert, 2001; UNDP, 2000), and partnership conditions referring to the actual cooperation practiced (*cf.* Johnson & Wilson, 2006; Spence & Ninnes, 2007; Tjandradewi et al., 2006; Jones & Blunt, 1999). Together these factors may provide a more holistic approach to understanding city-to-city cooperation, its strengths and weaknesses.

Overall, the analysis was sometimes ambivalent as to how municipal North-South cooperation should be approached. Has the practice of C2C led to shifts in North-South cooperation, and how can these shifts be interpreted? It is not easy to answer these questions. There appears to be a paradox resulting from the fact that municipal partnerships are embedded in North-South settings: there is a continuous tension in regarding North-South C2C as mechanisms of equal, horizontal exchange versus just another form of the classic linear model of aid flowing from North to South (*cf.* Baud, 2002). While the former implies learning and knowledge exchange that benefits each partner, which is popular rhetoric among C2C practitioners, the latter questions such reciprocity since unilateral flows of resources, technical knowledge and expertise from North to South appear to be practice, at least at first sight. To put it in other words: while C2C is based on the concept of 'twinning' which implies a high level of similarity among organisations operating in similar contexts, these partnerships are frequently contested as being structurally asymmetrical and incapable to overcome relentless inequalities in resources, knowledge, input and outcomes. Indeed, the findings revealed that there is in particular a discrepancy between the financial resources invested by the partner municipalities – virtually all C2C activities were found to be financed by the North. Also, the existence of international relations policies that provide a clear political-institutional mandate for international cooperation are a predominantly Northern issue. In the South however, international cooperation is usually a more important municipal affair than in the North, given its significance as source of income for municipal investments and the central position it may claim in the organisation and staff allocation.

These differences can be partly explained by the different roles municipalities take up in North-South C2C partnerships, which can arguably be seen as 'donor' versus 'recipient'.

The analysis has called for a flexible approach how North-South city partnerships should be regarded. The issue of capacity building and urban governance strengthening in local communities in the South, among common objectives set in North-South city-to-city cooperation, is clearly related to the donor-recipient view. It recognises donors' intentions to employ C2C partnerships as instruments for local public sector capacity building in developing countries. On the other hand city partnerships have been celebrated for their potential to act as sites for mutual learning, that appears to take place at the individual level (e.g. Van Ewijk & Baud, 2009; Devers-Kanoglu, 2009; Johnson & Wilson, 2006; 2009), the organisational level (e.g. De Villiers, 2009) and at city level (e.g. Campbell, 2009). Putting learning and mutuality central in the analysis of city-to-city cooperation calls for a more equitable approach, which should include an examination of real impacts with regard to shared costs, shared learning and shared benefits.

Hence, we should neither view city partnerships that operate in a North-South setting as twinning relations that bring together organisations with corresponding partnership input (i.e. roles and financial and technical backgrounds), nor should we neglect that they are institutions of the same kind, with relatively similar characteristics, activities and roles in communities. At the same time, North-South city partnerships are neither traditional donor-recipient relationships alone, nor do they bring about a completely mutual cooperation in terms of shared costs and shared benefits. Moreover, given the eclectic nature of participation and activities in C2C, the various dimensions may be applicable to one partnership at the same time. Peer-to-peer collaboration in municipal expertise sharing, which offers potential for mutuality, may e.g. co-exist in the same partnership with typical charity activities such as the donation of medical instruments or surplus equipment and fundraising activities.

Given the explorative character and the revelatory nature of the research and its case studies (see Annex I), due to limited knowledge prior to the research, and the corresponding attempt to present a high diversity among the cases, it can be said that the examples have collectively brought about a wide and solid evidence base, covering many different features. At the same time, valid questions can be prompted with regard to the relevance of the outcomes of these cases. Are the research findings relevant and applicable beyond these particular examples? This is especially of significance with regard to the central question how city-to-city cooperation may strengthen urban governance in the South, and it is apt to outline some limitations to the related analysis in Chapter 9. It was found that the potential of building civil society capacity is not as significant and systematic as one would expect from the twofold nature of C2C and its feature of representing and targeting a wide variety of urban stakeholders, including citizens. The replicability of the cases might be questioned. The specific architecture of these partnerships, of which some are particularly focused on municipal rather than civil society participation (e.g. Amstelveen-VES) may have biased the outcomes. A future step would therefore be to apply the analytical framework to other C2C experiences, with different features regarding the civil society participation in C2C arrangements, to see whether the potential impact on building civil society capacity would remain slight in other C2C experiences as well and whether the framework needs adjustment.

The replicability of the cases may further be challenged by the observation that local politics and political representation as elements of urban governance are absent in the analytical framework and optimal scenario model. The cases in this study have provided little insight into interventions dealing directly with local electoral systems and their political representatives. A possible explanation to this lack is that politics in the partner cities are a sensitive subject that municipalities in the North are reluctant to become involved in. Local politics are embedded in historical, socio-cultural contexts. It might be controversial to participate as external partners. Instead, it is often easier and more 'safe' to focus on technical capacity building, which delivers tangible outcomes. This is confirmed by Avskik (1999), who has similar observations in his examples of Norwegian twinning programmes. Still, the literature has increasingly paid attention to the part cities can play in (multi-party) democracy building and local conflict resolution, referring for example to the notion of 'city diplomacy'. Testing the framework on other C2C experiences may reveal more insight into the impact of partnership interventions that specifically seek to influence political dynamics.

All in all, the use of case studies as a research strategy is explicitly useful for analytic generalisation however, whereas generalising the outcomes to a larger research population (i.e. statistical generalisation) is not appropriate (see Annex I). Thus the strength of this research lies particularly in the sphere of identifying relevant features of the subjects under study, which help to sharpen the analytical frame that functions as a conceptual tool to (future) evidence building. The dynamics which have been revealed through this study and their systematisation may be a valuable starting point for a next step in research. It may serve to identify a set of measurable variables, which could be analysed in a more quantitative fashion, to test the outcomes of this study on a larger group of city-to-city partnerships and their cities.

10.3.2 Lessons learned

In relation to the literature on North-South (municipal) partnerships and urban governance, which lessons have been learned from this study? A first important lesson is that city-to-city cooperation can never be understood, nurtured nor facilitated without a proper assessment of the political factor. Since C2C interventions take place in a political setting, the contextual factors of local politics, power relations and decision-making through informal and formal arrangements should not be neglected. It is valuable here to reflect once more on the political nature and context which are inherent to municipal partnerships due to the mere fact that they are linked to public sector institutions that are represented by locally elected leaders. Given the focus on *local* processes in this study, the observations are confined to the dynamics of local politics, local political support (or lack thereof) and local political actors involved. City-to-city cooperation and politics are intrinsically connected, in at least three ways.

This first concerns the principal actors involved: Partner organisations are political institutions. Political will and commitment are of crucial importance to sustain partnership arrangements. Political factors that may undermine the sustainability of partnership efforts were found to be diverse. As local governments are by definition political institutions with a cyclic nature, the extent to which C2C is practiced and supported financially and institutionally is always subject to regime changes and political volatility. Moreover, local political turmoil may slow down the implementation of partnership projects (e.g. Oudtshoorn), and political leaders in the South maintain strong personal preferences and still exert a great deal of power in the young democratic systems under study. At the same time, their champion role in keeping the partnership alive has been found to be crucial, also in the North.

Secondly, city partnerships are political in terms of objectives. Partnership objectives are, in Koonings' (2007) words, politically value-laden. They are shaped by the nature of political regimes and their political programmes and (foreign) policies. The cases of Utrecht and Alphen suggest that municipal councils of a more right-wing nature are generally found to be more critical to the role of local government as development agent and donor. At the same time, local administrations in the South have their own policy objectives with partnership arrangements, either fed by existing planning policies or personal preferences of political leaders. When political dynamics thus shape partnership agenda-setting and implementation of activities, a conflicting situation may emerge in which long-term, development-oriented partnership objectives (expressed in cooperation agreements and defined jointly by partner cities), and short-term political objectives (defined by political leaders that are first and foremost accountable to their own constituents and not to partner cities), compete.

Thirdly, municipal partnerships are political in terms of beneficiaries of partnership initiatives. Chapter 7 provided some insight in informal and formal political contextual factors that largely shape relations among C2C actors in a given city, especially in the South. The example of Oudtshoorn, where the gap between local government and civil society is intensified by feelings of mistrust and resentment is illustrative. The eclectic nature of city partnerships, which brings about a set of parallel North-South structures targeting a range of beneficiaries may widen gaps between local government and civil society, and as such, may even be counterproductive to good governance practice at times. The question who benefits from aid and who is excluded from it, is usually a political one, influenced by local elite capture or patronage systems (cf. Gillespie et al., 1996; Baud, 2004) and therefore applies to C2C as well.

As Grindle (2006) already noted, development cooperation 'with a political twist' offers opportunities and is exposed to a number of dangers at the same time. In recent years for example, local administrations in the North that are engaged in long-term C2C partnerships have profited from general trends in society as regards global awareness, e.g. climate change and the negative effects of globalisation. The Utrecht administration has been successful to link activities in León to more mainstream popular themes including the need to reduce CO_2, contribute to the Millennium Development Goals and the general trend of increased global citizenship, making municipal politics more receptive to C2C. At the same time, divergent trends and developments may negatively affect the willingness of politicians in the North to be engaged in international affairs. In times of recession or economic decline, it may be controversial for municipal councils to account for citizen's tax money spent on projects overseas rather than on job creation and social support in the own city.

A second lesson learned is particularly applicable to municipalities in the North engaging in North-South city-to-city cooperation. An interesting point of discussion is the dual objective of cities in the North engaging in C2C partnerships. They aim to strengthen local institutions and foster local development in the South, while at the same time they intend to raise awareness and public support among their own citizens on development-related issues. Local level partnerships have traditionally been considered sites for development education in the North. As C2C is not confined to the work of local governments alone, it offers many opportunities for citizens to be exposed to development cooperation and issues related to global poverty and inequality, and the possibility to establish intercultural contacts and obtain greater global awareness. The dual objective however also creates tensions regarding the scope and content of C2C activities and projects. While donating school materials to educational institutes in the partner city may appeal to citizens and correspond to their idea of solidarity with the South, the developmental impact may in practice be rather limited. On the other hand, the technical exchanges between the partner municipalities do generally not appeal to citizens, especially when they are not 'visible' due to their focus on institutional or organisational aspects, e.g. financial administration, implementing IT systems or the design of new policies and plans. When results are not easily demonstrated it may be difficult for local governments to justify their international aspirations and investments towards their constituents, who want their local tax money to be well spent. Local authorities thus need to find a balance between generating visible, media attractive development results and employing their expertise niche in highly technical municipal cooperation efforts. The case of Utrecht and Alphen are good examples in this respect, where the municipalities have 'delegated' awareness-raising activities to civil society, while they simultaneously engage in technical cooperation with their respective partner municipalities.

A third lesson that can be learned from this study is that there is a danger that municipalities in the South become more concerned with being accountable to donors (their sister cities) than to their own constituents. Indeed, demanded 'donor accountability' dominates at times in North-South city partnerships over the quest to foster 'domestic accountability'. Through C2C arrangements, Northern municipalities enter the arena of local decision-making in the urban South. They may become powerful actors who exercise influence on the allocation of municipal investments. As such, preferences of international cooperation partners rather than the needs expressed by citizens may dictate how local governments go about in setting local development priorities. The proximity of decentralised cooperation actors to the local population poses moreover the danger that citizens seek to directly liaise with donors instead of local government to make their voices heard and express their needs. In León it has already been noted that instead of knocking at the Mayor's door (cf. Acioly et al., 2006), citizens knock at the door of the offices of the various sister cities that are locally represented. When C2C becomes too much absorbed in existing urban governance structures, it may thus disrupt rather than reinforce local government-civil society relations.

Donor accountability moreover applies here to the project and investment criteria set by the North that Southern counterparts need to meet. It was demonstrated that in the Dutch cases, the external funding provided by VNG-International has for some cities be too rigid and prescriptive, which has resulted in a lack of sustainable results and Southern partners cooperating in projects that were not a priority to them. Hence, the practice that municipalities in the North seek external funding – which was shown to generally exceed own resources invested in C2C – poses both advantages and disadvantages. On the one hand, there are more financial means available, which for some of the cities under study has been a determinant factor in C2C participation. On the other hand, partners in both North and South need to meet funding criteria and the extent to which ownership and demand-driven cooperation may generate more sustainable results may be undermined. In other words, while external funding is of great importance for local governments

THE CHALLENGE TO STRENGTHEN URBAN GOVERNANCE THROUGH NORTH-SOUTH CITY PARTNERSHIPS

engaging in development cooperation, at the same time it offers the risk of becoming over-dependent. For example from 2008, Amstelveen was no longer funded by VNG-I, which made continuation of the projects uncertain. If activities have to be stopped without a prior exit strategy as a result of decreasing funding opportunities, there is a risk that momentum gained in long-term cooperation arrangements may be lost.

It becomes clear that the principles of the Paris Agenda on Aid Effectiveness (2005) which is among the most important guidelines for development cooperation policy and practice today, are also applicable to the urban context and municipal partnerships. In order to find a balance between domestic and donor accountability, municipalities in the South need a clear and solid *locally owned* development strategy. Especially Municipal Development Plans, which have now become legally mandated for local governments in many countries in the South, could play an important role in this respect. They guarantee an institutional approach to setting development objectives based on community participation. These plans could moreover provide a framework for municipal donor *harmonisation* and *alignment* and serve to attract potential new donors. Moreover, regular evaluation by professional external independent bodies is needed for a critical assessment of the effectiveness of C2C arrangements. When municipalities in the South set development objectives in which they are accountable to their citizens needs, and municipalities in the North are in the position to respond the needs expressed by the South rather than defining how aid should be delivered, not in the least influenced by the parameters set by external funding partners, there is a great potential for a higher effectiveness in C2C arrangements.

A fourth lesson can be derived from the analysis of urban governance strengthening through city-to-city cooperation. The analysis implies an adjustment of the analytical framework, i.e. one should not only consider the *direct* impact of C2C interventions on the spheres of local government and civil society in isolation. The *indirect* impacts resulting from increased municipal effectiveness on the one hand and improved civil society skills on the other are also relevant to address. As was noted above, results in these separate spheres are not just an end of C2C interventions but also a means to further enhance the interaction and accountability between different urban actors. This calls for a more dynamic approach to understanding shifts in urban governance, and consequently the effects C2C can have in this respect.

A related issue stems from the observation made above that urban governance strengthening through C2C is mainly successful in the sphere of improving local government effectiveness and responsiveness, whereas civil society capacity building was not found to be frequently resulting directly from C2C interventions. Bearing in mind the multi-dimensional and multi-stakeholder nature of city-to-city cooperation, this may be regarded as a missed opportunity. One of the unique characteristics and comparative advantages of C2C as a form of development intervention is that it puts both public institutions and civil society centre stage, as partners and beneficiaries. As such, the results show that the potential of C2C to target urban governance strengthening from different angles is not sufficiently tapped. Especially city partnerships that are less technocratic and tend to focus more on civil society relations may offer strong possibilities for this simultaneous approach, or in the words of Gaventa (2001), to work on both sides of the equation. The weak results in the sphere of civil society strengthening may be explained by the nature of civil participation in C2C, which is mainly aimed at very practically improving living conditions through charity and donations, rather than working on more abstract issues of citizenship and empowerment. How can

C2C be effective in increasing 'voice' and skills for citizens to 'practice' their citizenship in the South and become more involved in urban collective decision-making? The literature used in this study offers some suggestions. It will be interesting to research the effects of promoting the role of CBOs as intermediary participation mechanisms to further bridge the gap between civil society and institutions as stated earlier by Mitlin (2004). C2C may aim to build strong networks and partnerships *among* civil society stakeholders in the South (Krishna, 2003), or may seek to facilitate education, resources and other means to enhance empowerment (Schneider, 1999) and increase civil skills (Gaventa & Valderrama, 1999) in civil society. The example of Utrecht put forward in Chapter 9 is promising in this respect, where it was attempted to strengthen CBOs to possibly allow them to obtain a stronger negotiating and advocacy position and in local decision-making structures. Although such interventions may at first sight not generate clear-cut outcomes that are easily measurable and quantifiable (and hence relevant to justify investments made to sponsors and make development cooperation 'visible' to sustain public support), they offer a promising strategy to more fully reap the benefits of the multidimensional nature of city-to-city cooperation and its potential to increase both the 'capacity to respond' and the 'capacity to demand' (*cf.* Romeo, 2003) in urban governance structures.

A fifth lesson of this study concerns the finding that partner municipalities in the North do not put learning from their partner in the South high on the cooperation agenda. Aren't Northern partners somewhat presumptuous in defining their experiences as relevant municipal expertise whereas the experiences in the South are not conceptualised as a potential source of learning? A new sound may evolve from the recent trend of the adoption in the North of innovations in democratic governance that have emerged from cities in the South (already briefly explained in Chapter 1). Exporting ideas and knowledge on urban governance from South to North may start a counter-trend to the perceptions in the North that are at times superior about their having advanced knowledge over their partners. Especially from the examples of Léon and Villa El Salvador, which build on a long tradition of community participation and have innovative forms of urban governance in place, there is much to be gained if Northern counterparts take these experiences more seriously. Cities in the North may start by attributing new values and meanings to knowledge exported by the South, to recognise potentials for learning and change in their own organisations, and arrive at true shifts in North-South cooperation.

A final lesson relates to relevance. How relevant is the role of cities and local governments in international (development) cooperation? In the light of an increased acknowledgment for the 'urban' in development thinking, ongoing urbanisation and the understanding that future poverty challenges need to be more and more tackled in the cities of the developing world, it appears that cities' and local governments' presence in the development cooperation arena is here to stay. This yet other 'shift in cooperation' is manifested in the ever growing number of cities engaged in international activities and the number of city networks that bring together cities to work on development issues. The participation of local public institutions in this field is not without pitfalls however. This study has shown that a more carefully balanced and nuanced appraisal is needed of the growing belief that city partnerships lead to local development in poor areas. It calls for a more realistic assessment of what especially donors and local government associations claim can be achieved through C2C. Much as it has proved difficult so far to find meaningful evidence to support a causal relationship between decentralisation and local development,

THE CHALLENGE TO STRENGTHEN URBAN GOVERNANCE THROUGH NORTH-SOUTH CITY PARTNERSHIPS

or between participation and poverty reduction, caution should be taken in drawing conclusions on the role of international city partnerships with regard to these processes of local development and poverty alleviation. This study has demonstrated that C2C can only partly meet the expectations of improving urban governance arrangements. The question how improved governance eventually results in opportunities for local development is even a more difficult one. Rather than seeing C2C as a panacea for a range of urban challenges, it is appropriate to take a more modest approach by seeing it as merely one of many potential catalysts for development and drivers of change.

When pitfalls will have been overcome, C2C's role as catalyst may be promising however. Municipalities in the North need to reduce the vulnerable position of international cooperation as a municipal task and meet the necessary organisational, technical, financial and political preconditions to engage in a sustainable way. Municipalities in the South need a solid understanding of their developmental needs and how international cooperation can be employed strategically to meet these needs. This study has shown that city-to-city cooperation can offer a niche in development cooperation and provide tailor-made support in the delivery of know-how, experience and expertise on highly specialised municipal affairs. When capacity building through municipal partnerships takes into account present structures and planning mechanisms, C2C arrangements explore new opportunities to collaborate with civil society in the South to strengthen their participation capacities, and cooperation is facilitated by political backing and acknowledgement of mutual objectives, C2C has the potential to considerably contribute to foster shifts towards improved urban governance in the South.

References

Abrahamsen, R. (2004) The power of partnerships in global governance. *Third World Quarterly* 25(8), pp. 1453-1467.

Acioly, C., J. Fransen, E. Makokha, J.G. Payot, R. Skinner, H. Teerlink & M. Zwanenburg (2006) *Knocking at the Mayor's door: Participatory urban management in seven cities*. Delft: Eburon.

Ahmad, M.M. (2006) The 'partnership' between international NGOs (Non-Governmental Organisations) and local NGOs in Bangladesh. *Journal of International Development* 18(5), pp. 629-638.

Algemeen Dagblad (2007) "Alphen herleeft in Zuid-Afrika". January 17, 2007.

Allegretti, G. & C. Herzberg (2004) *Participatory budgets in Europe: Between efficiency and growing local democracy.* Amsterdam: Transnational Institute.

Amstelveen Municipality (2006) Beleidskader internationale betrekkingen 2006-2010.

Amstelveens Nieuwsblad (2004) "Geen vertrouwen meer in Centrum voor Internationale Samenwerking". June 17, 2004.

Amstelveens Weekblad (2003) "Raad wil nieuw beleid internationale samenwerking". January 22, 2003.

Andrews, M. & A. Shah (2003) Assessing local government performance in developing countries. In: Shah, A. (ed.), *Measuring government performance in the delivery of public services,* Vol. 2 of *Handbook on public sector performance reviews.* Washington, D.C.: The World Bank.

Arellano Yanguas, J. (2008) A thoroughly modern resource curse? The new natural resource policy agenda and the mining revival in Peru. *IDS working papers* 300, 51 pp.

Argyris, C. (1996) *Organisational learning II. Theory, method and practice.* Cambridge: Addison-Wesley.

Argyris, C. (1999) *On organizational learning, second edition.* Oxford: Blackwell.

Arndt, C. & C. Oman (2006) *Uses and abuses of governance indicators.* OECD Development Center Study. Paris: OECD.

Ashman, D. (2000) Strengthening North-South partnerships: Addressing structural barriers to mutual influence. *Institute for Development Reports* 16(4), 21 pp.

Askvik, S. (1999) Twinning in Norwegian development assistance: A response to Jones and Blunt. *Public Administration and Development* 19(4), pp. 403-408.

Barten, F., R. Pérez Montiel, E. Espinoza & C. Morales (2002) Democratic governance – fairytale or real perspective? Lessons from Central America. *Environment and Urbanization* 14(1), pp. 129-144.

Baud, I.S.A., S. Grafakos, M. Hordijk & J. Post (2001) QOL and alliances in solid waste management: Contributions to urban sustainable development. *Cities* 18(1), pp. 1-10.

Baud, I.S.A. (2002) North-South partnerships in development research: An institutional approach. *International Journal of Technology Management and Sustainable Development* 1(3), pp. 153-170.

Baud, I.S.A. (2004) *Learning from the South: Placing governance in International Development Studies.* Inaugural address, Universiteit van Amsterdam.

Beall, J., O. Crankshaw & S. Parnell (2000) Local government, poverty reduction and inequality in Johannesburg. *Environment and Urbanization* 12(1), pp. 107-122.

Beall, J. (2005) Decentralizing government and decentering gender: Lessons from local government reform in South Africa. *Politics & Society* 33(2), pp. 253-276.

Bebbington, A. (2007) *Mining and development in Peru.* London: Peru support group.

Bergh, S. (2004) Democratic decentralization and local participation: A review of recent research. *Development in Practice* 14(6), pp. 780-790.

Blair, H. (2000) Participation and accountability at the periphery: Democratic local governance in six countries. *World Development* 28(1), pp. 21-39.

Boas, T.C. (2007) Conceptualizing continuity and change: The composite-standard model of path dependence. *Journal of Theoretical Politics* 19(1), pp. 33-54.

Bochove, J. van (2008) *Direct democracy in León, Nicaragua: Citizen participation, empowerment, and the influence on the democratic character of local governance.* Utrecht University: Unpublished MA thesis.

Boeije, H. (2005) *Analyseren in kwalitatief onderzoek: Denken en doen.* Amsterdam: Boom Onderwijs.

Bontenbal, M.C. (2006a) Understanding city-to-city cooperation: North-South partnerships of local authorities as development modality. *KNAG Geographical Studies of Development and Resource Use* 2006(2), 14 pp.

Bontenbal, M.C. (2006b) Dutch policy on city-to-city cooperation for improved local governance in South Africa. *Paper presented at the 10th International Winelands Conference, 5-7 April, University of Stellenbosch, South Africa.*

Bontenbal, M. & P. van Lindert (2006) Decentralised international cooperation: North-South municipal partnerships. In: Van Lindert, P., A. de Jong, G. Nijenhuis & G. van Westen (eds.), *Development matters. Geographical studies on development processes and policies*, pp. 301-314. Utrecht: Universiteit Utrecht.

Bontenbal, M. (2007) Internationale samenwerking: Gemeenten serieuze partner. *Geografie* 16(2), pp. 32-35.

Bontenbal, M.C. (2008) The role of European local governments in development cooperation: Examples from the Netherlands and Germany. *Paper presented at the 12th EADI General Conference, June 24-28, Geneva.*

Bontenbal, M. & E. van Ewijk (2008) General trends and policies with regard to municipal international cooperation in the Netherlands: Opportunities and threats in achieving the MDGs in Africa. *Presentation held at the 2008 International Symposium "City-to-city partnerships, achieving the millennium development goals in Africa", February 15-17, Stellenbosch, South Africa.*

Bontenbal, M. & P. van Lindert (2008a) Local players in a global field: Municipal international cooperation for local development. *Journal of Development Alternatives and Area Studies* 27(3-4).

Bontenbal, M. & P. van Lindert (2008b) Bridging local institutions and civic society in Latin America: Can city-to-city cooperation make a difference? *Environment & Urbanization* 20(2), pp. 465-482.

Bontenbal, M. (2009a) Understanding North-South municipal partnership conditions for capacity development: A Dutch-Peruvian example. *Habitat International* 33(1), pp. 100-105.

Bontenbal, M.C. (2009b) Strengthening urban governance in the South through city-to-city cooperation: Towards an analytical framework. *Article in press, Habitat International special issue on city-to-city cooperation, edited by Bontenbal & Van Lindert.*

Bontenbal, M. & P. van Lindert (2009) Transnational city-to-city cooperation: Issues arising from theory and practice. *Article in press, Habitat International special issue on city-to-city cooperation, edited by Bontenbal & Van Lindert.*

Bossuyt, J. (1994) Decentralised cooperation and the African public sector: Several players in search of a dramatist. *ECDPM Working Paper* 94(1), 18 pp.

Braun, M. & J.A. Harkness (2005) Text and context: Challenges to comparability in survey questions. In: Hoffmeyer-Zlotnik, J.H.P. & J.A. Harkness (eds.), *Methodological aspects in cross-national research*, pp. 95-107. Mannheim: Zentrum für Umfragen, Methoden und Analysen.

Bredenoord, J. (2005) *Urban development strategies in León, Nicaragua.* Amsterdam: Dutch University Press.

Brinkerhoff, J. (2002) Government-Nonprofit partnership: A defining framework. *Public Administration and Development* 22(1), pp. 19-30.

Buček, J & E. Bakker (1998) Slowaakse stedenbanden tegenwicht voor autoritair regime. *Geografie* 7(6), pp. 45-46.

Buis, H. (2009) The role of local government associations in increasing the effectiveness of city-to-city cooperation. *Article in press, Habitat International special issue on city-to-city cooperation, edited by Bontenbal & Van Lindert.*

Cabannes, Y. (2004) Participatory budgeting: A significant contribution to participatory democracy. *Environment and Urbanization* 16(1), pp. 27-46.

Cameron, R. (2001) The upliftment of South African local government? *Local Government Studies* 27(3), pp. 97-118.

Campbell, T. (2003) *The quiet revolution: Decentralisation and the rise of political participation in Latin America's cities.* Pittsburgh: University of Pittsburgh press.

Campbell, T. (2009) Learning cities: Knowledge, capacity and competitiveness. *Article in press, Habitat International special issue on city-to-city cooperation, edited by Bontenbal & Van Lindert.*

Cashdan, B. (2000) Local government and poverty in South Africa. *Background Research Series Municipal Services Project.* Available on: www.queensu.ca/msp/pages/Project_Publications/Papers/Local.pdf. Accessed January 2006.

CBS (2008) StatLine Databank Nederland. Voorburg: Centraal Bureau voor de Statistiek.

Census (2001) Statistics South Africa. Available on: www.statssa.gov.za. Accessed July 2006.

Cities Alliance (2001) Cities Alliance/GURI network meeting on urban poverty alleviation report. University of Toronto, October 6-7, 2001.

Cornelissen, W. (2004) Evaluation of the Netherlands Ministry of Foreign Affairs' inter-municipal co-operation programme for developing countries GSO. Working document, February 2004. In: IOB, *On solidarity and professionalisation. Evaluation of municipal international co-operation (1997-2001).* IOB Evaluations nr. 297. Den Haag: Policy and Operations Evaluation Department, Ministry of Foreign Affairs.

Cornwall, A. & J. Gaventa (2000) From users and choosers to makers and shapers: Re-positioning participation in social policy. *IDS Bulletin* 31(4).

Cornwall, A. & J. Gaventa (2001) Bridging the gap: Citizenship, participation and accountability. *PLA Notes* 40, pp. 32-35.

Cremer, R.D., A. de Bruin & A. Depuis (2001) International sister-cities: Bridging the global-local divide. *American Journal of Economics and Sociology* 60(1), pp. 377-401.

Crook, R.C. & A.S. Sverrisson (2001) Decentralisation and poverty-alleviation in developing countries: A comparative analysis or is West Bengal unique? *IDS Working Papers* 130.

THE CHALLENGE TO STRENGTHEN URBAN GOVERNANCE THROUGH NORTH-SOUTH CITY PARTNERSHIPS

Crook, R.C. & J. Manor (1998) *Democracy and decentralisation in South Asia and West Africa: Participation, accountability and performance.* Cambridge: CUP.

Crook, R.C. (2003) Decentralisation and poverty reduction in Africa: The politics of local-central relations. *Public Administration and Development* 23(1), pp. 77-88.

DBSA (2005) Global insight database 2005. Development Information Unit, Development Bank Southern Africa.

Devas, N. & C. Rakodi (1993) *Managing fast growing cities: New approaches to urban planning and management in the developing world.* Essex: Longman Scientific & Technical.

Devas, N. & U. Grant (2003) Local government decision-making – Citizen participation and local accountability: Some evidence from Kenya and Uganda. *Public Administration and Development* 23(4), pp. 307-316.

Development in Practice (2002) Special issue: Development and the learning organisation, edited by Roper, L. & J. Pettit, 12(3-4).

Development in Practice (2006) Special issue: Knowledge for development, edited by Eade, D. & M. Powell, 16(6).

Devers-Kanoglu, U. (2009) Municipal partnerships and learning: Remarks on a popular but still largely unexplored relationship. *Article in press, Habitat International special issue on city-to-city cooperation, edited by Bontenbal & Van Lindert.*

DfID (2001) *Making governance work for poor people: Building state capacity.* Strategy paper. London: DfID.

Dijkstra, A.G. (2004) Governance for sustainable poverty reduction: The social fund in Nicaragua. *Public Administration and Development* 24(3), pp. 197-211.

Dogliani, P. (2002) European municipalism in the first half of the twentieth century: The socialist network. *Contemporary European History* 11(4), pp. 573-596.

Doornbos, M. (2001) 'Good governance': The rise and decline of a policy metaphor? *Journal of Development Studies* 37(6), pp. 93-108.

Drew, R. (2002) Learning in partnership: What constitutes learning in the context of south-north partnerships? *Discussion paper jointly commissioned by BOND & the Exchange Programme.*

ECDPM (2004) Promoting local governance through municipal international cooperation. *Capacity.org* Issue 21, April 2004.

Evans, E. (2009) A framework for development? The growing role of UK local government in international development. *Article in press, Habitat International special issue on city-to-city cooperation, edited by Bontenbal & Van Lindert.*

Ewen, S. & M. Hebbert (2007) European cities in a networked world during the long 20th century. *Environment and Planning C: Government and Policy* 25(3), pp. 327-340.

Ewijk, E. van (2007*) Municipal international cooperation, Dutch municipalities and municipalities in migrant countries: First inventory.* Pre-research for PhD research, February-June 2007, University of Amsterdam, Amsterdam Institute for Metropolitan and International Development Studies.

Ewijk, E. van & I.S.A. Baud (2009) Partnerships between Dutch municipalities and municipalities in countries of migration to the Netherlands: Knowledge exchange and mutuality. *Article in press, Habitat International special issue on city-to-city cooperation, edited by Bontenbal & Van Lindert.*

FIDEG (2007) Transferencias municipales: ¿Motor eficiente o deficiente? *El Observador Económico,* August 7. Fundación Internacional para el Desafío Económico Global. Available on: www.elobservadoreconomico.com/articulo/304. Accessed September 2008.

Flores, A. (2005) El sistema municipal y la superación de la pobreza y precariedad urbana en el Perú. *Series Medio Ambiente y Desarrollo* 120. United Nations Publications: Economic Commission for Latin America and the Caribbean.

Fowler, A.F. (1998) Authentic NGDO partnerships in the new policy agenda for international aid: Dead end or light ahead? *Development and Change* 29(1), pp. 137-159.

Fowler, A. (2002) Beyond partnership: Getting real about NGO relationships in the aid system. In: Edwards, N. & A. Fowler, *The Earth Scan reader on NGO Management*, pp. 241-256. London: Earthscan.

Gaspari, O. (2002) Cities against states? Hopes, dreams and shortcomings of the European municipal movement, 1900-1960. *Contemporary European History* 11(4), pp. 597-621.

Gaventa, J. & C. Valderrama (1999) Participation, citizenship and local governance: Background note prepared for workshop on *strengthening participation in local governance,* Institute of Development Studies, June.

Gaventa, J. (1999) Crossing the great divide: Building links and learning between NGOs and community-based organisations in North and South. In: Lewis, D. (ed.), *International perspectives on voluntary action: Reshaping the third sector,* pp. 21-38. London: Earthscan.

Gaventa, J. (2001) Towards participatory local governance: Six propositions for discussion. Institute of Development Studies.

Giezen, M. (2008) Drie hoofdsteden en hun zustersteden. *Agora* 24(1), pp. 37-39.

Gillespie, P., M. Girgis & P. Mayer (1996) "This great evil": Anticipating political obstacles to development. *Public Administration and Development* 16(5), pp. 431-453.

Glasbergen, P., F. Biermann & A.P.J. Mol (eds.) (2007) *Partnerships, governance and sustainable development: Reflections on theory and practice.* Cheltenham: Edward Elgar Publishing.

Gómez Sabaini, J.C. & M. Geffner (2006) *Nicaragua: El papel de los municipios como instrumento para el combate de la pobreza.* Santiago de Chile: United Nations/CEPAL.

Grindle, M.S. & M.E. Hilderbrand (1995) Building sustainable capacity in the public sector: What can be done? *Public Administration and Development* 15(5), pp. 441-463.

Grindle, M.S. (ed.) (1997) *Getting good government: Capacity building in the public sector of developing countries.* Cambridge, Mass.: Harvard University Press.

Grindle, M.S. (2006) Modernising town hall: Capacity building with a political twist. *Public Administration and Development* 26(1), pp. 55-69.

Grindle, M.S. (2007) Good enough governance revisited. *Development Policy Review* 25(5), pp. 553-574.

Hafteck, P. (2003) An introduction to decentralized cooperation: Definitions, origins and conceptual mapping. *Public Administration and Development* 23(4), pp. 333-345.

Harpham, T. & K.A. Boateng (1997) Urban governance in relation to the operation of urban services in developing countries. *Habitat International* 21(1), pp. 65-77.

Have, P. ten (not dated) "Het hangt er maar van af...". Available on: www2.fmg.uva.nl/emca/hangt.htm. Accessed September 2005.

Heller, P. (2001) Moving the state: The politics of democratic decentralization in Kerala, South Africa and Porto Alegre. *Politics & Society* 29(1), pp. 131-163.

Helmsing, A.H.J. (2000) *Decentralisation and enablement: Issues in the local governance debate.* Inaugural address, Utrecht University.

Hewitt, W.E. (1999) Cities working together to improve urban services in developing areas: The Toronto-São Paulo example. *Studies in Comparative International Development* 34(1), pp. 27-44.

Hewitt, W.E. (2000) International municipal cooperation: An enabling approach to development for small and intermediate urban centres? *Third World Planning Review* 22(3), pp. 335-360.

Hewitt, W.E. (2004) Improving citizen participation in local government in Latin America through international cooperation: A case study. *Development in practice* 14(5), pp. 619-632.

Hobbs, H.H. (1994) *City hall goes abroad: The foreign policy of local politics.* Thousand Oaks: Sage.

Hoetjes, B. (2009) Trends and issues in municipal twinnings from the Netherlands. *Article in press, Habitat International special issue on city-to-city cooperation, edited by Bontenbal & Van Lindert.*

Hordijk, M. (2000) *Of dreams and deeds: The role of local initiatives for community based environmental management in Lima, Peru.* Amsterdam: Thela Theses.

Hordijk, M. (2005) Participatory governance in Peru: Exercising citizenship. *Environment and Urbanization* 17(1), pp. 219-236.

Howard, J. (2004) Citizen voice and participation in local government: Perspectives from Nicaragua. *Community Development Journal* 39(3), pp. 224-233.

Hyden, G., J. Court & K. Mease (2004) *Making sense of governance: Empirical evidence to the debate on fiscal decentralization.* Boulder: Lynne Rienner.

IDP (2005) *Greater Oudtshoorn Municipality revised Integrated Development Plan 2005/2006.* Oudtshoorn: Oudtshoorn Municipality.

Imparato, I. & J. Ruster (2003) Peru: The self-managed urban community of VES, Lima. In: Imparato, I. & J. Ruster, *Slum upgrading and participation: Lessons from Latin America,* pp. 73-76. Directions in Development Series. Washington, D.C.: The World Bank.

INEI (2007a) Medición de la pobreza 2004, 2005 y 2006: Informe Técnico. Lima: Instituto Nacional de Estadística e Informática. Available on: www.inei.gob.pe/web/ BoletinFlotantePrincipal.asp?file=7008.pdf. Accessed September 2008.

INEI (2007b) Censos Nacionales 2007: XI de población y VI de vivienda. Lima: Instituto Nacional de Estadística e Informática.

INIFOM & GTZ (2007) Anuario de finanzas municipales del 2005. Programa de Desarrollo Local y Transparencia Local (PRODELFIS). Available on: www.programas-gtz.org.ni/publicaciones. php?idcomponente=1. Accessed August 2007.

IOB (2004) *On solidarity and professionalisation. Evaluation of municipal international co-operation (1997-2001). IOB Evaluations nr. 297.* Den Haag: Policy and Operations Evaluation Department, Ministry of Foreign Affairs.

Irigoyen, M. & R. Machuca (1997) Inter-institutional consultation and urban environmental management in San Marcos Cajamarca. In: Edelman, D.J. (ed.), *Capacity building for the urban environment: A comparative research, training and experience exchange,* Project Paper 1. Rotterdam: Institute for Housing and Urban Development Studies.

Johnson, H. & G. Wilson (2006) North-South/South-North partnerships: Closing the 'mutuality gap'. *Public Administration and Development* 26(1), pp. 71-80.

Johnson, H. & A. Thomas (2007) Individual learning and building organisational capacity for development. *Public Administration and Development* 27(1), pp. 39-48.

Johnson H. & G. Wilson (2009) Learning and mutuality in municipal partnerships and beyond: A focus on Northern partners. *Article in press, Habitat International special issue on city-to-city cooperation, edited by Bontenbal & Van Lindert.*

Jones, M.L. & P. Blunt (1999) 'Twinning' as a method of sustainable institutional capacity building. *Public Administration and Development* 19(4), pp. 381-402.

Jong, A. de & A. Broekhuis (2004) The state, development policy and local communities in Mali. In: Kruijt, D. et al. (eds.), *State and development: Essays in honour of Menno Vellinga*, pp. 185-200. Amsterdam: Rozenberg Publishers.

Kaufmann, D., A. Kraay & M. Mastruzzi (2008) Governance matters VII: Aggregate and individual governance indicators for 1996-2007. Washington, D.C.: The World Bank.

Keiner, M. & A. Kim (2007) Transnational city networks for sustainability. *European Planning Studies* 15(10), pp. 1369-1395.

King, K. (2002) Banking on knowledge: The new knowledge projects of the World Bank. *Compare* 32(3), pp. 311-326.

Knack, S. (2006) Measuring corruption in Eastern Europe and Central Asia: A critique of the cross-country indicators. *Working Paper 3968*. World Bank Policy Research Department.

Knowles, E. & J. Materu (1999) *Partnerships for sustainable development. North-South cooperation within the framework of Local Agenda 21: Guide to good practice Africa*. Den Haag: IULA/Towns & Development.

Kolb, D., I. Rubin & H. McIntyre (1971) *Organisational psychology: An experiential approach*. Englewoord Cliffs: Prentice-Hall.

Koonings, K. (2007) Bringing politics into poverty: The political dimensions of poverty alleviation. In: *A rich menu for the poor: Food for thought on effective aid policies*. Den Haag: Ministry of Foreign Affairs Effectiveness and Quality Department (DEK).

Krishna, A. (2003) Partnerships between local governments and community-based organisations: Exploring the scope for synergy. *Public Administration and Development* 23(4), pp. 361-371.

Kruijt, D., P. van Lindert & O. Verkoren (eds.) (2004) *State and development: Essays in honour of Menno Vellinga*. Amsterdam: Rozenberg Publishers.

Kussendrager, N. (1985) *Case Studies for the first European conference on NGO and local community Joint action for North-South cooperation, Cologne, 18-20 September 1985*. Den Haag: Dutch National Committee for Information on Development Cooperation.

LA21TK (2004) Lokale Agenda 21 Treptow-Köpenick 2004. Bezirksamt Treptow-Köpenick von Berlin: Büro des Bezirksbürgermeisters.

Labordus, J.P. (1997) Tweemaal Oudshoorn. *De Viersprong* 53. Alphen aan den Rijn: Historische Vereniging Alphen aan den Rijn.

Land, T. (2000) Implementing institutional and capacity development: Conceptual and operational issues. *ECDPM Discussion paper 14*.

Larson, A.M. (2002) Natural resources and decentralisation in Nicaragua: Are local governments up to the job? *World Development* 30(1), pp. 17-31.

Leibler, C. & M. Ferri (2004) NGO networks: Building capacity in a changing world. USAID. Available on: www.usaid.gov/our_work/cross-cutting_programs/private_voluntary_cooperation/conf_leibler.pdf. Accessed September 2007.

Liesner, M. (2006) *Religion und Umwelt. Die Lokale Agenda 21 in Kirchengemeinden: Die Kommunale Ökumene in Treptow-Köpenick*. Freie Universität Berlin: Magister-arbeit Geschichts- und Kulturwissenschaften.

Lindert, P. van (2001) The Local Agenda 21 Charters Programme. The link between decentralised North-South cooperation and sustainable development planning. Evaluation of its experience. Utrecht: IDSUU.

Lindert, P. van & R. van Dooren (2001) Evaluatie gemeentelijke internationale samenwerking Eindhoven. Utrecht: IDSUU.

Lindert, P. van & G. Nijenhuis (2004) The challenge of participatory democracy in Latin America. In: Kruijt, D. et al. (eds.), *State and development: Essays in honour of Menno Vellinga,* pp. 163-184. Amsterdam: Rozenberg Publishers.

Lindert, P. van (2005a) Preface. In: Bredenoord, J., *Urban development strategies in León, Nicaragua,* pp. 6-11. Amsterdam: Dutch University Press.

Lindert, P. van (2005b) Participatory Budgeting. In: Forsyth, T. (ed.), *The encyclopaedia of international development,* pp. 505-506. London: Routledge.

Lindert, P. van (2005c) Local Government. In: Forsyth, T. (ed.), *The encyclopedia of international development,* pp. 415-417. London: Routledge.

Lindert, P. van (2006) From habitat to local governance: Urban development policy in debate. In: Van Lindert, P., A. de Jong, G. Nijenhuis & G. van Westen (eds.), *Development matters. Geographical studies on development processes and policies,* pp. 53-66. Utrecht: Universiteit Utrecht.

Lindert, P. van (2009) Transnational linking of local governments: The consolidation of the Utrecht-León municipal partnership. *Article in press, Habitat International special issue on city-to-city cooperation, edited by Bontenbal & Van Lindert.*

Lister, S. (2000) Power in partnership? An analysis of an NGO's relationships with its partners. *Journal of International Development* 12(2), pp. 227-239.

Litvack, J., A. Junaid & R. Bird (1998) *Rethinking decentralization in developing countries.* PREM Sector Studies Series. Washington, D.C.: The World Bank.

López Carrión, N.O., G. Espinoza & J.R. Palacios Mayorga (eds.) (2004) *Descentralización y desarrollo económico local en Nicaragua.* Managua: Fundación Friedrich Ebert.

LSE evaluation (2005) Interne evaluatie stedelijk uitbreidingsprogramma León Zuidoost: eindverslag. Utrecht: Utrecht Municipality.

Mamadouh, V. (2002) Twinning cities and towns: Localizing international relations or globalizing local ties? *Paper presented at the Fourth European Social Science History conference, Den Haag, The Netherlands.*

Marulanda, L. & J. Calderón (2001) La consulta ciudadana en Villa El Salvador, Lima, Perú. Municipalidad de Santa Cruz de la Sierra & Institute for Housing and Urban Development Studies, SINPA Program.

Marulanda, L. (2002) Planificación y gestión local participativa en Villa El Salvador. In: *Seguridad humana y desarrollo regional en América Latina.* UNCRD Research Report Series 44, pp. 357-395.

Mase, K. (2003) *Equitable share? An analysis of South Africa's system of fiscal transfers to local government in terms of how it addresses vertical and horizontal fiscal imbalances.* University of Birmingham School of Public Policy: MBA Thesis.

McCarney, P. (1996) Reviving local government: The neglected tier in development. In: McCarney, P. (ed.), *The changing nature of local government in developing countries,* pp. 5-30. Toronto: University of Toronto Press Inc.

McFarlane, C. (2006) Crossing borders: Development, learning and the North-South divide. *Third World Quarterly* 27(8), pp. 1413-1437.

MCLCP (2007) *Futuro sin pobreza: Balance de la lucha contra la pobreza y propuestas.* Lima: Mesa de Concertación para la Lucha contra la Pobreza.

MEF (2007) Ministerio de Economía y Finanzas – Perú: *Estadísticas Económicas.* Available on: www.minem.gob.pe/mineria/estad_inicio.asp. Accessed September 2008.

MEM (2007) *Informes Estadísticos*. Lima: Ministerio de Energía y Minas, Perú. Available on: www.minem.gob.pe/mineria/estad_inicio.asp. Accessed September 2008.

Merwe, I.J. van der (ed.) (2004) Growth potential of towns in the Western Cape, 2004: A research study undertaken for the Department of Environmental Affairs and Development Planning of the Western Cape Provincial Government. University of Stellenbosch: Centre for Geographical Analysis.

Milèn, A. (2001) What do we know about capacity building? An overview of existing knowledge and good practice. Geneva: WHO. Available on: www.popline.org/docs/1507/273392.html. Accessed December 2005.

MIM (2007) El Canon Minero en Cajamarca. *Boletín: Una mirada independiente al Canon Minero y a la inversión municipal* No. 6, p. 3. Cajamarca: Mecanismo Independiente de Monitoreo.

Miranda, L. & M. Hordijk (1998) Let us build cities for life: The national campaign of local agenda 21s in Peru. *Environment and Urbanization* 10(2), pp. 69-102.

Mitlin, D. (1999) Civil society and urban poverty. *Urban governance, partnership and poverty theme paper 5*. Birmingham: University of Birmingham, School of Public Policy.

Mitlin, D. (2004) Reshaping local democracy. *Environment and Urbanization* 16(1), pp. 3-8.

Mündel, K. & D. Schugurensky (2005) The 'accidental learning' of volunteers: The case of community-based organizations in Ontario. In: Künzel, K. (ed.), *International yearbook of adult education 31/32: Informelles Lernen – Selbstbildung und soziale Praxis*, pp. 183-205. Köln: Böhlau Verlag.

NCDO (2006) *Barometer Internationale Samenwerking 2006, trends en ontwikkelingen*. Amsterdam: Nationale Commissie voor Internationale Samenwerking en Duurzame Ontwikkeling.

Nel, E. & T. Binns (2001) Initiating 'developmental local government' in South Africa: Evolving local economic development policy. *Regional Studies* 35(4), pp. 355-370.

Nijenhuis, G. (2002) *Decentralisation and popular participation in Bolivia: The link between local governance and local development*. Utrecht: KNAG/Faculteit Ruimtelijke Wetenschappen.

Nitschke, U. & S. Wilhelmy (2009) Challenges of German city-to-city cooperation and the way forward to a quality debate. *Article in press, Habitat International special issue on city-to-city cooperation, edited by Bontenbal & Van Lindert*.

OEP (2005) Oudtshoorn Economic Profile. Oudtshoorn: Oudtshoorn Municipality.

Olowu, D. & J.S. Wunsch (eds.) (2004) *Local governance in Africa: The challenges of democratic decentralization*. Boulder: Lynne Rienner.

O'Toole, K. (2001) *Kokusaika* and internationalism: Australian and Japanese sister city type relationships. *Australian Journal of International Affairs* 55(3), pp. 403-419.

Paredes, R.I. (2007) Quince años del autogolpe de Fujimori: Entre la "dictablanda", la adicción al poder y la extradición. *MundoHispano* April, pp. 8-9.

Pérez Montiel, R. & F. Barten (1999) Urban governance and health development in León, Nicaragua. *Environment and Urbanization* 11(1), pp. 11-26.

PIA (2007) Plan de Inversiones Anual. León: Alcaldía de León.

Pierre, J. (ed.) (1998) *Partnerships in urban governance: European and American experience*. London: Macmillan.

Pierre, J. (2005) Comparative urban governance: Uncovering complex causalities. *Urban Affairs Review* 40(4), pp. 446-462.

Pluijm, van der, R. & J. Melissen (2007) *City diplomacy: The expanding role of cities in international politics*. Den Haag: Netherlands Institute of International Relations Clingendael.

THE CHALLENGE TO STRENGTHEN URBAN GOVERNANCE THROUGH NORTH-SOUTH CITY PARTNERSHIPS

Proctor, R. (2000) Twinning and the South Africa/Canada programme on governance: Some reflections on Blunt, Jones and Askvik. *Public Administration and Development* 20(4), pp. 319-325.

Rademaker, J. & A. van der Veer (2001) *Partnerships for sustainable development. North-South cooperation within the framework of Local Agenda 21: Final Report.* Den Haag: IULA/Towns & Development.

Ragin, C. (1994) *Constructing social research: The unity and diversity of method.* Thousand Oaks: Pine Forge.

Rhebergen, G. (2006) Capacity development for effective local government. *Presentation held at Knowledge for Development Symposium 'Local Governance for Development', November 8, Utrecht University.*

Romeo, L.G. (2003) The role of external assistance in supporting decentralisation reform. *Public Administration and Development* 23(1), pp. 89-96.

Rondinelli, D. (1999) What is decentralisation? In: Litvack, J. & J. Seddon (eds.), *Decentralization briefing note.* WBI Working Papers. Washington, D.C.: The World Bank.

Ros-Tonen, M.A.F., H. van den Hombergh & A. Zoomers (2007) *Partnerships in sustainable forest resource management: Learning from Latin America.* Leiden: Brill.

RSA (1998) The White Paper on Local Government. Republic of South Africa, Department of Constitutional Development, Pretoria.

Sabatini, C. (2003) Decentralization and political parties. *Journal of Democracy* 14(2), pp. 138-150.

SALGA (2005) Toolkit: Implementing a basic performance management system for municipalities. *Salga Performance Management Series* Vol. 1. Pretoria: South Africa Local Government Association.

Santiso, C. (2002) Good governance and aid effectiveness: The World Bank and conditionality. *Georgetown Public Policy Review* 7(1), pp. 1-23.

Sather, B. (1998) Retroduction: An alternative research strategy? *Business Strategy and the Environment* 7, pp. 245-249.

Schat, R. (2005) Verslag werkbezoek León, Nicaragua 27 februari/4 maart 2005. Utrecht: Utrecht Municipality.

Schep, G., F. Angenent, J. Wismans & M. Hillenius (1995) *Local challenges to global change: A global perspective on municipal international cooperation.* Den Haag: SDU.

Schneider, H. (1999) Participatory governance for poverty reduction. *Journal of International Development* 11(4), pp. 521-534.

Schneider, A. & R. Zúniga-Hamlin (2005) A strategic approach to rights: Lessons from clientelism in rural Peru. *Development Policy Review* 23(5), pp. 567-584.

SEOR (2003) Evaluation of the Dutch municipal international co-operation programme: Three independent projects. SEOR BV/Ecorys-NEI. In: IOB, *On solidarity and professionalisation. Evaluation of municipal international co-operation (1997-2001).* IOB Evaluations nr. 297. Den Haag: Policy and Operations Evaluation Department, Ministry of Foreign Affairs

Shah, A. & S. Shah (2006) The new vision of local governance and the evolving roles of local governments. In: Shah, A. (ed.), *Local governance in developing countries, Public sector governance and accountability series*, pp. 1-45. Washington, D.C.: The World Bank.

Shuman, M.H. (1994) *Towards a global village: International community development initiatives.* London: Pluto Press.

SKEW (2007) Städte als Partner für nachhaltige Entwicklung: Bilanz und Perspektiven 15 Jahre nach Rio. *Material 25.* Bonn: Service Agency Communities in One World/InWent GmbH.

Skinner, R. (2004) *Mapeo de procesos en Lima: Informe Final.* Alianza Cordaid-IHS, 57 pp.

Slutsky, M. (2003) Nicaragua: het spook van de hulp. Vice Versa 37(4).

Smoke, P. (2003) Decentralisation in Africa: Goals, dimensions, myths and challenges. *Public Administration and Development* 23(1), pp. 7-16.

Soberón, L. (1995) La mesa de concertación de Cajamarca: Un estudio de caso sobre políticas integradas en el Perú. In: Torres, M. & E. Mujica (eds.), *Políticas económicas, sociales y medioambiente integradas en América Latina: Informe final del seminario regional INTESEP,* pp. 69-103. Lima: Centro Internacional de la Papa.

Souza, C. (2001) Participatory budgeting in Brazilian cities: Limits and possibilities in building democratic institutions. *Environment and Urbanization* 13(1), pp. 159-184.

Spence, R. & F. Ninnes (2007) Building relationships across the Timor Sea: An evaluation of the Australian/Timorese friendship agreements. *Public Administration and Development* 27(4), pp. 333-340.

Steiner, S. (2007) Decentralisation and poverty: Conceptual framework and application to Uganda. *Public Administration and Development* 27(2), pp. 175-185.

Stoker, G. (1998) Governance as theory: Five propositions. *International Social Science Journal* 50(155), pp. 17-28.

Thomas, M. (2006) *What do the worldwide governance indicators measure?* Available on: http://ssrn.com/abstract=1007527. Accessed October 2008.

Tjandradewi, B.I., P.J. Marcotullio & T. Kidokoro (2006) Evaluating city-to-city cooperation: A case study of the Penang and Yokohama experience. *Habitat International* 30(3), pp. 357-376.

Tjandradewi, B.I. & P.J. Marcotullio (2009) City-to-city networks: Asian perspectives on key elements and areas for success. *Article in press, Habitat International special issue on city-to-city cooperation, edited by Bontenbal & Van Lindert.*

Turner, J.F.C. & R. Fichter (eds.) (1972) Freedom to build: Dweller control of the housing process. New York: MacMillan.

Ubels, J., T. Theisohn, V. Hauck & T. Land (2005) From local empowerment to aid harmonisation: A *tour d'horizon* of capacity development trends and challenges. *Capacity.org* Issue 26, pp. 3-6.

UCLG (2006) Press Kit United Cities and Local Governments. Available on: www.cities-localgovernments.org. Accessed November 2006.

Ugarte Ubilla, A. (2006) El proceso de descentralización en el Perú: Logros y agenda pendiente. *Diálogo Político* 23(1), pp. 81-112. Buenos Aires: Fundación Konrad Adenauer.

UNDP (1997a) Capacity development: Technical advisory paper II. In: *Capacity Development Resource Book.* Available on: http://magnet.undp.org/cdrb/default.htm. Accessed September 2007.

UNDP (1997b) *Governance for sustainable human development.* New York: UNDP.

UNDP (2000) The challenges of linking. UNDP Management Development and Governance Division – Bureau for Development Policy. Available on: http://mirror.undp.org/magnet/Docs/urban/City%20to%20city%20Linking/c2cfin.htm. Accessed March 2005.

UNDP (2006) United Nations and local development: Actions of United Nations programmes with and for local/regional Authorities. Geneva: UN Hub for Innovative Partnerships.

UN-Habitat (2002) The global campaign on urban governance concept paper. Available on: www.unchs.org/campaigns/governance/. Accessed February 2005.

UN-Habitat (2003) Partnership for local capacity development: Building on the experiences of city-to-city cooperation. Joint publication with WACLAC. Available on: www.unhabitat.org/pmss/getPage.asp?page=bookView&book=1187. Accessed March 2005.

UN-Habitat (2006) *Report Spring Workshop March 22-24*. Seville: UN-Habitat Best Practice Centre for City-to-City Cooperation.

United Nations (2008) *World urbanization prospects: The 2007 revision*. New York: UN Department of Economic and Social Affairs.

Utrecht Municipality (2007) Work plan International Affairs 2008.

Vagale, L.R. (2003) City to city cooperation. *ITPI Journal* 21(1), pp. 1-4.

Veen, G. van der (2008) *Low income housing in Oudthsoorn, South Africa: Catalyst towards development?* Utrecht University: unpublished MSc thesis

Ven, D. van de (2005) Stedenband sluit aan bij plannen León. *Nieuwsbrief Stichting Vriendschapsband Utrecht-León* 20(1), p. 8.

Ven, D. van de (2007) Verslag werkbezoek aan León, Nicaragua, juli 2006. Utrecht: Utrecht Municipality.

VES Municipality (2006) Plan integral de desarrollo concertado de Villa El Salvador al 2021. Versión popular.

Villiers, J.C. de (2005) *Strategic alliances between communities, with special reference to the twinning of South African provinces, cities and towns with international partners*. University of Stellenbosch Graduate School of Business Administration: Ph.D. dissertation.

Villiers, J.C. de (2009) Success factors and the city-to-city partnership management process: From strategy to alliance capability. *Article in press, Habitat International special issue on city-to-city cooperation, edited by Bontenbal & Van Lindert*.

Vion, A. (2002) Europe from the bottom up: Town twinning in France during the Cold War. *Contemporary European History* 11(4), pp. 623-640.

VNG (2000) *Gemeenten zonder grenzen: Een onderzoek naar de stand van zaken op het beleidsterrein Gemeentelijke Internationale Samenwerking 2000*. Den Haag: VNG/IPU.

VNG (2001) *Handboek Gemeentelijke Internationale Samenwerking*. Den Haag: VNG International.

VNG (2002) GSO Evaluatiemissie Zuid-Afrika. Den Haag: VNG International.

VNG (2005) LOGO South Country Programme South Africa: Housing in South Africa. Den Haag: VNG International.

VNG (2006) *Een wereld aan kansen, de stand van zaken op het beleidsterrein gemeentelijke internationale samenwerking in 2006*. Den Haag: VNG International.

VNG International & COS Rijnmond & Midden Holland (2005) Evaluatie van gemeentelijke internationale samenwerking van Alphen aan den Rijn, eindrapport. Den Haag: VNG International.

VUL Newsletter (2004) "Landbouwkundige levert bijdrage aan stedenbouw in León" – Interview met Dick Stiemer. In: *Nieuwsbrief Stichting Vriendschapsband Utrecht-León* 20(1), pp. 1-2.

WACAP (not dated) Brochure 'The Alliance: a response to the challenge of poverty'. Available on: http://mirror.undp.org/switzerland/wacap/download/pdf/brochure/brochure_en.pdf. Accessed September 2005.

Wijland, G. van (2003) Nicaragua: Verslaafd aan stedenbanden. *Vice Versa* 37.

Wilson, G. & H. Johnson (2007) Knowledge, learning and practice in North-South practitioner-practitioner municipal partnerships. *Local government studies* 33(2), pp. 253-269.

Wittenberg, M. (2003) Decentralisation in South Africa, first draft. Available on: http://sticerd.lse. ac.uk/dps/decentralisation/SouthAfrica.pdf. Accessed January 2006.

Work, R. (2002) Overview of decentralisation worldwide: A stepping stone to improved governance and human development. *Paper presented at the 2ⁿᵈ International Conference on Decentralisation, Manila, Philippines.*

World Bank (1998) Municipal administration and performance in Villa El Salvador, Peru. Case study of the World Bank/WBI's CBNRM Initiative. Washington, D.C.: The World Bank.

World Bank (2004) Policy note municipal decentralisation in Nicaragua: Fiscal and institutional issues. Washington, D.C.: The World Bank.

World Bank (2008) Public sector reform: What works and why? An IEG evaluation of World Bank support. Washington, D.C.: The World Bank.

Yin, R.K. (2003) Case study research design and methods, third edition. *Applied Social Research Methods Series* 5. Thousand Oaks: Sage.

Zanen, J.H.C. van (1993) Utrecht moet 'León' zorgvuldig afbouwen en samenwerking met Brno opbouwen. Utrechts nieuwsblad, 24 mei 1993.

Zelinsky, W. (1991) The twinning of the world: Sister cities in geographic and historical perspective. *Annals of the Association of American Geographers* 81(1), pp. 1-31.

Zolezzi, M. (2004) Participation in planning and budgeting in Villa El Salvador, Peru. In: Licha, I. (ed.), *Citizens in charge: Managing local budgets in East Asia and Latin America,* pp. 329-356. Washington, D.C.: Interamerican Development Bank.

Consulted websites

- Council of European Municipalities and Regions. www.ccre.org
- Federation of Canadian Municipalities, International Centre for Municipal Development. www.icmd-cidm.ca
- Local Government International Bureau. www.lgib.gov.uk
- Millenniumgemeenten: www.millenniumgemeente.nl
- Sister Cities International. www.sister-cities.org
- United Cities and Local Governments. www.cities-localgovernments.org
- VNG-International. www.vng-international.nl

Samenvatting

Steden als partners: de uitdaging lokaal bestuur te versterken door stedenbanden tussen Noord en Zuid

Lokale overheden worden in toenemende mate beschouwd als actieve spelers in internationale samenwerking. Naar schatting 70% van steden in de wereld is betrokken bij enige vorm van internationale samenwerking, stedenbanden, internationale stedennetwerken en programma's. Veel van deze samenwerkingsverbanden verbinden ontwikkelde en ontwikkelingslanden, of anders gezegd: het mondiale Noorden en het mondiale Zuiden. In deze vorm van internationale samenwerking staan steden centraal, als ontwikkelingspartners én als begunstigden. Tegen de achtergrond van wereldwijde voortgaande decentralisatie van bestuur, mondialisering en urbanisatie, een toenemend besef van wereldburgerschap, de veranderende rol van lokale overheden en een groeiende aandacht voor goed bestuur als voorwaarde voor ontwikkeling, wordt gemeentelijke internationale samenwerking steeds vaker ingezet door steden als instrument om kennis en expertise uit te wisselen en middelen over te dragen. Steden – zowel lokale overheden als het lokale maatschappelijke middenveld – gaan banden aan om bij te dragen aan een scala van doelen zoals armoedebestrijding, institutionele versterking, democratie en vredesopbouw.

Als gevolg van voortgaande urbanisatie – die vooral plaatsvindt in ontwikkelingslanden – en nieuw donorbeleid, heeft het 'urbane' een prominentere plaats gekregen in het ontwikkelingsdenken. Decentralisatie en de hervorming van openbaar bestuur in het Zuiden hebben geleid tot een belangrijkere positie voor lokale overheden. Een onderliggende gedachte is dat een bestuur dat dichter bij de burger staat, beter in staat is in te spelen op de behoeften van de burger. Het begrip 'participatief lokaal bestuur', dat steeds prominenter wordt in stedelijk beleid, verwijst naar het feit dat besluitvorming zowel binnen als buiten het domein van lokale overheden plaatsvindt. Als gevolg hiervan wordt het onderscheid tussen publieke en private partijen kleiner. De gedachte is dat 'goed', participatief lokaal bestuur bereikt kan worden als burgers en instituties dichter bij elkaar worden gebracht. Hiervoor is zowel een sterke lokale overheid als een sterk maatschappelijk middenveld nodig.

Tegen deze achtergrond heeft deze studie tot doel gehad inzicht te verschaffen in de relevantie en de mogelijkheden die gemeentelijke internationale samenwerking (GIS) biedt met betrekking tot het versterken van lokaal bestuur in het Zuiden. Daarnaast was het de bedoeling de verschillende factoren te identificeren die deze mogelijkheden beïnvloeden. Vijf onderzoeksvragen hebben centraal gestaan:

1. Welke institutionele en beleidscondities op nationaal en supranationaal niveau beïnvloeden de rol van lokale overheden in internationale samenwerking en in processen van lokale ontwikkeling?
2. Onder welke lokale politieke en institutionele omstandigheden opereren lokale overheden in internationale samenwerking en wat zijn de gevolgen voor gemeentelijke internationale samenwerking?

THE CHALLENGE TO STRENGTHEN URBAN GOVERNANCE THROUGH NORTH-SOUTH CITY PARTNERSHIPS

3. Welke actoren vormen GIS-netwerken in de partnersteden, wat is hun rol en verantwoordelijkheid, en welke relaties onderhouden zij?
4. Onder welke omstandigheden en in welke mate functioneert gemeentelijke internationale samenwerking als instrument voor capaciteitsopbouw en kennisuitwisseling?
5. In welke mate en op welke manier draagt gemeentelijke internationale samenwerking bij aan het versterken van lokaal bestuur in het Zuiden?

Een vergelijkend onderzoek is uitgevoerd van vier stedenbanden tussen Noord en Zuid, met steden uit Nederland, Duitsland, Peru, Nicaragua en Zuid-Afrika. In alle steden (vier in het Noorden en vier in het Zuiden) is een gestructureerde onderzoeksstrategie gehanteerd, die vergelijking tussen de cases mogelijk maakte. Het onderzoek vond plaats tussen 2005 en 2008 en was gestoeld op kwalitatieve methoden. De belangrijkste criteria voor het selecteren van de stedenbanden waren: a) zowel actoren van lokale overheden als het maatschappelijk middenveld zijn betrokken, b) de partnerstad in het Zuiden wordt gekenmerkt door recente decentralisatie of hervorming van openbaar bestuur, wat nieuwe uitdagingen en verantwoordelijkheden meebrengt voor zowel lokale overheden als burgers, en c) de doelen van de stedenband richten zich op institutionele versterking of lokale (duurzame) ontwikkeling.

De belangrijkste bevindingen worden hieronder per onderzoeksvraag besproken.

1. Institutionele en beleidscondities op nationaal en supranationaal niveau
Twee – op het eerste gezicht – onafhankelijke ontwikkelingen verklaren de beweegredenen en de groeiende erkenning voor gemeentelijke internationale samenwerking. Deze ontwikkelingen houden verband met ontwikkelingsbeleid (al dan niet van donoren) enerzijds en decentralisatiebeleid en verandering van de rol van gemeenten in het Zuiden anderzijds.

De eerste ontwikkeling betreft het feit dat de positie van lokale overheden in internationale samenwerking is versterkt, vooral in het Noorden. Drie trends illustreren en verklaren de toenemende rol van gemeenten als ontwikkelingspartners. Ten eerste is er groeiende erkenning van supranationale donoren, nationale en lokale overheden voor de positie van lokale overheden als partners in internationale samenwerking. Ten tweede richt het ontwikkelingsdenken en -plannen zich in toenemende mate op het belang van instituties en goed bestuur, ook op lokaal niveau. Ten derde is een scherpe toename waargenomen van zowel het aantal internationale stedennetwerken als van het belang van 'partnerschappen' in internationale samenwerking. De groeiende erkenning van GIS en de rol van lokale overheden in ontwikkeling uit zich tevens in een reeks donorprogramma's en -beleid op supranationaal en nationaal niveau die deze activiteiten ondersteunen.

De tweede institutionele ontwikkeling betreft de behoefte aan sterkere lokale overheden in het Zuiden. Gemeenten in het Zuiden zijn in korte tijd autonoom en proactief geworden op het gebied van lokale ontwikkeling. Ze hebben meer verantwoordelijkheden gekregen voor dienstverlening, armoedebestrijding en het verbeteren van de levensstandaard. Bestuurlijke veranderingen in Peru, Zuid-Afrika en Nicaragua hebben geleid tot een nieuw mandaat, nieuwe taken en meer financiële middelen voor gemeenten in deze landen. Deze studie onderschrijft dat bevolkingsparticipatie in deze landen wettelijk georganiseerd is als onderdeel van lokaal bestuur. Dit bevordert de mogelijkheden van lokale overheden om in te spelen op de behoeften van de burger, rekenschap af te leggen en ontwikkelingsgericht te handelen. Tegelijkertijd vormen de vaak snelle veranderingen een grote uitdaging voor lokale overheden door gebrek aan financiële middelen en adequaat personeel om nieuwe taken uit te voeren. GIS zou een manier kunnen zijn om bij te dragen aan de capaciteitsopbouw die hiervoor vereist is voor lokale overheden in het Zuiden.

2. *Lokale politieke en institutionele condities en de rol van lokale overheden in internationale samenwerking*

De positie en rol van lokale overheden in het Noorden om als partner in ontwikkelingssamenwerking op te treden via stedenbanden, wordt beïnvloed door het feit dat internationale samenwerking niet de *raison d'être* is van gemeenten. Het geeft gemeenten geen bestaansrecht en lokale overheden zijn niet wettelijk verplicht zich bezig te houden met GIS. Door deze vrijwillige aard van GIS is de betrokkenheid van lokale overheden kwetsbaar en onderhevig aan politieke schommelingen. Gemeenten die aan internationale samenwerking willen doen, moeten daarom aan een aantal politieke en institutionele voorwaarden voldoen:

- Gemeentelijk beleid en politieke programma's moeten GIS ondersteunen.
- Ambtenaren moeten over vaardigheden en expertise beschikken om betrokken te zijn bij internationale samenwerking.
- Het aantrekken van financiering van derden is essentieel en overstijgt meestal de eigen gemeentelijke bijdragen. Op deze manier wordt een veelvoud van de eigen middelen ingezet, waardoor (inter)nationale fondsen voor internationale samenwerking specifiek worden ingezet voor het lokale niveau in het Zuiden.
- Politieke steun is een cruciale factor.
- In het Zuiden is het hebben van een afdeling Internationale Samenwerking belangrijk om GIS als een volwaardige gemeentelijke taak te beschouwen. Ook kunnen deze afdelingen de behoeften wat betreft kennis en investeringen koppelen aan de beschikbare expertise en middelen van partnersteden, en het risico verkleinen dat stedenbanden te afhankelijk worden van één persoon.

De studie wijst uit dat het hebben van internationale contacten en voldoen aan de noodzakelijke organisatorische randvoorwaarden alleen niet voldoende is om de problemen van gemeenten in het Zuiden aan te pakken. Belangrijk is vooral de mate waarin gemeenten stedenbanden strategisch inzetten om hun gemeentelijke ontwikkelingsdoelen te realiseren. Gemeenten bleken hierin niet altijd succesvol te zijn. Het voorbeeld van León (Nicaragua) biedt inzicht in de onderliggende oorzaken waarom GIS onvoldoende gekoppeld wordt aan prioriteiten in lokaal bestuur en de ontwikkelingsrol van lokale overheden in het Zuiden. Ten eerste is er een gebrek aan organisatorisch vermogen (middelen en vaardigheden) om een GIS-strategie uit te zetten. Ten tweede is het een kwestie van politieke interesse. De politieke besluitvorming en bestedingen van internationale investeringsgelden worden dikwijls bepaald door persoonlijke voorkeuren – vooral van de zittende burgemeester – in plaats van institutioneel gestelde ontwikkelingsdoelen. Ten slotte is er sprake van onvoldoende institutioneel vermogen: de rol van gemeentelijke ontwikkelingsplannen om te fungeren als instrument voor stedelijke planning en de besteding van internationale fondsen is zwak.

3. *Actoren en hun positie in GIS-netwerken*

Lokale overheden zijn niet de enige deelnemers aan stedenbanden in de partnersteden in het Noorden en Zuiden. De voornaamste andere actoren zijn coördinerende instanties voor het maatschappelijk middenveld (in deze studie "CCSEs"[1] genoemd), donoren met een decentrale (semi-)overheidsachtergrond, externe en nationale ontwikkelingsinstanties, de private sector en het maatschappelijk middenveld. CCSEs nemen een unieke plaats in omdat hun bestaansrecht is ontleend aan de stedenband, terwijl de stedenband normaliter geen kernactiviteit is van de andere betrokken actoren. GIS-netwerken in partnersteden komen voort uit de onderlinge relaties tussen de actoren. Deze relaties bepalen bovendien in grote mate de rol en verantwoordelijkheden van de actoren binnen de stedenband. Voor GIS-relaties in het Noorden zijn zes verschillende functies gevonden: financiële ondersteuning, het bevorderen van bewustzijn, het leveren van kennis en expertise, het creëren van draagvlak, het toegang bieden tot ontwikkelingslanden en ontwikkelingssamenwerking en het uitvoeren van projecten en aangaan van zusterrelaties met de partnerstad. Het tweeledige doel van stedenbanden in het Noorden, namelijk lokaal bestuur versterken in het Zuiden en draagvlak en bewustzijn vergroten in het Noorden, ligt deels ten grondslag aan de onderlinge relaties tussen actoren.

De netwerken in Noord en Zuid vertonen een aantal verschillen. De relaties in Noordelijke netwerken lijken meer geformaliseerd. De samenwerking en coördinatie van actoren is helder en afgestemd. De relaties in het Zuiden daarentegen zijn informeler, minder zichtbaar en niet alle actoren maken onderdeel uit van eenzelfde GIS-netwerk. Daarnaast zijn de relaties die actoren onderhouden in het Noorden complementair, waarin actoren elkaar ondersteunen, terwijl in het Zuiden er soms meer sprake is van competitie en conflict dan samenwerking tussen actoren.

Hoewel het moeilijk is een causaal verband aan te tonen, kan in het geheel gesteld worden dat deelname van zowel de gemeente als het maatschappelijk middenveld de gunstigste omstandigheden biedt om stedenbanden te bevorderen en te onderhouden. Zonder deelname van de gemeente kunnen stedenbanden te lijden hebben onder een gebrek aan politieke steun, middelen, infrastructuur en mogelijkheden om het inzetten van overheidsgelden voor GIS te verantwoorden. Geen deelname van het maatschappelijk middenveld brengt echter het risico mee dat GIS uitmondt in technocratische, geïsoleerde samenwerking zonder maatschappelijk draagvlak en dialoog.

4. *Gemeentelijke internationale samenwerking als instrument voor capaciteitsopbouw en kennisuitwisseling*

Wie bepaalt de agenda en heeft zeggenschap in samenwerkingsverbanden? Deze studie toont aan dat beslissingen overwegend worden genomen door de Zuidelijke partnersteden. Dit biedt goede kansen voor samenwerking die afgestemd is op bestaande capaciteiten en behoeften van de 'ontvangende' organisatie. Tegelijkertijd bleek echter ook dat er een spanningsveld bestaat tussen de ambitie om zeggenschap te vergroten in het Zuiden en het feit dat financieel beheer in handen is van het Noorden. Dit laatste bepaalt tenslotte voor een groot deel het raamwerk waarbinnen samenwerking plaatsvindt.

Welke mechanismen worden ingezet voor uitwisseling en interactie tussen de steden? Deze bepalen of capaciteitsopbouw op een duurzame procesbenadering gebaseerd is. De meeste mechanismen beperken zich tot bezoeken van korte duur aan partnersteden. Als er hierdoor weinig interactie plaatsvindt tussen de bezoeken door, kan de procesbenadering ondermijnd worden. Uitwisselingsmissies lopen daarom het risico geïsoleerde momenten

---

[1]   'Coordinating civil society entities'

van contact te worden, wat negatief kan uitpakken voor het imago van de stedenband als vorm van langdurige samenwerking. Het kritisch volgen van voortgang en regelmatig evalueren zijn belangrijk om geboekte resultaten vast te houden en belangrijke toekomstige behoeften te identificeren.

Welke kansen bestaan er om te leren binnen stedenbanden? In zowel het Noorden als het Zuiden is er sprake van leren op het persoonlijke vlak, zoals persoonlijke vaardigheidstraining en het bewust worden van andere persoonlijke en professionele houdingen. Beroepsmatig leren in het Noorden betreft vooral het opdoen en verbeteren van werkvaardigheden en leren reflecteren op het eigen werk door in aanraking te komen met een andere culturele organisatorische context. Daarentegen is beroepsmatig leren in het Zuiden vooral gebaseerd op het vergaren van technische kennis in het specifieke vakgebied van deelnemers. In het algemeen hebben stedenbandprojecten in het Zuiden resultaten voortgebracht die het niveau van het individu overstijgen. Dit biedt kansen voor structurele veranderingen in de organisatie. De kennis en vaardigheden die in het Noorden worden opgedaan, hebben daarentegen geen noemenswaardige invloed op het dagelijkse werk.

Wederkerigheid is laatste factor van Noord-Zuidstedenbanden. Wederkerigheid is echter niet beperkt tot het aspect van leren. Steden in het Noorden zien het verbeteren van hun eigen organisatie of het vergroten van de kennis en vaardigheden van personeel niet als randvoorwaarden voor een 'goede' stedenband. In plaats daarvan zijn de (politieke en individuele) doelen in het Noorden vooral van altruïstische aard, gerelateerd aan het leveren van ontwikkelingshulp aan het Zuiden. Het feit dat leren in het Noorden geen doel is op zich, betekent dan ook dat de vraag of wederkerigheid van leren aanwezig is binnen stedenbanden niet relevant is, in elk geval niet vanuit een beleidsperspectief. In plaats van leren zijn er andere mogelijkheden voor wederkerigheid binnen stedenbanden, zoals de kansen die gemeenten in het Noorden creëren op strategisch politiek en organisatorisch gebied. Voorbeelden zijn het bevorderen van de loyaliteit en motivatie onder personeel, het vergroten van het mondiale bewustzijn binnen en buiten de gemeente, het genereren van positieve publiciteit en het scheppen van een sociaal imago van de gemeentelijke organisatie.

5. *In welke mate en op welke manier draagt gemeentelijke internationale samenwerking bij aan het versterken van lokaal bestuur in het Zuiden?*

Een eerste aspect van het versterken van lokaal bestuur is het verbeteren van de gemeentelijke organisatie. Deze studie vond hiervoor omvangrijke en diverse resultaten. Voor *individuele* ambtenaren komt vooral het trainen van personeel veel voor. Dit varieerde van het ontwikkelen van algemene vaardigheden tot het opdoen van meer specifieke technische kennis. Het versterken van de *organisatie* blijkt ook een resultaat van GIS, zoals technische opwaardering, het inzetten van nieuwe instrumenten en middelen, en het afstemmen en verbeteren van interne processen. Ten slotte hebben stedenbanden invloed op *institutionele* verandering. Dit heeft te maken met reorganisatie en het verbreden van het institutionele mandaat van gemeenten, bijvoorbeeld door nieuwe beleidsterreinen en vormen van dienstverlening te introduceren. Dit laatste verwijst ook naar de meer proactieve rol van gemeenten in lokale ontwikkelingsprocessen.

Het directe effect van GIS op het versterken van het maatschappelijk middenveld is aanzienlijk zwakker. Hoewel er een paar uitzonderingen zijn, hebben stedenbanden in het algemeen weinig directe invloed op het versterken van lokale gemeenschappen. Er is weinig bewijs dat het particulier initiatief in het Noorden de positie van burgers in de partnerstad heeft verstevigd. Het particulier initiatief binnen stedenbanden leidt niet altijd tot duidelijke en solide resultaten. Projecten zijn vaak kleinschalig en praktisch, gericht op het verbeteren van de levensomstandigheden in de partnerstad. Het werken aan abstracte zaken zoals burgerschap en burgerparticipatie komt minder aan bod.

Het onderzoek laat zien dat het versterken van het maatschappelijk middenveld hoofdzakelijk voortkomt uit gemeentelijke projecten, die in de eerste plaats gericht zijn op het versterken van de gemeentelijke organisatie, maar die een participatief karakter hebben. Deze projecten baseren zich bijvoorbeeld op de langdurige ervaring met burgerparticipatie zoals in León en Villa El Salvador (Peru), waarbij de burger niet slechts gebruiker maar ook vormgever van dienstverlening is. De voorwaarden om de betrokkenheid van burgers te stimuleren, worden door deze projecten verbeterd. Stedenbanden kunnen dus ook indirecte gevolgen hebben door wederkerige relaties tussen lokale overheid en andere lokale actoren te versterken.

Naast het versterken van lokale overheden enerzijds en het maatschappelijk middenveld anderzijds, staan ook het bevorderen van lokale multi-sectorale relaties centraal in de analyse. Resultaten zijn o.a. het opzetten van publiek-private samenwerking, wat nieuwe participatiekansen biedt; het verbeteren van het gemeentelijke vermogen te voorzien in lokale behoeften en verantwoordelijkheid af te leggen aan burgers, organisaties en bedrijven – bijvoorbeeld door verbeterde klantvriendelijkheid voor belastingbetalers en fiscale transparantie; betere instrumenten om het functioneren van de lokale overheid te beoordelen en controleren; een meer participatieve gemeentelijke planvorming, wat kansen biedt voor gemarginaliseerde bevolkingsgroepen hun behoeften kenbaar te maken; en het invoeren van nieuwe beleidsterreinen zoals sociale cohesie, zodat gemeenten hun rol als lokale ontwikkelaar meer serieus nemen.

Samenvattend kan gesteld worden dat stedenbanden vooral geschikt zijn om de effectiviteit van lokale overheden in het Zuiden te verbeteren, terwijl het verstevigen van het maatschappelijk middenveld beperkter is. Het lijkt erop dat de manier waarop *gemeentelijke* projecten uitgevoerd worden vooral belangrijk is om meer participatieve vormen van lokaal bestuur te ontwikkelen. Bij het evalueren van het versterken van lokaal bestuur via stedenbanden is het daarom nuttig niet alleen de directe gevolgen van projecten in acht te nemen. De *indirecte* resultaten, die het gevolg zijn van een meer burgergerichte overheid enerzijds en meer betrokkenheid van de gemeenschap anderzijds, zijn ook belangrijk. Deze indirecte resultaten zijn namelijk niet alleen een uitkomst van GIS-projecten, maar ook een middel om de uitwisseling en verantwoordelijkheid tussen verschillende actoren en collectieve planvorming te bevorderen.

Deze studie heeft getracht tot nieuwe inzichten te komen die gebaseerd zijn op empirisch bewijs, voornamelijk wat betreft de verschillende factoren die van invloed zijn op hoe internationale samenwerking tussen steden is georganiseerd en hoe het functioneert. Het onderzoek was soms ambivalent in de manier waarop Noord-Zuidsamenwerking benaderd zou moeten worden. Het lijkt erop dat er een paradox bestaat als gevolg van het feit dat stedenbanden ingebed zijn in een Noord-Zuidstructuur: er is een constant spanningsveld tussen het zien van Noord-Zuidstedenbanden als mechanismen van gelijkwaardige, horizontale uitwisseling enerzijds, en een vorm van het klassieke lineaire model van hulp van het Noorden naar het Zuiden anderzijds. Terwijl het eerste gezichtspunt impliceert dat beide partners profiteren van kennisuitwisseling – wat populaire retoriek is onder betrokkenen in het veld – worden bij het andere perspectief vragen gesteld bij de wederkerigheid van deze relaties, omdat in de praktijk blijkt dat er een grotendeels eenzijdige overdracht van middelen, kennis en expertise van Noord naar Zuid plaatsvindt. Het onderzoek wijst uit dat een flexibele benadering van Noord-Zuidstedenbanden op zijn plaats is, waarbinnen ruimte is voor beide gezichtspunten.

Er kan een aantal lessen worden getrokken uit deze studie en de achterliggende literatuuranalyse. In de eerste plaats kan gemeentelijke internationale samenwerking niet begrepen of bevorderd worden zonder een degelijke analyse van de politieke context. Omdat stedenbanden altijd opereren binnen een politieke structuur, mag een analyse van lokale politiek, machtsrelaties en informele en formele besluitvorming niet ontbreken. Stedenbanden en politiek zijn intrinsiek verbonden, op ten minste drie manieren: wat betreft actoren (partnerorganisaties zijn politieke instanties, waarvoor politieke steun cruciaal is om stedenbanden in stand te houden); wat betreft gestelde doelen (die politiek gekleurd zijn door collegeprogramma's en (internationaal) beleid van gemeenten); en wat betreft de begunstigden van stedenbandprojecten (de vraag wie profiteert en wie wordt buitengesloten van hulp is meestal een politieke kwestie).

Een tweede leerpunt vloeit voort uit de discussie over de tweeledige doelstelling van steden in het Noorden die Noord-Zuid stedenbanden onderhouden. Deze verwijst aan de ene kant naar het versterken van lokaal bestuur in het Zuiden en aan de andere kant naar het vergroten van het maatschappelijk draagvlak en bewustzijn in het Noorden omtrent ontwikkelingssamenwerking en mondiale armoede. Er kan door het tweeledige karakter spanning ontstaan bij het bepalen van de vorm en inhoud van activiteiten en projecten. Gemeenten moeten een balans vinden tussen het genereren van zichtbaar, mediageniek resultaat dat de eigen burger aanspreekt, en het inzetten van hun specifieke gemeentelijke expertise in technische uitwisselingen om institutionele en lokale ontwikkeling in de partnerstad te stimuleren.

Ten derde lopen gemeenten in het Zuiden het gevaar dat ze meer gespitst zijn op hun verantwoordelijkheid jegens donoren (hun zustersteden) dan jegens hun eigen burgers. De aandacht voor vereiste *donor accountability* prevaleert soms boven het streven naar *domestic accountability*. Noordelijke gemeenten worden via stedenbanden onderdeel van lokale besluitvormingsprocessen in het Zuiden. Ze kunnen grote invloed uitoefenen op bijvoorbeeld de besteding van gemeentelijke investeringsgelden. Op die manier worden prioriteiten van Zuidelijke gemeenten gebaseerd op de wensen van internationale samenwerkingspartners in plaats van op de behoeften van de lokale bevolking. De korte lijnen die op decentraal niveau bestaan tussen de donorgemeenschap en de lokale bevolking brengen daarnaast het risico mee dat burgers zich direct tot donoren wenden om hun situatie te verbeteren in plaats van tot hun eigen volksvertegenwoordigers. Als stedenbanden te veel onderdeel gaan uitmaken van het lokaal bestuur kunnen zij dus lokale burger-overheidrelaties verstoren in plaats van ze te bevorderen. Het wordt duidelijk dat de principes van de Parijs Agenda voor de effectiviteit van hulp (2005), die momenteel geldt als een van de belangrijkste richtlijnen in ontwikkelingsbeleid, ook van toepassing zijn op de urbane context en gemeentelijke internationale samenwerking. Om een balans te vinden tussen *domestic* en *donor accountability* moeten gemeenten in het Zuiden een heldere en solide *door zichzelf bepaalde* ontwikkelingsstrategie hebben, teneinde ontwikkelingsdoelen te stellen die institutioneel verankerd zijn en gebaseerd zijn op bevolkingsparticipatie. Een

THE CHALLENGE TO STRENGTHEN URBAN GOVERNANCE THROUGH NORTH-SOUTH CITY PARTNERSHIPS

dergelijke strategie kan bovendien dienen als leidraad voor gemeentelijke *donorharmonisatie* en *-afstemming*, en om potentiële donoren aan te trekken. De effectiviteit van stedenbanden kan aanzienlijk verbeteren mits gemeenten in het Zuiden eigen ontwikkelingsdoelen stellen die gebaseerd zijn op de behoeften van de bevolking, en gemeenten in het Noorden in staat zijn in te spelen op de behoeften van het Zuiden in plaats van zelf te bepalen hoe de hulp moet worden vormgegeven (vaak beïnvloed door de eisen die externe financiers stellen).

Een vierde leerpunt is gerelateerd aan de conclusie dat het directe effect van gemeentelijke internationale samenwerking op het versterken van het maatschappelijk middenveld mager is. Gezien het multi-dimensionale karakter van GIS waarbij verschillende actoren betrokken zijn, kan dit beschouwd worden als een gemiste kans. Een van de unieke kenmerken van stedenbanden als vorm van ontwikkelingssamenwerking is dat zowel de publieke sector als het particulier initiatief centraal staan, als partners en als begunstigden. De kansen om lokaal bestuur te versterken vanuit verschillende invalshoeken wordt onvoldoende benut. Om stedenbanden effectiever te maken, moeten nieuwe strategieën worden ontwikkeld om de positie van burgers en participatie in besluitvorming in het Zuiden te versterken.

Een vijfde leerpunt van dit onderzoek houdt verband met de bevinding dat partnergemeenten in het Noorden het leren van hun Zuidelijke partner niet centraal stellen in de samenwerking. De vraag rijst of het niet enigszins aanmatigend is van Noordelijke partners om hun eigen kennis en ervaring als relevante gemeentelijke expertise te beschouwen, terwijl ervaringen in het Zuiden niet als bron van nieuwe kennis worden gezien. Misschien dat de recente trend van innovatie in democratisch, participatief bestuur in het Zuiden, met name in Latijns-Amerika, een tegenwicht kan bieden in het exporteren van ideeën en kennis over lokaal bestuur van het Zuiden naar het Noorden. Steden in het Noorden zouden moeten beginnen met het anders waarderen en interpreteren van kennis uit het Zuiden, en nieuwe kansen scheppen om te leren en te veranderen.

Een laatste les die getrokken kan worden, heeft te maken met relevantie. Hoe relevant is de rol van steden en lokale overheden in internationale samenwerking? De toegenomen aandacht voor het 'urbane' in het ontwikkelingsdenken, urbanisatie en het besef dat armoede in de toekomst steeds meer een stedelijke kwestie wordt, doen vermoeden dat de positie van steden en lokale overheden in internationale samenwerking evident blijft. De deelname van gemeenten op dit gebied is echter niet zonder risico's. Deze studie heeft aangetoond dat een uitgebalanceerde en genuanceerde waardering van stedenbanden en stedennetwerken op zijn plaats is. Het beeld dat donoren en verenigingen van gemeenten scheppen van te bereiken resultaten moet realistischer. Voorzichtigheid is geboden bij het trekken van conclusies over stedenbanden en hun invloed op lokale ontwikkeling en armoedevermindering. Stedenbanden moeten niet beschouwd worden als een wondermiddel voor verschillende stedelijke problemen. Het verdient de voorkeur een bescheidener benadering te hebben en deze banden te zien als een mogelijk vliegwiel voor ontwikkeling en verandering.

Als de juiste condities gecreëerd worden, kan deze rol als vliegwiel echter veelbelovend zijn. Gemeenten in het Noorden moeten de positie van internationale samenwerking als gemeentelijke taak versterken en de noodzakelijke organisatorische, technische, financiële en politieke randvoorwaarden scheppen om op een duurzame manier betrokken te zijn. Gemeenten in het Zuiden moeten hun behoeften wat betreft lokale ontwikkeling goed in kaart brengen en bepalen hoe internationale samenwerking strategisch kan worden ingezet om in deze behoeften te voorzien. Dit onderzoek heeft aangetoond dat gemeentelijke internationale samenwerking een bijzondere plaats kan innemen in ontwikkelingssamenwerking door het leveren van kennis, ervaring en expertise op zeer gespecialiseerde gemeentelijke werkterreinen. Capaciteitsopbouw dient zich te baseren op bestaande structuren en planvorming. Stedenbanden moeten zoeken naar nieuwe mogelijkheden om het maatschappelijk middenveld in het Zuiden direct te betrekken en participatie te vergroten. Samenwerking moet worden gestimuleerd door politieke steun en het begrijpen van elkaars doelen. Als aan deze voorwaarden wordt voldaan, kunnen stedenbanden actief bijdragen aan het versterken van lokaal bestuur in het Zuiden.

Síntesis

Ciudades como socios: El desafío del fortalecimiento de la gobernanza local por medio de hermanamientos Norte-Sur

Durante las últimas décadas, gobiernos locales han venido siendo reconocidos como actores activos en la cooperación internacional al desarrollo. Según estimaciones, actualmente el 70% de las ciudades del mundo están involucradas en alguna forma de cooperación internacional, hermanamientos, redes internacionales entre ciudades, alianzas y programas. Muchos de estos vínculos – también llamados 'cooperación de ciudad a ciudad' (C2C, por sus siglas en inglés), un término introducido por el PNUD en el 2000 – establecen una conexión entre el mundo desarrollado y el en vías de desarrollo, o, formulándolo de otra forma, entre el Norte global y el Sur global. Las ciudades ocupan un lugar central en esta forma de cooperación internacional, como agente de desarrollo y al mismo tiempo como beneficiario. Considerando las tendencias continuas a nivel mundial de descentralización administrativa, globalización y urbanización, una consciencia creciente de *ciudadanía global*, el papel cambiante del gobierno local y una atención aumentada para la buena gobernanza como una precondición para el desarrollo, se está utilizando cada vez más la cooperación internacional entre municipios como un instrumento para ciudades y comunidades de dar asistencia mutua mediante el intercambio de conocimientos, la transferencia de recursos y tecnología, y la cooperación conjunta. Ciudades – tanto las administraciones locales como las sociedades civiles – se vinculan y a través de estas relaciones quieren contribuir a una variedad de objetivos, tales como aliviación de la pobreza, fortalecimiento institucional, construcción de democracia y paz.

La continua urbanización, especialmente en el mundo en desarrollo (el 'Sur'), y las cambiadas políticas de donantes han hecho que lo 'urbano' ocupara un lugar más prominente en el pensamiento sobre el desarrollo. La descentralización y el rediseño de la administración pública en el Sur resultaron en un papel más importante para el gobierno local. Un razonamiento subyacente es que cuánto más cerca esté el gobierno a la población más orientado será hacia las necesidades de sus ciudadanos. El concepto de gobernanza urbana, que está ganando terreno en las políticas municipales, reconoce que el poder de toma de decisiones existe tanto dentro como fuera de las instituciones gubernamentales locales, lo que disminuye la distinción entre las esferas pública y privada. Se ha sugerido que, para lograr una gobernanza local buena y participativa, se necesita acercar los ciudadanos y las instituciones, y para ello se requiere tanto un gobierno local fuerte como una sociedad civil fuerte.

Colocándolo en este trasfondo, la presente investigación tiene el objetivo de obtener entendimiento sobre la relevancia y las posibilidades de la cooperación Norte-Sur de ciudad a ciudad con respecto al fortalecimiento de la gobernanza urbana en el Sur. Además trata de obtener una mejor comprensión de los factores que afectan este potencial de la C2C. Cinco preguntas ocuparon un lugar central en esta investigación:

1. ¿Qué condiciones institucionales y políticas nacionales y supranacionales dan forma al papel de los gobiernos locales en los procesos de cooperación internacional y de desarrollo local?
2. ¿Bajo qué condiciones políticas e institucionales locales operan los gobiernos locales en la cooperación internacional y cuáles son las implicaciones para la cooperación de ciudad a ciudad?
3. ¿Qué actores constituyen las redes municipales de C2C en las ciudades hermanas, cuáles son sus papeles y responsabilidades y qué interrelaciones existen entre ellos?
4. ¿Bajo qué condiciones y en qué medida las relaciones de C2C funcionan como mecanismos para la construcción de capacidades y el intercambio de conocimientos?
5. ¿En qué medida y de qué forma las relaciones de C2C contribuyen al fortalecimiento de la gobernanza local en el Sur?

La investigación se basa en un estudio comparativo de cuatro hermanamientos Norte-Sur, en los que participan ciudades de los Países Bajos, Alemania, Perú, Nicaragua, y África del Sur. En cada una de estas ciudades (cuatro de ellas en el Norte y cuatro en el Sur) se aplicó una estrategia estructurada de investigación, lo que permitió la comparación cruzada de casos. Se realizó la investigación entre 2005 y 2008 mediante métodos cualitativos. Los principales criterios para la selección de los hermanamientos fueron a) tanto actores de los gobiernos locales como de la sociedad civil están participando, b) el contexto institucional de las ciudades en el Sur fue creado a través de un proceso reciente de descentralización o reformas en el sector público, lo que conlleva a nuevos desafíos y responsabilidades para tanto el gobierno local como los ciudadanos y c) los objetivos de los hermanamientos están vinculados al fortalecimiento institucional o al desarrollo local (sostenible).

A continuación, se presentan los principales hallazgos obtenidos de la investigación ordenados según las preguntas centrales de la investigación:

1. Condiciones institucionales y de políticas nacionales y supranacionales
Dos -a primera vista- desarrollos independientes, relacionados con la política de desarrollo (de los donantes) por un lado y las políticas de descentralización y el marco institucional cambiante de los gobiernos locales en el Sur por otro lado, explican los motivos y el creciente reconocimiento de la cooperación de ciudad a ciudad.

En primer lugar, la importancia de la posición del gobierno local en la cooperación internacional se aumentó, en la medida en que las ciudades en el Norte han venido involucrándose cada vez más en la arena de la cooperación internacional al desarrollo. Se identificaron tres tendencias que aclaran el creciente papel de las municipalidades como socios en el desarrollo: a) ha habido un creciente reconocimiento por parte de tanto donantes supranacionales como gobiernos nacionales y locales de gobiernos locales como socios en la cooperación al desarrollo; b) el pensamiento y la planificación con respecto al desarrollo se dirigen cada vez más a la importancia de instituciones y la buena gobernanza, también a nivel local; c) se demostró que ha habido un fuerte incremento en la cantidad de redes internacionales entre ciudades y una mayor importancia de hermanamientos en la cooperación internacional. El creciente reconocimiento de la C2C y el papel de los gobiernos locales en el desarrollo se ven reflejados en una amplia gama de políticas y programas de apoyo de donantes a nivel supranacional y nacional.

La segunda condición institucional que explica el razón fundamental de las relaciones de C2C guarda relación con la necesidad de tener gobiernos locales más fuertes en el Sur. Gobiernos locales y comunidades locales en el Sur se han convertido rápidamente en agentes más autónomos y proactivos de desarrollo, con mayores responsabilidades con respecto a la prestación de servicios, aliviación de la pobreza y el mejoramiento de la calidad de vida urbana. Cambios en los marcos institucionales en Perú, África del Sur y Nicaragua conllevaron a mandatos y responsabilidades nuevas y una base de recursos financieros más fuerte para sus respectivas municipalidades. Se demostró que las estructuras locales de administración en estos países están legalmente institucionalizadas y basadas en la participación ciudadana, lo que permite potencialmente a los gobiernos locales responder mejor a las necesidades de los ciudadanos, tener mayor capacidad de rendición de cuentas y una actuación orientada hacia el desarrollo. Al mismo tiempo, sin embargo, los muchas veces muy rápidos cambios legislativos significaron grandes desafíos para los gobiernos locales, que uniformemente continúan careciendo seriamente de recursos financieros y humanos para llevar a cabo adecuadamente sus tareas. Ello explica la necesidad de construcción de capacidades, que se podría lograr a través de la C2C.

2. *Condiciones políticas e institucionales locales del papel de los gobiernos locales en la cooperación internacional*

Con respecto a la posición y el papel de los gobiernos locales en el Norte para actuar como socios en la cooperación al desarrollo mediante hermanamientos, se encontró que la cooperación al desarrollo no es la razón de ser de los gobiernos locales. Su existencia no depende de ello, y no están legalmente obligados a participar en la cooperación internacional municipal. El carácter voluntario de la C2C hace que el involucramiento de gobiernos locales sea vulnerable y sujeto a cambios políticos (de régimen). Como resultado de ello, municipalidades que quieran participar en la cooperación internacional tendrán que cumplir varias condiciones políticas e institucionales:

- Se necesita contar con políticas municipales y programas políticos que apoyan la C2C
- Los funcionarios necesitan tener las destrezas y el peritaje necesarios para involucrarse en la C2C y la cooperación internacional al desarrollo
- El financiamiento de partes terceras generalmente excede las contribuciones propias de las ciudades hermanas. Los gobiernos locales en el Norte causan un efecto multiplicador en la obtención de fondos, lo que implica que, mediante la C2C, se descentralizan recursos (inter)nacionales y se los destinan directamente al nivel local en el Sur
- El interés y voluntad políticos son un factor crucial
- La presencia de un Departamento Municipal de Cooperación Internacional resultó ser de importancia en el Sur, para facilitar y mantener la C2C como una responsabilidad municipal plena, actuar como intermediario para acoplar las necesidades de capacidad humana e inversiones de la organización con el conocimiento y los recursos disponibles de la ciudad hermana, y reducir el riesgo de que los hermanamientos dependan demasiado de una sola persona.

De la investigación se desprende que, en las municipalidades en el Sur, el hecho de tener relaciones internacionales y disponer de las condiciones organizacionales necesarias no resuelve los desafíos relacionados con la capacidad municipal *per se*. Más bien, la medida en qué las municipalidades emplean sus relaciones de C2C como instrumentos estratégicos para lograr el desarrollo municipal y los objetivos de planificación es crucial. Se estableció que las municipalidades no siempre han tenido éxito en este respecto. El ejemplo de León (Nicaragua) mostró que las razones subyacentes por las que la C2C está vinculada insuficientemente a temas urgentes relacionados con la gobernanza urbana y el papel en el desarrollo de los gobiernos locales en el Sur son un asunto de capacidad organizacional (falta de recursos y destrezas para desarrollar estrategias para la C2C), intereses políticos (preferencias personales -del Alcalde de turno- predominan sobre objetivos de desarrollo definidos institucionalmente en la toma de decisiones a nivel político y en la asignación de inversiones (internacionales), y de capacidad institucional (el papel de los Planes Municipales de Desarrollo como instrumento para la planificación urbana y la asignación de fondos internacionales es débil).

3. *Actores, papeles y responsabilidades en las redes municipales de C2C*

En las ciudades hermanas en el Norte y en el Sur, la C2C va más allá de la participación del gobierno local, e incluye a otros actores también. Los principales actores reconocidos son las administraciones locales, entidades de coordinación de la sociedad civil (CCSEs, por sus siglas en inglés), donantes (descentralizados) del sector público, agentes de desarrollo externos o nacionales, el sector privado y actores de la sociedad civil. Las CCSEs fueron identificadas como ocupando una posición única, porque su existencia está basada primordialmente en el hermanamiento, mientras que el hermanamiento en general no es el quehacer principal de los otros actores involucrados. Redes municipales de C2C en ciudades hermanas son el resultado de las interrelaciones entre estos actores. Además, estas relaciones definen en gran medida los papeles y responsabilidades de los actores. Se encontraron seis tipos de relaciones funcionales dentro de las redes de C2C en el Norte; servicio de flujos financieros, fomento de la sensibilización, suministro de conocimientos y peritaje, creación de soporte social para el sostenimiento del hermanamiento, abrir una ventana hacia los países en vías de desarrollo y la cooperación al desarrollo, y la implementación de proyectos y hermanamientos con el Sur. El doble objetivo de la C2C que muchas veces se persigue en el Norte, o sea el fortalecimiento de la gobernanza local en el Sur y el fomento de la sensibilización en el Norte, es una explicación subyacente para las estructuras encontradas de estas redes.

Existen varias diferencias entre las redes establecidas en el Norte y en el Sur. Las relaciones dentro de las redes en el Norte parecen ser más formalizadas, y la cooperación y coordinación entre los actores están más armonizadas y cristalizadas. En el Sur, por el contrario, las relaciones son más informales, menos obvias y visibles, y no todos los actores están participando en la red. Además, mientras que las relaciones dentro de las redes en el Norte pueden ser caracterizadas generalmente como de apoyo mutuo y complementarias, en el Sur a veces se producen conflictos en vez de cooperación dentro de las redes de hermanamiento.

En términos generales, aunque una relación causal es difícil de demostrar, parece que una participación equilibrada del gobierno local y la sociedad civil ofrece las condiciones más favorables para el sostenimiento del hermanamiento. Sin la participación del gobierno local, el hermanamiento puede verse debilitado por la carencia del soporte político, de recursos, infraestructura y mecanismos para la justificación de la utilización de recursos públicos destinados a la cooperación internacional. La ausencia de la participación de la sociedad civil, por otro lado, significa el riesgo de una cooperación tecnocrática aislada con poco soporte público.

4. *La cooperación de C2C como mecanismo para la construcción de capacidades y el intercambio de conocimientos*

La apropiación y formulación de una agenda basada en la demanda fue la primera condición crítica identificada en las relaciones de hermanamiento. La toma de decisiones es, en general, llevada a cabo por las ciudades hermanas en el Sur, lo que ofrece mayores posibilidades de una cooperación hecha a la medida de la capacidad existente y las necesidades de las organizaciones 'receptoras'. Al mismo tiempo, sin embargo, se encontró que existe una tensión entre la ambición de aumentar la apropiación en el Sur y la realidad de que el control financiero está siendo ejecutado por el Norte, lo que determina en una medida considerable los parámetros para la cooperación.

Una segunda condición abordada son los mecanismos empleados para el intercambio y la interacción, los cuales definen si la construcción de capacidades se basa en el enfoque de un proceso sostenible. La mayoría de los mecanismos se limita a visitas de trabajo de corta duración a la ciudad hermana. El enfoque de proceso puede verse debilitado por el hecho de que haya poca interacción en el período entre las visitas realizadas. Las misiones técnicas, por lo tanto, presentan el riesgo de convertirse en eventos únicos aislados, lo que puede tener consecuencias negativas para la imagen del hermanamiento como una cooperación de largo plazo. Mecanismos de monitoreo y evaluación son instrumentos importantes para sostener los avances obtenidos y señalar necesidades futuras relevantes.

En tercer lugar, con respecto a las posibilidades de aprendizaje dentro de los hermanamientos, se puede llegar a varias conclusiones. El aprendizaje personal tiene múltiples dimensiones y se lo observó tanto en el Norte como en el Sur, por ejemplo el desarrollo personal (de destrezas); y adoptar actitudes diferentes hacia la vida y el trabajo. El aprendizaje profesional en el Norte está vinculado sobre todo a la adquisición y mejora de destrezas laborales y la reflexión sobre su propio trabajo, impulsada por estar expuesto a contextos organizacionales (culturales) diferentes. Por el contrario, el aprendizaje profesional en el Sur está basado sobre todo en adquirir conocimientos técnicos en el campo específico de peritaje de los participantes. En el Sur, proyectos realizados por los hermanamientos generalmente generaron resultados más allá de la esfera personal, creando oportunidades para cambios organizacionales. Contrariamente, los conocimientos y destrezas adquiridas no fueron manifiestamente implementadas en la práctica diaria laboral en el Norte.

De la cuarta condición, la mutualidad, se encontró que está presente en los hermanamientos Norte-Sur, pero que no estuvo limitada solamente a la dimensión de aprendizaje. Ciudades en el Norte no consideran el mejoramiento de su propio desempeño organizacional o el aumento de los conocimientos y destrezas de su personal por medio del aprendizaje como componentes necesarios de un 'buen' hermanamiento. En lugar de ello, los objetivos formulados en el Norte -tanto políticos como individuales- se los puede considerar como bastante altruistas y relacionados fuertemente con el ofrecimiento de asistencia técnica al desarrollo en el Sur. Si el aprendizaje en el Norte no es un objetivo en sí, implica que la pregunta de que la mutualidad en el aprendizaje es evidente en la C2C no es una pregunta relevante, por lo menos no desde una perspectiva de formulación de políticas. En lugar de mediante el aprendizaje, oportunidades más grandes para la mutualidad en los hermanamientos pueden ser ofrecidas por los beneficios que puedan obtener las municipalidades en el Norte en el ámbito estratégico político y organizacional, por ejemplo el fomento de la lealtad y motivación del personal, la creación de una sensibilización global dentro y fuera de la administración local, y la generación de publicidad positiva y una imagen social de la municipalidad.

5. ¿Hasta qué punto y de qué forma los hermanamientos de C2C contribuyen al fortalecimiento de la gobernanza urbana en el Sur?

En una primera categoría de fortalecimiento de la gobernanza urbana, tratándose de la capacidad del gobierno local, se encontró una gran riqueza y diversidad de resultados. A nivel individual de *recursos y capital humanos*, el entrenamiento del personal es un elemento encontrado en todos los ejemplos estudiados, que abarca desde el desarrollo de destrezas generales hasta la construcción de un peritaje técnico más específico. Con respecto al *fortalecimiento organizacional*, también se encontraron evidencias sustanciales, por ejemplo el aumento del nivel técnico y la introducción de nuevos instrumentos y herramientas, y la alineación y mejoramiento de procesos internos. También se identificaron resultados a nivel de *cambio institucional*, que se refieren a procesos de reorganización institucional, y la ampliación del alcance institucional de las administraciones, por ejemplo mediante la introducción de nuevas áreas de políticas municipales y de prestación de servicios. Este último además alude a la interpretación más amplia de los papeles de las municipalidades como 'desarrolladores de la comunidad' y no meramente como 'proveedores de servicios'.

Con respecto a una segunda categoría, es decir el impacto de las intervenciones realizadas por hermanamientos en la construcción de capacidades de la sociedad civil, la evidencia es considerablemente más variada y, además, bastante débil. Exceptuando algunos casos, las intervenciones hechas por los hermanamientos muestran en general pocos efectos *directos* en el fortalecimiento comunitario. Existe poca evidencia de iniciativas de la sociedad civil en las ciudades hermanas en el Norte que lograron empoderar la posición de los ciudadanos de la ciudad hermana en el Sur. El involucramiento de la sociedad civil en el hermanamiento no siempre lleva a resultados claros y sólidos debido a la ejecución de proyectos caracterizados como de pequeña escala y dirigidos a mejorar de forma muy práctica las condiciones de vida en la ciudad hermana, en vez de trabajar en temas más abstractos de ciudadanía y participación ciudadana.

En lugar de ello, se encontró que el fortalecimiento de la sociedad civil ocurre sobre todo como resultado de la naturaleza participativa de los proyectos de los hermanamientos municipales que se concentran en primer lugar en el fortalecimiento de los gobiernos locales. Estos proyectos no sólo reconocieron la experiencia de largo plazo de los ciudadanos como 'constructores y moldeadores' en vez de sólo 'usuarios y electores' especialmente en León y Villa El Salvador (Perú), sino que además crearon condiciones favorables para seguir estimulando el involucramiento de los ciudadanos. Por lo tanto, se puede llegar a la conclusión de que los hermanamientos también pueden tener efectos indirectos, es decir el reforzamiento de las relaciones mutuas entre el gobierno local y la sociedad civil.

Una tercera categoría de impacto reconoce estas relaciones y justifica un enfoque más dinámico para la evaluación de los efectos obtenidos por la C2C. Hallazgos de este tipo de impacto incluyen el surgimiento de coordinaciones multisectoriales, que ofrecen oportunidades de participación; el aumento de la capacidad del gobierno local de responder a las necesidades locales y rendir cuentas a los ciudadanos, por ejemplo al mejorar la atención al cliente con respecto a los contribuyentes locales, y el mejoramiento de la transparencia fiscal; mejores oportunidades para el control y monitoreo del desempeño del gobierno local tanto de parte de personas internas como externas a la administración local; un enfoque más participativo para la planificación municipal, al apelar a una mayor participación ciudadana que puede impulsar aún más a grupos marginalizados y pobres a hacer escuchar su voz y expresar sus necesidades; y la introducción de nuevas áreas dentro de la política municipal, por ejemplo la cohesión social y la participación comunitaria, que desafía a las administraciones locales de asumir más seriamente su papel como 'desarrollador comunitario'.

Resumiendo, se puede afirmar que la C2C parece ser especialmente aplicable para mejorar la eficacia de las administraciones locales en el Sur, mientras que el fortalecimiento directo de la sociedad civil es más limitado. En lugar de ello, la forma en qué se ejecutan las intervenciones *municipales* de los hermanamientos es de mayor importancia en la apertura de espacios para procesos de gobernanza urbana participativos y orientados a responder a las necesidades de los ciudadanos. Al hacer un análisis del fortalecimiento de la gobernanza local por medio de los hermanamientos, es útil, por lo tanto, no sólo tomar en consideración el impacto directo de estas intervenciones. Los impactos *indirectos*, que son el resultado de un gobierno local más orientado hacia las necesidades de sus ciudadanos por un lado y mejores destrezas participativas de la sociedad civil por el otro, también son cruciales para tomar en cuenta. No solamente significan el fin de las intervenciones de C2C, son también el medio para seguir mejorando la interacción y la capacidad de rendir cuentas entre los diferentes actores urbanos y para promover la planificación colectiva.

Esta investigación no sólo trató de recopilar conocimiento existente de una forma más sistematizada, sino también de ampliarlo, aportando nuevos entendimientos basados en hallazgos empíricos. De particular relevancia podrá ser el conjunto de factores que fue deshilachado como influyente en cómo se da forma a la cooperación internacional de ciudad a ciudad y cómo es su desempeño con respecto a los objetivos formulados. En general, el análisis a veces era ambivalente con respecto a cómo la cooperación municipal Norte-Sur debería ser abordada. No es fácil encontrar respuestas a estas preguntas. Parece haber una paradoja que es el resultado del hecho de que los hermanamientos estén enraizados en una estructura Norte-Sur; existe una constante tensión entre ver el hermanamiento Norte-Sur como mecanismos de intercambio equitativo y horizontal por un lado y como simplemente una forma diferente del modelo clásico lineal de ayuda que fluye del Norte hacia el Sur por otro lado. Mientras que lo primero implica un aprendizaje e intercambio de conocimientos que beneficia a ambas partes, lo que es la retórica popular entre los participantes en el hermanamiento, lo último cuestiona dicha reciprocidad, ya que el flujo unilateral de recursos, conocimientos y peritaje técnicos del Norte hacia el Sur muchas veces parece ser la práctica, por lo menos a primera vista. El análisis realizado aboga por un abordaje flexible de cómo se debería ver los hermanamientos Norte-Sur.

En relación con la literatura sobre hermanamientos (municipales) Norte-Sur y gobernanza urbana, se puede aprender varias lecciones identificadas a base de la presente investigación. En primer lugar, la cooperación de ciudad a ciudad nunca podrá ser entendida, nutrida ni facilitada sin una valoración apropiada del factor político. Ya que los hermanamientos siempre operan dentro de una estructura política, los factores contextuales de la situación política local, las relaciones de poder y la toma de decisiones mediante arreglos informales y formales no deberían ser descuidados. La cooperación de ciudad a ciudad y la política están intrínsecamente relacionadas, en por lo menos tres maneras; los principales actores involucrados (las organizaciones hermanas son instituciones políticas, para las que la

THE CHALLENGE TO STRENGTHEN URBAN GOVERNANCE THROUGH NORTH-SOUTH CITY PARTNERSHIPS

voluntad y el compromiso políticos son de crucial importancia para mantener las relaciones de hermanamiento); los objetivos formulados (en los que están incorporados valores políticos, moldeados por el carácter de los regímenes políticos, programas de gobierno y las políticas (internacionales) formuladas); y los beneficiarios de las iniciativas organizadas por el hermanamiento (la pregunta de quién se beneficiará de la ayuda ofrecida y quién es excluido de ello es muchas veces una pregunta política, y por lo tanto es aplicable también a la cooperación internacional de C2C).

Una segunda lección de aprendizaje surge de la discusión sobre el objetivo dual de las ciudades en el Norte involucradas en un hermanamiento, cuya meta es el fortalecimiento de las instituciones locales y el fomento del desarrollo local en el Sur, mientras que al mismo tiempo tratan de aumentar la sensibilización y el soporte público entre sus propios ciudadanos para temas relacionados con el desarrollo. Este doble objetivo causa algunas tensiones concernientes al alcance y contenido de las actividades y proyectos de los hermanamientos. Las autoridades locales deben encontrar el equilibrio entre la generación de resultados de desarrollo visibles y atractivos para los medios de comunicación, que son relevantes con respecto a la educación para el desarrollo, y el empleo de su peritaje específico en esfuerzos de cooperación municipal sumamente técnicos para lograr el objetivo de fomentar el desarrollo local en su ciudad hermana.

En tercer lugar, existe el peligro de que las municipalidades en el Sur se vuelvan más preocupadas por la rendición de cuentas a los donantes (sus ciudades hermanas) que a sus propios ciudadanos. Efectivamente, la 'rendición de cuentas a los donantes' exigida predomina a veces en los hermanamientos Norte-Sur sobre la búsqueda de 'rendición de cuentas doméstica'. Mediante arreglos de C2C, las municipalidades del Norte entran en la arena de la toma de decisiones a nivel local en el Sur urbano. Pueden convertirse en actores poderosos quienes ejercen influencia sobre la asignación de recursos municipales de inversión. Como tal, las preferencias de sus socios en la cooperación internacional en vez de las necesidades expresadas por sus ciudadanos pueden dictar la forma en que gobiernos locales formulan las prioridades locales de desarrollo. La cercanía de los actores de la cooperación descentralizada a la población local además implica el peligro que los ciudadanos busquen vincularse directamente con los donantes y no con el gobierno local para ser escuchados y expresar sus necesidades. Cuando el hermanamiento se vuelve demasiado absorbido en las estructuras existentes del gobierno urbano, puede más bien distorsionar en vez de reforzar las relaciones locales entre el gobierno y la sociedad civil. Está quedando claro que los principios de la Agenda de París sobre la Eficacia de Ayuda (2005), que se encuentra entre las directrices más importantes para la política y la práctica de cooperación al desarrollo hoy en día, también son aplicables al contexto urbano y a la cooperación internacional municipal. Para encontrar el equilibrio entre la rendición de cuentas doméstica y la rendición a los donantes, las municipalidades en el Sur requieren de una estrategia de desarrollo sólida formulada por ellas mismas con *apropiación local*, para garantizar un abordaje institucional para la formulación de objetivos de desarrollo basados en la participación ciudadana. Una estrategia de este tipo además puede proveer un marco para la *armonización* y *alineación* entre los donantes municipales y servir para atraer posibles donantes nuevos. Cuando las municipalidades en el Sur formulan objetivos de desarrollo basados en las necesidades de sus ciudadanos, y las municipalidades en el Norte están en la posición de poder dar respuesta a las necesidades expresadas por el Sur en vez de determinar cómo se debería proveer la ayuda, lo que muchas veces está siendo influenciado por los parámetros definidos por parte de los financiadores externos, existe un gran potencial para una mayor eficacia de los hermanamientos.

Como cuarta lección, el análisis efectuado del fortalecimiento de la gobernanza urbana mediante la cooperación de ciudad a ciudad reveló que la construcción de capacidades de la sociedad civil frecuentemente no fue el resultado de las intervenciones realizadas por el hermanamiento. Tomando en cuenta la naturaleza multidimensional y de múltiples partes interesadas de la cooperación de ciudad a ciudad, se lo puede considerar como una oportunidad perdida. Una de las características únicas y ventajas comparativas de los hermanamientos como forma de cooperación al desarrollo es que tanto las instituciones públicas como la sociedad civil ocupan el lugar central, como socios y como beneficiarios. Como tal, los resultados muestran que las posibilidades de los hermanamientos de dirigirse al fortalecimiento de la gobernanza urbana desde diferentes ángulos no están siendo aprovechadas suficientemente. Esto aboga por estrategias nuevas para que los hermanamientos sean más efectivos en el incremento de la capacidad de expresarse y de las destrezas de los ciudadanos para 'practicar' su ciudadanía en el Sur e involucrarse más en la toma colectiva de decisiones a nivel urbano.

Una quinta lección identificada en esta investigación concierne el hallazgo de que las municipalidades hermanas en el Norte no ponen el aprendizaje obtenido de sus socios en el Sur en un lugar prominente de su agenda de cooperación. ¿No están siendo los socios en el Norte algo presuntuosos en definir sus experiencias adquiridas como peritaje municipal relevante mientras que las experiencias obtenidas en el Sur no son conceptualizadas como una potencial fuente de aprendizaje? Tal vez ello cambiará a raíz de la tendencia reciente de la adopción en el Norte de innovaciones aplicadas a la gobernanza democrática que emergieron en ciudades en el Sur. La exportación de ideas y conocimientos sobre la gobernanza urbana del Sur hacia el Norte puede funcionar como una tendencia de contrapeso a las percepciones existentes en el Norte, que a veces son superiores con respecto a tener conocimientos más avanzados en comparación con sus socios. Ciudades en el Norte pueden empezar con atribuir valores y significados nuevos a los conocimientos exportados por el Sur, y reconocer el potencial de aprendizaje y cambio para sus propias organizaciones.

Una última lección se relaciona con el tema de la relevancia. ¿Qué relevante es el papel de ciudades y gobiernos locales en la cooperación internacional (al desarrollo)? Considerando el creciente reconocimiento de lo 'urbano' en el pensamiento sobre el desarrollo, la continua urbanización y el entendimiento de que los retos futuros concernientes a la aliviación de la pobreza tienen que ser asumidas cada vez más en las ciudades del mundo en desarrollo, parece que la presencia de ciudades y gobiernos locales en la arena de la cooperación al desarrollo seguirá siendo evidente. La participación de instituciones públicas locales en este terreno no es sin trampas, sin embargo. Esta investigación demostró que se necesita una valoración más cuidadosamente equilibrada y matizada de la convicción creciente de que los hermanamientos conllevan al desarrollo local en zonas de pobreza. Aboga por una valoración más realista de lo que especialmente donantes y asociaciones locales de municipios aseguran que se podrá lograr a través de la C2C. Se debe tener prudencia en llegar a conclusiones sobre el papel de los hermanamientos con respecto a estos procesos de desarrollo local y aliviación de la pobreza. En vez de considerar el hermanamiento como una panacea para un abanico de desafíos urbanos, es apropiado adoptar un enfoque más modesto viéndolo meramente como uno de los muchos posibles catalizadores de desarrollo y vehículos de cambio.

Si se superan las trampas, su papel como catalizador puede ser prometedor, no obstante. Las municipalidades en el Norte necesitan reducir la posición vulnerable de la cooperación internacional como tarea municipal y contar con las precondiciones organizacionales, técnicas y financieras necesarias para involucrarse de forma sostenible. Las municipalidades en el Sur necesitan un entendimiento sólido de sus necesidades de desarrollo y cómo la cooperación internacional puede ser empleada estratégicamente para dar respuesta a estas necesidades. Esta investigación mostró que la cooperación de ciudad a ciudad puede ofrecer un nicho de mercado en la cooperación al desarrollo y proveer ayuda hecha a la medida por medio del ofrecimiento de conocimientos, experiencias y peritaje en asuntos municipales altamente especializados. Si la construcción de capacidades a través de los hermanamientos se basa en las estructuras y mecanismos de planificación presentes, si los hermanamientos exploran nuevas oportunidades para colaborar con la sociedad civil en el Sur para reforzar sus capacidades de participación, y la cooperación está siendo facilitada por el soporte político y el reconocimiento mutuo de los objetivos, los hermanamientos pueden contribuir considerablemente al fortalecimiento de la gobernanza local en el Sur.

Zusammenfassung

Städte als Partner: die Herausforderung städtische Regierungsführung mithilfe von Nord-Süd-Städtepartnerschaften zu stärken

Während der vergangenen Jahrzehnte haben kommunale Verwaltungen in zunehmendem Maße als engagierte Akteure der internationalen Entwicklungszusammenarbeit Anerkennung gefunden. Schätzungen zufolge sind 70% aller Städte der Welt in verschiedenen Formen der internationalen Zusammenarbeit, Städte-Partnerschaften, internationalen Städtenetzwerken oder -programmen involviert. Viele dieser Verbindungen – auch City-to-City-Zusammenarbeit, ein Begriff, der im Jahr 2000 von der UNDP eingeführt wurde, genannt – stellen eine Verbindung zwischen Industrieländern und Entwicklungsländern oder, mit anderen Worten, dem globalen Norden und dem globalen Süden her. Städte werden hiermit in den Mittelpunkt der internationalen Zusammenarbeit, als Leistungsbringer und -empfänger im Rahmen der Entwicklungszusammenarbeit, gestellt. Angesichts der weltweit zunehmenden Dezentralisierung der Regierungen, Globalisierung und Verstädterung, dem wachsenden Bewusstsein für das Weltbürgertum, veränderten Aufgaben der kommunalen Verwaltungen und zunehmender Aufmerksamkeit für gute Regierungsführung als wesentliche Voraussetzung für Entwicklung, werden Kommunalpartnerschaften von Städten und Gemeinden zunehmend dazu benutzt, um einander auf dem Gebiet des Wissensaustausches, des Ressourcen- und Technologietransfers sowie der gemeinsamen Zusammenarbeit zu unterstützen. Städte – sowohl kommunale Verwaltungen als auch die Zivilgesellschaft – gehen mit der Absicht Partnerschaften ein, einen Beitrag zu einer Vielzahl von Zielsetzungen, einschließlich der Armutsbekämpfung, dem Stärken der Institutionen, der Demokratie und der Friedensarbeit, zu leisten.

Anhaltende Verstädterung, vor allem in Entwicklungsländern (dem „Süden"), und eine veränderte Politik der Geberländer haben dem Begriff des „Städtischen" im Entwicklungsdenken eine größere Bedeutung zukommen lassen. Die Dezentralisierung und Reformen der öffentlichen Verwaltungsaufgaben im Süden haben eine wichtigere Rolle der kommunalen Verwaltungen zur Folge gehabt. Das Grundprinzip dabei ist, dass eine zunehmende Bürgernähe der Regierungseinrichtungen zu einem größeren Verantwortungsbewusstsein gegenüber der Wählerschaft führen wird. Das Konzept der „städtischen Regierungsführung" (engl.: *urban governance*), welches eine zunehmende Bedeutung im Rahmen der städtischen Strategieplanung gewonnen hat, ist sich dessen bewusst, dass Entscheidungsgewalt sowohl innerhalb als auch außerhalb der kommunalen Verwaltungen existiert. Hierdurch wird es immer schwieriger, zwischen privaten und öffentlichen Sphären zu unterscheiden. Eine Möglichkeit, um gute, mitbestimmende kommunale Regierungsführung zu erreichen, besteht darin, Menschen und Institutionen zusammen zu führen. Hierfür sind starke kommunale Verwaltungen und eine starke Zivilgesellschaft nötig.

Vor diesem Hintergrund hat sich diese Untersuchung zum Ziel gesetzt, Einsicht in die Relevanz und das Potential der City-to-City-Partnerschaften (C2C) zwischen dem Norden und dem Süden, mit Blick auf das Stärken der städtischen Regierungsführung im Süden, zu erlangen. Ein weiteres Ziel ist es, eine tiefere Einsicht in die Faktoren, die das Potential der C2C beeinflussen, zu bekommen. Die folgenden fünf Forschungsfragen stehen dabei im Mittelpunkt dieser Untersuchung:

1. Welche nationalen und supranationalen institutionellen und politischen Bedingungen beeinflussen die Rolle der kommunalen Verwaltungen in der internationalen Zusammenarbeit und den kommunalen Entwicklungsprozessen?

2. Unter welchen kommunalen politischen und institutionellen Bedingungen agieren kommunale Verwaltungen in der internationalen Zusammenarbeit und welche Auswirkungen haben sie auf die City-to-City-Zusammenarbeit in der Praxis?

3. Welche Akteure sind Teil der kommunalen C2C-Netzwerke in Partnerstädten, welche Rolle spielen sie, welche Verantwortlichkeiten haben sie und welche Beziehungsverhältnisse gehen sie ein?

4. Unter welchen Bedingungen und in welchem Maße funktionieren C2C-Partnerschaften als Instrument des Aufbaus von Kapazitäten und des Wissensaustausches?

5. In welchem Maße und wie tragen C2C-Partnerschaften zur Stärkung der städtischen Regierungsführung im Süden bei?

Zur Beantwortung dieser Fragen wurde eine Vergleichsstudie zwischen vier Nord-Süd Städte-Partnerschaften in Deutschland, den Niederlanden, Peru, Nicaragua und Südafrika durchgeführt. Um die Fallstudien miteinander vergleichen zu können, wurde in all diesen Städten (vier im Norden und vier im Süden) einer strukturierten Forschungsstrategie gefolgt. Basierend auf qualitativen Untersuchungsmethoden wurden die Untersuchungen zwischen 2005 und 2008 durchgeführt. Die Hauptkriterien für die Auswahl der Partnerschaften waren, dass a) die involvierten Akteure sowohl kommunale Institutionen als auch die Zivilgesellschaft in den Partnerstädten repräsentieren und sich zur Zielgruppe nehmen, b) den institutionellen Rahmenbedingungen der Städte im Süden durch einen kürzlich erfolgten Dezentralisierungsprozess oder einer Reform des öffentlichen Sektors Form gegeben wurde, wodurch den öffentlichen kommunalen Entscheidungsträgern sowie der Zivilgesellschaft neue Herausforderungen gestellt und Verantwortung übertragen wurde und c) die Zielsetzungen der Partnerschaften an die institutionelle Stärkung oder kommunale (nachhaltige) Entwicklung geknüpft waren.

Die wichtigsten Untersuchungsergebnisse in Bezug auf diese Forschungsfragen sind nachstehend aufgeführt.

1. Nationale und supranationale institutionelle und politische Rahmenbedingungen
Zwei – auf den ersten Blick – von einander unabhängige Entwicklungen, die Bezug zu der Entwicklungspolitik (der Geber) einerseits und der Dezentralisierungspolitik und den sich ändernden institutionellen Rahmenbedingungen der kommunalen Verwaltungen im Süden andererseits nehmen, erklären das Grundprinzip und die wachsende Anerkennung der City-to-City-Zusammenarbeit.

Erstens hat die Bedeutung kommunaler Verwaltungen in der internationalen Zusammenarbeit zugenommen, während sich Städte des Nordens in zunehmendem Maße in der Arena der internationalen Entwicklungszusammenarbeit engagiert haben. Drei Trends verdeutlichen hierbei die immer wichtigere Rolle der Kommunalverwaltungen als Entwicklungspartner: a) supranationale Geber sowie nationale und kommunale Verwaltungen werden von kommunalen Verwaltungen in zunehmendem Maße als

Partner in der Entwicklungszusammenarbeit anerkannt; b) das Entwicklungsdenken und die Entwicklungsplanung ist sich der Bedeutung der Institutionen und der verantwortungsbewussten Regierungsführung, auch auf kommunaler Ebene, immer bewusster geworden; c) es hat sich gezeigt, dass es zu einer starken Zunahme der internationalen Städtenetzwerke und einer wachsenden Bedeutung der „Partnerschaften" in der internationalen Zusammenarbeit gekommen ist. Die wachsende Anerkennung der C2C und die Bedeutung der kommunalen Verwaltungen für die Entwicklung spiegelt sich in der Fülle an Programmen der Spenderpolitik und -unterstützung auf supranationaler und nationaler Ebene wider.

Die zweite institutionelle Rahmenbedingung, die das Grundprinzip der C2C erklärt, bezieht sich auf die zwingende Notwendigkeit zur Kompetenzentwicklung für kommunale Verwaltungen im Süden. Kommunale Verwaltungen und Gemeinden im Süden sind in kurzer Zeit selbständige und vorausschauende Agenten der Entwicklung, mit zunehmenden Verantwortlichkeiten hinsichtlich der Dienstleistung, der Armutsbekämpfung und der Verbesserung der städtischen Lebensqualität, geworden. Veränderungen der institutionellen Rahmenbedingungen in Peru, Südafrika und Nicaragua haben zu neuen Vollmachten, Verantwortlichkeiten und einer stärkeren finanziellen Reservenquelle für die jeweiligen Gemeinden geführt. Es hat sich gezeigt, dass kommunale Verwaltungsstrukturen in diesen Ländern rechtlich institutionalisiert sind und auf einer partizipativen Gemeinschaft aufbauen. Hierdurch haben die kommunalen Gebietskörperschaften die Möglichkeit, potentiell ansprechbar, rechenschaftspflichtig und entwicklungsorientiert zu sein. Gleichzeitig haben die häufig rasanten Gesetzesänderungen die kommunalen Verwaltungen vor viele Herausforderungen gestellt; Verwaltungen, die weiterhin geschlossen ernsthafte Mängel in ihren finanziellen und personellen Mitteln aufweisen und dadurch ihren Aufgaben nicht nachkommen können. Dies erklärt die Notwendigkeit der Kompetenzentwicklung, die durch eine C2C erreichte werden könnte.

2. *Kommunale politische und institutionelle Rahmenbedingungen der Rolle kommunalen Verwaltungen in der internationalen Zusammenarbeit*

In Bezug auf die Position und die Rolle der kommunalen Verwaltungen im Norden, als Partner in der Entwicklungszusammenarbeit durch C2C-Partnerschaften zu agieren, haben die Untersuchungen gezeigt, dass Entwicklungszusammenarbeit nicht der Daseinsgrund der kommunalen Gebietskörperschaften ist. Ihre Existenz hängt nicht davon ab, und sie sind gesetzlich nicht verpflichtet, sich in C2C zu engagieren. Aufgrund der Freiwilligkeit der Teilnahme an C2C ist das Engagement der kommunalen Verwaltungen anfällig und politischen Änderungen (oder Regimewechseln) ausgesetzt. Dies hat zur Folge, dass Gemeinden bestimmte politische und institutionelle Bedingungen erfüllen müssen:

- den C2C förderliche kommunale Richtlinien und politische Programme müssen etabliert sein
- Verwaltungsmitarbeiter müssen über die erforderlichen Kenntnisse und Expertise, um sich in C2C und internationaler Entwicklungszusammenarbeit zu engagieren, verfügen.
- die Menge der Drittmittel übersteigt in der Regel die eigenen Beiträge der Partnerstädte. Kommunale Verwaltungen im Norden erzeugen Multiplikatoreffekte im Bereich der Finanzierungen. Voraussetzung hierfür ist, dass (inter)nationale Ressourcen durch C2C dezentralisiert werden und direkt auf kommunaler Ebene im Süden angewandt werden.
- Politisches Interesse und Wille sind ausschlaggebende Faktoren.

- Es hat sich gezeigt, dass die Anwesenheit kommunaler internationaler Entwicklungsabteilungen im Süden wichtig ist, um C2C in vollständiger Verantwortung der Kommunen zu ermöglichen und zu erhalten, um als Vermittler die Kapazitäten und notwendigen Investitionen der Organisation mit dem verfügbaren Know-how und der Ressourcen der Partnerstädte abzustimmen, und um das Risiko der Abhängigkeit der Partnerschaften von Einzelpersonen zu reduzieren.

In Gemeinden des Südens ist man zu dem Schluss gekommen, dass internationale Beziehungen und die anwesenden notwendigen organisatorischen Voraussetzungen die Kapazitätsherausforderungen der Kommunen nicht von selbst lösen. Von Bedeutung ist eher, inwiefern Kommunen von ihren C2C-Partnerschaften als strategische Instrumente, um kommunale Entwicklungs- und Planungsziele zu erreichen, Gebrauch machen. Die Untersuchung hat gezeigt, dass Kommunen diesbezüglich nicht immer erfolgreich waren. Das Bespiel Leóns (Nicaragua) zeigt, dass die Ursachen für die unzureichende Verknüpfung von C2C mit den gegenwärtigen Problemen der städtischen Regierungsführung und der Rolle der kommunalen Verwaltungen des Südens bei Entwicklungsprozessen eine Angelegenheit der organisatorischen Kapazität (fehlende Ressourcen und Kenntnisse bei der Entwicklung von Strategien für C2C), des politischen Interesses (persönliche Vorzüge – des Bürgermeisters – dominieren gegenüber den institutionell vorgegebenen Entwicklungsrichtlinien bei politischen Entscheidungsprozessen und der Zuteilung von (internationalen) Investitionen) und institutioneller Angelegenheiten (schwache Amtsgewalt der kommunalen Entwicklungspläne als Instrument der Stadtplanung und der Zuteilung internationaler Finanzmittel) ist.

3. Akteure, Funktionen und Verantwortlichkeiten in kommunalen C2C-Netzwerken

In Partnerstädten des Nordens und des Südens geht C2C über die Beteiligung der kommunalen Verwaltungen hinaus und schließt auch andere Akteure mit ein. Die wichtigsten anerkannten Akteure sind kommunale Verwaltungen und Behörden, Koordinierungsorgane der Zivilgesellschaft (in dieser Studie CCSEs[1] genannt), (dezentralisierte) Geber des öffentlichen Sektors, externe oder nationale Entwicklungsagenten, der private Sektor und Akteure der Zivilgesellschaft. CCSEs nehmen hierbei eine ganz besondere Position ein, da sie in erster Linie aufgrund der C2C-Partnerschaft existieren, während die Partnerschaft für die betroffenen Akteure im Allgemeinen keine Kernfrage ist. Kommunale C2C-Netzwerke in Partnerstädten sind das Ergebnis der Beziehungen zwischen diesen Akteuren. Diese Beziehungen definieren außerdem in hohem Grade die Funktionen und Verantwortlichkeiten der Akteure. Man kann sechs funktionelle Beziehungstypen bei C2C-Netzwerken im Norden unterscheiden: Beziehungen, die den Finanzströmen dienen, der Bewusstseinsbildung, der Förderung von Know-how und Expertise, der Schaffung von Unterstützung zur Erhaltung der C2C Partnerschaften, Zugang zu Entwicklungsländern und der Entwicklungszusammenarbeit schaffen sowie der Durchführung von Projekten und Städtepartnerschaften im Süden. Die zweiseitige Zielsetzung der C2C im Norden, d.h. die Stärkung der kommunalen Regierungsführung im Süden und die Bewusstseinsbildung im Norden, ist die, den gefundenen Netzwerkstrukturen zugrundeliegende, Erklärung.

Es existieren diverse Unterschiede zwischen den Netzwerken des Nordens und des Südens. Die Beziehungen innerhalb der Netzwerke des Nordens scheinen formeller zu sein,

---

1   "Coordinating civil society entities"

und die Zusammenarbeit und Koordination zwischen den Akteuren ist besser abgestimmt und auskristallisiert. Dem gegenüber sind die Beziehungen im Süden informeller, weniger deutlich erkennbar bzw. sichtbar und nicht alle Akteure im Netzwerk integriert. Während sich Netzwerkbeziehungen im Norden im Allgemeinen gegenseitig unterstützen und ergänzen, treten im Süden innerhalb der Partnerschaftsnetzwerke manchmal Konflikte anstelle der Zusammenarbeit auf.

Zusammenfassend kann man sagen, dass es scheint – auch wenn man nicht ganz sicher sagen kann, dass es einen ursächlichen Zusammenhang gibt – als ob eine ausgewogene Partizipation kommunaler Verwaltungen und der Zivilgesellschaft die günstigsten Voraussetzungen für den Erhalt der C2C-Zusammenarbeit darstellt. Ohne die Partizipation der kommunalen Verwaltungen könnte die Arbeit der C2C durch einen Mangel an politischer Unterstützung, Ressourcen, Infrastruktur und Mechanismen, die die öffentlichen Ausgaben verantworten, untergraben werden. Andererseits birgt das Fehlen einer partizipierenden Zivilgesellschaft das Risiko einer technokratischen und isolierten Zusammenarbeit mit geringer öffentlicher Unterstützung.

4   C2C Partnerschaften als Instrument der Kapazitätsaufbaus und des Wissensaustausches
Eigentümerschaft und eine nachfrageorientierte Zielsetzungsstrategie waren die ersten identifizierten Partnerschaftsvoraussetzungen. Die Entscheidungsfindung wird im Großen und Ganzen von den Partnerstädten im Süden verfolgt, wodurch ein größeres Potential für eine Zusammenarbeit, die auf die bestehenden Kapazitäten und Bedürfnissen der Geberorganisationen abgestimmt ist, entsteht. Gleichzeitig hat es sich allerdings gezeigt, dass ein Spannungsfeld zwischen dem Wunsch, Eigentümerschaft zu verbessern und der Tatsache, dass sich die finanzielle Kontrolle in den Händen des Nordens befindet, besteht. Dies bestimmt letztendlich in beträchtlichem Maße die Rahmenbedingungen der Zusammenarbeit.

Eine zweite Voraussetzung sind die Mechanismen, die für den Austausch und das Zusammenwirken angewandt werden und die darüber entscheiden, ob ein nachhaltiger Prozess des Kapazitätsaufbaus stattfindet. In der Mehrzahl beschränken sie sich auf kurze Arbeitsbesuche bei den Partnerstädten. Der Prozessansatz kann untergraben werden, wenn zwischen den Treffen zu wenig Austausch stattfindet. Die Treffen drohen Einzelereignisse zu werden, und der Schwung der langfristigen Partnerschaftsabsprachen kann verloren gehen. Monitoring und Evaluationsmechanismen sind wichtige Werkzeuge um die verbuchten Fortschritte zu erhalten und relevante zukünftige Bedürfnisse aufzuzeigen.

Drittens kann man in Bezug auf das Lernpotential in C2C-Partnerschaften eine Anzahl von Schlussfolgerungen ziehen. Persönliche Bildung umfasst verschiedene Dimensionen und wurde im Norden als auch im Süden beobachtet, z.B. persönlicher (Kompetenz)Aufbau und das Prüfen verschiedener Lebens- und Arbeitseinstellungen. Berufliche Bildung im Norden ist hauptsächlich mit dem Erwerb und der Verbesserung der fachlichen Qualifikation und dem Nachdenken über die eigene Arbeit verknüpft. Dies ist eine Folge des unterschiedlichen (kulturellen) organisatorischen Umfeldes. Demgegenüber baut berufliche Bildung im Süden auf dem Erwerb technischen Wissens in dem spezifischen Fachgebiet der Teilnehmer auf. Im Süden haben C2C-Projekte in der Regel zu Ergebnisse jenseits des Wirkungsbereiches des Einzelnen geführt, wodurch sich Möglichkeiten für organisatorische Veränderungen ergeben haben. Im Gegensatz dazu wurden erworbene Kenntnisse und Fähigkeiten im Norden nicht in nennenswertem Maße in der täglichen Arbeitspraxis angewandt.

Die vierte Voraussetzung, Beidseitigkeit, war zwar den Ergebnissen der Untersuchung zufolge in Nord-Süd Städte-Partnerschaften anwesend, beschränkte sich aber nicht auf den Bereich der Bildung. Städte des Nordens messen der Verbesserung ihrer eigenen organisatorischen Leistung oder der Erweiterung des Wissens und der Kenntnisse ihres Mitarbeiterstabes durch Bildungsmaßnahmen als notwendige Komponenten einer „guten" Partnerschaft nicht viel Bedeutung bei. Stattdessen können die Zielsetzungen im Norden – sowohl politisch als auch individuell – als eher altruistisch und als in großem Maße auf die Lieferung von Entwicklungshilfe für den Süden abzielend, betrachtet werden. Wenn man davon ausgeht, dass Bildung im Norden kein vorrangiges Ziel ist, bedeutet das, dass die Fragestellung, ob Beidseitigkeit in Bildungsmaßnahmen im Rahmen der C2C nicht relevant ist; zumindest nicht aus einer politischen Perspektive. Anstelle solcher Bildungsmaßnahmen, bieten sich innerhalb der Städtepartnerschaften andere Möglichkeiten der Beidseitigkeit, z.B. die Möglichkeiten, die Gemeinden im Norden auf der strategischen politischen und organisatorischen Ebene schaffen. Typische Beispiele sind die Förderung von Loyalität und Motivation des Mitarbeiterstabes, die Schaffung eines globalen Bewusstseins innerhalb und außerhalb der kommunalen Verwaltung und indem man positive Werbung für die Gemeinde macht und ein soziales Image kreiert.

5. *In welchem Maße und wie tragen C2C Partnerschaften zur Stärkung der städtischen Regierungsführung im Süden bei?*

Zum ersten Aspekt im Bereich der Stärkung der städtischen Regierungsführung, der mit den Kapazitäten der kommunalen Verwaltungen zu tun hat, wurde ein Vielzahl an unterschiedlichen Ergebnissen gefunden. Einer der wichtigsten Aspekte auf der individuellen Ebene der Humanressourcen und des -kapitals – ein Aspekt, der in allen untersuchten Städtepartnerschaften eine Rolle spielt – ist die Ausbildung des Mitarbeiterstabes, von den allgemeinen Fähigkeiten bis hin zu spezifischeren technischen Qualifikationen. Was die Stärkung der Organisation angeht, wurden deutliche Hinweise gefunden, so z.B. die technische Aufwertung bzw. Einführung neuer Instrumente und Werkzeuge und die Abstimmung und Verbesserung interner Prozesse. Außerdem wurden Ergebnisse auf der Ebene der institutionellen Veränderung, die auf Prozesse der institutionellen Umstrukturierung und einer Erweiterung der institutionellen Aufgaben der Verwaltung und Behörden, z.B. durch das Einführen neuer Gebiete der politischen Richtlinien und Dienstleistungen, gefunden. Letztere richtete sich auch an die Aufgaben der Gemeinden als „Gemeinschaftsentwickler" im weiteren Sinne, und nicht nur als „Dienstleister".

In Bezug auf die zweite Kategorie, d.h. die Auswirkungen der C2C-Interventionen auf die Kapazitätsförderung der Zivilgesellschaft, sind die Belege gemischt und eher schwach. Abgesehen von einigen Ausnahmen haben C2C-Interventionen in der Regel kaum direkte Auswirkungen auf die Stärkungen der Communities. Es gibt kaum Belege dafür, dass Initiativen der Zivilgesellschaft in den Partnerstädten des Nordens dazu geführt hätten, dass in Übersee Verantwortung an Bürger übertragen worden wäre. Die Einbindung der Zivilgesellschaft in C2C führt nicht immer zu eindeutigen und soliden Erfolgen. Projekt verharren meist im kleinen Maßstab und gehen auf pragmatische Art und Weise Probleme, wie die Lebensbedingungen in der Partnerstadt zu verbessern, an, als dass man sich um abstraktere Themen wie Bürgerrechte und Partizipation kümmern würde.

Es hat sich gezeigt, dass das Stärken der Zivilgesellschaft eher ein Ergebnis der partizipativen Eigenschaften derjenigen C2C Projekte ist, die sich vor allem um die Stärkung kommunaler Verwaltungen kümmern. Diese Projekte waren nicht nur diejenigen, die den Erfahrungsschatz der Bürger als Anbieter und nicht nur als Nutzer von Dienstleistungen vor allem in León und Villa El Salvador (Peru) respektierten, sondern auch günstige Voraussetzungen für die zukünftige Einbindung der Bürger schufen. Es kann also zusammenfassend gesagt werden, dass C2C auch indirekte Effekte haben können, d.h. die Stärkung beidseitiger Beziehungen zwischen den kommunalen Verwaltungen und der Zivilgesellschaft.

Eine dritte Kategorie der Auswirkungen erkennt diese Beziehungen an und rechtfertigt einen dynamischeren Ansatz, mit dem C2C-Auswirkungen evaluiert werden können. Ergebnisse dieser Art umfassen das Entstehen multisektoraler Partnerschaften, die Möglichkeiten der Partizipation eröffnen; eine Zunahme des Entgegenkommens und der Rechenschaftspflicht der Verwaltungen und Behörden, indem man z.B. die Kundenbetreuung der örtlichen Steuerzahler verbessert und die fiskale Transparenz erhöht; verbesserte Möglichkeiten der Beaufsichtigung und Monitorings des internen und externen Auftretens der kommunalen Verwaltungen und Behörden; eines partizipativen Ansatzes der Kommunalplanung, ein Aufruf zu stärkerer Bürgerbeteiligung, um dadurch marginalisierte und armen Bevölkerungsteilen zu veranlassen, ihre Stimme zu erheben und ihre Bedürfnisse zu äußern; und die Einführung neuer Bereiche der Politik – einschließlich des sozialen Zusammenhalts und der Beteiligung der Gemeinschaften – um damit die kommunalen Verwaltungen und Behörden herauszufordern, ihre Rolle als Gemeindeentwickler ernster zu nehmen.

Zusammenfassend kann man sagen, dass C2C seine Anwendung vor allem im Bereich der Verbesserung der Effizienz kommunaler Verwaltungen, und weniger in der unmittelbaren Stärkung der Zivilgesellschaft, finden kann. Stattdessen ist es ausschlaggebend, wie *kommunale* C2C-Interventionen durchgeführt werden, um dadurch Raum für partizipative und entgegenkommende städtische Verwaltungsprozesse zu schaffen. Bei der Analyse der Stärkung der städtischen Regierungsführung ist es also nützlich, nicht nur die direkten Auswirkungen dieser Interventionen zu berücksichtigen. Es ist außerordentlich wichtig, die indirekten Auswirkungen, die ein Ergebnis des Entgegenkommens der kommunalen Gebietskörperschaften einerseits und der verbesserten partizipativen Fähigkeiten der Zivilgesellschaft andererseits sind, zu berücksichtigen. Sie sind nicht nur Zweck der C2C-Interventionen, sondern auch ein Mittel um die Interaktion und Rechenschaftspflicht zwischen verschieden städtischen Akteuren zu verbessern und kollektive Planung zu voranzutreiben.

Das Ziel dieser Untersuchung war nicht nur, dass das bestehende Wissen in einer systematischeren Weise zusammen zu führen und es zu ergänzen, indem sie zu neuen Einsichten, die auf empirischen Untersuchungen aufbauen, gekommen ist. Von besonderer Bedeutung könnten hierbei die Faktoren sein, die sich als besonders einflussreich auf die Art und Weise, wie internationale Zusammenarbeit zwischen Städten Form gegeben wird und inwiefern die Zusammenarbeit die gesteckten Ziele erreicht hat, erwiesen haben. Insgesamt ist die Analyse manchmal, hinsichtlich der Art und Weise wie kommunale Nord-Süd-Zusammenarbeit angegangen werden sollten, doppeldeutig gewesen. Diese Frage lässt sich nicht leicht beantworten. Es scheint, als ob sich eine paradoxe Situation aus der Tatsache, dass kommunale Partnerschaften in Nord-Süd Schauplätzen eingebettet sind, ergeben würde. Diese Situation führt zu einer andauernden Spannung, bei der einerseits

Nord-Süd Partnerschaften als Mechanismen des gleichwertigen, horizontalen Austauschs gesehen werden, während andererseits diese Partnerschaften nur eine andere Form des klassisch-linearen Modells der Hilfe darstellen, die der Norden dem Süden zukommen lässt. Während das Ziel des gleichwertigen Austausches darauf abzielt, dass Lernprozesse und Wissensaustausch beiden Partnern zugute kommt – und besonders unter C2C-Verantwortlichen populär ist – zweifelt das klassisch-lineare Modell diesen beidseitigen Nutzen an, da Ressourcen, technisches Wissen und Know-how doch, zumindest auf den ersten Blick, einseitig vom Norden in Richtung Süden fließen. Die Untersuchung hat gezeigt, dass Nord-Süd Städtepartnerschaften flexibler betrachtet werden müssen.

In Bezug zu der Literatur, die sich mit (kommunalen) Nord-Süd Partnerschaften und städtischer Regierungsführung auseinandersetzt, kann aus dieser Studie eine Anzahl von Schlussfolgerungen gezogen werden: erstens kann die C2C-Zusammenarbeit nie ohne eine anständige Einschätzung der politischen Faktoren verstanden oder gefördert werden. Da C2C-Interventionen innerhalb eines politischen Umfeldes stattfinden, dürfen die kontextbezogenen kommunalen politischen Umstände, Machtverhältnisse und informellen und formellen Entscheidungsprozesse nicht vernachlässigt werden. C2C- Zusammenarbeit und Politik sind in drei Bereichen eng miteinander verwoben, hinsichtlich a) der Hauptakteure (Partnerorganisationen sind politische Institutionen, bei denen politischer Wille und Engagement von außerordentlicher Bedeutung sind, um partnerschaftliche Übereinkünfte aufrecht zu erhalten), b) der gesetzten Ziele (die politisch geladen sind, da sie unter dem Einfluss politischer Regimes, politischer Programme und (außen)politischer Richtlinien stehen) und c) der Empfänger der Partnerschaftsinitiativen (die Frage, wer von der Hilfe profitiert und wer ausgeschlossen wird, ist häufig politisch und trifft daher auch auf C2C zu).

Eine weitere Schlussfolgerung lässt sich aus der Diskussion zu den doppelten Zielsetzungen der Städte des Nordens, die in C2C-Partnerschaften involviert sind, ziehen: während sie einerseits darauf abzielen, kommunale Institutionen zur Entwicklung im Süden zu fördern, bemühen sie sich gleichzeitig, aufzuklären und die öffentliche Unterstützung unter der eigenen Bevölkerung zu Themen im Bereich der Entwicklungszusammenarbeit zu vergrößern. Diese doppelte Zielsetzung stellt kommunale Verwaltungen und Behörden vor einige Herausforderungen in Bezug auf den Umfang und den Inhalt der C2C-Aktivitäten und Projekte. Kommunale Verwaltungen müssen ein Gleichgewicht zwischen zwei Aufgaben finden: einerseits müssen sie sichtbare, medienwirksame Entwicklungsergebnisse, die für Entwicklungsbildung relevant ist, vorweisen können, andererseits müssen sie ihre besondere Fachkenntnis in den Bemühungen zu hochtechnischer kommunaler Zusammenarbeit einbringen, um das Ziel der kommunalen Entwicklung in der Partnerschaft zu erreichen.

Drittens besteht die Gefahr, dass Kommunen im Süden sich mehr darum sorgen, den Gebern (den Partnerstädten) als der eigenen Wählerschaft gegenüber Rechenschaft abzulegen. Tatsächlich ist es so, dass die Rechenschaftspflicht gegenüber den Gebern in Nord-Süd Städtepartnerschaften manchmal gegenüber der Rechenschaftspflicht im Inland Priorität genießt. Durch C2C-Absprachen betreten Kommunen des Nordens die Arena der kommunalen politischen Entscheidungen der Städte des Südens. Dadurch können sie als mächtige Akteure die Zuteilung kommunaler Investitionsmittel beeinflussen. Dies kann dazu führen, dass anstelle der Bedürfnisse, die die örtliche Bevölkerung ausdrückt, die Vorzüge der internationalen Kooperationspartner bestimmen, wie kommunale Verwaltungen Entwicklungsprioritäten identifizieren und angehen. Die Nähe der Bevölkerung zu den dezentralisierten Kooperationspartnern und -akteuren kann dazu führen, dass sich die Bevölkerung nicht an die kommunalen Verwaltungen wendet, sondern direkt mit den Gebern in Kontakt tritt, um ihre Bedürfnisse und Probleme zu äußern. Wenn C2C zu sehr in bestehenden städtischen Verwaltungsstrukturen verwickelt wird, kann es dazu führen, dass das Verhältnis von Zivilgesellschaft zu der örtlichen Verwaltung nicht gestärkt, sondern gestört wird.

Es versteht sich, dass die Grundsätze der Erklärung von Paris über die Wirksamkeit der Entwicklungszusammenarbeit (2005), die zu den wichtigsten Richtlinien der Politik und Praxis im Bereich der Enwicklungszusammenarbeit zählen, auch im städtischen Kontext und den kommunalen Partnerschaften angewandt werden müssen. Um ein Gleichgewicht zwischen der Rechenschaftspflicht gegenüber der eigenen Bevölkerung und gegenüber den Gebern zu finden, brauchen Kommunen im Süden eine klare und solide *den Kommunen eigene* Entwicklungsstrategie, um einen institutionellen Ansatz zur Erstellung auf Bürgerbeteiligung basierender Entwicklungsziele zu garantieren. Eine solche Strategie könnte dazu dienen, potentielle Geber anzuziehen und außerdem die Rahmenbedingungen für die *Harmonisierung* und *Angleichung* bzw. Partnerausrichtung von kommunalen Gebern schaffen. Wenn sich Kommunen im Süden Entwicklungsziele setzen, bei denen sie den Bedürfnissen der Bürger gegenüber Rechenschaft ablegen müssen, und wenn Kommunen im Norden in der Lage sind, auf die vom Süden selber definierten Bedürfnisse einzugehen, anstatt von außen zu bestimmen, wie Hilfe durchgeführt werden sollte, und dabei in keinster Weise durch externe Geber beeinflusst werden, gibt es ein großes Potential für eine höhere Wirksamkeit von C2C-Vereinbarungen.

Viertens hat die Analyse der Stärkung von städtischer Regierungsführung durch C2C-Kooperation ergeben, dass der Kapazitätsaufbau der Zivilgesellschaft häufig nicht das Ergebnis von C2C-Interventionen war. Wenn man den multidimensionalen und multi-stakeholder Charakter der C2C-Kooperation berücksichtigt, kann man das als eine verpasste Chance betrachten. Eine der Besonderheiten der C2C als Entwicklungsintervention ist die Tatsache, dass sie öffentliche Einrichtungen und Zivilgesellschaft, als Partner und als Empfänger, in den Mittelpunkt stellen. Von daher zeigen die Ergebnisse, dass das Potential der Stärkung von städtischer Regierungsführung von verschiedenen Seiten mithilfe von C2C nicht ausreichend genutzt wird. Neue Strategien sind also vonnöten; Strategien, um die C2C dabei effizienter machen, den Bürgern eine Stimme zu geben und Kenntnisse zu vermitteln, um ihre Bürgerrechte im Süden zu praktizieren und sich bei den kollektiven Entscheidungen im städtischen Raum einzubringen.

Bei der fünften Schlussfolgerung dieser Studie geht es darum, dass Partnerkommunen im Norden dem Lernprozess ihrer Partner im Süden keine Priorität auf der Kooperationsagenda einräumen. Ist es von Seiten der Partner im Norden nicht ein gewisses Zeichen von Überheblichkeit, dass sie ihre eigenen Erfahrungen als relevantes Fachwissen betrachten, während die Erfahrungen im Süden nicht als potentielle Lernquelle angesehen werden? Eine neue Perspektive könnte sich ergeben, wenn es dazu kommen sollte, dass der Norden Innovationen im Bereich der demokratischen Regierungsführung, die sich in den Städten des Südens entwickelt haben, übernehmen sollte. Der Export von Ideen und Wissen im Bereich der städtischen Regierungsführung von Süd nach Nord könnte eine Gegenbewegung zu der Auffassung im Norden, dass der Norden über höherwertiges Wissen verfügt, darstellen. Städte im Norden könnten anfangen, dem Wissen, das aus dem Süden importiert wird, neue Werte und Bedeutungen zuzuschreiben und Möglichkeiten des Lernens und der Veränderung in ihren eigenen Organisationen anerkennen.

Eine letzte Lektion bezieht sich auf das Thema der Relevanz. Wie relevant ist die Rolle der Städte und der kommunalen Verwaltung in der internationalen Entwicklungszusammenarbeit? Angesichts einer zunehmenden Anerkennung des „städtischen" in Entwicklungstheorien, anhaltender Verstädterung und der Einsicht, dass zukünftige Herausforderungen der Armutsbekämpfung immer mehr in Städten der Entwicklungsländer angegangen werden müssen, scheint es, als ob die Anwesenheit von Städten und kommunalen Verwaltungen in der Arena der Entwicklungszusammenarbeit auf Dauer Bestand hat. Die Partizipation der örtlichen öffentlichen Einrichtungen in diesem Bereich verursacht aber auch Probleme. Diese Untersuchung hat gezeigt, dass eine ausgewogenere und nuanciertere Bewertung der (zunehmenden) Auffassung, dass Städtepartnerschaften zu kommunaler Entwicklung in Armutsgebieten führen, notwendig ist. Man braucht eine realistischere Einschätzung dessen, was Geber und kommunale Verwaltungsverbände von den Möglichkeiten der Städtepartnerschaften behaupten. Man sollte nicht voreilig Schlüsse aus der Rolle internationaler Städtepartnerschaften hinsichtlich der kommunalen Entwicklungsprozesse und Armutsbekämpfung ziehen. Anstatt C2C als Allheilmittel für eine Vielzahl städtischer Herausforderungen zu sehen, wäre es angemessen, einen bescheideneren Ansatz zu wählen, indem man sie nur als einen von mehreren potentiellen Auslösern für Entwicklung und Veränderung betrachtet.

Sobald die Probleme überwunden worden sind, kann ihre Rolle als Auslöser jedoch vielversprechend sein. Kommunen im Norden müssen die verletzliche Position der internationalen Zusammenarbeit als kommunale Aufgabe verringern und die notwendigen organisatorischen, technischen, finanziellen und politischen Voraussetzungen erfüllen, um sich nachhaltig einbringen zu können. Kommunen im Süden müssen ein klares Verständnis für ihre Entwicklungsbedürfnisse haben und bestimmen, wie internationale Zusammenarbeit dafür eingesetzt werden kann haben. Diese Untersuchung hat gezeigt, dass C2C- Kooperation eine Nische in der Entwicklungszusammenarbeit darstellt und dass sie maßgeschneiderte Unterstützung im Bereich des Lieferung von Know-how, Erfahrung und Expertise zu hoch spezialisierten kommunalen Aufgabenbereichen anbieten kann. Wenn der Kapazitätsaufbau mithilfe kommunaler Partnerschaften gegenwärtige Strukturen und Planungsmechanismen berücksichtigt, C2C-Absprachen neue Möglichkeiten der Zusammenarbeit mit der Zivilgesellschaft im Süden entdecken, um deren Partizipationsvermögen zu stärken, und wenn Zusammenarbeit durch politische Unterstützung und Anerkennung der beidseitigen Zielsetzungen ermöglicht wird, kann C2C eine entscheidenden Beitrag hin zu einer verbesserten städtischen Regierungsführung im Süden leisten.

Annex I – Research design and methodology

In this Annex, the research design and methodology used in this study are clarified. The research has made use of qualitative methods and takes a multiple-case study strategy. First, the use of case studies in social science research is considered, and the implications it has with regard to the selection of cases, the number of cases studied, and the units of analysis applied in the cases under study. Secondly, this Annex reviews the various qualitative methods that have been used within the framework of the case studies, and the opportunities and limitations experienced in the employment of these methods. The latter moreover addresses some observations with regard to doing cross-cultural and multi-lingual research.

The use of case studies in research: selection and methodological implications

Taking a multiple-case study approach as a research strategy
The choice for using the case study as research strategy can be explained by its definition: a case study is "an empirical inquiry that investigates a contemporary phenomenon within its real-life context, especially when the boundaries between phenomenon and context are not clearly evident" (Yin, 2003, p. 13). This applies to the practice of city-to-city cooperation and the concept of urban governance, which are embedded in social, cultural, economical, political and institutional contexts. It is not only impossible to isolate these contexts or control for them, it is also relevant to consider contexts in order to gain a deeper understanding of the subjects under study. Contextual conditions are thus deliberately included. This implies that a unlimited number of variables and choice of evidence is available, which requires the researcher to rely on multiple methods to converge data in a triangular fashion. Case studies are celebrated to have the unique strength to simultaneously deal with a full variety of evidence and methods.

Furthermore, the choice for using the case study has been influenced by the type of research questions put central in this study, the extent to which the researcher can control (behavioural) events and the extent to which the focus of the research is on contemporary as opposed to historical events (Yin, 2003). The prevalence of 'how' and 'why' questions in this research, in which operational links and context are relevant, favour the use of case studies. This very context, which takes into account political and policy frameworks, organisational systems and countless other variables used in evidence that cannot be controlled, and the fact that the relevant 'behaviours' in this study cannot be manipulated, calls for a multi-method approach, e.g. direct observations and the use of interviews. The case study approach moreover has a distinct advantage to examine the contemporary nature of the research subject (which applies to this study and its research questions).

The use of more than one case study is preferable as the use of a single case may be vulnerable to misinterpretation or may not be appropriate to replicate or to allow for analytical generalisation (see below). Evidence from multiple cases is usually considered

THE CHALLENGE TO STRENGTHEN URBAN GOVERNANCE THROUGH NORTH-SOUTH CITY PARTNERSHIPS

Box 1: A model for social research: retroduction

Retroduction is an alternative research model which makes it possible to link evidence (induction) and social theory (deduction) in a continually evolving, dynamic process (Sather, 1998). Introduced by Charles Ragin (1994), retroduction may be especially suitable for case study research where the dualism between theory and practice may be explicit and could be bridged using the retroduction model as research framework. Ragin believes the research process can be seen as a dialogue between *ideas* (theories) and *evidence* (data). Ideas serve as a framework to clarify and understand evidence, while evidence can be used to expand, revise or test ideas (Ten Have, n.d.). This dialogue results in a 'representation of social life', based on empirical data and constructed by theory. In his model, Ragin introduces the concepts *analytic frames* and *images*. They serve as intermediate stages to overcome the distance between ideas and evidence. Analytic frames are what most social scientists make use of when they have a specific research question in mind and then approach social theory (Sather, 1998). Analytic frames are detailed descriptions of ideas (categories of phenomena), that through deduction provide conceptual tools to articulate ideas, and classify and characterise phenomena (Ten Have, n.d.; Sather, 1998). Images, on the other hand, imply a synthesis of empirical data that results from an inductive process. They are 'idealised cases'. This process makes it possible to link data constructed as cases to theoretical ideas expressed in analytical terms. Throughout the research process, images and analytic frames interact and match, resulting in retroduction – a representation of social life (see Figure).

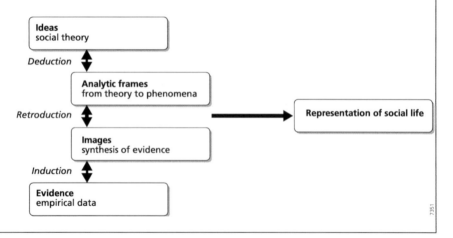

more convincing, making studies generally more powerful and robust (Herriott & Firestone, 1983, quoted in Yin, 2003). Not only may the use of more than one case provide a wider evidence base for revelatory purposes (to reveal significant issues and data), a multiple case study strategy also allows for identifying commonalities and differences among the cases, which may contain important implications for the theoretical framework.

The model of retroduction introduced by Ragin (1994) is useful to refer to in this respect (Box 1). Retroduction is a research process that combines both induction and deduction in social research, and as such, it is believed to increase the quality of research where it has proved difficult to combine theory and empirical data. As the choice of what evidence to use is limitless in qualitative research, case studies may be used to link data constructed as cases to theoretical ideas in a more systematised way. Theory is transformed into 'analytic frames' which function as points of inspiration and provide the cognitive structure to the evidence. Theory and evidence are thus in a symbiotic relationship, reinforcing each other's presence. Applying these conceptualisations to this study, by examining various examples of city-to-city cooperation arrangements and phenomena of urban governance in cities in the South, including contextual conditions in relation to the cases, a wide evidence base is generated. At the same time, this research has several theoretical starting points, not in the least place because two concepts (C2C and urban governance) are central in this study, each with their own knowledge base and theoretical insights. While these theoretical ideas provide conceptual tools to approach, classify and categorise the evidence, the evidence is applied to feed the theoretical ideas, and challenge or complete them. As such, Ragin's model has served as a methodological tool of reference throughout all stages of the research process.

The process of linking evidence to theoretical ideas refers to "analytic generalisation", which is, as Yin (2003) notes, distinct from "statistical generalisation" used in quantitative research based on statistical samples. Case studies are generalisable to theoretical propositions and not to populations or 'universes'. It is incorrect to assume that the case study represents a sample. The aim of using case studies is thus to "generalise theories and not to enumerate frequencies" (Yin, 2003, p. 10). Cases should not be selected as 'sampling units', and the choice of selection should not be based on this reasoning. Instead, cases are to be seen as a set of individual experiments. The role of theory is to serve as a framework for the comparison of these cases and as such it provides a vehicle for generalising the results of the case studies.

How can a 'representative' set of case studies be selected to allow for analytic generalisation? This question refers both to the number of cases to be included, and how the cases can be compared amongst one another based on their characteristics or 'features'. With regard to the number of cases, as the sampling logic should not be used in case study design, the typical criteria regarding sampling size are also irrelevant. Ragin (1994) distinguishes different research strategies characterised by the number of cases and the number of features, ranging from quantitative research on relationships among variables (which calls for a large number of cases but a few features), to qualitative research of commonalities (requesting a small number of cases with many different features). The latter is particularly suitable in situations where knowledge is still lacking and the aim to find commonalities among the cases may help increase the understanding of the phenomenon (Sather, 1998). This applies to a considerable extent to this research, as the phenomenon of city-to-city cooperation has been found to be lacking a broad empirical knowledge base (see Introduction). As a result, the study has an explorative character. In this study, four North-South C2C partnership case studies have been selected. A number of four case studies is small enough to deal with a large number of features and large enough to find commonalities and possibly differences between the cases – which can then be used to improve the analytic frame of the research. The next paragraph deals with the selection of these particular four cases in more detail.

Selection of case studies: city-to-city partnerships
The case studies in the research included refer to C2C partnerships. They are briefly introduced in Box 0.1 of the Introduction, and Chapter 5 provides a more detailed background to the cities and respective partnerships. The cases are:
- Amstelveen (The Netherlands) – Villa El Salvador (Peru)
- Treptow-Köpenick (Germany) – Cajamarca (Peru)
- Utrecht (The Netherlands) – León (Nicaragua)
- Alphen aan den Rijn (The Netherlands) – Oudtshoorn (South Africa).

The selection of these particular cases was based on a combination of factors:
1. **Existing knowledge base**. This study builds on previous work by Rademaker & Van der Veer (2001), Van Lindert (2001) and Knowles & Materu (1999) which was performed in the framework of the joint IULA and ICLEI Local Agenda 21 Charters Programme. In this programme, which is discussed in more detail in the literature review of Chapter 1, 10 North-South city-to-city partnerships – that had the objective to strengthen local governance in the participating cities – were examined and compared. Among them were the cases of Treptow-Köpenick/Cajamarca and Utrecht/León. This study has made use of the existing knowledge on these cases which provided the possibility to indicate relevant features, conditions and observations to feed the theoretical framework and to compare with other experiences in a later stage.
2. **Theory driven considerations**. The research questions that have been derived from the analytic frame have been an important guideline to the selection of cases. First, the unique multi-stakeholder dimension of C2C needed to be emphasised, as a key question to the research was how various actors participate in C2C both as partners and beneficiaries. Therefore, a main selection criterion was that a wide range of urban actors be involved, representing and targeting both local institutions and civic society in both partner cities. Secondly, an important theoretical consideration concerned the capacity imperative that exists in local governments in the South, which to a large extent explains the possible contributions C2C can make to overcome these capacity needs. A next criterion of cases was therefore based on the fact that the institutional context of the cities in the South is currently shaped by a process of recent decentralisation or public sector reform, which brings about new challenges and responsibilities to local state and citizens alike. Chapter 4 provides the evidence that justifies the selection of cities in Peru, South Africa and Nicaragua, as these countries have undergone vast and recent changes in this respect in recent years, which has increased local government capacity demand. Thirdly, the literature distinguishes development-oriented city-to-city cooperation from other forms of city twinning, and there was a need to select case studies that corresponded to this developmental aspect, also in the light of the aim of the research i.e. understanding the link between C2C and (developmental) urban governance in the South. Therefore, the cases needed to include the criterion that the objectives of the partnerships (e.g. expressed in cooperation agreements) are linked to institutional strengthening, poverty alleviation or local development. The four cases in this study meet these criteria.
3. **Allowing for analytic generalisation**. In the selection of cases, it was important to find a balance between commonalities and differences among the cases. It was thus attempted to gain analytical benefits from finding both comparing and contrasting

CITIES AS PARTNERS

outcomes. A comparison on commonalities shows the different features of the cases (relating to the research questions and conceptual model) and their respective quality in relation to the four case studies. Finding commonalities allows for replication and extends the external generalisability of the findings. Focusing on differences, or *diversity* among the cases, may be useful for theoretical replication and strengthening the theoretical framework. If seen from this perspective, attention would be paid to the different localities and contexts of the respective case studies. Conclusions then largely reflect how contextual factors affect the outcomes, e.g. with regard to the effectiveness of C2C partnerships. Diversity in local realities, context and values is then no longer an obstacle to the comparison; rather this diversity is used as explanatory factor to the results found (Ragin, 1994). A balanced selection was thus made of case studies with a number of common characteristics while recognising the wide variety in context. Examples include the age of the partnerships, its complexity (e.g. with regard to actors involved), perceived level of success prior to the research, level of (external) resources and expertise available, regional and thematic scope of partnerships, size of participating local administrations, etc.

4. **Access to the field**. A factor of a more practical nature was the access to the field in both the Northern and Southern city of partnerships. Initially, the partnerships between Haarlem (The Netherlands) – Mutare (Zimbabwe) and Leuven (Belgium) – Nakuru (Kenya) were among the case studies selected, as they were also part of the LA21 Charters programme which, as shown above, served as an important starting point in the research. The ever deteriorating political conditions in Zimbabwe however made it not only complicated to perform fieldwork in the Southern partner city, but it would also prove difficult to do a meaningful analysis of local ('democratic and participatory') governance in Mutare under the totalitarian regime of Robert Mugabe. The partnership between Leuven and Nakuru was abruptly terminated in November 2005. Although it would be interesting to understand the reasons behind this decision, it also meant a more difficult access to interview respondents and other research data, as with its termination, the partnership became more of a historical rather than a contemporary event. It was therefore decided to replace these two cases with alternative partnerships.

Finally, some observations should be made on the unit of analysis of the case studies. It is important to point out that the case studies in this research refer to city-to-city partnerships, and not to individual cities. Therefore, each case study consist of two geographical and administrative components, i.e. the Northern and the Southern city of the partnerships. Moreover, in each of the case studies, more than one unit of analysis is involved. Within a single case, various subunits are thus considered. Whereas the C2C partnerships are the main units of analysis, this is also a rather abstract concept that is composed of a number of elements. These include local administrations (the level of the organisation), C2C partnership networks (the level of the city) and staff members that e.g. partake in C2C partnership missions (the level of the individual). These various elements are the *embedded units*, and moving the analysis to the level of these subunits allows to examine these phenomena in operational detail to deliver significant data (Yin, 2003).

THE CHALLENGE TO STRENGTHEN URBAN GOVERNANCE THROUGH NORTH-SOUTH CITY PARTNERSHIPS

Data collection: methods and experiences

Research was performed between 2005 and 2008. Data collection was carried out in the two partner cities of each case study. Bearing in mind that academic knowledge on C2C is limited on the one hand, and that the research subject is complex with many features and dimensions on the other hand, Ragin's model (Box 1) suggested that an appropriate research strategy corresponding to these considerations is of a qualitative nature. During fieldwork, various qualitative research techniques have been applied, which has enabled method and data triangulation (Boeije, 2005). The methods are reviewed below.[1]

Methods

Interviews
Semi structured (in-depth) interviews have been used to explore various topics and to allow interviewees to share their knowledge and express their opinions and views. A prepared topic list ascertained that the important topics (guiding concepts) be covered. Semi-structured interviews were done with all possible informants and experts. The design and content of topic lists varied, depending on the interviewees' background, position, function and knowledge. In total, over 100 in-depth interviews have been held, of which the majority were conducted in the South.[2] Roughly speaking targets have included individuals and representatives of organisations that are either involved in C2C partnerships, affect it or experience impact from it: Local politicians, local government officials, representatives of public-private partnerships, (twinning) development projects, local government associations, civic society groups, NGOs, embassies, etc. A list of respondents is included in Annex II, which provides more detail on the actual number of interviews per case study and the background of the interview respondents. With some minor exceptions, interviews have been transcribed *verbatim*, i.e. word for word, that together with the prepared topic lists, contributed to the reliability of the research.

Survey
A survey was held among 42 respondents to assess the individual characteristics, motivations, learning experiences and visions with regard to their participation in municipal exchanges and delegation missions. Respondents were interviewed from municipal councils and local administrations in both Northern and Southern case study cities, and entrepreneurs (6) from Oudtshoorn that undertook a trade mission to Alphen in 2005. Whereas Annex II provides an overview of interview respondents, no such record of survey respondents is provided, due to the small sample in some of the cities and the aim to guarantee confidentiality of participants' responses. Instead, below a more general typology of respondents is presented.

The survey took the form of semi-structured interviews, with a standardized topic list. The questions were open ended; but a set of statements was included on which respondents indicated their level of agreement. The survey was mainly aimed at collecting

---

1   The number of interviews, observation opportunities and documents has varied per case.

2   This included 17 interviews in Lima/Villa El Salvador, 15 in Cajamarca, 18 in South Africa/Oudtshoorn, and 22 in Nicaragua/León.

data with regard to individual characteristics of participants taking part in municipal exchanges.[3] It focused on the thematic areas, funding and mechanisms of exchanges, their origins, objectives and outcomes. An important aim of the survey was to unravel general effects of the exchanges regarding personal and professional learning, at the level of the individual and of the organisation, and which benefits have accrued to both North and South in terms of skills development, organisational change and institutional development. The survey furthermore aimed to shed light on the issue of mutuality, e.g. with regard to how the balance of benefits between North and South was perceived and who was taking the lead in partnership activities.

In terms of characteristics of the sample, 19 of the 42 participants (45%) were women and 23 (55%) men; 30 persons (71%) held a university degree, 6 had followed other post-secondary education (14%) and another 6 had completed secondary school. The majority (80%) was in the 30-49 age group, nobody was younger than 29. In both Amstelveen and Utrecht 6 respondents were interviewed, in Alphen 2, in León and Villa El Salvador 7, and in Oudtshoorn 8 in the municipality and 6 local business owners. No data was gathered in Cajamarca and Treptow-Köpenick, since municipal technical exchanges have not systematically taken place between these cities. Instead, individual experiences of this partnership were registered through other research methods, such as interviews and reviewing personal mission reports of participants' journeys and through informal talks in both cities.

Of the 36 respondents from local government, 2 were councillor, 16 participants (44%) were local administrators,[4] while 18 participants (50%) were local administrators with a leadership or senior management position in the municipal organisation.[5] The majority (20 respondents or 56%) had worked between 4 and 7 years in the local administration at the time of research, 6 respondents between 8 and 10 years, 5 between 11 and 20 years and 5 had worked for more than 20 years in the organisation. Fourteen respondents were from the North and 22 from the South. In the South, the large majority of respondents (19 out of 22, or 86%) had a university degree against 71% (10 out of 14) in the North.

A separate survey was conducted in Oudtshoorn to sample the target group of officials and councillors who had been trained in the framework of joint project with Alphen aan den Rijn on Performance Management. At the time of fieldwork in Oudtshoorn (April and May 2006), the PMS project was in full swing, which made it relatively easy to approach participants and reflect on their recent partaking in the project. The 9 respondents of the survey had all participated in training sessions and other activities that were organised in the framework of this particular project.

---

3   This includes a range of capacity building, advisory and other partnership activities that involved direct interaction with participants from the partner city. It usually referred to participation in technical missions overseas but also included attending training sessions, workshops and conferences (e.g. organised by VNG), and doing internships in partner organisations.

4   This category includes a range of staff positions, such as policy officers, policy advisors, project managers and project assistants, coordinators and technical staff. In this study they are collectively referred to as 'officials'.

5   This group is classified as having positions in which they manage people in subdivisions of the administration, such as heads of departments. Also, participants with key strategic positions (e.g. Municipal Managers) are part of this category. In this study they will be referred to as 'senior officials'.

THE CHALLENGE TO STRENGTHEN URBAN GOVERNANCE THROUGH NORTH-SOUTH CITY PARTNERSHIPS

It should be noticed that the survey was not intended to generate statistical value, given the small number of respondents. Instead, it has served as a tool to systematically collect data on a number of selected features to allow for a more categorised comparison in a qualitative fashion.

Observations

The opportunity to do observation largely depended on whether situations occurred during the fieldwork period that were relevant to the research. Examples include shadowing members of delegations visiting their partner cities (which was possible in León, Oudtshoorn, Alphen, Utrecht and Amstelveen), being present at workshops and meetings organised in the light of the partnership or institutional learning, attending public forums such as public consultation for approval of the annual municipal budget and other mechanisms of public participation. The implementation of observation as a research strategy has varied significantly among the cities researched and in some cases have not been a suitable or sufficient means of data collection. Observation therefore functioned as an additional tool to further understand information acquired through interviews and documents. Of many observation events, an observation protocol was prepared, which included details on observation setting, rationale, content, impression and notes on reflection and observation quality. Other observations were included in the logbooks that were kept during each fieldwork period.

Document collection

Documents that have been used include policy documents, C2C partnership evaluations (external and internal), urban strategic plans, urban development plans, reports from civic organisations, speeches, local newspaper articles, etc. As with observation, document collection has varied from case to case. Some partnerships are better documented than others and some local authorities have more extensive policy documentation where others have not. The differences were especially felt between North and South. Whereas in the North, policies, plans, partnership activities, and even personal experiences are relatively well documented, in the South much of this documentation was not available. Instead, research in the cities in the South relied more on interviews and observations, which also explains the high number of interviews conducted in the South compared to the North (Annex II).

Desk research

To assess contextual conditions, detailed desk research has been conducted to document country and regional information prior to fieldwork, functioning as background to understanding the local context of the research areas. It included political-governmental backgrounds, government systems, positions of local government and intergovernmental relations, national development policies and international donor and aid assistance, and geographical, socio-ethnic and historical backgrounds on the country and cities under study.

Dissemination and feedback workshops

In a number of the cities under study, there were opportunities to organise dissemination and feedback workshops in the final stages of the research project. Sharing the research findings and results with the respondents is not only of ethical and societal importance,

Table 1: Overview of fieldwork periods per location

	Fieldwork in the North	Fieldwork in the South
Utrecht-León	2005: March 23, April 19, May 10,12, June 22, July 12, September 29, October 6,7, December 19. 2006: September 22,29, October 9,13 2007: October 30, November 19 2008: January 23,28, April 23, May 13	2005: October 22 – November 24 2008: July 3 – 12
Alphen-Oudtshoorn	2005: September 21, October 12 2006: January 17, February 22, March 7,15, July 12 2007: October 23 2008: June 11,17	2006: April 10 – May 21 2008: February 17-20
Amstelveen-Villa El Salvador	2006: October 18 2007: January 18, May 22, July 5,10, October 2	2007: February 3 – March 2
Treptow-Köpenick – Cajamarca	2005: February 10,11 2007: January 8 – 12 2008: May 11	2007: March 2 – 26

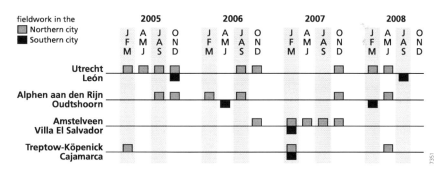

Figure 1 Overview of fieldwork periods per location

it proved also to be an unique method to fine-tune and reflect on the research outcomes, as the meetings allowed to directly incorporate feedback from respondents. As such it also served as a strategy to increase the construct validity and reliability of the study (Yin, 2003; Boeije, 2005) and reduce possible subjective judgements and biases in the analysis. Sharing the findings with respondents in the field have occurred in Amstelveen (October 2007), Oudtshoorn (February 2008), Treptow-Köpenick (May 2008), and León (July 2008). Additional workshops are envisaged in Utrecht and Alphen aan den Rijn in March 2009.

Research experiences and limitations
Fieldwork in the Northern cities has taken approximately 2-3 weeks per city. Due to the proximity of Utrecht, Alphen aan den Rijn and Amstelveen, visits could take place on a regular basis, and a rigidly defined fieldwork period therefore did not apply. Fieldwork in the Southern cities has taken approximately 6 weeks per city. Fieldwork has been conducted from 2005 until 2008. Table 1 and Figure 1 give an overview of the research periods in each of the locations. In the Figure, circular markers indicate fieldwork in the Northern city, rectangular markers refer to field research in the Southern city. Only the actual time of visit is indicated (and no preparation or analysis phases).

In general, a generous willingness of respondents and informants to collaborate was experienced, with some exceptions, for which alternative sources of information were found. There were in the main no constraints to observe in meetings and events, e.g. to shadow delegation visits or to be present at citizen consultation meetings. Although it proves difficult to assess, the researcher has not felt that her presence had in any sense influenced the course and interaction of the various events observed. Throughout the course of data collection and analysis, some issues emerged that deserve more attention here.

First, the research has been performed in a cross-cultural, cross-lingual[6] context, and as a result, a number of challenges arise. These challenges are for example related to issues of method use to measure across countries or localities, dealing with differences in social and political systems under study, and the translation from one language to another and from one culture to another. When questions are posed to informants and respondents, these questions are perceived in the cultural context in which the respondent is embedded. In other words: questions are understood differently in different cultures. Cultural contexts frame not only the respondents' understanding of questions, but also that of the researcher. Differences may appear between the intended and the perceived meaning of questions, triggered by cognitive and communicative processes (Braun & Harkness, 2005).

In cross-lingual, cross-cultural studies, appropriate language and translation thus play a key role to secure comparability (indifferent of whether commonalities or differences are sought). In this study, it was important to take into account these aspects during the stages of data collection and analysis. Although the effects of a language system, its usage, and the specific cultural context are frequently difficult to disentangle (Braun & Harkness, 2005), and although these processes were confined to the cultural and language abilities of the researcher, it has been attempted to consider at all times the influence of (cultural and language) context when posing questions and comprehending and interpreting answers.

Secondly, it should be noted that respondents are often influenced in the process of interpreting questions, generating an opinion and formulating a response by the (perceived) social desirability of optional answers. As a result, the data of this study have been subject to possible biases in this respect. Given the – although arguable – donor/recipient character of the C2C partnerships under study, it was felt that especially in the South (the 'recipient' partner), opinions were at times biased towards the desirable outcomes of C2C projects and towards 'what the partner city in the North wants to hear'. Although it was always emphasised that interviews were confidential and that the researcher took an impartial, objective position – not representing the partner city in the North, it was still felt that at times respondents in the South perceived the research as an evaluative exercise performed under auspices of the Northern partner or donor/funder of C2C projects. This was for example noticed when respondents thanked the researcher at the end of an interview for the aid given and projects implemented with assistance from the partner city, putting the researcher in a perceived donor position. Again, it proved important to consider these aspects during the stages of data collection and analysis, and act accordingly to attempt to reduce this bias where possible.

---

6   Research was conducted in five different countries, and as a result, the researcher has communicated in Dutch, German, Spanish, English and Afrikaans.

Annex II – List of interview respondents

Peru

Villa El Salvador and Lima

J. Zea	Mayor Villa El Salvador
L. Castro	Councillor Villa El Salvador
J. Rodríguez	Councillor Villa El Salvador
G. Soto	Councillor Villa El Salvador
J. Bueno	Municipal Manager, VES Municipality
J. Ordoñez	Head of International Cooperation, VES Municipality
A. Paredes	Head of Finances, VES Municipality
C. Zela	Former Head of Environmental Services, VES Municipality
J. Portugal	Proyecto Woongroep Holland, VES Municipality
M. Mendoza	Proyecto Woongroep Holland, VES Municipality
L. Miranda	Foro de Ciudades para la Vida
A. Ugarte	Instituto de Investigación y Capacitación Municipal (INICAM)
M. Zolezzi	Centro de Estudios y Promoción del Desarrollo (DESCO)
E. Roof	Dutch Embassy in Peru
L. Cortez	Ecociudad
F. Narrea	Asociación de Municipalidades del Perú (AMPE)
C. Cordero	Independent consultant/urban expert

Cajamarca

L. Saenz	Municipal Manager, Cajamarca Provincial Municipality
V. Montenegro	Planning and Technical Cooperation, Cajamarca Provincial Municipality
J. Gonzalez	Tourism, Cajamarca Provincial Municipality
R. Machuca	Head of Economic Development, Regional Government Cajamarca
A. Centurión	Municipal Manager, Baños del Inca District Municipality
N. Alburuqueque	Representative Working Group Treptow-Köpenick
S. Sánchez	Representative Working Group Treptow-Köpenick
C. Stark	Representative Working Group Treptow-Köpenick
N. Kalafatovich	Instituto de Investigación y Capacitación Municipal (INICAM) Cajamarca
J. Vigo	Asociación para el Desarrollo Local (ASODEL)
P. Rojas	Grupo de Formación e Intervención para el Desarrollo Sostenible (GRUFIDES)
E. Sánchez	Mesas de Concertación Cajamarca
N. Ortiz	Director kindergarten #17

THE CHALLENGE TO STRENGTHEN URBAN GOVERNANCE THROUGH NORTH-SOUTH CITY PARTNERSHIPS

| M. Paredes | Director kindergarten #105 |
| J. Trigoso | St. Vicente de Paúl School, Otuzco |

South Africa

J. Swartbooi	Mayor Oudtshoorn
P. Nel	Speaker Oudtshoorn
M. May	Municipal Manager, Oudtshoorn Municipality
L. Coetzee	IDP Manager, Oudtshoorn Municipality
A. Bekker	Head of Planning, Oudtshoorn Municipality
K. Hude	Head of Health Department, Oudtshoorn Municipality
C. Scheepers	Head of Human Resources, Oudtshoorn Municipality
Ph. Nel	Manager PMS, Oudtshoorn Municipality
G. Baartman	LED Manager, Oudtshoorn Municipality
P. Luiters	Councillor Eden District Municipality
K. Van der Molen	School of Public Management and Planning, Stellenbosch University
B. Ketel	School of Public Management and Planning, Stellenbosch University
C. Pieterse	Former representative *gespreksforum*
H. Oosthuizen	Former representative *gespreksforum*
K. Grootboom	Oudtshoorn Development and Information Centre
R. Klein	Entrepreneur; representative Civic Forum
A. Killian	Entrepreneur
A. Van Greunen	Entrepreneur

Nicaragua

T. Téllez	Mayor León
V. Gutiérrez	Councillor León
E. López	Director León Sur Este urban expansion programme, León Municipality
C. Blandón	Head of Urban Planning, León Municipality
M. Solis	Head of Strategic Planning and External Cooperation (until 2006), León Municipality
H. Chavarrías	Head of Strategic Planning and External Cooperation (from 2006), León Municipality
L. García	Department of Local Development, León Municipality
I. Barrantes	Fundación DIA
C. Chávez	Consejo de Desarrollo Departamental de León (CONDELEON)
R. Sampson	Former Mayor León; Rector UNAN
D. Pérez	Instituto Nicaragüense de Fomento Municipal (INIFOM)
A. Salinas	Asociación de Municipios de Nicaragua (AMUNIC)
J. Castillo	Consejo Nacional de los Hermanamientos Holanda – Nicaragua
B. Van der Meulen	Dutch Embassy in Nicaragua
M. Schaapveld	Friendship Foundation Utrecht – León
O. Ara	City partnership Zaragoza – León; ECODES
D. Grüneberg	City partnership Hamburg – León

I. Arteagoitia	City partnership Basque Country – León (LEONEKIN)
M. Quesada	Environmental Education Project Utrecht-León
C. Santovenia	Consultant Local Agenda 21; UNAN
D. Zavala	Asociación Comunitaria Los Poetas (ACOPOE)
V. Salazar	Fundación para la Promoción de Technologías Alternativas (FUNPROTECA)

The Netherlands
H. Buis	VNG-International
A. Musch	VNG-International
W. Prins	Stichting Habitat Platform
G. Rhebergen	PSO – Capaciteitsopbouw in ontwikkelingslanden

Amstelveen
J. van Zanen	Mayor Amstelveen
Y. Tan	Councillor Amstelveen
R. Schurink	Municipal Manager, Amstelveen Municipality
E. Weijers	Head of Policy Dept., Amstelveen Municipality
H. Jansen	International Cooperation, Policy Dept., Amstelveen Municipality
R. Vos	Head of Resource Management, Amstelveen Municipality
N. Bijl	Waste management/public infrastructure, Amstelveen Municipality
A. Kaiser	Waste management/public infrastructure, Amstelveen Municipality
C. Willems	VES Neighbourhood Group Amstelveen

Utrecht
M. van Dongen	International Affairs (until 2005), Utrecht Municipality
D. van de Ven	International Affairs (from 2005), Utrecht Municipality
E. Kroese	Coordinator León Sur Este Programme
H. Sakkers	Head of Strategic and International Affairs, Utrecht Municipality
H. Kloosterman	Coordinator Sustainable Development, Utrecht Municipality
D. Koppenberg	Friendship Foundation Utrecht-León
T. Daggers	International Bicycle Consultant

Alphen aan den Rijn
N. Schoof	Mayor Alphen aan den Rijn
J. Eshuis	Municipal Manager, Alphen aan den Rijn Municipality
H. Tangerink	International Cooperation, Welfare and Education, Alphen aan den Rijn Municipality
H. van Arkel	Controller, Alphen aan den Rijn Municipality
K. van Arkel	Chairman Platform Twinning Alphen-Oudtshoorn

Germany

S. Eichmann	European and International Affairs, Treptow-Köpenick District Municipality
K. Jakobi	Education and Youth, Berlin Senate
M. Schrick	Representative Working Group Cajamarca
I. Beier	Representative Working Group Cajamarca
J. Querengässer	Förderverein Lokale Agenda 21 Treptow-Köpenick
K. Wazlawik	Ökumenische Initiativgruppe Eine Welt/Lokale Agenda 21 Treptow-Köpenick

Curriculum Vitae

Marike Bontenbal (1978) graduated in 2003 from the Faculty of Geosciences at Utrecht University. She earned an MSc in Human Geography and Urban and Regional Planning, with a specialisation in Development Geography. She worked as project assistant at the Urban Governance Unit of the European Secretariat of ICLEI-Local Governments for Sustainability in Freiburg, Germany (2003), and completed an administrative internship at the European Commission's International Co-operation Office, EuropeAid in Brussels (2004). She has further worked in short term elections missions in Kosovo (with the Organisation for Security and Cooperation in Europe – OSCE) and for the Iraq Out-of-Country Voting Programme (with the International Organisation for Migration – IOM). She started her PhD research in January 2005, and has conducted research in Nicaragua, South Africa, and Peru. Since 2007 she has worked as a trainer at the The Hague Academy for Local Governance/VNG-International in courses for Dutch local government officials on working in municipal partnerships and local governance. She has also worked at the Ministry of Foreign Affairs' Department of Aid Effectiveness and Quality (2009). Marike Bontenbal has published several articles in the field of development geography and urban planning.